D1244367

Image, Language, Brain

Image, Language, Brain

Papers from the First Mind Articulation Project Symposium

edited by Alec Marantz, Yasushi Miyashita, and Wayne O'Neil

The MIT Press
Cambridge, Massachusetts
London, England

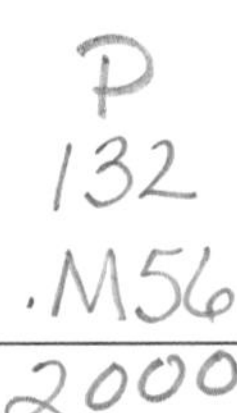

This book was set in Times New Roman by Asco Typesetters, Hong Kong in '3B2', and was printed and bound in the United States of America.

Library of Congress Cataloging-in-Publication Data

Mind Articulation Project Symposium (1st : 1998 : Tokyo)
Image, language, brain : papers from the First Mind Articulation Project Symposium / edited by Alec Marantz, Yasushi Miyashita, and Wayne O'Neil.
p. cm.
Revised papers from a symposium held November 16–17, 1998 in Tokyo.
Includes bibliographical references and index.
ISBN 0-262-13371-7 (hc.)
1. Biolinguistics—Congresses. I. Marantz, Alec. II. Miyashita, Y. (Yasushi), 1949–
III. O'Neil, Wayne. IV. Title.
P132.M56 1998
401—dc21 00-032889

Contents

Preface

The chapters in this volume,[1] now extensively revised for publication, were first presented in Tokyo 16–17 November, 1998, at the first symposium of the Mind Articulation Project, a joint MIT/JST (Japan Science and Technology) research project conducted under the auspices of JST's program of international cooperative research (ICORP).

The Mind Articulation Project, codirected by two of the editors of these proceedings (Yasushi Miyashita and Wayne O'Neil), arose largely through the efforts of the third editor, Alec Marantz. This first symposium, a joint undertaking of the three of us, brought together eleven linguists and cognitive neuroscientists (in addition to Marantz, Miyashita, and O'Neil): Noam Chomsky and Edward Gibson (both of MIT), Robert Desimone (NIMH), Richard Frackowiak (University College London), Angela Friederici (Max Planck Institute/Leipzig), Masao Ito (RIKEN), Willem Levelt (Max Planck Institute/Nijmegen), Jacques Mehler (CNRS), Helen Neville (University of Oregon), David Poeppel (University of Maryland at College Park), and Hiroshi Shibasaki (Kyoto University).

One goal of the symposium was to examine the recent attempts to unify linguistic theory and brain science that have grown out of the increasing awareness that a proper understanding of language in the brain must reflect the steady advances in linguistic theory of the past forty years. How can the understanding of language provided by linguistic research be transformed through the study of the biological basis of language? How can our understanding of the brain be transformed through the same research? The best model of such interaction between cognitive science and neurobiology is research on vision. Abilities such as visual awareness, attention, and imagery generation are the first higher cognitive abilities to have been firmly localized in the brain. Key findings on these matters have been enhanced by the recent explosion of noninvasive brain-monitoring techniques that have been most successfully applied in the investigation of the functional anatomy of the visual system.

The long-term goals of the project are, on the one hand, to integrate linguistics and brain science in the way that has been attempted in the study of the visual system, and, on the other hand, to formulate a cognitive theory that more strongly constrains visual neuroscience.

The chapters in this volume explore some of the topics just sketched, addressing the goals both of the symposium and of the project. Thus, some chapters examine the current status of the cognitive/neuroscience synthesis in the study of the visual system. Other chapters address whether and how linguistics and neuroscience can be integrated, given the paradigm of cognitive neuroscience emerging from work on vision. Still other chapters, though focused on vision, are primarily concerned to illustrate "how integrative brain mechanisms can be studied" through the use of the various noninvasive brain-imaging techniques (see chapter 8).

For example, in chapter 11, Reynolds and Desimone integrate these approaches and propose that attentional modulation depends on two interacting neural mechanisms: one, an automatic competitive mechanism within a cortical area, and the other, feedback from outside a cortical area that biases the competition in favor of the neuronal population activated by the attended stimulus. They present a simple computational circuit that provides a good fit to the data and makes easily testable predictions.

Miyashita begins chapter 12, on the neural mechanism of visual imagery, by quoting Alain: "Create an image of the Pantheon in your mind. Can you count the columns that support its pediment?" The basic neural circuit of imagery generation is drawn in comparison with the cognitive model of Stephen Kosslyn. Two predictions of the circuit were directly tested by neurophysiological approaches in animal models: activation of internal representation of objects in the inferotemporal cortex and its executive control by the prefrontal cortex.

As for the chapters on language, we will not comment on all of them, but let us at least note that Levelt and Indefrey's reanalysis (in chapter 4) of fifty-eight reports of brain-imaging experiments on word production from the point of view of an independently arrived at theory of lexical access in speech production reveals a remarkable convergence between the theory and the experimental data. This convergence leads them to wonder about "how much more can be achieved if a processing theory is used beforehand to guide the planning of functional brain-imaging studies of language?" And in chapter 6, Friederici presents "a tentative model of the neuronal dynamics of auditory language comprehension" according to which "early syntactic processing is independent of lexical-semantic information [, which] only comes into play when thematic roles are assigned. If initial syntactic structure and thematic structure map well, comprehension has taken place adequately." Her results have clear implications for psycholinguistic models of language comprehension.

Finally, consider the research by Poeppel and Marantz on the perception of the sounds of language, presented in detail in chapter 2. The preliminary results of this work, firmly based in the theory of phonology, suggest that the interface between the sounds of language and the cognitive system of language is embedded in the articulatory-perceptual system. Part of auditory cortex thus appears to be language dedicated, a surprising result if supported by further research.

In chapter 1, Chomsky expresses some caution, however. Commenting on the work of the past fifty years, he points out that although

> there has been intensive and often highly productive inquiry into the brain, behavior, and cognitive faculties of many organisms [, t] he goal that has aroused the most enthusiasm is also likely to be the most remote, probably by orders of magnitude: an understanding of the human brain and human higher mental faculties, their nature, and the ways they enter into action and interaction.
>
> From the outset, there has been no shortage of optimistic forecasts, even declarations by distinguished researchers that the mind-body problem has been solved by advances in computation, or that everything is essentially understood apart from the "hard problem" of consciousness. Such conclusions surely do not withstand analysis. To an objective outside observer—say, a scientist from Mars—the optimism too might seem rather strange, since there is also no shortage of much simpler problems that are poorly understood, or not at all.

Chapter 5, by Gibson, is in part an illustration of Chomsky's last point. Working on problems of complex sentence processing that Chomsky, together with George Miller (in Miller and Chomsky 1963), addressed over thirty-five years ago, Gibson reports progress that results entirely from behavioral studies, and not at all from brain-imaging technology.

Thus, the conclusion to Chomsky's paper serves as a fitting and challenging end to this prefatory essay as well:

> Exactly how the story unfolds from here depends on the actual facts of the matter.... A primary goal is to bring the bodies of doctrine concerning language into closer relation with those emerging from the brain sciences and other perspectives. We may anticipate that richer bodies of doctrine will interact, setting significant conditions from one level of analysis for another, perhaps ultimately converging in true unification. But we should not take truisms for substantive theses, and there is no place for dogmatism as to how the issues might move toward resolution. We know far too little for that, and the history of modern science teaches us lessons that I think should not be ignored.

To say that the chapters of this volume originated at the *first* Mind Articulation Project symposium is to presuppose that there will be at least a second symposium, at which time we hope to know better how far we have traveled along the path toward the unification of the brain and cognitive science, if at all.

Wayne O'Neil (MIT)
Yasushi Miyashita (University of Tokyo)

Note

1. This volume contains one paper not presented at the symposium, the paper by Kensuke Sekihara, David Poeppel, Alec Marantz, and Yasushi Miyashita, and lacks a paper that was presented, a paper by Helen Neville.

Reference

Miller, George A., and Noam Chomsky. 1963. In *Handbook of Mathematical Psychology*, volume 2, ed. R. Duncan Luce, Robert R. Bush, and Eugene Galanter, 419–491. New York: John Wiley and Sons.

Introduction: Mind Articulation

Alec Marantz, Yasushi Miyashita, and Wayne O'Neil

Since the term *mind articulation* may seem vague or even opaque to some—suggesting a number of interrelated topics—we turn first to an explication of the relevant meanings the term has for the Mind Articulation Project.

Perhaps foremost is the notion of "articulating the mind"—that is, investigating the functional anatomy of the mind and the brain, figuring out what the functional pieces of the mind are and how they work in the brain. We "articulate the structure of the mind" by identifying specialized modules of computational machinery. For example, there seems to be a special module of mind devoted to recognizing faces.

For linguists, *mind articulation* also suggests the "articulating" or "speaking" mind, the study of language in the minds and brains of humans. Since language is a uniquely human mental capacity, mind articulation is then the investigation of what makes us human, of what makes all humans the same. Among the complex mental capacities of humans or of any species, language is perhaps the best understood; the cognitive models that linguists and psycholinguists have developed for language are the richest cognitive models for any cognitive function. Studying the articulating mind in the articulating brain allows highly developed cognitive theories to help us understand the brain as a computational machine.

Human Brains/Animal Brains

The capacity for language is unique to humans—a product of our genetic endowment. However, humans are genetically quite close to other primates, the genetic distance between a human and a chimpanzee being small. The evidence suggests that the specialized human capacity for language involves a small number of genes that have an effect on the functional structure of the brain and perhaps also on the motor and perceptual systems. The nature of the genetic basis for language provides a special role for animal studies in the Mind Articulation Project. Since other species lack human language, investigations of the articulating mind must use humans and must find methods to investigate the human articulating brain—methods such as the various noninvasive brain-imaging techniques employed in the research reported on in many of the chapters that follow: positron emission tomography (PET), functional magnetic resonance imaging (fMRI), magnetoencephalography (MEG), and event-related (brain) potential (ERP). However, the small genetic difference between humans and other primates suggests that, in evolution, language built heavily on preexisting structures and capacities. Animal models should illuminate which aspects of language are part of a shared primate structure and which are language-particular innovations.

Language as a Symbolic Computational System

Linguists study language as a symbolic computational system, internal to the minds and brains of humans. Language connects form and meaning—where *form* is, at least, the sounds of spoken language or the movements of the body that are the expression of sign languages. As is well known, the units of language do not involve an iconic relation between form and meaning: the sound of the word *cat* does not sound like any aspect of a cat, not its size, color, shape, or vocalizations. The smallest units of language, then, are noniconic symbols. Small pieces of language like words are combined into larger constructions like phrases and sentences. Combinations of words have meanings that are also noniconic. If one considers the hierarchical structure of a sentence as in (1), there is nothing about the structural relations among the elements in the sentence that transparently or iconically reflects the meaningful relations among the constituents. For example, there is nothing about the juxtaposition of *the* and *cat* to suggest the semantic effect that the definite determiner *the* has on the common noun *cat*.

(1) a. The man saw the cat.
b.

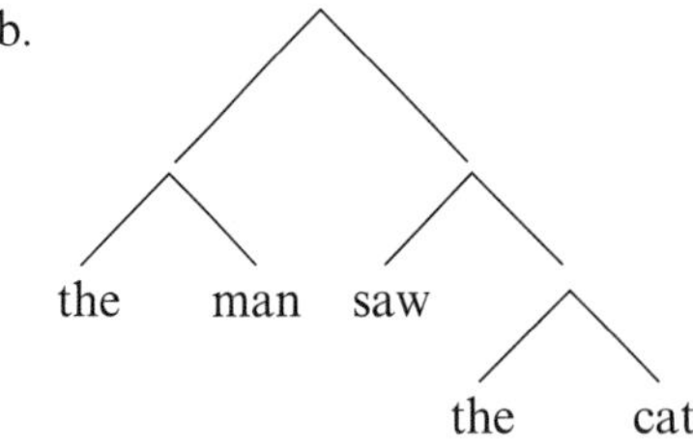

The computational system of language has the structure shown in (2):

(2)

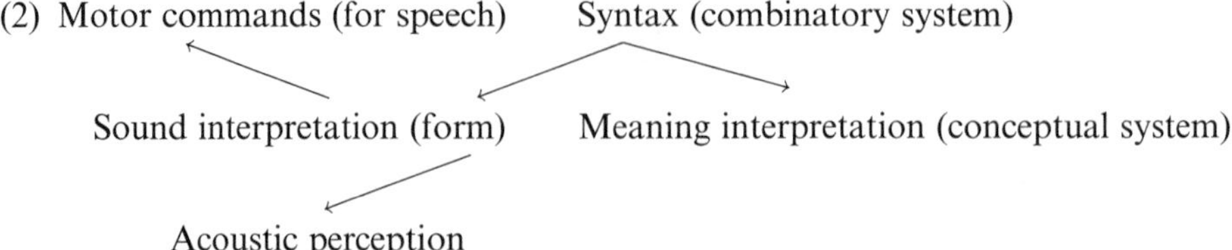

There is a combinatoric engine, called the *syntax*, that puts the elementary pieces of language together into the kind of hierarchical structure shown in the tree graph (1) for the English sentence *The man saw the cat*. The units combined by the syntax have features or properties that make them subject to interpretation both in form and in meaning. Structures built by the syntax are thus subject to phonological or *sound* interpretation, either in terms of the sounds or acoustics of language or in terms of the motor commands necessary to produce speech (or sign language). The same structures are subject to interpretation in terms of the meaningful concepts of our mental life. The representations of language *interface* with nonlinguistic systems, then, at two points or interfaces—with the perceptual and motor systems involved in speech production and perception and with the conceptual system involved in meaningful language comprehension.

There is some question about the capacity of nonhumans to use symbols at all, whether iconic or noniconic. But the special nature of human language goes beyond the simple use of symbols. The combination of units in language is recursive: in (1), when we put *the* and *cat* together, the result of the combination becomes a unit for further combination, here with the word *saw*. The recursive nature of linguistic computations gives rise to what Chomsky has called the "discrete infinity" of language: the potentially infinite use of finite means. In addition, although the units of language have features interpretable in terms of sound (or movements) and in terms of meaningful concepts, the combinatoric system of language combines the units to a large extent independently of their interpretation. Thus, although the units themselves consist largely of features with concrete interpretations, the computational system of language treats these units as abstract symbols. Compare how computers manipulate commands in computer languages. Such commands might be interpreted as instructions to draw, say, a particular character on the computer screen, but internal to the computations of the computer, the commands are strings of 1s and 0s, manipulated as binary numbers. Similarly, the elements of language are treated internal to the linguistic system according to their internal form—that is, according to their feature structure considered abstractly, independent of their interpretation in sound or meaning.

Transformational Grammar/Articulating Minds

The theory of language schematically diagrammed in (2) holds important implications for how language works in the brain and for how brains work at language. Note that in this diagram, the combinatoric or generative engine of language is in the syntax, which creates structures subject to interpretation in sound and meaning. There is no independent combinatoric engine on either the sound or the meaning side of the diagram. Theories of language that contain this single generative engine have been called *transformational*.

The version of transformational grammar schematically diagrammed in (2) also makes certain claims about language production and understanding within a human using grammatical knowledge in language behavior. Because there is no combinatoric system exclusive to the sound side of language, sentence comprehension cannot be viewed as the construction of a sound representation based on the auditory input followed by a mapping of such a representation onto a meaning representation. Rather, the construction of a sound representation requires the combinatoric system of the syntax, and thus successful building of a sound representation for a sentence already provides the listener with a representation for semantic interpretation.

Similarly, language production cannot be the creating of a meaningful representation for a sentence followed by the mapping of this representation onto some representation that can be pronounced. There is no independent generative engine for semantic representations. Rather, the successful construction of a semantic representation requires the generative engine of syntax, which provides something that can be pronounced directly whenever it constructs a meaningful representation.

Language production and language comprehension, then, involve essentially the same generative cognitive machinery. In language perception, the goal is to generate a representation consistent with the acoustic clues coming into the ears, as well as all the contextual clues as to the semantic content of the incoming speech. In language production, the goal is to generate a representation consistent with one's internal mental state as well as with one's construction of the linguistic and semantic context both for oneself and for one's audience.

Interfaces, Animals, and the Dynamic Aspect of Representations

The model of linguistic knowledge shown in (2) places the species-specific adaptation for language in the generative engine of syntax and in the interfaces between the combinatoric system of language and the interpretative systems that take linguistic representations into other modules of mind. Thus, in looking at animal models for understanding language in the brain, we should be looking at specialization in the acoustic perception abilities, in the motor control of the speech apparatus, and in the conceptual representational systems. The combinatoric engine called *syntax* is perhaps the best candidate from linguistics for a mind module that might be instantiated within a specialized location in the cerebral cortex of humans. However, this language- and species-specific module of mind might be instantiated within brain areas that subserve other functions. We should be looking in the brains of humans for the specialized computations of syntax, but we need not be looking for a specialized location for these computations. The generative engine of syntax might be instantiated by a special mode of processing within neural circuits or within brain areas that perform other functions.

Although linguistics does not provide a functional anatomy of language in the brain that necessarily maps onto a structural anatomy of specialized brain areas, still linguistic accounts of language provide a direct account of brain activity in language perception and production. The linguistic account of sentence structure is dynamic and generative—it provides a detailed description of the mental operations necessary in constructing a representation of a sentence. As a first hypothesis about the way that mind maps onto brain, we have no reason not to suppose that each mental operation implied by linguistic theory corresponds to a computation carried out by the brain.

Much current linguistic research concerns the interfaces between syntax and meaning—semantics—on the one hand and between syntax and form—phonetics and phonology—on the other. Since these investigations involve the interaction of language systems with extralinguistic systems, they provide a good basis for the study of language in the brain. The extralinguistic systems that interface with language can be studied independently of language and in nonhuman species, allowing linguistic research to make contact with animal models of brain function.

Articulating the Mind in Brain Space

The standard image of language in the brain involves the localization of different language functions to various structural landmarks in the physical structure of the brain and a spatial coding of linguistic features within these functional centers. The most influential view until twenty years ago, for example, had language production localized in Broca's area, in the frontal lobe of the left hemisphere, and language perception in Wernicke's area, in the temporal lobe of the left hemisphere. Spatial coding meant, for instance, the localization of different semantic categories of words in different regions of the temporal lobe.

Functional separation and spatial coding as visions of the way the brain works fit in naturally with contemporary brain-imaging techniques such as PET and fMRI, which are best at pinpointing the location of brain activity accompanying particular mental events. But the standard image of language in the brain—an image we inherit from the late nineteenth century—fails in many respects to account for what we know both about how the brain works and about how language works. The brain is, among other things, a computational device that combines and transforms information. Language in the brain requires computations over representations. The *where* of brain activity tells us something about the way computations work, since separation of function is a basic clue to function itself. But the key to computation is the transformation of information, and to understand computation one must study the representation and transformation of information. Spatial coding might be one method the brain uses to represent information, but spatial spread of coding elements is not the same thing as a spatial code, as we will see. The spatial organization of brain regions is an inevitable result of the three-dimensional physicality of the brain, with the particular organization of tuned receptor cells resulting from the nature of brain development. *Coding* in the brain seems a function of the pattern of firing of tuned cells, and of the patterns of their interconnections.

Functional Anatomy and Organs in the Brain

The notion that the brain is organized into subparts specialized for different functions was a breakthrough in our understanding of the brain. Consider as an analogy the discovery of the various internal organs of the body—the heart, the lungs, the liver, the circulatory system. The discovery that the lungs transfer oxygen to the blood is at once part of a functional understanding of the circulatory system of the body and the beginning of an investigation of how the lungs perform this function.

Functional organization can be investigated through *deficit-lesion* studies—the correlation between a lesion or damage to some particular area of the brain and a marked deficit in some behavior or capacity of the afflicted animal. The discovery of supposed language areas such as Broca's and Wernicke's areas came from such deficit-lesion studies. In animals, brain areas necessary for particular functions can be pinpointed by systematic removal of such areas. Moreover, once an area has been implicated in a particular process, neuronal activity in that area can be measured with depth electrodes. Within animals, then, clues from deficit-lesion studies that point to an answer to the question of what this area does can be followed up with invasive direct recordings in an effort to answer questions about how the area does this and how information is processed in this area by neurons and neuronal connections.

In humans, on the other hand, deficit-lesion studies are the results of accidents or accidents of nature, and tentative conclusions from such studies can rarely be followed by invasive recordings to examine information processing.

Where in the Brain vs. How in the Brain?

The confusion between *where* and *how* can be illustrated by a classic result in brain mapping, the "map" of the body in the somatosensory cortex. Stimulation of the skin at a particular location on the body causes activity at the corresponding site on the somatosensory cortex. Although space on the body is mapped onto space on the brain, it is not clear that the brain is using a spatial code to map space. That is, does the brain use distance and direction between sites on the somatosensory cortex to code for distance and direction on the body? Since the body map on the somatosensory cortex clearly results from brain development, it is not clear whether it is functional in the computational system of the human brain or merely a by-product of development.

Similarly, many areas of visual processing in the brain are organized retinotopically—that is, particular regions on the retina at the back of the eye correspond to particular regions of the cortex in visual areas, starting with the primary visual cortex at the occipital lobe at the back of the head. Here again, spatial organization does not necessarily mean spatial coding. A human observer watching the activity of brain cells on the cortex sees spatial information preserved in the spatial organization of the active cells, but that does not indicate how the brain itself might exploit this information or whether it is information for the brain at all.

To understand better the difference between the where and the how, consider how the brain does color vision. Colors can be mapped into a space, perhaps a three-dimensional space, of hue, brightness, and saturation. If spatial coding were the primary means the brain used to represent features of sensory input, one might expect to find *chromotopic* maps in the visual cortex where one or more of these color dimensions is mapped onto a physical dimension of the brain. However, color-processing cells seem to be retinotopically organized, just like other feature-detecting cells in the visual system. As is well known, color vision works with the help of cells tuned in particular ways to the frequency of light hitting small patches of the retina. The differential firing of these types of cells yields the color percept. The detection of features of sensory inputs—light, sound, touch, smell—depends on cells tuned to fire at particular values along physical continua (for example, at particular frequencies along the continua of frequencies of electromagnetic waves that are light). The spatial organization of these tuned detector cells in sensory cortical areas of the brain usually reflects the spatial organization of the sensory cells at the sense organs. So touch-sensitive cells in the skin relay information to somatosensory cells in the cerebral cortex whose organization reflects the spatial organization of the touch-sensitive cells at the surface, and visual processing cells reflect the spread of light-sensitive cells on the retina of the eye.

For hearing, the cochlea of the ear does a rough form of frequency analysis according to its own resonant properties. Frequency-sensitive neurons in the cochlea are also roughly distributed according to the frequency to which they are tuned. Thus a cochleotopic distribution of cells in the auditory cortex corresponds also to a rough mapping of frequency onto space—the so-called tonotopic organization of the auditory cortex. Rather than *tonotopy*, we should say *cochleotopy*, since this organization simply follows the general pattern of the spatial organization of sensory neurons in the cortex mirroring the spatial organization of receptor cells at the sense organs themselves.

The animal model of brain research has us identifying functional regions of the brain and studying the functional anatomy of these regions, including the response characteristics and interconnectivity of the neurons they contain. But in human brain mapping, the correlation of structure and function often stops at the identification of areas somehow involved in a particular mental activity. Localization of activity associated with a function is often useful if much is already known about an area. However, a simple observation that a particular function is associated with activity in a particular area is not by itself particularly useful—the observation awaits further study of the area.

Temporal Dynamics of Brain Activity

If localization of brain activity during the performance of some cognitive act is not by itself very revealing of the way the brain functions as a computational device, what tools can we employ to understand the how of brain computation?

Brain activity has a temporal as well as a spatial dimension. Groups of neurons firing at particular locations in the cerebral cortex are firing at particular rates, and at particular times with respect to the firing of other neurons. Electrophysiological brain imaging techniques such as ERP and MEG allow us to record the activity over time of large ensembles of neurons in the brain. The activity of large groups of neurons over time potentially provides us with two sorts of information. In terms of functionally identified areas in the brain, the time course of activation provides clues as to the flow of information across the areas. Such clues help us match up functional brain areas with pieces of functional cognitive models of thought. For detailed discussion, see chapters 4 and 6.

Perhaps more crucially, the time course of activation of large ensembles of cells also might reveal temporal coding of information in the brain. Morse code is a simple example of a temporal code—a long sustained sound contrasts with a short sound, and combinations of short and long sounds code for letters. Given that cognition is dynamic, a product of brain activity over time, there is no reason to rule out Morse code–type of codings of features for mental computation. Information might also be coded in the rate of firings of groups of cells—that is, in the frequency of neuronal activity.

To return to the example of color vision, a paper in *Nature* (Cottaris and De Valois 1998) illustrates the potential of temporal coding in an area removed from language. The tuning curve we discussed in the preceding section involved a cell in the lateral geniculate nucleus, in the pathway from eye to cortex. Cottaris and De Valois reveal the properties of the response of color processing cells in the primary visual cortex of a macaque, and show that information about the wavelength of light hitting the retina can be read off the latency to peak firing of some cell types in the primary visual cortex. There is an exact correlate for sound from the MEG studies of Roberts and Poeppel (e.g., 1996) where the latency of the peak response from an ensemble of cells in the auditory cortex correlates with the pitch of tone played to a listener. Since information about color is available in the latency of peak firing of cells, it is possible that the brain might use this temporal information to code for color. Similarly, latency to peak firing in the auditory cortex may code for sound frequency (see chapter 2, this volume).

We conclude by providing an example of two sorts of temporal information for language: one that shows the flow of information between different areas of the brain and one that points to the possibility of temporal coding of information for brain computation. An experiment reported by Poeppel and Marantz in chapter 2 looks at a response to the discrepancy between sounds different only in the phonological feature [+/−voice], a feature that has an interpretation in the motor commands to the articulatory muscles during speech production and an interpretation in terms of the acoustic structure of speech sounds relevant to speech perception. Data from this experiment show a response to the change of this feature that peaks around 180 ms after the onset of the sound and localizes to a position along the top of the temporal lobe, near the primary auditory cortex. This result shows that information about the linguistic category of a speech sound is processed by a particular brain area at a particular point in time, and such a result can be used to map out the flow of information in speech comprehension, from ear to semantic interpretation.

From the results of another experiment on the distinction between [+voice] and [−voice] sounds, Lukka, Schoner, and Marantz (2000) have looked at the temporal dynamics of the response from the primary auditory cortex in the time interval around 100 ms after the onset of a speech sound, and have found that there is information in this 100 ms response that distinguishes the response to voiced sounds like /da/ from voiceless sounds like /ta/. The difference in firing pattern between the response to voiced and voiceless sounds might in this case be a temporal code for the linguistic category.

These and other results, reported in chapter 2 and elsewhere, suggest that there is a point in articulating the mind in the way we have outlined.

References

Cottaris, N., and R. De Valois. 1998. Temporal dynamics of chromatic tuning in macaque primary visual cortex. *Nature* 395:896–900.

Lukka, Tuomas, Bernd Schoner, and Alec Marantz. 2000. Phoneme discrimination from MEG data. *Neurocomputing* 31:153–165.

Roberts, T. P. L., and D. Poeppel. 1996. Latency and auditory evoked M100 as a function of tone frequency. *NeuroReport* 7:1138–1140.

Part I

Language and the Brain

Chapter 1

Linguistics and Brain Science

Noam Chomsky

In the past half century, there has been intensive and often highly productive inquiry into the brain, behavior, and cognitive faculties of many organisms. The goal that has aroused the most enthusiasm is also likely to be the most remote, probably by orders of magnitude: an understanding of the human brain and human higher mental faculties, their nature, and the ways they enter into action and interaction.

From the outset, there has been no shortage of optimistic forecasts, even declarations by distinguished researchers that the mind-body problem has been solved by advances in computation, or that everything is essentially understood apart from the "hard problem" of consciousness. Such conclusions surely do not withstand analysis. To an objective outside observer—say, a scientist from Mars—the optimism too might seem rather strange, since there is also no shortage of much simpler problems that are poorly understood, or not at all.

Despite much important progress in many areas, and justified excitement about the prospects opened by newer technologies, I think that a degree of skepticism is warranted, and that it is wise to be cautious in assessing what we know and what we might realistically hope to learn.

The optimism of the early postwar period had many sources, some of them a matter of social history, I believe. But it also had roots in the sciences, in particular, in successful integration of parts of biology within the core natural sciences. That suggested to many people that science might be approaching a kind of "last frontier," the mind and the brain, which should fall within our intellectual grasp in due course, as was soon to happen with DNA.

Quite commonly, these investigations have adopted the thesis that "Things mental, indeed minds, are emergent properties of brains," while recognizing that "these emergences are not regarded as irreducible but are produced by principles that control the interactions between lower level events—principles we do not yet understand." The last phrase reflects the optimism that has been a persistent theme throughout this period, rightly or wrongly.

I am quoting a distinguished neuroscientist, Vernon Mountcastle of the Johns Hopkins University Institute of Mind/Brain. Mountcastle is introducing a volume of essays published by the American Academy of Arts and Sciences, with contributions by leading researchers, who review the achievements of the past half century in understanding the brain and its functions ("The Brain" 1998). The thesis on emergence is widely accepted in the field, often considered a distinctive contribution of the current era. In the last few years, the thesis has repeatedly been presented as an "astonishing hypothesis," "the bold assertion that mental phenomena are entirely natural and caused by the neurophysiological activities of the brain" and "that capacities of the human mind are in fact capacities of the human brain." The thesis has also been offered as a "radical new idea" in the philosophy of mind that may at last put to rest Cartesian dualism, some believe, while others express doubt that the apparent chasm between body and mind can really be bridged.

Within the brain and cognitive sciences, many would endorse the position expressed by Harvard evolutionary biologist E. O. Wilson in the same American Academy issue on the brain: "Researchers now speak confidently of a coming solution to the brain-mind problem," presumably along the lines of Mountcastle's thesis on emergence. One contributor, the eminent neurobiologist Semir Zeki, suggests that the brain sciences can even confidently anticipate addressing the creative arts, thus incorporating the outer limits of human achievement within the neurosciences. He also observes that the ability to recognize "a continuous vertical line is a mystery that neurology has not yet solved"; perhaps the word *yet* is a bit more realistic here.

As far as I am aware, the neural basis for the remarkable behavior of bees also remains a mystery. This behavior includes what appear to be impressive cognitive feats and also some of the few known analogues to distinctive properties of human language, notably the regular reliance on "displaced reference"—communication about objects not in the sensory field (Griffin 1994). The prospects for vastly more complex organisms seem considerably more remote.

Whatever one may speculate about current prospects, it is worth bearing in mind that the leading thesis about minds as emergent properties of brains is far from novel. It revives eighteenth-century proposals put forth for compelling reasons, by, among others, the famous English scientist Joseph Priestley, and before him, the French physician Julien Offray de la Mettrie. As Priestley formulated the thesis, "The powers of sensation or perception and thought" are properties of "a certain organized system of matter." Properties "termed mental are the result [of the] organical structure" of the brain and "the human nervous system" generally.

In other words, "Things mental, indeed minds, are emergent properties of brains" (Mountcastle). Priestley of course could not say how this emergence takes place, and we are not much better off after 200 years.

The reasons for the eighteenth-century conclusions about emergence were indeed compelling. I think the brain and cognitive sciences can learn some useful lessons from the rise of the emergence thesis 200 years ago, and from the ways the sciences have developed since, right up to mid-twentieth century, when the assimilation of parts of biology to chemistry took place. The debates of the early part of this century about atoms, molecules, chemical structures and reactions, and related matters are strikingly similar to current controversies about mind and brain. I would like to digress for a moment on these topics—instructive and pertinent ones, I think.

The reasoning that led to the eighteenth-century emergence thesis was straightforward. The modern scientific revolution was inspired by the "mechanical philosophy," the idea that the world is a great machine that could in principle be constructed by a master artisan and that is therefore intelligible to us, in a very direct sense. The world is a complex version of the clocks and other intricate automata that fascinated the seventeenth and eighteenth centuries, much as computers have provided a stimulus to thought and imagination in recent years—the change of artifacts has limited consequences for the basic issues, as Alan Turing demonstrated sixty years ago.

In that context, Descartes had been able to formulate a relatively clear mind-body problem: it arose because he observed phenomena that, he plausibly argued, could not be accounted for in terms of automata. He was proven wrong, for reasons he could never have guessed: nothing can be accounted for within the mechanical philosophy, even the simplest terrestrial and planetary motion. Newton established, to his great dismay, that "a purely materialistic or mechanistic physics ... is impossible" (Koyré 1957:210).

Newton was bitterly criticized by leading scientists of his day for reverting to the mysticism from which we were at last to be liberated by the scientific revolution. He was condemned for reintroducing "occult qualities" that are no different from the mysterious "sympathies" and "antipathies" of the neoscholastic Aristotelian physicists, which were much ridiculed. Newton agreed. He regarded his discoveries as an utter "absurdity," and for the rest of his life sought some way around them: he kept searching for a "certain most subtle spirit which pervades and lies hid in all gross bodies," and would account for motion, interaction, electrical attraction and repulsion, properties of light, sensation, and the ways in which "members of animal bodies move at the command of the will"—comparable mysteries, he felt.

Similar efforts continued for centuries, but always in vain. The absurdity was real, and simply had to be accepted. In a sense it was overcome in this century, but only by introducing what Newton and his contemporaries would have regarded as even greater absurdities. We are left with the "admission into the body of science of incomprehensible and inexplicable 'facts' imposed upon us by empiricism" (Koyré 1957:272).

Well before Priestley, David Hume wrote that "Newton seemed to draw off the veil from some of the mysteries of nature," but "he shewed at the same time the imperfections of the mechanical philosophy; and thereby restored [Nature's] ultimate secrets to that obscurity, in which they ever did and ever will remain" (Hume [1778] 1983:542). The world is simply not comprehensible to human intelligence, at least in the ways that early modern science had hoped and expected. In his classic study of the history of materialism, Friedrich Lange observes that their expectations and goals were abandoned, and we gradually "accustomed ourselves to the abstract notion of forces, or rather to a notion hovering in a mystic obscurity between abstraction and concrete comprehension." Lange describes this as a "turning-point" in the history of materialism that removes the surviving remnants of the doctrine far from those of the "genuine Materialists" of the seventeenth century, and deprives them of much significance (Lange 1925:308).

The turning point also led gradually to a much weaker concept of intelligibility than the one that inspired the modern scientific revolution: intelligibility of theories, not of the world—a considerable difference, which may well bring into operation different faculties of mind, a topic some day for cognitive science, perhaps.

A few years after writing the introduction to the English translation of Lange's history, Bertrand Russell illustrated the distinction with an example reinvented recently and now a centerpiece of debates over consciousness. Russell pointed out that "a man who can see knows things which a blind man cannot know; but a blind man can know the whole of physics," so "the knowledge which other men have and he has not is not part of physics" (Russell 1929:389). Russell is referring to the "qualitative knowledge which we possess concerning mental events," which might not simply be a matter of conscious awareness, as the phenomenon of blindsight suggests. Some leading animal researchers hold that something similar may be true of bees (Griffin 1994). Russell's own conclusion is that the natural sciences seek "to discover the causal skeleton of the world," and can aim no higher than that. "Physics studies percepts only in their cognitive aspect; their other aspects lie outside its purview" (Russell 1929:391–392).

These issues are now very much alive, but let us put them aside and return to the intellectual crisis of eighteenth-century science.

One consequence was that the concept of "body" disappeared. There is just the world, with its many aspects: mechanical, chemical, electromagnetic, optical, mental—aspects that we may hope to unify somehow, but how no one knows. We can speak of "the physical world," if we like, but for emphasis, without implying that there is some other world—rather the way we speak of the "real truth," without meaning that there is some other kind of truth. The world has occult properties, which we try to comprehend as best we can, with our highly specific forms of intelligence, which may leave much of nature a mystery, at least if we ourselves are part of the biological world, not angels. There is no longer a "mind-body problem," because there is no useful notion of "body," of the "material" or "physical" world. The terms simply indicate what is more or less understood and assimilable in some manner to core physics, whatever that turns out to be. For individual psychology, the emergence hypothesis of contemporary neuroscience becomes a truism: there is no coherent alternative, with the abandonment of materialism in any significant sense of the concept.

Of course, that leaves all empirical problems unsolved, including the question of how bees find a flower after watching the "waggle dance," and how they know not even to leave the hive if the directions lead to the middle of a lake, it has been reported (Gould 1990). Also included are questions about the relation between the principles of human language and properties of cells. Included as well are the much more far-reaching problems that troubled Descartes and Newton about the "commands of the will," including the normal use of language—innovative, appropriate, and coherent, but apparently uncaused. It is useful to remember that these problems underlie Descartes's two-substance theory, which was put to rest by Newton, who showed that one of the two substances does not exist: namely body.

How do we address the real problems? I know of no better advice than the recommendations of the eighteenth-century English chemist Joseph Black: "Chemical affinity must be accepted as a first principle, which we cannot explain any more than Newton could explain gravitation, and let us defer accounting for the laws of affinity until we have established such a body of doctrine as Newton has established concerning the laws of gravitation" (Black, quoted in Schofield 1970:226). That is pretty much what happened. Chemistry proceeded to establish a rich body of doctrine, "its triumphs ... built on no reductionist foundation but rather achieved in isolation from the newly emerging science of physics" (Thackray 1970). That continued until recently. What was finally achieved by Linus Pauling sixty years ago was unification, not reduction. Russell's observation in 1929 that chemical laws "cannot at present be reduced to physical laws" turns out to have been misleading, in an important way (Russell 1929). Physics had to undergo fundamental changes, mainly in the 1920s, in order to be unified with basic chemistry, departing even more radically from commonsense notions of "the physical." Physics had to "free itself" from "intuitive pictures" and give up the hope of "visualizing the world," as Heisenberg put it (quoted in Holton 1996:191), another long leap away from intelligibility in the sense of the scientific revolution of the seventeenth century, which brought about the "first cognitive revolution" as well.

The unification of biology and chemistry a few years later can be misleading. That was genuine reduction, but to a newly created physical chemistry; some of the same people were involved, notably Pauling. True reduction is not so common in the history of science, and need not be assumed automatically to be a model for what will happen in the future.

Prior to the unification of chemistry and physics in the 1930s, it was commonly argued by distinguished scientists, including Nobel Prize winners in chemistry, that chemistry is just a calculating device, a way to organize results about chemical reactions, sometimes to predict them. Chemistry is not about anything real. The reason was that no one knew how to reduce it to physics. That failure was later understood: reduction was impossible, until physics underwent a radical revolution. It is now clear—or should be clear—that the debates about the reality of chemistry were based on fundamental misunderstanding. Chemistry was "real" and "about the world" in the only sense of these concepts that we have: it was part of the best conception of how the world works that human intelligence had been able to contrive. It is impossible to do better than that.

The debates about chemistry a few years ago are in many ways echoed in the philosophy of mind and the cognitive sciences today—and theoretical chemistry, of course, is hard science, merging indistinguishably with core physics. It is not at the periphery of scientific understanding, like the brain and cognitive sciences, which are trying to study systems vastly more complex. I think these recent debates about chemistry, and their surprising outcome, may be instructive for the brain and cognitive sciences. We should follow Joseph Black's good advice and try to construct "bodies of doctrine" in whatever terms we can, unshackled by commonsense intuitions about how the world must be—we know that it is not that way—and untroubled by the fact that we may have to "defer accounting for the principles" in terms of general scientific understanding. This understanding may turn out to be inadequate to the task of unification, as has regularly been the case for 300 years. A good deal of discussion of these topics seems to me misguided, perhaps seriously so, for reasons such as these.

Other similarities are worth remembering. The "triumphs of chemistry" offered useful guidelines for the eventual reconstruction of physics: they provided conditions that core physics would have to meet, in some manner or other. In a similar way, discoveries about bee communication provide conditions that have to be met by some account in terms of cells. In both cases, it is a two-way street: the discoveries of physics constrain possible chemical models, as those of basic biology should constrain models of insect behavior.

There are familiar analogues in the brain and cognitive sciences: the issue of computational, algorithmic, and implementation theories emphasized particularly by David Marr, for example. Or Eric Kandel's work on learning in marine snails, seeking "to translate into neuronal terms ideas that have been proposed at an abstract level by experimental psychologists," and thus to show how cognitive psychology and neurobiology "may begin to converge to yield a new perspective in the study of learning" (Hawkins and Kandel 1984:380, 376). Very reasonable, though the actual course of the sciences should alert us to the possibility that the convergence may not take place because something is missing—where, we cannot know until we find out.

Questions of this kind arise at once in the study of language and the brain. By *language* I mean "human language," and understand each particular language to be a state of a subcomponent of the brain specifically dedicated to language—as a system that is; its elements may have other functions. It seems clear that these curious brain states have computational properties: a language is a system of discrete infinity, a procedure that enumerates an infinite class of expressions, each of them a structured complex of properties of sound and meaning.

The recursive procedure is somehow implemented at the cellular level, how no one knows. That is not surprising; the answers are unknown for far simpler cases. Randy Gallistel observes that "we clearly do not understand how the nervous system computes," even "how it carries out the small set of arithmetic and logical operations that are fundamental to any computation." His more general view is that in all animals, learning is based on specialized mechanisms, "instincts to learn" in specific ways. These "learning mechanisms" can be regarded as "organs within the brain [that] are neural circuits whose structure enables them to perform one particular kind of computation," as they do more or less reflexively apart from "extremely hostile environments." Human language acquisition is instinctive in this sense, based on a specialized "language organ." This "modular view of learning" Gallistel takes to be "the norm these days in neuroscience" (Gallistel 1997:77, 82, 86–89).

Rephrasing in terms I have sometimes used (Chomsky 1975), the "learning mechanisms" are dedicated systems LT(O, D) (*learning theories* for organism O in domain D); among them is LT(Human, Language), the specialized "language organ," the *faculty of language* FL. Its initial state is an expression of the genes, comparable to the initial state of the human visual system, and appears to be a common human possession to close approximation. Accordingly, a typical child will acquire any language under appropriate conditions, even under severe deficit and in "hostile environments." The initial state changes under the triggering and shaping effect of experience, and internally determined processes of maturation, yielding later states that seem to stabilize at several stages, finally at about puberty. We can think of the initial state of FL as a device that maps experience into state L attained, hence a *language acquisition device* (LAD). The existence of such a LAD is sometimes regarded as controversial, but it is no more so than the (equivalent) assumption that there is a dedicated *language module* that accounts for the linguistic development of an infant as distinct from that of her pet kitten (or chimpanzee, or whatever), given essentially the same experience. Even the most extreme "radical behaviorist" speculations presuppose (often tacitly) that a child can somehow distinguish linguistic materials from the rest of the confusion around it, hence postulating the existence of

FL = LAD. As discussion of language acquisition becomes more substantive, it moves to assumptions about FL that are richer and more domain specific, without exception to my knowledge.

It may be useful to distinguish modularity understood in these terms from Jerry Fodor's influential ideas (Fodor 1983). Fodorian modularity is concerned primarily with input systems. In contrast, modularity in the sense just described is concerned with cognitive systems, their initial states and states attained, and the ways these states enter into perception and action. Whether the processing (input/output) systems that access such cognitive states are modular in Fodor's sense is a distinct question.

As Fodor puts the matter, "The perceptual system for a language comes to be viewed as containing quite an elaborate theory of the objects in its domain; perhaps a theory couched in terms of a grammar of the language" (and the same should hold for the systems of language use) (Fodor 1983:51). I would prefer a somewhat different formulation: Jones's language L is a state of FL, and Jones's perceptual (and production) systems access L. Theories of L (and FL) are what the linguist seeks to discover; adapting traditional terms, the linguist's theory of Jones's L can be called *a grammar of L*, and the theory of FL can be called *universal grammar*, but it is the linguist, not Jones, who has a theory of L and FL, a theory that is partial and partially erroneous. Jones has L, but no theory of L (except what he may believe about the language he has, beliefs that have no privileged status, any more than what Jones may believe about his visual system or problem-solving capacities).

When we look more closely, we see that more is involved here than choice of terminology, but let us put that aside. Clearly the notions of modularity are different, as are the questions raised, though they are not incompatible, except perhaps in one sense: FL and L appear to be "central systems" in Fodor's framework, distinctive components of the central "architecture of mind," so that the "central systems" would not be unstructured (what Fodor calls "Quinean and isotropic"), containing only domain-neutral properties of inference, reasoning, and thought generally.

For language, this "biolinguistic" approach seems to me very sound (see Jenkins, 2000, on the state of the art). But elementary questions remain to be answered before there will be much hope of solving problems about the cellular implementation of recursive procedures, and mechanisms for using them, that appear to have evolved recently and to be isolated in the biological world in essential respects.

Problems become still more severe when we discover that there is debate, which appears to be substantive, as to how to interpret the recursive procedure. There are so-called derivational and representational interpretations, and subvarieties of each. And although on the surface the debates have the character of a debate over whether 25 is 5 squared or 5 is the square root of 25, when we look more closely we find empirical evidence that seems to support one or another view.

These are difficult and subtle questions, at the borders of inquiry, but the striking fact is that they do appear to be empirical questions. The fact is puzzling. It is far from clear what it means to say that a recursive procedure has a particular interpretation for a cognitive system, not a different interpretation formally equivalent to the first; or how such distinctions—whatever they mean—might be implemented at the cellular level. We find ourselves in a situation reminiscent of that of post-Newtonian scientists—for example, Lavoisier, who believed that "the number and nature of elements" is "an unsolvable problem, capable of an infinity of solutions none of which probably accord with Nature." "It seems extremely probable that we know nothing at all about ... [the] ... indivisible atoms of which matter is composed," and never will, he thought (Lavoisier, quoted in Brock 1992:129).

Some have reacted to these problems much in the way that leading natural scientists did in the era before unification of chemistry and physics. One influential proposal is the *computer model of the mind.* According to this view, cognitive science "aims for a level of description of the mind that abstracts away from the biological realizations of cognitive structures." It does so in principle, not because of lack of understanding we hope will be temporary, or to solve some problem for which implementation is irrelevant, or in order to explore the consequences of certain assumptions. Rather, for cognitive science "it does not matter" whether one chooses an implementation in "gray matter ..., switches, or cats and mice." Psychology is therefore not a biological science, and given the "anti-biological bias" of this approach, if we can construct automata in "our *computational* image," performing as we do by some criterion, then "we will naturally feel that the most compelling theory of the mind is one that is general enough to apply to both them and us," as distinct from "a biological theory of the *human* mind [which] will not apply to these machines" (Block 1990:261).

So conceived, cognitive science is nonnaturalistic, not part of the natural sciences in principle. Notice that this resembles the view of chemistry, not long ago, as a calculating device, but is far more extreme: no one proposed that "the most compelling theory of chemistry is one general enough to apply" to worlds with different physical laws than ours, but with phenomena that are similar by some criterion. One might ask why there should be such a radical departure from the practice of the sciences when we turn to the study of mind.

The account of the computer model is a fair description of much of the work in the cognitive sciences; for example, work that seeks to answer questions framed in terms of the Turing test—a serious misinterpretation of Turing's proposals, I think, but that is another matter. For the computer model of the mind, the problems I mentioned do not arise. It also follows that nothing discovered about the brain will matter for the cognitive sciences. For example, if it is some day discovered that one interpretation of the recursive procedure can be implemented at the cellular level, and another cannot, the result will be irrelevant to the study of human language.

That does not seem to me to be a wise course.

Another approach, influential in contemporary philosophy of mind and theoretical cognitive science, is to hold that the relation of the mental to the physical is not *reducibility* but *supervenience*: any change in mental events or states entails a "physical change," though not conversely, and there is nothing more specific to say. The preunification debates over chemistry could be rephrased in these terms: those denying the "reality" of chemistry could have held that chemical properties supervene on physical properties, but are not reducible to them. That would have been an error, for reasons already mentioned: the right physical properties had not yet been discovered. Once they were, talk of supervenience becomes irrelevant and we move toward unification. The same stance seems to me reasonable in this case.

Still another approach is outlined in a highly regarded book by neuroscientist Terrence Deacon (1997) on language and the brain. He proposes that students of language and its acquisition who are concerned with states of a genetically determined "module" of the brain have overlooked another possibility: "that the extra support for language learning," beyond the data of experience, "is vested neither in the brain of the child nor in the brains of parents or teachers, but outside brains, in language itself." Language and languages are extrahuman. "Languages have evolved with respect to human brains"; "The world's languages evolved spontaneously" and have "become better and better adapted to people," apparently the way prey and predator coevolve in the familiar cycle. Language and languages are not only extrahuman organisms but are outside the biological world altogether, it would seem. Infants are "predisposed to learn human languages" and "are strongly biased in their choices" of "the rules underlying language," but it is a mistake to try to determine what these predispositions are, and to seek their realization in brain mechanisms (in which case the extrahuman organisms vanish from the scene). It is worse than a mistake: to pursue the course of normal science in this case is to resort to a "magician's trick" (Deacon 1997: chap. 4).

I have been giving quotations, because I have no idea what this means, and understanding is not helped by Deacon's unrecognizable account of "linguistics" and of work allegedly related to it. Whatever the meaning may be, the conclusion seems to be that it is a waste of time to investigate the brain to discover the nature of human language, and that studies of language must be about the extrahuman—and apparently extrabiological—organisms that coevolved with humans and somehow "latch on" to them, English latching on some, Japanese to others.

I do not recommend this course either; in fact could not, because I do not understand it.

Within philosophy of language and mind, and a good part of theoretical cognitive science, the consensus view also takes language to be something outside the brain: it is a property of some social organism, a "community" or a "culture" or a "nation." Each language exists "independently of any particular speakers," who have a "partial, and partially erroneous, grasp of the language." The child "borrows" the language from the community, as a "consumer." The real sound and meaning of the words of English are those of the lender and are therefore outside of my head, I may not know them, and it would be a strange accident if anyone knew them for "all of English." I am quoting several outstanding philosophers of mind and language, but the assumptions are quite general, in one or another form.

Ordinary ways of talking about language reinforce such conceptions. Thus we say that a child is learning English but has not yet reached the goal. What the child has acquired is not a language at all: we have no name for whatever it is that a four-year-old has acquired. The child has a "partial, and partially erroneous, grasp" of English. So does everyone, in fact.

Learning is an achievement. The learner has a goal, a target: you aim for the goal and if you have not reached it, you have not yet learned, though you may be on the way. Formal learning theory adopts a similar picture: it asks about the conditions that must be satisfied for the learner to reach the target, which is set independently. It also takes the "language" to be a set of sentences, not the recursive procedure for generating expressions in the sense of the empirical study of language (often called the *internalized grammar*, a usage that has sometimes been misleading). In English, unlike similar languages, one also speaks of "knowing a language." That usage has led to the conclusion that some cognitive relation holds between the person and the language, which is therefore outside the person: we do not know a state of our brains.

None of this has any biological interpretation. Furthermore, much of it seems to me resistant to any explicit and coherent interpretation. That is no problem for ordinary language, of course. But there is no reason to suppose that common usage of such terms as *language* or *learning* (or *belief* or numerous others like them), or others belonging to similar semantic fields in other linguistic systems, will find any place in attempts to understand the aspects of the world to which they pertain. Likewise, no one expects the commonsense terms *energy* or *liquid* or *life* to play a role in the sciences, beyond a rudimentary level. The issues are much the same.

There have been important results in the study of animal behavior and communication in a variety of species, generally in abstraction from the cellular level. How much such work advances us toward an understanding of human higher mental faculties seems unclear. Gallistel introduced a compendium of review articles on the topic a few years ago by arguing that representations play a key role in animal behavior and cognition. Here *representation* is to be understood in the mathematical sense of isomorphism: a one-one relation between mind/brain processes and "an aspect of the environment to which these processes adapt the animal's behavior"—for example, when an ant represents the corpse of a conspecific by its odor (Gallistel 1990b:2).

The results are extremely interesting, but it is not clear that they offer useful analogues for human conceptual representation, specifically, for what is called *phonetic* or *semantic representation.* They do not seem to provide a useful approach to the relation of phonology to motions of molecules, and research does not follow this course. Personally, I think the picture is more misleading than helpful on the meaning side of language, contrary to most contemporary work about meaning and reference. Here particularly, I think we can learn a good deal from work on these topics in the early modern period, now mostly forgotten. When we turn to the organization and generation of representations, analogies break down very quickly beyond the most superficial level.

The "biolinguistic" approach is at the core of the modern study of language, at least as I understand it. The program was formulated with relative clarity about forty years ago. As soon as the first attempts were made to develop recursive procedures to characterize linguistic expressions, it instantly became clear that little was known, even about well-studied languages. Existing dictionaries and grammars, however extensive, provide little more than hints and a few generalizations. They tacitly rely on the unanalyzed "intelligence of the reader" to fill in the rest, which is just about everything. Furthermore the generalizations are often misleading or worse, because they are limited to observed phenomena and their apparent structural arrangements—morphological paradigms, for example. As has been discovered everywhere in the sciences, these patterns mask principles of a different character that cannot be detected directly in arrangement of phenomena.

But filling in the huge gaps and finding the real principles and generalizations is only part of the problem. It is also necessary to account for the fact that all children acquire their languages: their own private languages, of course, from this point of view, just as their visual systems are their own, not a target they are attempting to reach or a community possession or some extrahuman organism that coevolved with them.

It quickly became clear that the two basic goals are in conflict. To describe the state attained, it seemed necessary to postulate a rich and complex system of rules, specific to the language and even specific to particular grammatical constructions: relative clauses in Japanese, verb phrases in Swahili, and so on. But the most elementary observations about acquisition of language showed that that cannot be even close to accurate. The child has insufficient (or no) evidence for elementary properties of language that were discovered, so it must be that they reflect the initial state of the language faculty, which provides the basic framework for languages, allowing only the kinds of marginal variation that experience could determine.

The tension between these two goals set the immediate research agenda forty years ago. The obvious approach was to try to abstract general properties of the complex states attained, attribute them to the initial state, and show that the residue is indeed simple enough to be acquired with available experience. Many such efforts more or less crystallized fifteen to twenty years ago in what is sometimes called the *principles-and-parameters* approach. The basic principles of language are properties of the initial state; the parameters can vary in limited ways and are set by experience.

To a large extent, the parameters furthermore seem to be lexical, in fact properties of a small subcomponent of the lexicon, particularly inflectional morphology. Some recent work suggests that an even smaller subpart of inflectional morphology may be playing the central role in determining both the functioning and the superficial variety of language: inflectional morphology that lacks semantic interpretation. This narrow subcomponent may also be what is involved in the ubiquitous and rather surprising "dislocation" property of human language: the fact that phrases are pronounced in one position in a sentence, but understood as if they were in a different position, where their semantic role would be transparent.

Here there is some convergence with other approaches, including work by Alfonso Caramazza and others. These investigators have found dissociation of inflectional morphology from other linguistic processes in aphasia, and have produced some intriguing results that suggest that dislocation too may be dissociated (Caramazza 1997). A result of particular interest for the study of language is the distinction that Grodzinsky and Finkel report between dislocation of phrasal categories and of lexical categories (Grodzinsky 1990; Grodzinsky and Finkel 1998). That result would tend to confirm some recent ideas about distinctions of basic semantic, phonological, and syntactic properties of these two types of dislocation: head movement and XP-movement in technical terms.

Other recent linguistic work has led to a sharper focus on the "interface" relations between extralinguistic systems and the cognitive system of language—that is, the recursive procedure that generates expressions. The extralinguistic systems include sensorimotor and conceptual systems, which have their own properties independent of the language faculty. These systems establish what we might call "minimal design specifications" for the language faculty. To be usable at all, a language must be "legible" at the interface: the expressions it generates must consist of properties that can be interpreted by these external systems.

One thesis, which seems to me much more plausible than anyone could have guessed a few years ago, is that these minimal design specifications are also maximal conditions in nontrivial respects. That is, language is a kind of optimal solution to the minimal conditions it must meet to be usable at all. This *strong minimalist thesis*, as it is sometimes called, is highly controversial, and should be: it would be quite surprising if something like that turned out to be true. I think the research program stimulated by this thesis is promising. It has already yielded some interesting and surprising results, which may have suggestive implications for the inquiry into language and the brain. This thesis brings to prominence an apparent property of language that I already mentioned, and that might prove fundamental: the significance of semantically uninterpretable morphological features, and their special role in language variety and function, including the dislocation property.

Other consequences also suggest research directions that might be feasible and productive. One major question of linguistic research, from every perspective, is what George Miller years ago called *chunking*: what are the units that constitute expressions, for storage of information, and for access in production, perception, retrieval, and other operations? Some are reasonably clear: something like syllables, words, larger phrases of various kinds. Others that seem crucial are harder to detect in the stream of speech: phonological and morphological elements, dislocation structures, and semantically relevant configurations that may be scarcely reflected in the sound of an expression, sometimes not at all, and in this sense are "abstract." That is, these elements are really present in the internal computation, but with only indirect effects, if any, on the phonetic output.

Very recent work pursuing minimalist theses suggests that two types of abstract phrases are implicated in a special way in linguistic processes. The two types are the closest syntactic analogues to full propositions, in the semantic sense. In more technical terms, these are clauses with tense/event structure as well as force-mood indicators, and verbal phrases with a full argument structure: full CPs and verbal phrases with an external argument, but not finite or infinitival Tense-headed phrases without complementizer or verbal phrases without external argument (Chomsky 2000).

It is impossible to spell out the details and the empirical basis here, but the categories are clearly defined, and there is evidence that they have a special role with regard to sound, meaning, and intricate syntactic properties, including the systems of uninterpretable elements, dislocation, and the derivational interpretation of the recursive function. It would be extremely interesting to see if the conclusions could be tested by online studies of language use, or from other approaches.

To the extent that the strong minimalist thesis holds, interface conditions assume renewed importance. They can no longer simply be taken for granted in some inexplicit way, as in most empirical work on language. Their precise nature becomes a primary object of investigation—in linguistics, in the brain sciences, in fact from every point of view.

Exactly how the story unfolds from here depends on the actual facts of the matter. At the level of language and mind, there is a good deal to say, but this is not the place. Again, I think it makes sense to think of this level of inquiry as in principle similar to chemistry early in the twentieth century: in principle that is, not in terms of the depth and richness of the "bodies of doctrine" established.

A primary goal is to bring the bodies of doctrine concerning language into closer relation with those emerging from the brain sciences and other perspectives. We may anticipate that richer bodies of doctrine will interact, setting significant conditions from one level of analysis for another, perhaps ultimately converging in true unification. But we should not mistake truisms for substantive theses, and there is no place for dogmatism as to how the issues might move toward resolution. We know far too little for that, and the history of modern science teaches us lessons that I think should not be ignored.

References

Block, N. 1990. "The Computer Model of the Mind." In D. N. Osherson and Edward E. Smith, eds., *An Invitation to Cognitive Science*, vol. 3: *Thinking*. Cambridge, Mass.: MIT Press.

"The Brain." *Daedalus*, Spring 1998 (special issue).

Brock, William H. 1992. *The Norton History of Chemistry*. New York: Norton.

Caramazza, A. 1997. "Brain and Language." In M. S. Gazzaniga, *Conversations in the Cognitive Neurosciences*. Cambridge, Mass.: MIT Press.

Chomsky, N. 1975. *Reflections on Language*. New York: Pantheon. Reprint. New York: New Press, 1998.

Chomsky, N. 2000. "Minimalist Inquiries: The Framework." In R. Martin, D. Michaels, and J. Uriagereka, eds., *Step by Step: Essays on Minimalist Syntax in Honor of Howard Lasnik*. Cambridge, Mass.: MIT Press.

Deacon, T. W. 1997. *The Symbolic Species: The Co-Evolution of Language and the Brain*. New York: Norton.

Fodor, J. A. 1983. *The Modularity of Mind*. Cambridge, Mass.: MIT Press.

Gallistel, C. R. 1997. "Neurons and Memory." In M. S. Gazzaniga, *Conversations in the Cognitive Neurosciences*. Cambridge, Mass.: MIT Press.

Gallistel, C. R., ed. 1990a. "Animal Cognition." *Cognition* 37 (special issue), 1–2.

Gallistel, C. R. 1990b. "Representations in Animal Cognition: An Introduction." In C. R. Gallistel, ed., "Animal Cognition." *Cognition* 37 (special issue), 1–22.

Gazzaniga, M. S. 1997. *Conversations in the Cognitive Neurosciences*. Cambridge, Mass.: MIT Press.

Gould, J. L. 1990. "Honey Bee Cognition." In C. R. Gallistel, ed., "Animal Cognition." *Cognition* 37 (special issue), 83–104.

Griffin, D. R. 1994. "Animal Communication as Evidence of Animal Mentality." In D. C. Gajdusek and G. M. McKhann, eds., *Evolution and Neurology of Language: Discussions in Neuroscience* X, 1–2.

Grodzinsky, Y. 1990. *Theoretical Perspectives on Language Deficits*. Cambridge, Mass.: MIT Press.

Grodzinsky, Y., and L. Finkel. 1998. "The Neurology of Empty Categories: Aphasics' Failure to Detect Ungrammaticality." *Journal of Cognitive Neuroscience* 10(2): 281–292.

Hawkins, R. D., and E. R. Kandel. 1984. "Is There a Cell-Biological Alphabet for Simple Forms of Learning?" *Psychological Review* 91: 376–391.

Holton, G. 1996. "On the Art of Scientific Imagination." *Daedalus*, Spring 183–208.

Hume, David. [1778] 1983. *History of England*. Vol. 6, chap. 71. Indianapolis: Liberty Fund.

Jenkins, L. 2000. *Biolinguistics*. Cambridge, England: Cambridge University Press.

Koyré, A. 1957. *From the Closed World to the Infinite Universe*. Baltimore: Johns Hopkins University Press.

Lange, Friedrich A. 1925. *The History of Materialism*. London: Kegan Paul.

Russell, B. 1929. *The Analysis of Matter*. Leipzig: Teubner.

Schofield, Robert E. 1970. *Mechanism and Materialism: British Natural Philosophy in an Age of Reason*. Princeton: Princeton University Press.

Thackray, A. 1970. *Atoms and Powers*. Cambridge, Mass.: Harvard University Press.

Chapter 2

Cognitive Neuroscience of Speech Processing

David Poeppel and Alec Marantz

In the context of cognitive neuroscience, in general, and research on the neural basis of speech and language, in particular, a focus on speech processing provides some compelling advantages over other possible objects of study. First, the inputs to the speech perception system are well-understood signals from the perspective both of the physical structure of the signals and of the psychophysical responses associated with them (Liberman 1996; Stevens 1998). Second, a body of research on animals exists that has shown what types of neuronal responses are associated with processing speech sounds in the mammalian central nervous system (Steinschneider et al. 1995). Insofar as it is possible to connect human experimental data to that literature in plausible ways, a solid neurobiological grounding for human speech processing is realistic. Finally, speech processing offers the possibility of understanding how attributes of a physical signal are transformed into symbolic mental representations that enter into further computation. Phonetics and phonology constitute domains of knowledge in which linguists have made explicit how computations are performed on the representations that derive from speech perception. Beyond being interesting in its own right, then, and considered in the larger context of cognitive neuroscience, the speech processing system can illuminate how (acoustic) sensory input is transformed into the abstract representations that form the basis of the computational system that constitutes language. From that perspective, research on speech perception is directly relevant to questions of the architecture of cognitive systems in general.

Most recent research examining the neural basis of speech processing has focused on functional anatomy. A variety of studies, typically deficit-lesion studies and hemodynamic imaging experiments, attempt to delineate the anatomic organization of the speech perception system. The regions most often implicated include the left and right superior temporal cortical areas (Binder et al. 1997; Démonet et al. 1992; Fiez et al. 1995; Petersen et al. 1989; Price et al. 1996), the left supramarginal gyrus (Caplan, Gow, and Makris 1995; Paulesu, Frith, and Frackowiak 1993; Petersen et al. 1989), and (left) frontal cortical fields, including Broca's area (Zatorre et al. 1992). Often, these studies have been performed with the goal of isolating "phonetic processing" or "phonological processing." While some degree of consensus is beginning to emerge in the field, there is no unified view of the cortical functional anatomy of the speech processing system. Indeed, the research has led to some controversy (Poeppel 1996; Démonet et al. 1996), and only recently have there been attempts to unify the findings. To the extent that one can find convergence in the field, there are now models of speech processing that explicitly try to incorporate observations from neuroscience within the constraints provided by linguistics and speech science (Hickok and Poeppel 2000; chap. 4, this volume).

According to one view, deriving from deficit-lesion work, neuroimaging, and clinical studies, the network supporting speech processing consists of the left and right superior temporal cortices, the left supramarginal gyrus, and left frontal areas including parts of Broca's area and possibly parts of the anterior insula (Hickok and Poeppel 2000). In this model, the superior temporal cortex (particularly areas in the superior temporal gyrus, STG; Brodmann's area 22) *bilaterally* supports the construction of sound-based representations of the speech signal. Beyond this initial elaboration of the input signal, there are two "interfaces" that these sound-based representations must serve. On the one hand, listeners need to recover lexical information in order to derive meaningful interpretations from the signal. That means that the system must be able to interface with the format used in, say, inferior temporal areas including the middle and inferior temporal gyri (see chapter 4), where a variety of perceptual and conceptual representations appear to be stored or processed. On the other hand, speech signals have associated articulatory information (maybe even for perception proper; see Liberman and Mattingly 1985). Consequently, one needs a representation that allows both sound-based and articulation-based processing. A second interface thus requires that one can easily translate between auditory and articulatory representations. Motivated by the assumption that the frontal cortical fields implicated in speech are involved in articulatory processing (not necessarily for overt speech only), we hypothesize that the supramarginal gyrus mediates the "coordinate transformation" from auditory to articulatory representations. This may mean a transformation between a specifically acoustic representation to a specifically articulatory one or the transformation into detailed articulatory features of a representation that is neutral between perception and production, much like the distinctive feature representations of phonological theory. The position of the supramarginal gyrus in the parietal cortex suggests such a transformational role. Parietal areas have been argued to play a privileged role in sensorimotor transformations in a variety of contexts, and a similar role for the supramarginal gyrus in speech would bring this region in line functionally with other parietal areas (Andersen 1997; Caminiti, Ferraina, and Johnson 1996). It is worth considering that the role of the angular gyrus might also fit into such a framework. The angular gyrus is typically implicated in reading and writing, and one could imagine that the ("coordinate") transformation from visual word form to other linguistic representations is mediated by the angular gyrus.

Needless to say, virtually every area implicated in speech processing is controversial. What is uncontroversial is that the auditory cortices participate at some stage in speech processing. The research program we describe here is focused on the auditory cortex. The work attempts to understand the role that early auditory cortical areas, including A1, play in creating the representations that form the basis for further linguistic computation.

In the discussion of perception and neural coding, one needs to make a distinction between (all) "representations" and "symbolic representations." In some sense, any pattern of cerebral activation in response to an external stimulus can be said to be a representation of the stimulus. The word *representation* is usually reserved, however, for a pattern of activation characteristic of the particular external stimulus or some property of the stimulus, such that we can say that the pattern of activity is a representation of this stimulus as opposed to some other stimulus. Along these lines, the pattern of activation at visual area V1 in response to some visual stimulus presented to the eyes of a human could constitute a representation of the stimulus at V1 for that person.

The results of linguistics have shown that language processing manipulates not just any kind of representations but specifically representations consisting of abstract symbols. The connection between sound and meaning in language is not simply a mapping between a distinct representation of sound and one of meaning; rather, language involves computations over representations of linguistic units that transform one representation into another of the same kind. Phonological computations, for example, treat a linguistic feature such as [+voice] independently of any interpretation of this feature in acoustics or articulation, although such features do hold both acoustic and articulatory interpretations. Such features can be said to be "abstract" or "symbolic." Phonological computations map representations consisting of phonological features into other representations consisting of the same features. When we search for the physical instantiation of linguistic computation in the brain, then, we are looking for symbolic representations, not just any representations of language.

Looking for symbolic representations requires investigating the nature of coding in the brain—that is, the form of representations for linguistic units. Most neuroscientists make at least the tacit assumption that the brain uses spatial coding for mental representations. In spatial coding, the spatial distribution of coordinated neural activity constitutes the code. A simple example of a spatial coding is the coding of letters in Braille, where the pattern of raised dots versus flat surface over an array of possible dot positions codes for the symbols of the Latin alphabet. The spatial mapping of the body onto the somatosensory cortex, the spatial (retinotopic) mapping of the retina onto the visual cortices, and the spatial mapping of the cochlea onto the auditory cortices leads naturally to the assumption of spatial coding, since neural computation is easily viewed as a successive transformation of spatial maps from one stop to another along some processing pathway in the brain. Much crucial information in language, however, unfolds over time rather than space; even when the spectral properties of speech are spatially mapped by the cochlea and auditory cortex, it is primarily the changing spectral information over time that distinguishes speech sounds, particularly the consonants. Given that the information in the speech input is spread out over time, it is natural to consider the possibility that the brain codes and manipulates linguistic information in a form also spread out over time—that is, in a temporal code. The Morse code used in telegraphy is an example of a temporal code, in which the pattern of dots and dashes (short and long tones or signals) over time codes for the letters of the Latin alphabet.

In our work, we have focused on the temporal rather than the spatial domain, looking for evidence of temporal representation and coding both for the spectral information and the timing information in the speech signal. Central to speech processing is the transformation of continuous acoustic information into the discrete categories employed in linguistic computation. The letters of the Roman alphabet represented in Braille or Morse code are a kind of discrete category used in orthographic representations. A letter is a "t" or is not a "t." The system of language does not employ graded categories in most computations and so does not care, for example, how "good" a "t" a given letter is, just whether or not it falls into the "t" category. The work to be described centers around the transformation of the acoustic input into discrete linguistic categories and the possible coding of these categories in neural responses for the computational system of language.

2.1 Noninvasive Recording Methodologies

In the investigation of speech and language processing, one is generally tied to noninvasive recording methods. The technique of recording activity from neurons or groups of neurons with penetrating electrodes has ideal temporal and spatial resolution, but it is highly invasive (see chapter 12). It is, of course, a tool with which to explore in animal models the perceptual or articulatory interfaces that are potentially common to higher primates and humans, but it is not a technique that can be used to investigate human brain function except in clinically motivated studies (e.g., Boatman, Lesser, and Gordon 1995; Nobre, Allison, and McCarthy 1994; Ojemann 1991).

The techniques of choice to obtain images of brain activity with high *spatial* resolution are the hemodynamic methods, principally positron emission tomography (PET) and functional magnetic resonance imaging (fMRI). Figure 2.1 summarizes the noninvasive methods currently in use and highlights some of their major charac-

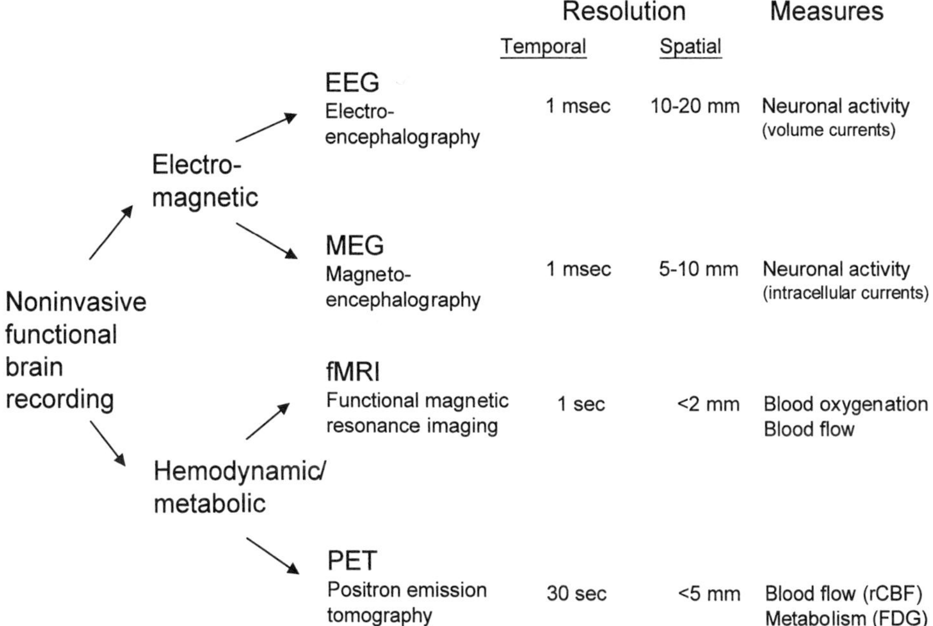

Figure 2.1
Summary of imaging methods.

teristics. A number of reviews discussing the details of the techniques are available. EEG is discussed by, for instance, by Gevins et al. (1994), PET and fMRI by Kwong (1995) and Frackowiak (chapter 8, this volume), MEG by Hämäläinen et al. (1993) and Roberts, Poeppel, and Rowley (1998).

The hemodynamic imaging methods are based on a coupling between neuronal activity and blood flow, oxygen consumption, and other physiologic parameters. These methods offer excellent spatial resolving power, but they are based on signals whose time course ranges from tens of milliseconds (fMRI) to tens of seconds (PET). Even with fMRI, the time course of the signal is slow from the perspective of neuronal activity.

A variety of recent results in neuroscience and cognitive neuroscience suggest a central role for neural information representation in the (millisecond) time domain (Bialek and Rieke 1992; Joliot, Ribary, and Llinas 1994; Singer 1993). The recording methods that can be used to investigate timing in the central nervous system are necessarily based on the electromagnetic signals associated with neuronal activity. Since we are concerned with the timing of neuronal activity associated with speech sound processing, the noninvasive recording methods available include electroencephalography (EEG) and magnetoencephalography (MEG). As shown in figure 2.1, these techniques have the millisecond temporal resolution appropriate to the recording of neuronal activity. The issue of spatial resolution for these methods is more complex. The localization of neuronal activity depends heavily on the nature of the activity itself (e.g., whether it is focal or spread over larger brain regions) and on the type of model used in the analysis. In addition, localization accuracy is limited by the quality of the anatomic and physiologic information fed into the given model. However, it is worth noting that even relatively simplistic source models, such as a single dipole in a spherical conductor, can yield localizations that place the neuronal activity in a useful anatomic context (spatial resolution approximately 5–10 mm). Magnetoencephalography (MEG), an electrophysiologic method especially well suited to study the human auditory system, will be introduced in more detail later.

2.2 Examples of Typical Time-Based Phenomena

Focusing on the temporal aspect of information, one can observe a variety of types of data noninvasively in studies of speech and language processing.

The best-known data, derived largely from the literature on event-related potentials (ERPs), are the peaks and valleys in electrical potential or magnetic field strength over time observed in evoked response recordings. Peaks with characteristic latencies and amplitudes are argued to be associated with specific mental operations, and sometimes with specific brain regions. Peaks (components) that have received much attention in studies of speech and language include the electric N1/magnetic M100 or N1m that is associated with features of an acoustic input signal (Gage et al. 1998; Hari 1990; Näätänen and Picton 1987; Poeppel et al. 1997; Poeppel et al. 1996), and the mismatch negativity response (MMN/MMF) that reflects the automatic integration of a signal and change detection between signals in memory (Dehaene-Lambertz 1997; Näätänen 1995; Phillips et al., forthcoming). Also receiving considerable attention are the following: the left anterior negativity (LAN), which is argued to correlate with a rapid structural analysis of sentences (Friederici, Hahne, and Mecklinger 1996; Neville et al. 1991; Osterhout and Holcomb 1995; chapter 6, this volume); the N400, which reflects the semantic integration of lexical information (Kutas and Hillyard 1980; Osterhout and Holcomb 1995); and the P600, which reflects analysis of sentence structure (chapter 6, this volume; Osterhout and Holcomb 1995).

A powerful approach toward combining this type of temporal peak analysis with spatial localization is exemplified in the work of Salmelin and her colleagues (Helenius et al. 1998; Levelt et al. 1998; Salmelin et al. 1994). In a technique they call the measurement of *cortical dynamics* using MEG, they identify the various peak responses and localize the sources of the sequence of peaks. Such an approach reveals the location and timing of signals associated with a particular language-processing operation. Data from a picture-naming experiment, for example, show that there are isolable responses from the occipital cortex, the left and right posterior temporal cortices, and bilateral frontal regions, all with different latencies relative to the presentation of the picture (Salmelin et al. 1994; see also chapter 4, this volume). Presumably the response peaks originating from different cortical areas are associated with distinct processes involved in executing the task at hand. The promise of this style of research is that one can follow the course of processing in space and time through the brain, matching responses to stages and modules of cognitive theories of the experimental task with a temporal resolution of milliseconds.

A second type of timing-based phenomenon are the rhythmic, or oscillatory, responses that one can observe in electrophysiologic signals (Basar et al. 1999; Llinas 1988; Steriade 1998). Oscillatory neuronal activity and synchronized firing patterns are the focus of much current neuroscience research. It has been argued that oscillations in particular frequency bands (for example the gamma band, in the range 30–60 Hz) provide the coordinating, temporal infrastructure for binding information together into the representations that form the basis of our sensory and cognitive experience. Oscillatory neuronal behavior might provide a framework to coordinate information within and across brain areas into unified percepts—much like the role of the timing clock and computational cycles of a computer. In the domain of speech perception and language processing, it has been argued that particular patterns of oscillatory activity in specific brain regions reflect a variety of subprocesses (Eulitz et al. 1996; Pulvermüller et al. 1996).

A third type of data illustrating potential information encoding in the time domain is the systematic latency variation of a specific peak or component in the response within particular areas of the brain. As explained in the introduction to this book, response latency variation can form the basis of a temporal code in the brain, much like Morse code serves as a temporal code in telegraphy. In our research, we have been investigating one specific response, the auditory evoked M100, for correlations between stimulus attributes and response peak latencies. The auditory M100 is a very early response from the human auditory cortex, presumably generated beginning at a poststimulus latency of about 70 msec. The actual peak latency of the M100 reflects specific properties of the input signals, including sound frequency. This response offers a time-based measure that supplements the (spatial) tonotopic code typically taken as the primary representational medium in audition. We will describe the data in section 2.4.

2.3 Introduction to Magnetoencephalography (MEG)

All the current state-of-the-art functional imaging modalities have tremendous intuitive appeal, although the underlying measurement technology, physiology, signal processing, and data analysis are extremely sophisticated. The basis of MEG recording lies in a simple fact of physics: wherever there is current flow, there is an associated magnetic field. The signal measured by MEG is generated by current flow in the apical dendrites of pyramidal cells in the cortex. Because of (1) the geometric "right-hand rule" relation between current and magnetic fields, (2) the orientation of pyramidal cells in the cortex, and (3) the timing and summation of postsynaptic currents in apical dendrites, it is possible to measure the magnetic fields generated by (at least some) neuronal activity outside the head.

The fields generated by even thousands of cells with overlapping activity are extremely small in amplitude. For example, the difference between sensory brain activity and the magnetic activity associated with the urban environment is about six or seven orders of magnitude. How can one measure systematic neuronal activity in the face of such measurement obstacles?

The solution has been the development of extremely sensitive magnetic field detectors. These detectors are known as *superconducting quantum interference devices*, or SQUIDS. SQUID-based detectors act as high-gain, low-noise amplifiers for the small magnetic field signals. The detectors are positioned in a dewar filled with liquid helium to maintain superconductivity. A typical contemporary MEG machine does not have just one or a few SQUID-based detectors, but large arrays, ranging from 37 to 300 sensors recording signals from large portions of the brain simultaneously.

The output of the detectors is a measurement of time-varying magnetic field strength that looks very much like an EEG recording. Each channel records the time-varying signal from one position outside the skull. The recording shown in figure 2.2a, made with a 37-channel system, shows a typical response averaged over 100 presentations of the same stimulus, with the "epochs" to be averaged together lined up temporally according to the onset of the stimulus. Such averaged responses time-locked to a stimulus are called *evoked responses*. Evoked responses measured by EEG are called *event-related potentials* or ERPs. The analysis and interpretation of stimulus-evoked MEG data is similar to what is found in the ERP literature. Notice in figure 2.2a that there is a cluster of coordinated responses in the top traces and a cluster in the bottom traces. Notice, also, that the clusters are reversed in polarity—that is, in one cluster you can see an "up-before-down" pattern, while in the other the response is "down-before-up." This configuration of responses suggests that the data were produced by an underlying dipolar source. In other words, the aggregate neuronal activity we are measuring here can be approximated as an electromagnetic dipole.

A useful way to visualize these data is as a contour map analogous to a weather map (figure 2.2b). In such a map, each line shows a region of equal field strength. These maps can be created for each sample in time—for example, each millisecond. The map in figure 2.2b, created at the largest peak of the response in figure 2.2a, is very dipolar—half the channels are recording the field exiting the head, half are recording the field entering the head (solid versus dashed lines). One can imagine a

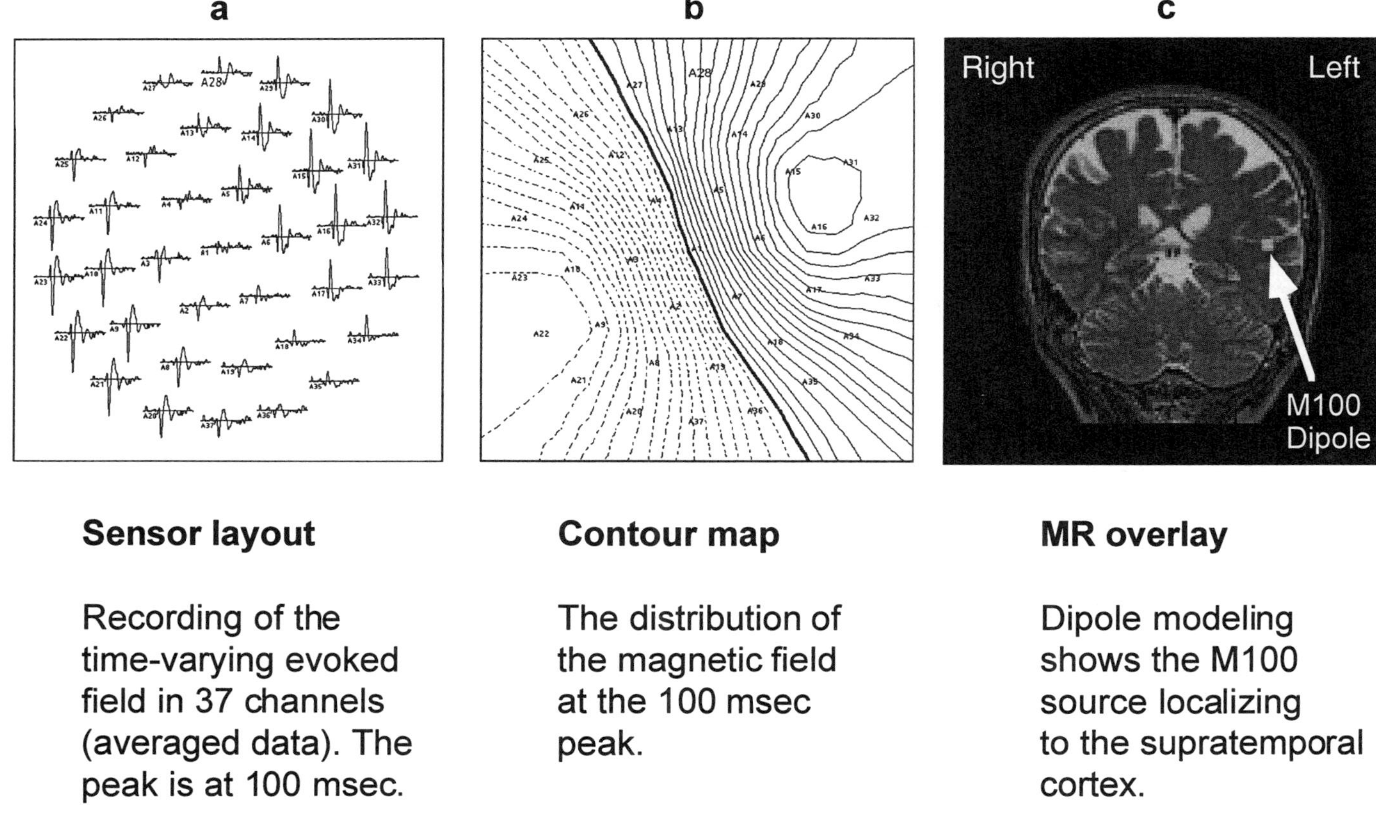

a
b
c
Right
Left
M100
Dipole
Sensor layout
Recording of the time-varying evoked field in 37 channels (averaged data). The peak is at 100 msec.
Contour map
The distribution of the magnetic field at the 100 msec peak.
MR overlay
Dipole modeling shows the M100 source localizing to the supratemporal cortex.

Figure 2.2
(*a*) Sensor layout. (*b*) Contour map. (*c*) MR overlay.

current source underlying this data pattern lying along the zero field contour line between the contour mountain and valley and pointing in one direction (the direction of the underlying source can be inferred by the right-hand rule relation).

The goal for MEG field-strength data such as these is to model the origin of the current source at each point in time. What sort of underlying neuronal activity is responsible for the observed measurement? The simplest possible model—or the most extreme idealization—is the single *equivalent current dipole* (ECD) model. In this model, the assumption is that just one electromagnetic dipole generated the extracranially measured field. The goal is to determine for every sample of time where in the head the dipole is, what its orientation is, and how strong it is (the so-called dipole moment). Of course, it is most valuable to know the location in a real anatomic context. Therefore, it is customary to coregister the source information with MR images obtained from the same subject. Figure 2.2c shows the dipole computed for the data in figure 2.2a (at the 100-msec peak) overlaid on the subject's MRI. This form of coordinating MEG-derived data with MR structural images is called *magnetic source imaging* or MSI. MSI permits the visualization of electromagnetic activity millisecond by millisecond.

ECD modeling is most appropriate for localizing focal cortical activity in which thousands of pyramidal cells are firing in synchrony in a small brain region. Such activity yields the sort of bipolar field seen in the contour map in figure 2.2b. When sources do not match the ECD ideal and/or the recorded fields are not dipolar, as is more commonly the case, more complex localization algorithms come into play. A variety of algorithms have been developed for source localization in such cases. Sekihara, for example, has developed elegant new analysis methods to best capture underlying activity (Sekihara et al. 1997, 1998, 1999).

The intuitive appeal of MEG and MSI lies in the fact that one can create images that reflect millisecond-by-millisecond brain activity in three dimensions. MEG recordings are, at present, perhaps the closest one can get to a type of noninvasive electrophysiology that is like recording from animals with penetrating electrodes. More important, we are beginning to see close correspondences between the kind of data obtained by invasive physiologic recordings in the auditory cortex of macaques and our MEG recordings from the auditory cortex. Given the temporal resolution of MEG and its ability to localize fields in a useful anatomic context, the technique thus offers a real bridge between the high-spatial-resolution data obtained with fMRI on the one hand and invasive electrophysiology on the other.

2.4 The Mismatch and M100 Experimental Paradigms

We have been using two measures in our electrophysiologic MEG studies, the magnetic mismatch response (or magnetic mismatch field MMF) and the M100 latency paradigm. The two approaches are briefly described in this section. The motivation for our experiments is the same regardless of the tools: Can we develop an understanding of how speech input is transformed into linguistic categories, how these categories are represented, and, ultimately, how computation with categories is carried out in the human brain? To get to these questions, we have been performing a variety of simple auditory experiments, some with speech sounds and some with nonspeech tonal stimuli.

2.4.1 Magnetic Mismatch Negativity or Mismatch Field (MMN/MMF)

The event-related mismatch response is a very sensitive indicator of change in a stream of acoustic information. As an ERP response, it is characterized by a negative-going wave in the response to an infrequent stimulus as compared to the response to a frequent stimulus in a sequence. This mismatch negativity or MMN is seen as a bipolar field in MEG recordings and called the MMF. It is elicited whether or not the subject attends to the stimuli. A typical example of an experimental design eliciting the MMF would be to have the subject listen to sequences of tonal stimuli at two different pitches, like [boop] [boop] [boop] [boop] [beep] [boop] [boop] [boop] [beep] and so on, where the frequent stimulus occurs more often than the infrequent in a seven-to-one ratio. When one records the event-related potential to a sequence of auditory stimuli in such a frequent/rare or standard/deviant design, the deviant sounds elicit a mismatch response (as compared to the response to the same stimulus heard outside the mismatch paradigm) that typically peaks around 200 ms after the onset of the deviant stimulus. The use of the MMN response has been developed by Näätänen and colleagues and has been used in hundreds of studies (Dehaene-Lambertz 1997; Näätänen 1995; Phillips et al., in press).

In research on speech processing it has been shown, for example by Aulanko et al. (1993), that simple consonant-vowel syllables, when presented in this sort of standard-deviant setup, elicit a mismatch field. MEG recordings of the mismatch field and subsequent reconstruction of the generators have established that the mismatch response is generated in the supratemporal auditory cortex. It has further been shown that the mismatch generator can be influenced by native phonology (Dehaene-Lambertz 1997; Näätänen et al. 1997).

Our group (Marantz, Phillips, Poeppel) has been interested in an even more specific issue. In particular, we explore whether the auditory cortex is not simply sensitive to acoustic differences among speech sounds—even when those differences reflect differences across native phonology—but whether there is evidence that category-specific labels can play a role at this stage in processing. In other words, we use the mismatch measure to test the idea that the auditory cortex at this stage of the auditory processing pathway (and this latency) has access to the discrete categorical representations relevant to speech sound processing—the phonological categories.

Led by Colin Phillips, our MEG group has designed a mismatch protocol that tests this hypothesis. Aulanko et al. (1993) showed that it is possible to introduce acoustic variation among sets of standard and deviant stimuli in the mismatch paradigm as long as the standards share a perceptual feature in contrast to the deviants. For example, two contrasting syllables will yield a MMF in a mismatch design even if both syllables are presented at a number of different pitches such that no individual stimulus token (particular syllable at a particular pitch) is especially frequent or infrequent over the length of the experiment. In the study by Aulanko and colleagues, the phonological features that held the standard and the deviant sets together were signaled by an invariant acoustic cue for each set. Thus, the phonological feature that united the sets was also an acoustic feature within the experiment. To test whether sharing a phonological feature but no acoustic feature is sufficient to unite the sets in a mismatch experiment, we needed to find a way to vary tokens within each set along the same dimension that serves as the cue to the phonological contrast between the sets. The goal is to generate stimulus sets such that only a phonological feature but no acoustic feature both unites the standards and the deviants and distinguishes one set from the other.

We chose the feature [+/−voice], a feature that distinguishes, for example, the [−voice] stop consonants [p], [t], and [k] from the [+voice] stop consonants [b], [d], and [g]. For English speakers, the primary acoustic cue to [voice] for stop consonants in word-initial position is the latency between the noise burst that signals the release of the consonant and the onset of the sound associated with the following vowel. For each [+voice]/[−voice] pair of consonants made with the same part of the mouth—[b/p], [d/t], and [g/k]—a particular latency between noise burst and vowel marks the boundary between the two sounds. For example, for English speakers a *voicing onset time* (VOT) of about 30 msec marks the boundary between [d] and [t], with VOTs shorter than 30 msec giving rise to [d] perceptions and VOTs longer than 30 msec giving rise to [t] perceptions. For VOT values between 0 and 25 msec or so on one side of the boundary and between 35 and 90 msec or so on the other side, VOT variation is not generally perceptible.

Given that we could vary VOT both to obtain token variation within each [+/−voice] category and to obtain the phonological difference between the categories, we could construct the stimulus sets needed to test whether the MMF could be generated by a phonological category alone. Figure 2.3a shows the basic design of the experiment. Again, unlike in canonical mismatch designs, both standards and deviants are drawn from a set of tokens that differ acoustically. If, given such a design, one clearly observes the mismatch response, it must be due to the fact that the stimuli have been grouped and labeled as a category. In our design, the acoustic variation within each category, [+voice] and [−voice], is along the same dimension that dis-

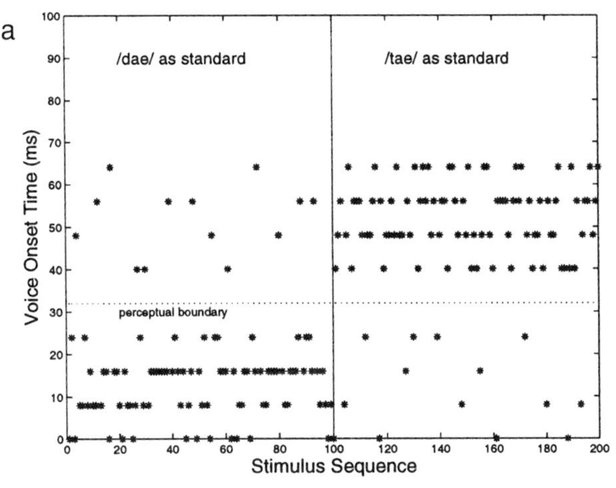

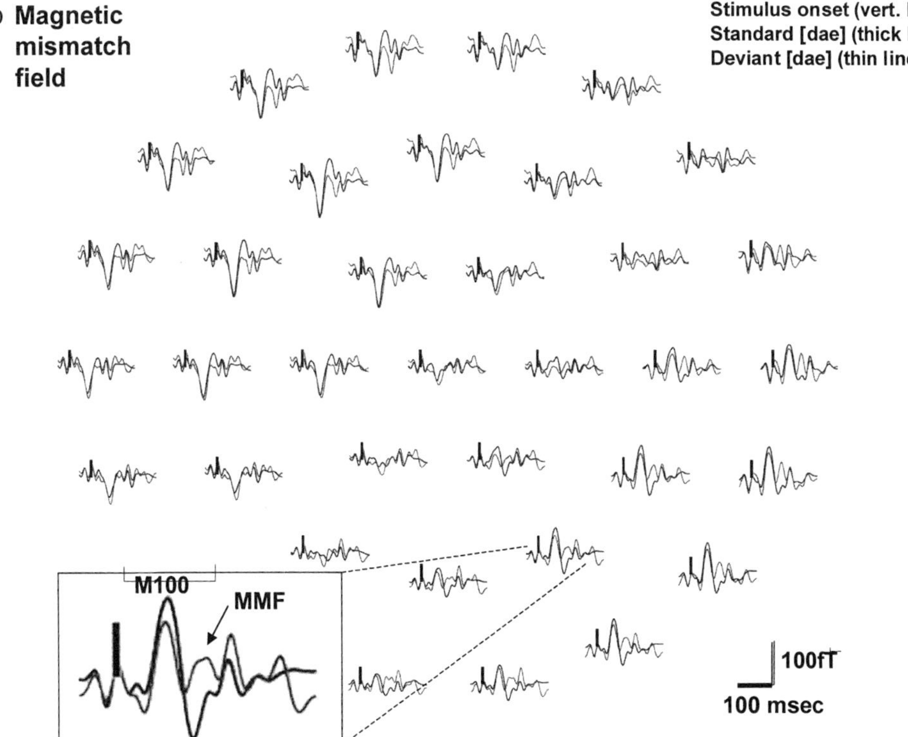

Figure 2.3
(*a*) Mismatch design. (*b*) Mismatch field in sensor layout.

tinguishes the categories. There is thus no acoustic constant that divides the sets, only the phonological category distinction.

Figure 2.3b shows the core result. The array of 37 MEG channels is pictured. The thick traces show the response to the voiced stimuli as standards; the thin traces show the response to the same set of sounds when presented as the deviant stimuli. The mismatch field shows up here as the difference between the two sets of traces. Crucial to understanding these data is the fact that a mismatch response is seen at all. It suggests that the standards and deviants, despite being different acoustically, are grouped into categories with phonological consequences—they are labeled or categorized into discrete symbolic units. To control for the possibility that our results could be attributed to subjects forming "low" and "high" VOT acoustic categories during the experiment, we repeated the experiment with a new set of stimuli created from the old set by adding a fixed amount of VOT to each stimulus. In this control experiment, the boundary separating [d] and [t] now fell in the middle of the low-VOT set. For the control, then, the two sets of stimuli still consisted of a low- and a high-VOT set, but in terms of the phonological categories [+voice] and [−voice], the stimuli failed to fall into the frequent/infrequent ratio necessary to generate a mismatch response. In contrast to the results from the original experiment, no MMF was observed in the control, confirming that an acoustic high- versus low-VOT grouping cannot account for the original results. Rather, the experiment supports the claim that the generator of the MMF has access to the phonological categorization [+/−voice].

In a follow-up experiment using the whole-head KIT MEG machine at MIT, Phillips and colleagues added additional variation within the [+voice] and [−voice] categories, including variation in point of articulation (labial ([b/p]), alveolar ([d/t]), and velar ([g/k])) along with the within-category VOT variation of the earlier experiment, for a total of twelve different tokens differing along two acoustic dimensions within each set of stimuli, [+voice] and [−voice]. This new study confirmed that the MMF could be generated based solely on a phonological feature distinction between standards and deviants and also yielded an intriguing left-right asymmetry: the MMF for this distinction between consonant categories was seen only in the left hemisphere, not the right.

2.4.2 M100 Latency Paradigm

Based on the results using the mismatch design, we hypothesize that the supratemporal auditory cortex has access to phonological representations at a latency of ~180 msec. We interpret these data to be evidence for the idea that at this point in time, on the supratemporal plane, listeners are no longer computing with acoustically defined tokens but rather with linguistic (phonological) representations. If this is correct, what is the status of even earlier cortical responses to speech sounds? The earlier responses presumably provide mechanisms for categorization that we can measure. Our group has approached this problem by looking at the major early auditory cortical response measured by MEG, and its variation, as a consequence of the stimulus features that relate to how linguistically motivated categories are formed.

The most prominent response from the human auditory cortex, whether recorded with EEG or MEG, is the response that peaks approximately 100 msec after the onset of an acoustic stimulus (N1 or M100 response). The response is elicited by virtually any auditory stimulus and can be evaluated reliably in individual subjects. Pantev and colleagues have used the magnetically recorded M100 to demonstrate the tonotopic organization of human auditory cortex (Pantev et al. 1988).

A variety of recent EEG and MEG recordings have shown that the timing of this early response (probably generated in the auditory cortex beginning at approximately 70–80 msec) varies in systematic ways. In particular, it has been shown that the peak latency of the N1 and M100 varies as a function of frequency of the signal (Forss et al. 1993; Roberts and Poeppel 1996; Woods et al. 1995). Figure 2.4a shows the relation between signal frequency (sinusoidal signals) and the peak latency of the M100 as described by Roberts and Poeppel (1996). At low frequencies (100–300 Hz), the peak latency is typically 25 msec later than for frequencies of 500 Hz and higher. Crucially, this relation appears whether the signals are presented at equal acoustic energy or at equal perceived loudness. For speech research, this fractionation of response latencies into a frequency range corresponding to fundamental frequencies or pitch of a voice (80–250 Hz) versus a range corresponding to formant frequencies (300–5000 Hz) is, of course, suggestive. The frequency dependence of the M100 is

a

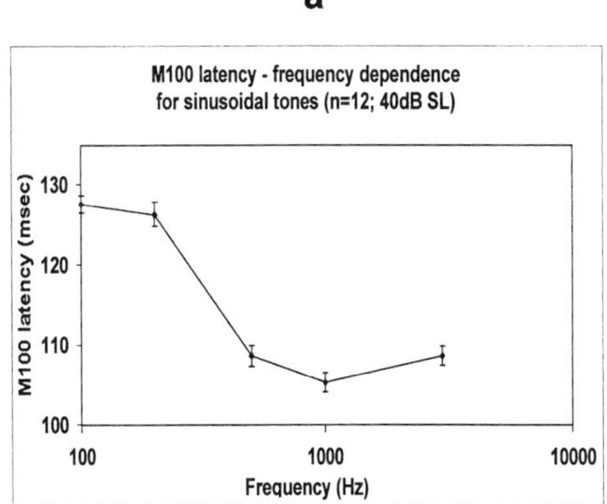

b

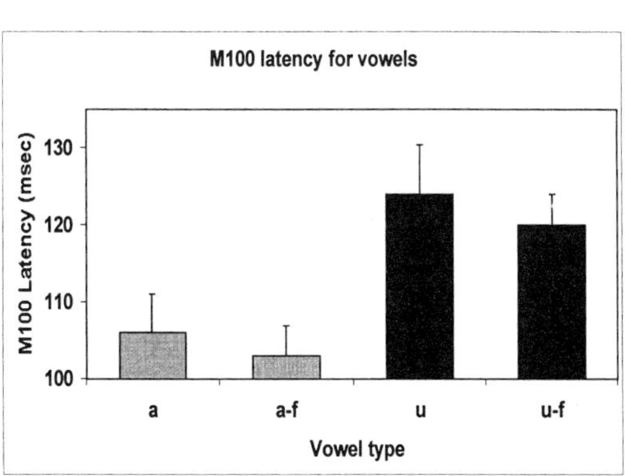

Figure 2.4
(*a*) M100 latency with frequency. (*b*) F1 dominates in vowels.

very robust, and one can easily document it in individual subjects. Importantly, this relationship holds across signal amplitudes.

Specifically, it can be shown that in a given amplitude regime (e.g., 10 dB, 20 dB, or 40 dB above threshold) the precise relation between frequency and latency is maintained (Stufflebeam et al. 1998). The robustness of this phenomenon is important because it contrasts with spatial tonotopy. Tonotopic, or more precisely, cochleotopic mapping is not robust at higher signal levels, particularly at levels typical for spoken language. Cochleotopy is most readily observed at near-threshold levels. In contrast, the frequency-latency relation holds across the range of amplitudes characteristic of spoken language. Cochleotopic maps thus do not provide good frequency representations for speech processing, while temporal coding of frequency, reflected in M100 latency variation, could serve such a function.

The M100 latency-frequency relation appears thus to reflect a "tono-chronic" method of analysis in the auditory cortex that at least supplements the tonotopic spatial mapping. The timing of the M100 response reflects cortical mechanisms that seem to use the precise timing of cortical ensembles to analyze and represent acoustic information. If the latency variation we assess noninvasively reflects a timing code in a specific cortical field, it would be an example of the same type of time-based representation described for the case of color vision (Cottaris and De Valois 1998). The view suggested by the vision work and our auditory research is that the spatial codes typically assumed for cerebral processing may be supplemented by latency-based timing codes that make use of the precise timing of cortical ensembles. In our case, this timing becomes visible as the noninvasively assessed latency variation in the M100.

Can we use this time-based representation to probe early cortical processing of speech sounds? Frequency information serves a variety of phonetic functions in language. The fundamental frequency of the speech signal—the pitch—helps identify the speaker and carries information relevant to the tones of tonal languages and to intonation patterns. Average or stable fundamental frequency reflects physical aspects of a speaker's vocal apparatus. Male speakers tend to speak with lower fundamental frequencies than females. Changing or relative fundamental frequency is important for intonation and tone. Intonational patterns signaled by fundamental frequency contours include the rising final intonation of English yes/no questions.

The vocal tract above the larynx acts as a series of connected resonance chambers to enhance certain harmonics of the fundamental frequency of the speech sounds created at the vocal cords. The enhanced harmonics creates bands of energy along the frequency dimension called *formants*. These formants reflect the resonant properties of the mouth as determined by the position of the lips and tongue. The identity of vowel sounds—for example, the distinction between [a] and [u] or between [u] and [i]—is carried acoustically in the formant structure of the vowel sounds.

Since fundamental frequency and formant structure carry different information in the speech input along the same frequency dimension, we have asked whether the M100 latency is determined by the pitch of a vowel or by its formants—that is, its linguistic identity. One experiment on this issue is summarized here (Poeppel et al. 1997). We asked whether the latency variation in the M100 will provide some clear index of what happens in vowel processing at the (early) cortical level. Evidence that the M100 tracks formant structure (vowel quality) rather than fundamental frequency (speaker identity) would suggest that the auditory system is zeroing in early on the features of the speech input that are crucial for linguistic categorization.

To test this, subjects listened to vowels made with a Klatt synthesizer while the auditory evoked neuromagnetic field was measured. We synthesized a male and a female version of the vowels [a] and [u] (fundamental frequencies 100 Hz or 200 Hz). The vowels were chosen because of their particular formant patterns. The first two formants (F1 and F2) for [a] were at 710 Hz and 1100 Hz—both values quite close to 1000 Hz, the pure tone frequency associated with the fastest M100 latencies (figure 2.4a). F1 and F2 for the [u] were at 310 Hz and 870 Hz. Because the peak in spectral density lies near F1, or some weighted average of F1 and F2, [a] and [u] differ in where their peak energy lies. Both the absolute value of F1 and the peak in spectral density lie considerably lower for [u] than for [a]. Based on previous recordings, we were able to make numerical predictions about the M100 latency, depending on whether it is determined by the fundamental or the formants. If the M100 latency is primarily conditioned by the fundamental frequency F0, the male [a] and male [u] should generate the longest M100 latencies, say around 125–130 msec (given that 100-Hz tones generate longest latencies; see figure 2.4a); the female [a] and female [u] should be associated with slightly faster M100 latencies, say 120–125 msec. In contrast, if the M100 latency is determined by the formant structure, in general, and by the dominant formant F1, in particular, a different pattern is predicted: the male and female [a] will be associated with the fastest latencies (near that of an M100 evoked by a 1000-Hz tonal signal), and the male and female [u] (with F1 quite low in frequency) should generate considerably delayed latencies. Figure 2.4b shows data from this experiment. The data are consistent with the second prediction. The [a] stimuli yielded faster latencies than the [u] stimuli, regardless of fundamental frequency. The latency pattern suggests that the response is primarily driven by the formant structure, in a numerically predictable way. In fact, follow-up studies with more artificial single-formant vowels show that the relation between M100 latency and F1 is extremely tight.

Our observations contrast sharply with a related experiment reported by Ragot and Lepaul-Ercole (1996). Like our study, theirs separated and examined the relative contributions of the pitch and spectral composition of complex auditory signals on the ERP. The authors synthesized harmonic complexes using peak spectral density values close to those of vowel formants. In particular, the stimuli were approximations of the vowels [o], [a], [i], which also varied in pitch (from 100 to 330 Hz). In contrast to our result, in their study the auditory evoked N1 followed the pitch of the stimuli, not the "formants" that they synthesized.

There is an intriguing possible explanation for the discrepancy between these studies. An important feature of our stimuli is that they were synthesized to resemble natural speech quite closely. In particular, the formant structure was such that both the frequency spacing and the relative amplitudes between formants followed from a vocal-tract model motivated by human anatomy and physiology (the model of the Klatt synthesizer). This contrasts with the stimuli used by Ragot and Lepaul-Ercole (1996). Although their harmonic complexes have spectral peaks related to the spectral peaks of natural vowels, the amplitudes of the spectral peaks were not related to the corresponding values for vowels. Crucially, the stimuli utilized by Ragot and Lepaul-Ercole do not sound like speech, but rather like buzzes. That is, despite their frequency organization, they are not perceived as speech. In summary, stimuli that are not speech, even though they resemble speech in some of their spectral characteristics, generate evoked responses that are clearly different from stimuli that are speech.

The interpretation of these experiments (and particularly the difference between our results and those of Ragot and Lepaul-Ercole) is that timing mechanisms, in particular a latency-based auditory mechanism, might provide one way to generate, early in the processing stream, categories that we argue, based on the mismatch results, are the basis for computation at slightly later times. The provocative aspect of the finding is that there is such a close relationship between the part of a speech sound that determines its phonetic identity and the brain response to speech—so close that these brain responses might be systematically and specifically related to speech processing, for example, to the extraction of formants. These results suggest experiments in which one contrasts speech and nonspeech in ways that makes differential predictions for the neurophysiologic response.

2.5 Conclusion

Three points were emphasized. First, in the context of contemporary brain imaging methods, MEG is extraordinarily useful for investigating the temporal dimension of responses. Because it is a noninvasive electrophysiologic method that nevertheless gives localization information, it provides a bridge between invasive electrophysiology as practiced in animal studies and PET and fMRI imaging, which provide good functional localization in humans but little temporal information at the millisecond scale. Second, it was argued that the auditory cortex, at least at the brain region and temporal latency associated with the generator of the MMF, has access to phonological categories. That is, at this processing stage some 100–200 msec post-stimulus onset, the brain is well beyond an acoustic analysis of differences and has reached a level at which phonological categories seem to operate in the computation. Third, we have observed that there is an alternative to spatial tonotopic coding associated with the M100 response: response peak latency correlates with stimulus properties in a consistent way across subjects and could facilitate a "tono-chronic" coding system. We have used this response to show that a simple temporal latency-based code provides a possible base for building the categorical representations of vowels in the auditory system that enter into phonological computation.

The theoretical motivation underlying the research is that language processes are computations over discrete categories organized into symbolic representations. The long-term aims of the program of research are, then, to develop an understanding of how categories are implemented in the brain and how computation is done with these categories by neuronal structures. The tools of cognitive neuroscience, including experimental paradigms and imaging machines, allow us to exploit the results of cognitive sciences like linguistics to learn about brain function. Motivated and guided by observations about language, we are learning about computation in the brain.

References

Andersen, R. 1997. Multimodal integration for the representation of space in the posterior parietal cortex. *Philosophical Transactions of the Royal Society of London, Series B: Biological Sciences*, 352, 1421–1428.

Aulanko, R., Hari, R., Lounasmaa, O. V., Näätänen, R., and Sams, M. 1993. Phonetic invariance in the human auditory cortex. *NeuroReport*, 4(12), 1356–1358.

Basar, E., Basar-Eroglu, C., Karakas, S., and Schurmann, M. 1999. Are cognitive processes manifested in event-related gamma, alpha, theta, and delta oscillations in the EEG? *Neuroscience Letters*, 259, 165–168.

Bialek, W., and Rieke, F. 1992. Reliability and information transmission in spiking neurons. *Trends in Neurosciences*, 15(11), 428–434.

Binder, J. R., Frost, J. A., Hammeke, T. A., Cox, R. W., Rao, S. M., and Prieto, T. 1997. Human brain language areas identified by functional magnetic resonance imaging. *Journal of Neuroscience*, 17(1), 353–362.

Boatman, D., Lesser, R., and Gordon, B. 1995. Auditory speech perception in the left temporal lobe: An electrical interference study. *Brain and Language*, 51, 269–290.

Caminiti, R., Ferraina, S., and Johnson, P. 1996. The sources of visual information to the primate frontal lobe: A novel role for the superior parietal lobule. *Cerebral Cortex*, 6(3), 319–328.

Caplan, D., Gow, D., and Makris, N. 1995. Analysis of lesions by MRI in stroke patients with acoustic-phonetic processing deficits. *Neurology*, 45(2), 293–298.

Cottaris, N., and De Valois, R. 1998. Temporal dynamics of chromatic tuning in macaque primary visual cortex. *Nature*, 395, 896–900.

Dehaene-Lambertz, G. 1997. Electrophysiological correlates of categorical phoneme perception in adults. *NeuroReport*, 8(4), 919–924.

Démonet, J.-F., Chollet, F., Ramsay, S., Cardebat, D., Nespoulous, J.-L., Wise, R., Rascol, A., and Frackowiak, R. 1992. The anatomy of phonological and semantic processing in normal subjects. *Brain*, 115, 1753–1768.

Démonet, J.-F., Fiez, J., Paulesu, E., Petersen, S., and Zatorre, R. 1996. PET studies of phonological processing: A critical reply to Poeppel. *Brain and Language*, 55, 352–379.

Eulitz, C., Maess, B., Pantev, C., Friederici, A., Feige, B., and Elbert, T. 1996. Oscillatory neuromagnetic activity induced by language and nonlanguage stimuli. *Cognitive Brain Research*, 4, 121–132.

Fiez, J., Raichle, M. E., Miezin, F. M., Petersen, S. E., Tallal, P., and Katz, W. F. 1995. Studies of auditory and phonological processing: Effects of stimulus characteristics and task demands. *Journal of Cognitive Neuroscience*, 7(3), 357–375.

Forss, N., Makela, J., McEvoy, L., and Hari, R. 1993. Temporal integration and oscillatory responses of the human auditory cortex revealed by evoked magnetic fields to click trains. *Hearing Research*, 68, 89–96.

Friederici, A., Hahne, A., and Mecklinger, A. 1996. Temporal structure of syntactic parsing: Early and late event-related brain potential effects. *Journal of Experimental Psychology: Learning, Memory, and Cognition*, 22(5), 1219–1248.

Gage, N., Poeppel, D., Roberts, T., and Hickok, G. 1998. Auditory evoked M100 reflects onset acoustics of speech sounds. *Brain Research*, 814(1–2), 236–239.

Gevins, A., Le, J., Martin, N. K., Brickett, P., Desmond, J., and Reutter, B. 1994. High resolution EEG: 124-channel recording, spatial deblurring, and MRI integration methods. *Electroencephalography and Clinical Neurophysiology*, 90(5), 337–358.

Hämäläinen, M., Hari, R., Ilmoniemi, R., Knuutila, J., and Lounasmaa, O. V. 1993. Magnetoencephalography—theory, instrumentation, and applications to noninvasive studies of the working human brain. *Reviews of Modern Physics*, 65(2), 413–497.

Hari, R. 1990. The neuromagnetic method in the study of the human auditory cortex. In F. Grandori, M. Hoke, and G. Romani (Eds.), *Auditory evoked magnetic fields and electric potentials* (vol. 6, pp. 222–282). Basel: Karger.

Helenius, P., Salmelin, R., Service, E., and Connolly, J. 1998. Distinct time courses of word and context comprehension in the left temporal cortex. *Brain*, 121, 1133–1142.

Hickok, G., and Poeppel, D. 2000. Towards a functional neuroanatomy of speech sound processing. *Trends in Cognitive Sciences*, 4, 131–138.

Joliot, M., Ribary, U., and Llinas, R. 1994. Human oscillatory brain activity near 40 Hz coexists with cognitive temporal binding. *Proceedings of the National Academy of Sciences of the USA*, 91(24), 11748–11751.

Kutas, M., and Hillyard, S. 1980. Reading senseless sentences: Brain potentials reflect semantic incongruity. *Science*, 207, 203–205.

Kwong, K. K. 1995. Functional magnetic resonance imaging with echo planar imaging. *Magnetic Resonance Quarterly*, 11(1), 1–20.

Levelt, W., Praamstra, P., Meyer, A., Helenius, P., and Salmelin, R. 1998. An MEG study of picture naming. *Journal of Cognitive Neuroscience*, 10(5), 553–567.

Liberman, A. 1996. *Speech: A special code*. Cambridge, Mass.: MIT Press.

Liberman, A., and Mattingly, I. 1985. The motor theory of speech perception revised. *Cognition*, 21, 1–36.

Llinas, R. 1988. The intrinsic electrophysiological properties of mammalian neurons: Insights into central nervous system function. *Science*, 242, 1654–1664.

Näätänen, R. 1995. The mismatch negativity: A powerful tool for cognitive neuroscience. *Ear and Hearing*, 16(1), 6–18.

Näätänen, R., Lehtokoski, A., Lennes, M., Cheour, M., Huotilainen, M., Iivonen, A., Vainio, M., Alku, P., Ilmoniemi, R., Luuk, A., Allik, J., Sinkkonen, J., and Alho, K. 1997. Language-specific phoneme representations revealed by electric and magnetic brain responses. *Nature*, 385, 432–434.

Näätänen, R., and Picton, T. 1987. The N1 wave of the human electric and magnetic response to sound: A review and analysis of the component structure. *Psychophysiology*, 24(4), 375–425.

Neville, H., Nicol, J., Barss, A., Forster, K., and Garrett, M. 1991. Syntactically-based processing classes: Evidence from event-related brain potentials. *Journal of Cognitive Neuroscience*, 3, 151–165.

Nobre, A. C., Allison, T., and McCarthy, G. 1994. Word recognition in the human inferior temporal lobe. *Nature*, 372, 260–263.

Ojemann, G. A. 1991. Cortical organization of language. *Journal of Neuroscience*, 11(8), 2281–2287.

Osterhout, L., and Holcomb, P. 1995. Event-related potentials and language comprehension. In M. Rugg and M. Coles (Eds.), *Electrophysiology of mind: Event-related brain potentials and cognition*. Oxford, England: Oxford University Press.

Pantev, C., Hoke, M., Lehnertz, K., Lütkenhöner, B., Anogianakis, G., and Wittkowski, W. 1988. Tonotopic organization of the human auditory cortex revealed by transient auditory evoked magnetic fields. *Electroencephalography and Clinical Neurophysiology*, 69, 160–170.

Paulesu, E., Frith, C. D., and Frackowiak, R. S. J. 1993. The neural correlates of the verbal component of working memory. *Nature*, 362, 342–345.

Petersen, S., Fox, P., Posner, M., Mintun, M., and Raichle, M. 1989. Positron emission tomographic studies of the processing of single words. *Journal of Cognitive Neuroscience*, 1(2), 153–170.

Phillips, C., Marantz, A., Yellin, E., Pellathy, T., McGinnis, M., Wexler, K., Poeppel, D., and Roberts, T. P. L. Forthcoming. Auditory cortex accesses phonological categories: An MEG mismatch study. *Journal of Cognitive Neuroscience*.

Poeppel, D. 1996. A critical review of PET studies of phonological processing. *Brain and Language*, 55, 317–351.

Poeppel, D., Phillips, C., Yellin, E., Rowley, H. A., Roberts, T. P. L., and Marantz, A. 1997. Processing of vowels in supratemporal auditory cortex. *Neuroscience Letters*, 221, 145–148.

Poeppel, D., Yellin, E., Phillips, C., Roberts, T. P. L., Rowley, H. A., Wexler, K., and Marantz, A. 1996. Task-induced asymmetry of the auditory evoked M100 neuromagnetic field elicited by speech sounds. *Cognitive Brain Research*, 4, 231–242.

Price, C., Wise, R., Warburfon, E. A., Moore, C., Howard, D., Patterson, K., Frackowiak, R., and Friston, K. 1996. Hearing and saying: The functional neuro-anatomy of auditory word processing. *Brain*, 119, 919–931.

Pulvermüller, F., Eulitz, C., Pantev, C., Mohr, B., Feige, B., Lutzenberger, W., Elbert, T., and Birbaumer, N. 1996. High-frequency cortical responses reflect lexical processing: An MEG study. *EEG and Clinical Neurophysiology*, 98, 76–85.

Ragot, R., and Lepaul-Ercole, R. 1996. Brain potentials as objective indices of auditory pitch extraction from harmonics. *NeuroReport*, 7, 905–909.

Roberts, T. P. L., Poeppel, D., and Rowley, H. 1998. Magnetoencephalography and magnetic source imaging. *Neuropsychiatry, Neuropsychology, and Behavioral Neurology*, 11(2), 49–64.

Roberts, T. P. L., and Poeppel, D. 1996. Latency of auditory evoked M100 as a function of tone frequency. *NeuroReport*, 7, 1138–1140.

Salmelin, R., Hari, R., Lounasmaa, O. V., and Sams, M. 1994. Dynamics of brain activation during picture naming. *Nature*, 368(6470), 463–465.

Sekihara, K., Poeppel, D., Marantz, A., Koizumi, H., and Miyashita, Y. 1997. Noise covariance incorporated MEG-MUSIC algorithm: A method for multiple-dipole estimation tolerant of the influence of background brain activity. *IEEE Transactions on Biomedical Engineering*, 44, 839–847.

Sekihara, K., Poeppel, D., Marantz, A., and Miyashita, Y. 1998. Comparison of Covariance-Based and Waveform-Based Subtraction Methods in Removing the Interference from Button-Pressing Finger Movements. *Brain Topography*, 11(2), 95–102.

Sekihara, K., Poeppel, D., Miyauchi, S., Takino, R., Fujimaki, N., and Miyashita, Y. 1999. MEG Spatio-Temporal Analysis Using a Covariance Matrix Calculated from Non-Averaged Multiple-Epoch Data. *IEEE Transactions on Biomedical Engineering*, 46(5), 515–521.

Singer, W. 1993. Synchronization of cortical activity and its putative role in information processing and learning. *Annual Review of Physiology*, 55, 349–374.

Steinschneider, M., Schroeder, C. E., Arezzo, J. C., and Vaughan, H. G. 1995. Physiologic correlates of the voice onset time boundary in primary auditory cortex (Al) of the awake monkey: Temporal response patterns. *Brain and Language*, 48, 326–340.

Steriade, M. 1998. Corticothalamic networks, oscillations, and plasticity. *Advances in Neurology*, 77, 105–134.

Stevens, K. 1998. *Acoustic phonetics*. Cambridge, Mass.: MIT Press.

Stufflebeam, S., Poeppel, D., Rowley, H. A., and Roberts, T. P. L. 1998. Peri-threshold encoding of stimulus frequency and intensity in the M100 latency. *NeuroReport*, 9, 91–94.

Woods, D., Alain, C., Covarrubias, D., and Zaidel, O. 1995. Middle latency auditory evoked potentials to tones of different frequencies. *Hearing Research*, 85, 69–75.

Zatorre, R., Evans, A., Meyer, E., and Gjedde, A. 1992. Lateralization of phonetic and pitch discrimination in speech processing. *Science*, 256, 846–849.

Chapter 3

How Infants Acquire Language: Some Preliminary Observations

Jacques Mehler, Anne Christophe, and Franck Ramus

Humans are helpless at birth, but in the space of only a few years, they learn many things—for example, motor and perceptual skills as well as language and numerical abilities. How does this change in competence come about? Despite the large number of investigations devoted to answering these questions, the underlying mechanisms responsible for the change remain largely unknown. Psychologists, physicians, and others have remarked on the speed and predictability with which growth takes place. They have determined, for instance, that the tridimensional organization of visual space emerges sixteen to eighteen weeks after birth (Held, Birch, and Gwiazda 1980) and that bipedal gait is attained without any coaching at the end of the first year of life (see Adolph 1995). Likewise, they have documented that language unfolds gradually. After only a few years of growth, the child becomes like the adults around it. Moreover, major deviations from these developmental landmarks usually signal neurological impairment. Below, we review the main landmarks that characterize the growth of language (see Brown 1973; Pinker 1994). Before proceeding with this, however, we will outline some of the main positions that characterize our domain of inquiry.

The changes observed as the newborn infant develops from a helpless creature into a competent adult are both physical and psychological. The ways the properties of the mind unfold are so predictable that they match embryological changes like those that take place when an egg is fertilized and begins to turn into a complete organism. Psychologists, however, only recognized the importance of this parallel after Piaget demonstrated the predictability of cognitive development. Up until that time, most psychologists believed that living creatures learned simply by extracting regularities from their environment through association. It is not readily obvious, however, how association can explain the origin of species-specific behavior (see Tinbergen 1951; Gallistel 1990). Even when one studies two species with equally complex brains, behaviors specific to each can be readily observed. Moreover, different species attain different competencies even when they are raised in similar environments.

In the last fifty years our conception of the mind has undergone a profound transformation that stems from the work of Turing and Chomsky. Turing argued that mental processes could be equated with computation by a digital computer (Turing 1950). Chomsky (1957) demonstrated that the speaker-hearer's knowledge of language entails a grammatical system, a system that can be described as a "discrete infinity": a system that can generate an infinite number of sentences and meanings with a finite number of lexical items and a handful of rules with which to combine them.

The first question that comes to mind is how such a grammatical system is learned. Chomsky (1965) proposed that humans can learn language because they, and only they, are endowed with Universal Grammar (UG). UG captures the underlying similarities found in all languages, despite the obvious surface differences that descriptive linguists have identified. UG is a hypothesis about the knowledge that the human infant must have in order to learn any natural language. Although a few cognitive scientists are still not convinced of this, much of this knowledge would appear to be innate to humans.

Skeptical psychologists typically argue that language can only be the product of learning. Humans can learn languages as different as French, English, Quechua, or Japanese. Thus, they argue, language cannot be an instinct: it is simply the product of learning the language that is spoken around one when one is a child. How can anyone imagine that so much learning stems from an instinct that is as stereotyped and rigid as animal instincts, the skeptics ask. Language, but not narrow animal-specific behaviors, has to be learned afresh by every human being without exception.

There is much common sense to these objections, but they are based on misunderstanding or error. Indeed, generative grammarians never thought or proposed that languages are not learned. What they deny is that natural languages are solely the product of learning. Infants, they claim, are endowed with innate knowledge about the properties that all natural languages share and the devices that make it possible to learn the specific structures that characterize and distinguish the language in their surroundings from other natural languages. Yet generative grammarians and many behavioral scientists are confronted with the skepticism of those who still believe that learning is all that is needed to explain language acquisition. The skeptics are convinced that in the end learning will also explain why even the most evolved apes do not learn language. This tension is healthy in that it has prompted more and better research. Chomsky's proposals have encouraged many of us to study what makes language and other mental processes possible in the infant. Likewise, other researchers are attempting to show that neural nets can learn language without the postulation of innate knowledge (McClelland and Rumelhart 1986; Elman et al. 1996).

Let us now turn to the presentation of empirical studies that on balance, we believe, are compatible with the conjecture that language is a species-specific behavior made possible by the genetic endowment conferred on our species. We review experimental work carried out to determine whether humans have a specialized organ that makes it possible for them to acquire and represent language. Next we review some of the dispositions (or knowledge structures) that infants bring to the language acquisition situation and describe how these are refined throughout the first year of life. We then examine work that suggests that languages can be clustered in classes according to their prosodic and, in particular, rhythmic properties. We conclude that rhythm is one of the essential properties initially represented by infants. Finally, we speculate on the role played by prosodic properties in language acquisition.

3.1 Investigating the Biology of Language

Chomsky's *Syntactic Structures* (1957) and Eric Lenneberg's *Biological Foundations of Language* (1967) challenged the dominant antibiological stance representative of psychology during the first half of the twentieth century. Lenneberg was familiar with Chomsky's critique of empiricism (Chomsky 1959) and supplemented it with a rich description of the biological foundations of language. Furthermore, he documented a generally disregarded fact, namely, that language learning is not strictly correlated with the learner's intelligence, contrary to the empiricist position. Lenneberg showed that children born with a low IQ (children with Down's syndrome, for example) acquire language at a normal pace provided they are not too intellectually impoverished. Children with a lower IQ, namely, with scores suggesting a diagnosis of severe cognitive impairment, demonstrate language development correlated with the severity of their impairment. Otherwise, IQ has little correlation with language acquisition. For example, children with high IQs do not learn language faster than average.

Lenneberg went on to enumerate criteria for evaluating whether a faculty is largely genetically controlled or has to be acquired from scratch by each individual. He argued that a faculty present in all members of a species, despite environmental differences, is likely to be genetically controlled. This conviction is strengthened once one finds a specific organ that mediates the faculty in question. Lenneberg also pointed out that a faculty largely under genetic control will unfold in ways modulated by the environment.

Lenneberg provided evidence that children learn language spontaneously and apparently without effort. Language arises in the deaf (Klima and Bellugi 1979) and in the blind (Landau and Gleitman 1985) in spite of deprived input. Even more remarkable is the fact that some children who are congenitally both deaf and blind can acquire language using the Tadoma method based on touch (see Chomsky 1986). The fact that children can learn language with such diminished sensory input suggests that the brain is preprogrammed to acquire the structures that the community uses to package grammatical systems. How this happens is a crucial aspect of the research being carried out by psycholinguists.

Language takes many different forms in speakers from different communities. There are thousands of languages in the world, but one can only understand the languages one has learned. Clearly, every language must be learned, and humans are the only animals who have the ability to learn them. Hence, Chomsky postulates a special human endowment, the *language acquisition device* (Chomsky 1968). Contrary to the view that language is an arbitrary code that each speaker has to learn, he demonstrates that all languages share remarkable underlying regularities in spite of huge superficial differences. As Chomsky states in the present volume:

> The obvious approach was to try to abstract general properties of the complex states attained, attribute them to the initial state, and show that the residue is indeed simple enough to be acquired with available experience. Many such efforts more or less crystallized fifteen to twenty years ago in what is sometimes called the *principles-and-parameters* approach. The basic principles of language are properties of the initial state; the parameters can vary in limited ways and are set by experience.

Chomsky has argued that we grow up in surroundings too impoverished for the child to learn syntax solely by extracting regularities from the input. The solution to the child's quandary is presented in the principles-and-parameters proposal. Without elaborating on this proposal here, we can simply say that UG is equipped with switches that can be set to specify a syntactic property of a given language. A relatively restricted number of binary parameters are supposed to specify syntactic differences between the grammars of all natural languages.

The principles-and-parameters approach underlies the work that many linguists have pursued over the past several years.

3.2 An Organ for Language?

Since Broca's famous 1861 communication, psychologists and neuropsychologists have devoted considerable time and effort trying to discover whether there is a language organ located in the human brain. After reviewing the evidence available in the mid-1960s, Lenneberg reached the conclusion that the brain is not specialized at birth—that is, any of its parts can learn to accomplish a given task, including language, given the proper conditions. Lenneberg scrutinized the aphasiological data available at the time and discovered that there was a consensus attributing language to the left hemisphere in adults, but not in children under the age of four. He correlated this observation with the emergence of foreign accents and other difficulties encountered by people who learn a foreign language after puberty. From these observations Lenneberg concluded that the association of the left hemisphere with language is an epiphenomenon due to the mode and the timing of language acquisition, a view that Bever (1980) has also defended. Woods and colleagues (Woods and Teuber 1978; Woods and Carey 1979) critically reviewed the data on which Lenneberg based his conclusions and surveyed several studies carried out since. They concluded that the incidence of aphasias following a left-hemisphere lesion in right-handers is similar in young children and adults. Moreover, recovery of language is not as total as had been claimed. Thus, Lenneberg's conclusion that language delays or aphasia are equally likely in very young children following right- or left-brain injuries has not received unconditional support. Twenty years later the association of language with the left hemisphere in young children remains unclear. For instance, Aram, Meyers, and Ekelman (1990) found that both right and left lesions produced more nonfluency in young patients compared to matched controls. Similarly, reports from Vargha-Kadhem's and Bates's laboratories (see Muter, Taylor, and Vargha-Khadem 1997; Reilly, Bates, and Marchman 1998) suggest that Lenneberg's view may be closer to the truth than the more recent revision.

Fortunately, in the last twenty years new methods have become available that are helping us to understand the emergence of language and hemispheric lateralization. For instance, Muller and colleagues (Muller et al. 1998) have used PET with young children who had suffered early unilateral lesions. They found evidence that the right hemisphere takes over some of the functions of the damaged left hemisphere and also that there is little intrahemispheric reorganization, with other areas in the left hemisphere taking over the function initially represented in the left hemisphere's perisylvian region. Studies of this kind will allow us to gain a better understanding of initial brain organization, plasticity, and structural determination. In the meantime, other methods have become available and suggest an initial specialization of the left hemisphere for language. Indeed, dichotic-listening experiments carried out on neonates reveal that, even at birth, humans show a disposition to process and represent languagelike stimuli preferentially with the left hemisphere. This does not apply to other acoustic stimuli. Dichotic-listening tasks have been used to study language lateralization in adults, and the outcome is generally that most right-handed adults have a right-ear advantage for syllables or words and a left-ear advantage for musiclike sequences. Best, Hoffman, and Glanville (1982) used dichotic presentations in conjunction with the heart-rate orienting reflex on four-month-old infants and found that they have a right-ear advantage for languagelike stimuli and a left-ear advantage for musiclike stimuli. Bertoncini and colleagues (1989) also used dichotic presentation in conjunction with the nonnutritive sucking paradigm to test neonates. Using syllables, they found a larger response to a change in the right ear than to a change in the left ear. With music stimuli they found the converse, namely, a left-ear superiority. Segalowitz and Chapman (1980) and Molfese (1984), among others, have reported results suggesting that in very young infants and in neonates, the left hemisphere is specialized for the processing of languagelike contrasts but not for other acoustic stimuli. If anything, the opposite is true for the right hemisphere.

Studies using improved behavioral methods coupled with brain imaging would be helpful here. A study in this direction has been carried out by Dehaene-Lambertz and Dehaene (1994) using event-related potentials (ERPs). They observed a greater left hemisphere response to a phonetic contrast (ba/ga) in very young infants. However, in more recent studies using the same technique, Dehaene-Lambertz (2000) explicitly compared the electrical responses to linguistic and nonlinguistic changes (using syllables and tones) and observed a greater left hemisphere response in both conditions, although different neuronal networks within the left hemisphere handled the phonetic and timbre changes. This suggests an early intrahemispheric specialization, but no language-specific left advantage. One should note however that imaging studies with adults were able to uncover a strong asymmetric activation for syllables and words only when the stimuli were presented dichotically. Binaurally presented words did not give rise to a left hemisphere advantage (O'Leary et al. 1996; but see chapter 2). It is thus possible that, if the baby experiments were carried out with dichotic stimulation, a left hemisphere advantage would arise for syllables. The advent of improved brain-imaging technology that makes the study of neonates possible will advance our understanding of the brain structures programmed for the acquisition of language. As the preceding review shows, an intrinsic relation between the left hemisphere and language may be preprogrammed, although better studies will have to be carried out before we can understand how brain structures support a given faculty of mind.

With the background just provided, we can now turn to another claim made by Lenneberg, namely, that the older we get the harder it is to learn a language. If there is a critical period for learning language, three consequences should arise. First, once language is acquired, the initial plasticity of brain structures should vanish and there should therefore be a greater risk of a permanent language deficit following a brain lesion. Second, as brain structures become less flexible, the ability to acquire a new language should diminish. One assumes that this claim must be right every time one hears a speaker who has a foreign accent in a second language acquired late in life. Third, individuals who did not learn their first language in the crib should encounter difficulties. What happens in those rare cases when a first language is acquired late in life? An interesting review of a few feral children appeared in Brown's *Words and things* (1958) and Curtiss (1977) published an important study about Genie, a feral child found when she was thirteen years old.

Feral children, however, are not necessarily a good source of information about late first-language acquisition. They have been deprived of so much for so long (including social interaction and proper care) that several different problems may be at the root of the observed deficits. Taking a different approach, Mayberry and her colleagues studied a population of deaf infants born to hearing parents (Mayberry 1989, 1993). This population gained access to sign language rather late but, in contrast to feral children, had been raised under favorable social and emotional conditions. Mayberry and colleagues found that such children do not become as proficient as children who have learned their first language in the first two years of life. Why should this be? We usually observe more and better learning of most topics at the normal school or university ages than in the crib. These data suggest that language learning is a special kind of learning, and that it occurs best during the first few years of life.

Can we speak of a critical age or period after which it is very difficult and unnatural to acquire language? Or rather, should we talk about a window of opportunity or a period of life when, all other things being equal, it is easier to acquire language? If so, how long does this window remain open for language learning to proceed smoothly? The evidence bearing on the acquisition of a second language is fairly clear, or at any rate, much better than that for a first language. This is due to the fact that modern life favors the acquisition of more than one language, and it is easy to find highly proficient speakers of more than a single language. It is difficult, however, to assess whether speakers are as good at their first as at their second language. Indeed, careful psycholinguistic assessments have shown that in general, one language becomes dominant (Cutler et al. 1989). Second languages learned late are usually spoken with an accent and perceived via the phonology of the first language (see Dupoux et al. 1999, 1997). Problems with morphology and syntax (see Weber-Fox and Neville 1996) are also frequent sequels to late learning.

The later in life one learns a second language, the more pronounced the accent. As we mentioned above, we are not sure that there really is a *critical age* for language acquisition.[1] Flege, Munro, and MacKay (1995) have shown that pronunciation of a second language acquired after the age of three is increasingly deviant.[2] They have claimed that poor pronunciation of the second language is inversely related to age of acquisition, but more research would be needed to ground such an assertion. Individual differences in the ease with which one acquires a foreign language may be important. Likewise, comprehension and production routines may have different windows of opportunity across speakers. In a study that focused on syntactic and semantic rather than on phonological aspects, Weber-Fox and Neville (1996) showed that Chinese native speakers who live in the United States and use English more than any other language, perform less well in English than native speakers of English. For some measures, this observation is valid even for people who arrived in the United States before the age of three.

Speech perception itself seems to get adjusted to the first language acquired, not the second one, even when it is acquired very early (between the ages of three and six years). Thus, Pallier et al. (1998) studied highly bilingual adults, who had been exposed to Spanish and Catalan from early childhood (with exposure to the second language starting between the ages of three and six). They showed that subjects organized their vocalic space differently depending on whether they had acquired Spanish before Catalan or vice versa. The findings by Cutler et al. (1989) with highly proficient English-French bilinguals point in the same direction. Although all the subjects they tested felt equally fluent and at ease in both languages, they were able to split the group into French-dominant and English-dominant subjects and observe different behaviors for the two populations. Subjects behaved either like English monolinguals or French monolinguals but could not change their processing mode to match the language presented.

These and other studies suggest that the ability to acquire a language decreases with age. It is, however, unclear whether the capacity to learn decays gradually or abruptly. Only in the latter case would one be entitled to speak of a critical age per se. Regardless of the ultimate outcome of these investigations, it seems judicious to speak of a window of opportunity for learning a second language with a performance comparable to the performance we observe in matched monolinguals. This conclusion is close to Lenneberg's conjecture.

Brain imaging studies have complemented the above explorations of bilingual processing. Positron emission tomography (PET) and functional magnetic resonance imaging (fMRI) have made it possible to explore the cortical representation of first and second languages in healthy bilinguals. In a series of experiments, bilingual subjects were selected controlling the age of second language acquisition, the proficiency attained, and the distance between the first and second language. A number of studies have shown that the first language is bilaterally represented in the perisylvian cortex across different languages. In all studies, however, clear left hemisphere dominance for the first language was observed (see Dehaene et al. 1997; Mazoyer et al. 1993; Perani et al. 1996, 1998). Moreover, the cortical representation of the second language varies greatly in high- and low-proficiency bilinguals. In low-proficiency bilinguals, representation of the second language is quite variable from one subject to the next, some subjects having the second language predominantly represented in the right hemisphere (Dehaene et al. 1997). In high-proficiency bilinguals, in contrast, the first and second languages occupy comparable cortical regions of the left hemisphere, apparently irrespective of age of acquisition of L2 (Perani et al. 1998).

The above studies used Spanish-Catalan, Italian-English, and French-English bilinguals. Even though Spanish and Catalan may be closer to each other than the languages in the other pairs, in all cases the languages involved were fairly closely related. What would happen in bilinguals who spoke extremely distant languages? This question was partially answered in a study by Kim and colleagues (Kim et al. 1997). They explored implicit speech production in bilinguals from a variety of languages and found results comparable to the ones just mentioned. In contrast, Neville et al. (1998) studied high-proficiency bilinguals who spoke both English and American Sign Language (ASL), two languages that differ even in the modality involved (auditory/oral vs. visual/manual) and found that the representation of English and ASL remain only partially similar in spite of the fact that the bilinguals were as proficient as the Spanish-Catalan bilinguals mentioned. As Paulesu and Mehler (1998) have argued, more research is needed to understand whether bilinguals who speak an oral language and ASL constitute a special case when compared to people who speak two oral languages. Further research should clarify the variables that determine the cortical representations of the first and second language in bilinguals.

In summary, when the first language is acquired in the crib it is mastered to perfection, barring neurological deficit. In contrast, when it is learned after the age of three the competence attained differs from the norm. It remains unclear whether the difficulties with a second language learned after the age of two or three are due to interference from the first language or to the closing of the window of opportunity. One way to answer this query may be through the study of infants exposed to two languages from the outset. We might conjecture that such bilinguals acquire two maternal languages. In contrast, if these infants do not master both languages equally well, we might hypothesize that this is due to reciprocal interference. Another way to address this issue is to study adults who have forgotten their first language (for instance, children adopted outside their linguistic community). In such cases, the first language is not active when the second is acquired and therefore cannot interfere with the second language. Data from both research lines are now starting to be gathered, and we may hope to soon know more about these issues.

3.3 First Adjustments to the Maternal Language

Two months before birth and thereafter, infants encounter all kinds of noise, including that made by the vocal tracts of other humans. It seems reasonable to speculate that nature provides our species with a means of distinguishing stimuli relevant for language learning from other incoming stimuli. Other animals also have special mechanisms for recognizing sounds made by conspecifics. Researchers have questioned whether humans prefer languagelike sounds to other sounds (see Colombo and Bundy 1983). Whatever the findings may be, they lend themselves to many different interpretations. Indeed, they leave open the possibility of finding a nonlinguistic sound that infants may prefer to utterances produced by a speaker. Even though it is, to say the least, difficult to know what auditory stimulus an infant prefers, we know that infants are particularly well equipped to process speech sounds. In particular, they have the ability to establish that a previously unheard set of utterances belongs to the same language. This finding has been a central preoccupation of ours for a long time.

In the next section we turn to a related issue that may shed light on the normal course of first-language acquisition. We review work that clarifies the age at which the first adjustments to the language in the surrounding environment are made. We also review the nature of these adjustments in the hope of gaining a better understanding of the capacities and processes that make it possible for humans to acquire language.

A decade ago it was discovered that neonates react when a speaker suddenly switches from one language to another (Mehler et al. 1988). Maternity ward anecdotes were being told suggesting that when their foreign mother switched to French, infants often showed signs of distress. It was unclear whether these anecdotes were true or not. Still, our team began asking if and at what age infants treat a part of the auditory input as if it constituted a natural language and whether they can by some means or other distinguish one natural language from another. In the 1980s newborns were tested with natural sentences to try to understand at what point in their development they act as if they know that sentences belong to an abstract construct, namely, a natural language. Research in the visual modality has revealed that rather early in life infants represent visual objects as belonging to natural categories (Quinn, Eimas, and Rosenkrantz 1993), and it is equally likely that before the end of the first year they also represent a language as a natural category.

Research was carried out with neonates confronted with their parental language after they had listened to a foreign language. Their reaction to the language switch was compared to that of control infants who were tested with a novel set of sentences in the same language as the one to which they had been habituated. The results of this study established that neonates distinguish a change in language. The discrimination response persists when the sentences are low-pass filtered but vanishes when they are played backward.[3] Mehler and colleagues concluded that infants are attending to acoustic cues that differ for French and Russian, the languages used in the study. Studies presented in the same paper also showed that neonates born in France to French-speaking parents distinguish sentences in English from sentences in Italian, languages to which they had never been exposed prior to the experiment (see Mehler and Christophe 1995). This suggests that infants do not need to be familiar with one of the languages in the pair to react to a shift. We take these results as an indication that discrimination is facilitated by salient acoustic properties of the languages rather than only by experience.[4]

What are the limits of this ability to distinguish pairs of languages? Which cues determine its fulfillment and what role, if any, does it play in the course of language acquisition? The first question is rather rhetorical since, from the outset, it did not seem likely that infants could notice a switch between any two languages randomly drawn from the thousands of inventoried languages. In fact, adults often fail to notice when someone switches from one foreign language to another unknown language.

Why then, can one ask, would infants do better than adults? Rather, it seems more likely that infants, like adults, will miss some shifts while readily detecting others. Thousands of languages are spoken around the world, making it impossible to explore their ability to discriminate systematically. Yet, some clear cases of failure were first noticed and then reported by Nazzi, Bertoncini, and Mehler (1998). They found that French neonates distinguish Japanese from English but fail to discriminate Dutch from English. These contrasting results indicate that to newborn babies' ears, Dutch and English are more similar than Japanese and English. Mehler, Dupoux, Nazzi, and Dehaene-Lambertz (1996) have suggested that prosodic properties of languages, and in particular rhythmic properties, may be most salient to very young infants, and would form the basis of the first representations infants build for speech signals. Before we spell out this proposal in more detail, we will examine how the language discrimination ability evolves during the first few months of life.

Two- to three-month-old American infants discriminate English from Italian (Mehler et al. 1988) and English from French (Dehaene-Lambertz and Houston 1998). Once again, performance is preserved with low-pass-filtered sentences, indicating that the discrimination is made on the basis of prosodic properties of the speech signal. Dehaene-Lambertz, in addition, showed that the discrimination collapsed when the speech signals presented to the infant were shorter than phonological phrases. However, one striking behavioral change was observed between birth and two to three months of age: two-month-olds, in contrast to neonates, fail to notice a language switch between two foreign languages. Mehler et al. (1988), already noted that two-month-old American infants failed to discriminate Russian from French, even though neonates reacted positively to the same contrast. Similarly, two-month-old English-born infants failed to discriminate French from Japanese, two very different foreign languages, even though they were able to discriminate English from Japanese (Christophe and Morton 1998).[5] In contrast, as mentioned above, French neonates were able to detect a change from English to Italian (Mehler et al. 1988) or from Japanese to English (Nazzi, Bertoncini, and Mehler 1998). This behavioral change, which takes place during the first two months of life, may be one of the earliest adjustments the infant makes in response to the maternal language. Both Werker and her colleagues (Werker and Polka 1993; Werker and Tees 1984) and Kuhl and her colleagues (Kuhl et al. 1992) showed that infants start to specify the phonemes of their language between six and twelve months of age. Now we know that it takes infants barely two months to make an initial adjustment to the "native" language. We take this adjustment to involve the identification of some characteristic prosodic properties of their maternal language.

What happens with language pairs that newborns cannot distinguish? Christophe and Morton (1998) found that two- to three-month-old British infants show marginally significant discrimination with both a switch between English and Dutch, and between Japanese and Dutch. They interpreted this result as indicating that some babies of that age still confound Dutch and English (therefore failing in the Dutch-English comparison but succeeding in the Dutch-Japanese one, since it becomes a native vs. a foreign distinction) while others have already decided that Dutch sentences are nonnative (therefore succeeding in the Dutch-English comparison but failing in the Dutch-Japanese one, which involves two foreign languages). Consonant with this interpretation, Nazzi and Jusczyk (forthcoming) observed that when they reach five months of age, a group of American infants successfully distinguish between English and Dutch.

More data on this issue come from studies carried out in Barcelona with Spanish and Catalan using the same technique as Dehaene-Lambertz and Houston (1998). These two languages also appear very close prosodically, possibly as close as English and Dutch. Bosch and Sebastián-Gallés (1997) observed that four-month-old Spanish babies (that is, born in Spanish-speaking families) were able to distinguish between Spanish and Catalan. Specifically, they oriented faster to Spanish, their native language, than to Catalan; symmetrically, Catalan babies oriented faster to Catalan than to Spanish. In addition, preliminary results suggest that French newborns are unable to distinguish between Spanish and Catalan sentences (Ramus 1999). These results thus suggest that by four months of age, infants who have had some experience with at least one of the languages in a pair are able to make finer discriminations than infants for whom both languages are foreign.

The data we have presented so far suggest that babies are able at birth to distinguish between pairs of languages that are sufficiently different prosodically, even when none of these languages is familiar to them. This suggests that they are endowed with an ability to categorize prosodic representations of language. During the first few months of life, babies refine their representation of their mother tongue and lose the ability to distinguish between two foreign languages, while they gain the ability to distinguish their mother tongue from foreign languages similar to it. What might be the use of such a representation? We suggest that infants may use it to discover some of the phonological and syntactic properties of their maternal language. This view is consonant with the *prosodic bootstrapping* approach, which was initially advocated by Gleitman and Wanner (1982). More recently, Morgan coined the term *phonological bootstrapping* (Morgan and Demuth 1996) to convey the idea that some formal properties of languages, either phonological or syntactic, can be discovered through a purely phonological analysis of the speech input, without reference to, for instance, the context in which utterances are spoken.

Mazuka (1996) first pointed out some problems that arise within the standard formulation of the principles-and-parameters approach to language acquisition. She noticed that it is difficult to understand how the head-complement parameter, which governs the order of words in a sentence, can be set unless the child has first acquired the meaning of words. However, she goes on, if the child already knows the meaning and the lexical role of the words in the language, setting the head-complement parameter is not necessary anymore, in that it is difficult to understand how the child can acquire the words in the lexicon without some notion of the order in which the parts of the sentence are organized in the language (see Gleitman 1990). Hence, the child needs to set the parameter at a prelexical stage. To break loose from this quandary, Mazuka suggested that the child might find some help in the phonology of her or his language. This version of phonological bootstrapping was presented without providing any decisive hint on how it might function.

A precise account of how phonology might determine the setting of the head-complement parameter was developed by Nespor, Guasti, and Christophe (1996; see also Christophe et al. 1997). The head-complement parameter captures the fact that in human languages, complements either consistently follow their heads, as in English, French, or Italian, or they consistently precede them, as in Japanese, Turkish, or Bengali. The first set of languages is called *head-complement*, the second *complement-head*. In head-complement languages, the main prominence of each phonological phrase (a small prosodic unit generally containing one or two content words) falls on its last word, while it falls on the first word in complement-head languages. As a consequence, if babies can hear prominence within phonological phrases and can segment speech input into such phrases, they might use this information to decide about the word order of their native language. To gather empirical support for this hypothesis, we used sentences in French and Turkish, two languages that are well matched for a number of prosodic features (such as syllabic structure, word stress, absence of vowel reduction), but differ in their head direction. A first experiment found that two-month-old babies could distinguish between sentences in French and Turkish on the basis of their prosody alone, suggesting that babies this age can hear the difference of prominence within phonological phrases (Guasti et al., forthcoming). Further experiments are in progress to confirm this result.

Before we end this section, we wish to present more empirical data on how much of the phonology of their native language children acquire before they reach the end of their first year. Peter Jusczyk and his colleagues have shown, for instance, that American babies know the preferred stress pattern for words in their language by the age of nine months (Jusczyk, Cutler, and Redanz 1993). Also at nine months, babies prefer to listen to native words than to words that contain either nonnative phonemes or illegal strings of phonemes (Friederici and Wessels 1993; Jusczyk et al. 1993; Jusczyk, Luce, and Charles-Luce 1994). During the last few months of the first year of life, babies also show some ability to recover spoken words from whole sentences (Jusczyk and Aslin 1995; Jusczyk, Houston, and Newsome 1999). To this end, they may use their knowledge of typical word patterns and phonotactics, as well as an ability to compute distributional regularities between strings of adjacent phonemes or syllables (Brent and Cartwright 1996; Morgan 1994; Saffran, Aslin, and Newport 1996). Finally, there is evidence that by the age of ten to eleven months, infants may already know some of the function words of their language, since they react to the replacement of these words by nonsense words (Shafer et al. 1998).

Taken together, these results (and many others) suggest that when they reach the end of their first year, babies have acquired most of the phonology of their mother tongue. In addition, phonology seems to be acquired before the lexicon contains many items. In fact, phonology appears to help lexical acquisition (for instance, both phonotactics and typical word pattern may help in segmenting sentences into words), rather than the converse, whereby phonology would be acquired by considering a number of lexical items. Therefore, one wonders how infants learn about the phonological properties of their mother language in the absence of a sizable lexicon. One may think that the path to learning phonology is simple, and not different from the acquisition of many other skills. This may indeed be true of certain properties that are evident on the surface, like rhythm. However, other phonological properties may not be accessible through a direct analysis of the speech signal, and may therefore need to be acquired, in much the same way already proposed for certain syntactic properties. We now present a possible scenario of this sort.

3.4 The Phonological Class Hypothesis

In the previous section we reviewed the remarkable ability of newborns to discriminate between languages. Here, we would like to emphasize an even more remarkable phenomenon—that they do not discriminate all possible pairs of languages. Newborns have been shown to discriminate between French and Russian, English and Italian (Mehler et al. 1988), English and Spanish (Moon, Cooper, and Fifer 1993), English and Japanese (Nazzi, Bertoncini, and Mehler 1998), Dutch and Japanese (Ramus, Nespor, and Mehler 1999), but not between English and Dutch (Nazzi, Bertoncini, and Mehler 1998) nor Spanish and Catalan (Ramus 1999).

Moreover, Nazzi and associates (1998) showed evidence of discrimination between *groups of languages*. They habituated one group of French newborns to a mixed set of English and Dutch sentences, and tested them with a set of Spanish and Italian sentences. Another group was habituated to English and Italian, then tested with Dutch and Spanish. What Nazzi and colleagues discovered is that only the former group reacted to a change in the pair of languages. That is, newborns reacted as if they perceived English and Dutch as belonging to one family, and Spanish and Italian as belonging to another. On the other hand, pairing English with Italian and Dutch with Spanish did not seem to elicit any discrimination behavior.

Thus all these studies concur, suggesting that infants may represent languages in a space where English is closer to Dutch than to Spanish or Italian. Also, Spanish and Italian are closer to one another than either is to English or Dutch. This is strongly reminiscent of the typological research done by linguists like Pike or Abercrombie. For example, Pike (1945) suggested that languages can be classified into two major classes on the basis of the units of time on which these languages rely: he described Romance languages, as well as Yoruba and Telugu, as syllable-timed, and Germanic and Slavic languages, as well as Arabic, as stress-timed languages. Pike and also Abercrombie (1967) believed that syllable-timed languages have syllable isochrony and stress-timed languages have interstress intervals that are isochronous. This typology was later expanded by Ladefoged (1975), who argued that languages like Japanese (or Tamil) have mora timing.

This typology suggests that newborns could in fact be sensitive to the rhythmic properties of languages and could classify them with respect to their rhythm type. All the studies just reviewed are consistent with the view that infants primarily discriminate between languages presenting different types of rhythm, and confound languages sharing the same type of rhythm. We conjecture that in such experiments, the infant first identifies the rhythm class of the utterances, then is able to detect large deviations in rhythm when listening to utterances that belong to another class.

However, the notion that languages can be grouped into a few rhythm classes is not uncontroversial. Indeed, these linguistic intuitions were not corroborated by subsequent precise measurement. Phoneticians have consistently failed to find empirical evidence for the isochrony hypothesis, and Nespor (1990) suggested that languages cannot be sorted into groups since their properties vary almost continuously. Today, a consensus has been built around the notion that languages do not cluster in this way at all. In contrast, we will attempt to defend the reality of the rhythm class hypothesis with relevant recent evidence.

Ramus, Nespor, and Mehler (1999) explored in great detail the proposal that neonates begin by representing utterances as a succession of vowels (Mehler et al. 1996). According to this view, the quality of the vowels is ignored; only their duration and energy are mapped onto a grid. In between vowels the infant represents the distance between the offset of a vowel and the onset of the following one. Using a large corpus of utterances in eight different languages,[6] Ramus and associates studied all utterances measuring the duration of vowels and the duration of the intervening time taken up by consonants. Next, a simple calculation allowed them to determine, for each utterance and each language, the proportion of time taken up by vowels (%V), the standard deviation of the vocalic intervals (ΔV), and the standard deviation of the consonantal intervals (ΔC).

As can be seen in figure 3.1, when %V is plotted against ΔC the languages pattern in a way compatible with the rhythm classes. Indeed, the four syllable-timed

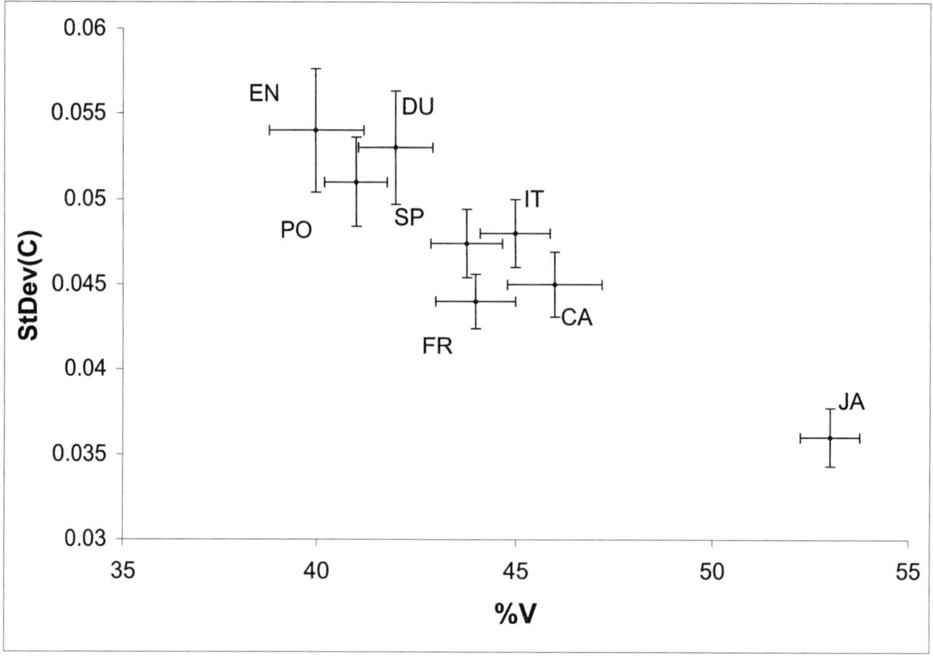

Figure 3.1
Average %V and ΔC for each language. Error bars represent ±1 standard error of the mean, over twenty 3-second-long sentences per language. Adapted from Ramus, Nespor, and Mehler 1999.

languages cluster together. The three stress-timed languages are next to one another but separate from the syllable-timed languages. Japanese appears as a singleton in another part of the graph.

More than a graphic representation of the three rhythm classes, these data allow us, through simulations and statistical tests, to predict the results observed in language discrimination experiments (see Ramus, Nespor, and Mehler 1999). Thus, even though the number of languages studied is small, we find in these data good reason to believe that rhythm, conceived as the alternation of vowel and consonant duration, is an essential property that is used to discriminate between unknown languages. We are also confident that, thanks to their sensitivity to rhythm, infants can classify languages into a few rhythm classes.

This leads us to formulate the *Phonological Class Hypothesis*[7] (PCH). We propose that the rhythm classes are in fact phonological classes, in the sense that they group languages that share a number of phonological properties, rhythm being only one of them. The privileged role of rhythm lies in the fact that it is the property most readily perceived by infants, possibly enabling them to acquire the other properties.

So what are these other properties tied to rhythm? The linguistic literature provides a wealth of possible candidates. At present we can elaborate on only one such scenario, which was originally proposed by Ramus (1999). Syllable complexity seems to be a parameter that is firmly tied to speech rhythm. Indeed, linguists like Dasher and Bolinger (1982) and Dauer (1983) had already noticed that stress-timed languages allow syllables that are more complex than in syllable-timed languages, and a fortiori than in mora-timed languages. Different degrees of syllable complexity are even invoked as the cause for the different types of rhythm. This is mostly evident in figure 3.1, since the variables %V and ΔC actually are correlates of syllable complexity: stress-timed languages, having more complex syllables, have more consonants in their syllables, thus lower %V. At the same time, they also allow simple syllables, which means that the size of consonant clusters is more variable, hence higher ΔC.

Thus, it is clear that an early determination of the rhythm class can enable infants to partly specify the syllable types of their native language. Note that this is true regardless of the linguistic theory one uses to describe syllable structure. Within the principles-and-parameters framework (Chomsky 1981), infants can use rhythm class as a *trigger* (Gibson and Wexler 1994) to set parameters like complex-onset and complex-coda. This aspect can be equally well captured within Optimality Theory (Prince and Smolensky 1993), where markedness, thus syllable complexity, is directly apparent in the level of faithfulness constraints with respect to structural constraints. In this formulation, knowing the type of rhythm can enable the child to set the faithfulness constraints at the appropriate level. In typological work Levelt and van de Vijver (1998) have proposed five levels of markedness for syllable structure, three of which seem to correspond to the current rhythm classes, the other two possibly falling in between.

PCH has been presented to account for the earliest adjustments infants make during language acquisition. In addition to its value as an account of language learning, PCH may also explain some properties of the adult speech processing system. For instance, when exposed to highly compressed sentences (up to 50%), subjects find it difficult to understand them at first; then they gradually improve and finally reach asymptotic performance after a dozen sentences (Mehler et al. 1993; Voor and Miller 1965). Furthermore, this performance seems to transfer across speakers (Dupoux and Green 1997) and languages (Mehler et al. 1993; Pallier et al. 1998). Subjects are always tested with compressed sentences from their L1. Interestingly, regardless of whether subjects understand the habituation sentences or not, transfer seems to occur only between languages belonging to the same rhythm class. This suggests that the mechanisms that enable listeners to normalize for speech rate may depend on the phonological class of the language. More research is needed to understand the precise nature of these mechanisms and in which respect they depend on phonological classes. But this last example allows us to conjecture that PCH might have a much broader scope than just being a starting point for the acquisition of syllable structure.

3.5 Conclusion

Chomsky stimulated interest in the earliest stages of language acquisition by formulating a detailed theoretical framework for how the young child learns the grammar of his or her language. Crucially, to solve the logical problem posed by language acquisition, Chomsky postulated the existence of an innate human disposition, Universal Grammar (UG), a theory about the minimal innate disposition needed for the acquisition of natural language. This view, consistent with the discoveries of scientists focusing on the biological foundations of language, has led to fairly broad rejection of the empiricist position that reigned in the early twentieth century.

While Chomsky and many other linguists posit an organ responsible for language competence, neuropsychologists are studying how this organ materializes in the cortex. The locus of the language organ, however, remains elusive. Even though it is relatively easy to delineate a network of neural areas actively involved when adults use language, it is still not known whether developing infants utilize similar structures when they use or acquire language.

Several reasons can be advanced to explain why it is so difficult to establish whether young children use a network for language similar to that of adults. First, younger brains are quite plastic and brain lesions often do not have lasting consequences. Thus, developmental neuropsychology, and in particular the neurolinguistic study of very young children, is not a very well developed area of research. Also, it is hard to interpret the outcome of learning in infants who have suffered early brain damage. Moreover, the brain-imaging techniques that have provided important data about cortical organization in healthy subjects are not generally appropriate for studying infants and children below the age of six. Despite these difficulties, existing empirical work shows that infants, from birth on, are remarkably well adapted to acquiring language. Indeed, infants have been shown to have a great many abilities that assist them in learning the language spoken around them. Whether some or all of these abilities are unique to humans is the object of empirical investigation. But even if some of these abilities are shared by other organisms, it may well be that only humans exploit them in the acquisition of language.

What lessons should we draw from the facts presented in this chapter? We think that they mostly contribute toward questioning the validity of the traditional learning models that psychologists have relied on to explain language acquisition. Standard learning models presuppose that the age at which one learns one's first language should not affect the outcome of the learning process. Moreover, learning theorists assume that one's first language and the languages that one acquires later in life are learned the same way, largely by association between stimuli or between behavior and stimulating configurations. We presented some evidence suggesting that first-language learning is qualitatively different from later-language learning. The exact causes of these differences (e.g., age of acquisition, interference among languages, and so on) and their relative importance remain to be precisely assessed in future work. But we know now that we need to continue research in order to clarify these issues, particularly since theories once seen as correct are no longer tenable.

Regardless of the preceding negative comments, we do have some positive news as well. Psycholinguists have shown that infants use statistical procedures to segment speech signals (Saffran, Aslin, and Newport 1996). The fact that a statistical approach is used to build language-specific representations is not in itself surprising. After all, infants have to extract regularities from the incoming message and computing statistics is one efficient way to do this. The essential question, however, is whether statistical procedures are sufficient for language learning, or as Chomsky and others have claimed, whether more is required. Marcus and his associates (Marcus et al. 1999) have argued that infants use algebraic rules to characterize the lexical regularities that arise in three-word utterances. In their 1999 paper, they show that infants who have listened to trisyllabic "sentences" spoken without prosody extract characteristic structural properties exemplified by these words. In fact, if the words have an ABB structure—that is, if the second and third (monosyllabic) words are identical—infants treat novel ABB sentences as if they are familiar. Marcus and his colleagues conclude that infants use algebraic rulelike reasoning to extract structural representations. The work of Saffran, Aslin, and Newport and of Marcus and his associates characterizes two learning procedures that might be used by infants in the course of language acquisition.

In our work we explore learning procedures related to Chomsky's principles-and-parameters approach to grammar. Chomsky's proposal is that humans are born with basic notions of phrase structure and parameters that determine the particular value that a structure can assume. However, actually setting the parameters is not necessarily easy (see Dresher and Kaye 1990; Fodor 1998; Mazuka 1996).

Psycholinguists have tried to extricate themselves from this quandary by proposing that phonological properties of languages provide cues to bootstrap the acquisition process (see Gleitman and Wanner 1982; Morgan and Demuth 1996). For instance, Nespor, Guasti, and Christophe (1996) have proposed that certain prosodic properties of sentences may allow infants to set the head-complement parameter before they acquire words. The language discrimination experiments presented in the context of the phonological class hypothesis can also be appraised using the phonological bootstrapping hypothesis. It seems likely that the determination of the rhythmic class facilitates the acquisition of the sound pattern of the native language (Ramus, Nespor, and Mehler 1999).

In summary, we think that now is the time for researchers to formulate relatively specific learning algorithms for language acquisition, and to determine empirically which is closer to the child's actual developmental path. Therefore, we hope to provide experimental answers to questions such as whether a purely statistical learning mechanism allows the acquisition of a given part of language (say, word stress), and which innate language-universal constraints allow us to account for the data. The domain of phonology, involving simpler representations than syntax, has lent itself nicely to such an endeavor. Other developments are within reach. Thus we predict that in the near future we will see remarkable discoveries that will help us understand the specificity of language acquisition.

Notes

1. This is true whether one is talking about learning the first or a second language.

2. We do not know whether this would also be the case for the first language.

3. As mentioned, it is difficult to judge whether infants prefer linguistic stimuli to other acoustic sounds. Backward speech is, however, an excellent stimulus to contrast with speech. It has the same spectrum as speech but backward temporally. Nonetheless, infants show sophisticated behaviors to speech that they fail to display with backward speech.

4. Some investigators (including Mehler et al. 1988; Moon, Cooper, and Fifer 1993) have also found that neonates prefer the familiar language to an unfamiliar language. These studies suggest that during the first days of life and/or the last two months of pregnancy, infants are already sensitized to some properties of their "native" language.

5. Note that for this conclusion to be fully warranted, one needs to obtain the reverse pattern of results with French babies, namely, discrimination of French-Japanese, but no discrimination of English-Japanese (two foreign languages for the French babies). To date, an attempt to obtain French-Japanese discrimination with French babies has failed (French babies also did not discriminate between English and Japanese). This experiment is currently being replicated.

6. The languages were four syllable-timed languages, French, Spanish, Italian, and Catalan; three stress-timed languages, English, Polish, and Dutch; one mora-timed language, Japanese.

7. An earlier version, called the *periodicity bias*, can be found in Cutler and Mehler (1993).

References

Abercrombie, D. 1967. *Elements of general phonetics*. Chicago: Aldine.

Adolph, K. A. 1995. Psychophysical assessment of toddlers' ability to cope with slopes. *Journal of Experimental Psychology: Human Perception and Performance, 21*(4), 734–750.

Aram, D. M., S. C. Meyers, and B. L. Ekelman. 1990. Fluency of conversational speech in children with unilateral brain lesions. *Brain and Language, 38*, 105–121.

Bertoncini, J., J. Morais, R. Bijeljac-Babic, S. McAdams, I. Peretz, and J. Mehler. 1989. Dichotic perception and laterality in neonates. *Brain and Language, 37*, 591–605.

Best, C. T., H. Hoffman, and B. B. Glanville. 1982. Development of infant ear asymmetries for speech and music. *Perception and Psychophysics, 31*, 75–85.

Bever, T. G. 1980. Broca and Lashley were right: Cerebral dominance is an accident of growth. In D. Caplan (Ed.), *Biological studies of mental processes* (pp. 186–232). Cambridge, Mass.: MIT Press.

Bosch, L., and N. Sebastián-Gallés. 1997. Native language recognition abilities in 4-month-old infants from monolingual and bilingual environments. *Cognition, 65*, 33–69.

Brent, M. R., and T. A. Cartwright. 1996. Distributional regularity and phonotactic constraints are useful for segmentation. *Cognition, 61*, 93–125.

Brown, R. 1958. *Words and things*. New York: Free Press.

Brown, R. 1973. *A first language*. Cambridge, Mass.: Harvard University Press.

Chomsky, C. 1986. Analytic study of the Tadoma method: Language abilities in three deaf-blind subjects. *Journal of Speech and Hearing Research, 29*, 332–347.

Chomsky, N. 1957. *Syntactic structures*. The Hague: Mouton.

Chomsky, N. 1959. A review of Skinner's *Verbal Behavior. Language, 35*, 26–58.

Chomsky, N. 1965. *Aspects of the theory of syntax*. Cambridge, Mass.: MIT Press.

Chomsky, N. 1968. *Language and mind*. New York: Harcourt Brace & World.

Chomsky, N. 1981. *Lectures on government and binding*. Dordrecht: Foris.

Christophe, A., M. T. Guasti, M. Nespor, E. Dupoux, and B. van Ooyen. 1997. Reflections on phonological bootstrapping: Its role for lexical and syntactic acquisition. *Language and Cognitive Processes, 12*, 585–612.

Christophe, A., and J. Morton. 1998. Is Dutch native English? Linguistic analysis by 2-month-olds. *Developmental Science, 1*(2), 215–219.

Colombo, J., and R. S. Bundy. 1983. Infant response to auditory familiarity and novelty. *Infant Behavior and Development, 6*, 305–311.

Curtiss, S. 1977. *Genie: A psycholinguistic study of a modern "wild-child."* New York: Academic Press.

Cutler, A., and J. Mehler. 1993. The periodicity bias. *Journal of Phonetics, 21*, 103–108.

Cutler, A., J. Mehler, D. Norris, and J. Segui. 1989. Limits on bilingualism. *Nature, 340*, 229–230.

Dasher, R., and D. Bolinger. 1982. On pre-accentual lengthening. *Journal of the International Phonetic Association, 12*, 58–69.

Dauer, R. M. 1983. Stress-timing and syllable-timing reanalyzed. *Journal of Phonetics, 11*, 51–62.

Dehaene, S., E. Dupoux, J. Mehler, L. Cohen, E. Paulesu, D. Perani, P. F. van der Moortele, S. Lehiricy, and D. L. Bihan. 1997. Anatomical variability in the cortical representation of first and second languages. *NeuroReport, 8*, 3809–3815.

Dehaene-Lambertz, G. 2000. Cerebral asymmetry in 2-month-olds. *Journal of Cognitive Neuroscience, 12*, 1–12.

Dehaene-Lambertz, G., and S. Dehaene. 1994. Speed and cerebral correlates of syllable discrimination in infants. *Nature, 370*, 292–295.

Dehaene-Lambertz, G., and D. Houston. 1998. Faster orientation latency toward native language in two-month-old infants. *Language and Speech, 41*, 21–43.

Dresher, B. E., and J. D. Kaye. 1990. A computational learning model for metrical phonology. *Cognition, 34*, 137–196.

Dupoux, E., and K. Green. 1997. Perceptual adjustment to highly compressed speech: Effects of talker and rate changes. *Journal of Experimental Psychology: Human Perception and Performance, 23*, 914–927.

Dupoux, E., K. Kakehi, Y. Hirose, C. Pallier, and J. Mehler. 1999. Epenthetic vowels in Japanese: A perceptual illusion? *Journal of Experimental Psychology: Human Perception and Performance, 25*, 1568–1578.

Dupoux, E., C. Pallier, N. Sebastián-Gallés, and J. Mehler. 1997. A destressing "deafness" in French? *Journal of Memory and Language, 36*, 406–421.

Elman, J. L., E. Bates, M. H. Johnson, A. Karmiloff-Smith, D. Parisi, and K. Plunkett. 1996. *Rethinking innateness: A connectionist perspective on development*. Cambridge, Mass.: MIT Press.

Flege, J. E., M. J. Munro, and I. R. A. MacKay. 1995. Effects of age of second-language learning on the production of English consonants. *Speech Communication, 16*(1), 1–26.

Fodor, J. D. 1998. Unambiguous triggers. *Linguistic Inquiry, 29*, 1–36.

Friederici, A. D., and J. M. I. Wessels. 1993. Phonotactic knowledge of word boundaries and its use in infant speech-perception. *Perception and Psychophysics, 54*, 287–295.

Gallistel, C. R. 1990. *The organization of learning*. Cambridge, Mass.: MIT Press.

Gibson, E., and K. Wexler. 1994. Triggers. *Linguistic Inquiry, 25*, 407–454.

Gleitman, L. R. 1990. The structural sources of verb meaning. *Language Acquisition, 1*, 3–55.

Gleitman, L. R., and E. Wanner. 1982. Language acquisition: The state of the state of the art. In E. Wanner and L. R. Gleitman (Eds.), *Language acquisition: The state of the art*. New York: Cambridge University Press.

Guasti, M., M. Nespor, A. Christophe, and B. van Ooyen. Forthcoming. Pre-lexical setting of the head complement parameter through prosody. In J. Weissenborn and B. Höhle (Eds.), *Signal to syntax II*. Amsterdam: Benjamins.

Held, R., E. Birch, and J. Gwiazda. 1980. Stereoacuity of human infants. *Proceedings of the National Academy of Sciences of the USA, 77*, 5572–5574.

Jusczyk, P. W., and R. N. Aslin. 1995. Infants' detection of the sound patterns of words in fluent speech. *Cognitive Psychology, 29*, 1–23.

Jusczyk, P. W., A. Cutler, and N. J. Redanz. 1993. Infants' preference for the predominant stress patterns of English words. *Child Development, 64*, 675–687.

Jusczyk, P. W., A. D. Friederici, J. M. I. Wessels, V. Y. Svenkerud, and A. M. Jusczyk. 1993. Infants' sensitivity to the sound pattern of native language words. *Journal of Memory and Language, 32*, 402–420.

Jusczyk, P. W., D. M. Houston, and M. Newsome. 1999. The beginnings of word segmentation in English-learning infants. *Journal of Cognitive Psychology, 39*, 159–207.

Jusczyk, P. W., P. A. Luce, and J. Charles-Luce. 1994. Infants' sensitivity to phonotactic patterns in the native language. *Journal of Memory and Language, 33*, 630–645.

Kim, K. H. S., N. R. Relkin, L. Kyoung-Min, and J. Hirsch. 1997. Distinct cortical areas associated with native and second languages. *Nature, 388*(July 10), 171–174.

Klima, E., and U. Bellugi. 1979. *The signs of language*. Cambridge, Mass.: Harvard University Press.

Kuhl, P., K. Williams, F. Lacerda, K. Stevens, and B. Lindblom. 1992. Linguistic experience alters phonetic perception in infants by 6 months of age. *Science, 255*, 606–608.

Ladefoged, P. 1975. *A course in phonetics*. New York: Harcourt Brace Jovanovich.

Landau, B., and L. Gleitman. 1985. *Language and experience: Evidence from a blind child.* Cambridge, Mass.: Harvard University Press.

Lenneberg, E. 1967. *Biological foundations of language*. New York: Wiley.

Levelt, C., and R. van de Vijver. 1998. *Syllable types in cross-linguistic and developmental grammars*. Paper presented at the Third Biannual Utrecht Phonology Workshop, Utrecht.

Marcus, G. F., S. Vijayan, S. Bandi Rao, and P. M. Vishton. 1999. Rule-learning by seven-month-old infants. *Science, 283*, 77–80.

Markson, L., and P. Bloom. 1997. Evidence against a dedicated system for word learning in children. *Nature, 385*, 813–815.

Mayberry, R. I. 1989. Looking through phonological shape to lexical meaning: The bottleneck of non-native sign language processing. *Memory and Cognition, 17*, 740–754.

Mayberry, R. I. 1993. First-language acquisition after childhood differs from second-language acquisition: The case of American Sign Language. *Journal of Speech and Hearing Research, 36*, 1258–1270.

Mazoyer, B. M., S. Dehaene, N. Tzourio, V. Frak, N. Murayama, L. Cohen, G. Salamon, A. Syrota, and J. Mehler. 1993. The cortical representation of speech. *Journal of Cognitive Neuroscience, 5*, 467–479.

Mazuka, R. 1996. How can a grammatical parameter be set before the first word? In J. L. Morgan and K. Demuth (Eds.), *Signal to syntax: Bootstrapping from speech to grammar in early acquisition* (pp. 313–330). Mahwah, N.J.: Erlbaum.

McClelland, J. L., and D. E. Rumelhart. 1986. *Parallel distributed processing: Explorations in the microstructures of cognition*, Vol. 2: *Psychological and biological models*. Cambridge, Mass.: MIT Press.

Mehler, J., and A. Christophe. 1995. Maturation and learning of language in the first year of life. In M. S. Gazzaniga (Ed.), *The cognitive neurosciences* (pp. 943–954). Cambridge, Mass.: MIT Press.

Mehler, J., E. Dupoux, T. Nazzi, and G. Dehaene-Lambertz. 1996. Coping with linguistic diversity: The infant's viewpoint. In J. L. Morgan and K. Demuth (Eds.), *Signal to syntax: Bootstrapping from speech to grammar in early acquisition* (pp. 101–116). Mahwah, N.J.: Erlbaum.

Mehler, J., P. Jusczyk, G. Lambertz, N. Halsted, J. Bertoncini, and C. Amiel-Tison. 1988. A precursor of language acquisition in young infants. *Cognition, 29*, 143–178.

Mehler, J., N. Sebastián-Gallés, G. Altmann, E. Dupoux, A. Christophe, and C. Pallier. 1993. Understanding compressed sentences: The role of rhythm and meaning. *Annals of the New York Academy of Sciences, 682*, 272–282.

Molfese, D. 1984. Left hemisphere sensitivity to consonant sounds not displayed by the right hemisphere: Electrophysiological correlates. *Brain and Language, 22*, 109–127.

Moon, C., R. Cooper, and W. Fifer. 1993. Two-day-olds prefer their native language. *Infant Behavior and Development, 16*, 495–500.

Morgan, J. L. 1994. Converging measures of speech segmentation in preverbal infants. *Infant Behavior and Development, 17*, 389–403.

Morgan, J. L., and K. Demuth. 1996. *Signal to syntax: Bootstrapping from speech to grammar in early acquisition*. Mahwah, N.J.: Erlbaum.

Morgan, J. L., and K. Demuth. 1996. Signal to syntax: An overview. In J. L. Morgan and K. Demuth (Eds.), *Signal to syntax: Bootstrapping from speech to grammar in early acquisition* (pp. 1–22). Mahwah, N.J.: Erlbaum.

Muller, R.-A., R. D. Rothermel, M. E. Behen, O. Muzik, T. J. Mangner, P. K. Chakraborty, and H. T. Chugani. 1998. Brain organization of language after early unilateral lesion: A PET study. *Brain and Language, 62*, 422–451.

Muter, V., S. Taylor, and F. Vargha-Khadem. 1997. A longitudinal study of early intellectual development in hemiplegic children. *Neuropsychologia, 35*(3), 289–298.

Nazzi, T., J. Bertoncini, and J. Mehler. 1998. Language discrimination by newborns: Towards an understanding of the role of rhythm. *Journal of Experimental Psychology: Human Perception and Performance, 24*(3), 1–11.

Nazzi, T., and P. W. Jusczyk. Forthcoming. Discriminating languages from the same rhythmic class: Data from 5-month-old English-learners. *Journal of Memory and Language*.

Nespor, M. 1990. On the rhythm parameter in phonology. In I. M. Roca (Ed.), *Logical issues in language acquisition* (pp. 157–175). Dordrecht: Foris.

Nespor, M., M. T. Guasti, and A. Christophe. 1996. Selecting word order: The Rhythmic Activation Principle. In U. Kleinhenz (Ed.), *Interfaces in phonology* (pp. 1–26). Berlin: Akademie Verlag.

Neville, H. J., D. Bavelier, D. Corina, J. Rauschecker, A. Karni, A. Lalwani, A. Braun, V. Clark, P. Jezzard, and R. Turner. 1998. Cerebral organization for language in deaf and hearing subjects: Biological constraints and effects of experience. *Proceedings of the National Academy of Sciences, 95* (Feb. 1988), 922–929.

O'Leary, D., N. C. Andreasen, R. R. Hurtig, R. D. Hichiwa, G. L. Watkins, L. L. B. Ponto, M. Rogers, and P. T. Kirchner. 1996. A positron emission tomography study of binaurally and dichotically presented stimuli: Effects of level of language and directed attention. *Brain and Language, 53*, 20–39.

Pallier, C., N. Sebastián-Gallés, E. Dupoux, A. Christophe, and J. Mehler. 1998. Perceptual adjustment to time-compressed speech: A cross-linguistic study. *Memory and Cognition, 26*, 844–851.

Paulesu, E., and J. Mehler. 1998. "Right on" in sign language. *Nature, 392*, 233–234.

Perani, D., S. Dehaene, F. Grassi, L. Cohen, S. F. Cappa, E. Dupoux, F. Fazio, and J. Mehler. 1996. Brain processing of native and foreign languages. *NeuroReport, 7*, 2439–2444.

Perani, D., E. Paulesu, N. Sebastián-Gallés, E. Dupoux, S. Dehaene, V. Bettinardi, S. Cappa, F. Fazio, and J. Mehler. 1998. The bilingual brain: Proficiency and age of acquisition of the second language. *Brain, 121*, 1841–1852.

Pike, K. L. 1945. *The intonation of American English*. Ann Arbor: University of Michigan Press.

Pinker, S. 1994. *The language instinct*. New York: Morrow.

Prince, A., and P. Smolensky. 1993. *Optimality Theory: Constraint interaction in generative grammar* (TR-2). New Brunswick, N.J.: Rutgers University Press.

Quinn, P. C., P. D. Eimas, and S. L. Rosenkrantz. 1993. Evidence for the representation of perceptually similar natural categories by 3-month old and 4-month old infants. *Perception, 22*, 463–475.

Ramus, F. 1999. Rythme des langues et acquisition du langage. Doctoral dissertation, Ecole des Hautes Etudes en Sciences Sociales, Paris.

Ramus, F., M. Nespor, and J. Mehler. 1999. Correlates of linguistic rhythm in the speech signal. *Cognition, 73*, 265–292.

Reilly, J. S., E. A. Bates, and V. A. Marchman. 1998. Narrative discourse in children with early focal brain injury. *Brain and Language, 61*, 335–375.

Saffran, J. R., R. N. Aslin, and E. L. Newport. 1996. Statistical learning by 8-month-old infants. *Science, 274*, 1926–1928.

Segalowitz, S. J., and J. S. Chapman. 1980. Cerebral asymmetry for speech in neonates: A behavioral measure. *Brain and Language, 9*, 281–288.

Shafer, V. L., D. W. Shucard, J. L. Shucard, and L. Gerken. 1998. An electrophysiological study of infants' sensitivity to the sound patterns of English speech. *Journal of Speech, Language, and Hearing Research, 41*, 874–886.

Tinbergen, N. 1951. *The study of instinct*. Oxford, England: Oxford University Press.

Turing, A. M. 1950. Computing machinery and intelligence. *Mind, 49*, 433–460.

Voor, J. B., and J. M. Miller. 1965. The effect of practice on the comprehension of worded speech. *Speech Monographs, 32*, 452–455.

Weber-Fox, C. M., and H. J. Neville. 1996. Maturational constraints on functional specializations for language processing: ERP and behavioral evidence in bilingual speakers. *Journal of Cognitive Neuroscience, 8*(3), 231–256.

Werker, J. F., and L. Polka. 1993. The ontogeny and developmental significance of language-specific phonetic perception. In B. de Boysson-Bardies, S. de Schonen, P. W. Jusczyk, P. MacNeilage, and J. Morton (Eds.), *Developmental neurocognition: Speech and face processing in the first year of life* (pp. 275–288). Dordrecht: Kluwer.

Werker, J. F., and R. C. Tees. 1984. Cross-language speech perception: Evidence for perceptual reorganization during the first year of life. *Infant Behavior and Development, 7*, 49–63.

Woods, B. T., and S. Carey. 1979. Language deficits after apparent clinical recovery from childhood aphasia. *Annals of Neurology, 3*, 273–280.

Woods, B. T., and H. L. Teuber. 1978. Changing patterns of childhood aphasia. *Annals of Neurology, 3*, 273–280.

Chapter 4

The Speaking Mind/Brain: Where do Spoken Words Come From?

Willem J. M. Levelt and Peter Indefrey

The scientific study of how we speak saw substantial progress in the late twentieth century, but it has not been a major information source for functional brain-imaging studies of language production. First, these studies have been largely restricted to the production of isolated words. Second, even with this limitation in mind, the choice of experimental and control tasks has not been much informed by psycholinguistic theorizing on how we generate a phonological word from a conceptual base. The present chapter begins with a synopsis of such a theory of word production. It involves various processing components that function largely in staged succession, such as conceptually driven lexical selection and phonological encoding. That theory is used to reanalyze the experimental tasks used in a set of fifty-eight reported brain-imaging experiments on word production, tasks such as picture naming or spoken-word repetition. This task analysis is then used in a meta-analysis of the brain-activation data reported in all these studies. The exercise reveals that the cerebral network subserving the core processes in the production of words is almost strictly left-lateralized, with the exception of the bilateral involvement of sensorimotor and cerebellar areas. The midpart of the middle temporal gyrus has an involvement in conceptually driven lexical selection, Wernicke's area in the retrieval of phonological codes, Broca's and adjacent areas in phonological encoding (such as syllabification), the sensorimotor areas in phonetic encoding and articulation, and the midsuperior temporal lobe in phonological encoding and/or self-monitoring. There is no involvement of occipital, parietal, and prefrontal brain regions in the core processes of word production.

Nothing is more useful in cognitive neuroscience than a well-founded processing theory. This is particularly true for the study of the brain's ability to produce and understand language. Each linguistic task, such as understanding a relative clause or naming a picture, involves various component processes that run in some temporal relation to each other. These component processes perform particular linguistic functions—phonological, morphological, syntactic, semantic, and so on—making use of knowledge of various kinds. A sophisticated processing theory specifies the computations performed by these component processes, the representations they generate, and the information exchange between them, as well as the time course of their functioning. Given such a theory, the cognitive neuroscientist can experimentally vary linguistic tasks in such a way that a particular component is more or less involved and then register the concomitant variation in brain-activation patterns. If the theory is specific enough about the time course of the process, one can in addition relate the time course of the activation pattern to the independently established time course of the component processes.

In the initial phase of linguistic brain-imaging research, experimental subjects were perhaps inevitably presented with linguistic tasks whose componential structure is opaque. What, for instance, does one do if asked to generate as many words as possible beginning with "t"? Nobody has ever analyzed that task to find out. It involves some form of lexical access, to be sure, but does it also involve visual word imaging, and if so, is the visual activation necessary for lexical retrieval? How does the task relate to "normal" generation of language? Is it mostly a metalinguistic task? More often than not the choice of linguistic experimental and control tasks in PET and fMRI research has been based on global, ad hoc task analyses. The composition of a new task has hardly ever been independently analyzed as a prerequisite to the imaging study. The situation has, however, been much better in ERP research, where there is a "human performance" tradition of careful task analysis.

In this chapter we will report some core findings of a more extensive study (Indefrey and Levelt 2000) in which we reanalyzed the imaging data obtained in fifty-eight word-production experiments. This meta-analysis was guided by a detailed processing theory of word production, a theory that helped us decompose the main tasks used in the imaging studies. The theory, moreover, has sufficient temporal detail to allow for a further analysis of some activation timing data in the literature. We will first outline the processing theory, which is followed by the task analysis we based on it. In the third section we present some of the main findings of the componential and temporal analyses.

4.1 A Theory of Lexical Access in Speech Production

Most of the utterances we normally produce are multiword utterances. Words are typically generated as parts of phrases, clauses, and sentences. Any theory of word generation should be embedded in a theory of speaking—that is, in an account of how we formulate utterances in a larger discourse context. That holds for the theory of lexical access adopted here. It figures in the theory of speaking outlined in Levelt (1989) and has been further developed since (see Levelt 1999). We will not review that theory here, but rather focus on the lexical access aspect of it, making occasional reference to the way it is embedded in the larger framework. Also, we will be relatively concise with respect to the lexical access theory itself, because a comprehensive statement of the theory, with all its experimental and computational detail, is available (Levelt, Roelofs, and Meyer 1999).

A first step in the generation of any utterance is *conceptual preparation*. There are always multiple ways to reveal a communicative intention to an interlocutor or audience. As speakers we continually make rhetorical decisions on what information to express for what purposes (Clark 1996). One aspect of this process is "perspective taking"—the way we decide to refer to some state of affairs (Levelt 1989, 1996; Clark 1997). I can refer to the same person as *the woman, the phonologist, my daughter* and so on. The lexical concept[1] I select for the expression (woman, phonologist, daughter) depends on the discourse context. If I am aware that my interlocutor knows the person as a phonologist but is not privy to her being my daughter, opting for "phonologist" rather than for "daughter" would be logical. Choosing a particular lexical concept for expression is the beginning of lexical access. This first stage is depicted in figure 4.1 as *conceptual preparation*.

Whatever the information we select for expression, it must become encoded grammatically. This involves two major operations. The first is to select the appropriate words from the mental lexicon, among them one for each lexical concept to be expressed. The second is to generate a syntactic representation in which these words participate. There is good experimental evidence now that what we select in this first stage are not yet fully specified words, but rather *lemmas*—syntactic words. The activation of the words' phonological properties is a subsequent step. The lemma specifies a word's syntax, its syntactic category and subcategory (mass noun, transitive verb, and so on), and the way it maps argument structure onto syntactic relations. For instance, the lemma for the mental verb *hate* specifies how the argument structure *somebody hates something* should be syntactically realized: the *somebody* (or experiencer) argument should end up in subject position and the *something* (or stimulus) argument in object position. This mapping is verb specific. Other mental verbs, such as *scare*, do it the other way around (*something scares somebody*). On retrieval of the lemma, such lexically specified syntactic information will drive further grammatical encoding: the construction of phrase and clause structure and the linear ordering and inflection of selected lexical material. The lexical part of grammatical encoding is called *lexical selection*; it is depicted as the second stage in figure 4.1. Roelofs (1992) developed a detailed computational model of lexical selection. The model, which predicts the time course of lexical selection, has survived extensive experimental testing.

Once grammatical encoding is under way, by and large generating the syntactic pattern incrementally (Kempen 1997)—that is "from left to right"—*phonological code retrieval* follows as closely as possible. For each word entered into the budding syntactic frame, the phonological code is retrieved from the mental lexicon. The delay

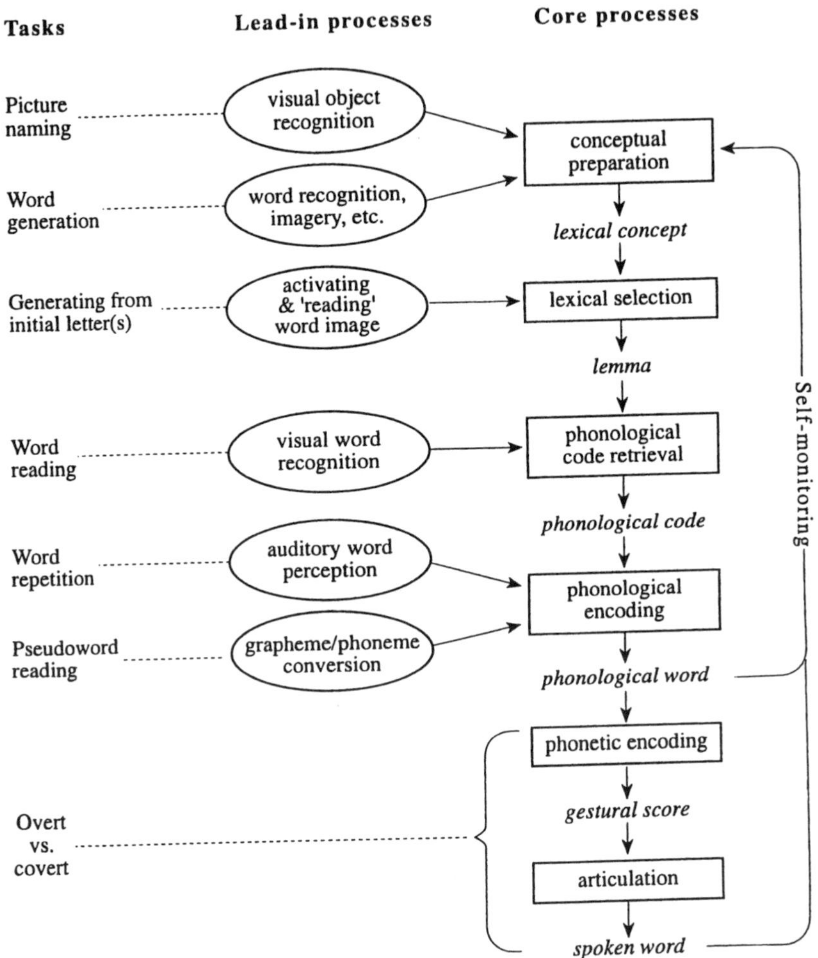

Figure 4.1
Processing stages involved in the generation of words (right column) and "lead-in" processes for various experimental word production tasks (left columns).

between retrieving the lemma and retrieving its phonological code may well be on the order of a mere 40 ms (van Turennout, Hagoort, and Brown 1998). The word's phonological code specifies (among other things) the phonological segments of which it is composed and their ordering. For instance, the phonological code of *hate* contains the string of segments /h/, /eɪ/, and /t/. Experimental measurements support the notion that a word's segments are retrieved simultaneously (though "strung together" successively—see below). Phonological codes are morphologically "packaged." The code of a monomorphemic word, such as *hate*, is a single package. However, when we retrieve a multimorphemic word, such as *blackboard*, we access the phonological code for *black* and another code for *board*. The speed of accessing these morpheme-size packages depends on the frequency of usage of the morpheme (which, in turn, is highly correlated with age of acquisition). For more detail on the process of morphological composition, see Levelt, Roelofs, and Meyer (1999).

As phonological codes become available, they become the ingredients of phonological encoding. This is the generation of the utterance form, from syllabic and phonological word composition to metrical phrasing and intonation. From the point of view of word production, the core process is the construction of phonological words. Phonological words are the domains of syllabification, and these often do not coincide with lexical words. For instance, in uttering the sentence *they hate us*, *hate* and *us* will blend into a single phonological word: a speaker will cliticize *us* to *hate*, which leads to the syllabification *ha-tus*. Here the last syllable *tus* straddles the lexical boundary between verb and pronoun. In *they hate ugliness*, however, *hate* keeps its integrity as a phonological word and becomes a whole syllable. In other words, the way a word syllabifies depends on the context in which it appears, which makes it unlikely that a word's syllables are specified in its stored phonological code. They are, rather, generated on the fly in the process of phonological encoding. There is good experimental evidence that this syllabification-in-context proceeds incrementally, from the first to the last segment of a phonological word (Levelt, Roelofs, and Meyer 1999).

Another aspect of encoding a phonological word is assigning word stress. The way this is done depends on the language. In French, for instance, it is always the last syllable that gets stressed. In English it tends to be the first full-voweled syllable. Syllabification and word stress are both aspects of word-form encoding that follow the retrieval of phonological word codes. In figure 4.1 this processing stage is labeled *phonological encoding*. As far as word formation is concerned, its output is a syllabified phonological word. In the larger utterance context it will be a constituent of a phonological phrase and of an intonational phrase.

The next processing component deals with *phonetic encoding*: the specification of articulatory gestures for syllables and phonological words in the larger utterance context. A major function of phonological encoding is to prepare a pronounceable utterance. The context dependency of syllabification, for instance, serves to create syllables of moderate complexity. There is always a sonorous nucleus (mostly a vowel) in a syllable, and consonants are as much as possible grouped "to the left" of it, with increasing sonority from syllable onset to syllable nucleus. These are properties that facilitate the articulatory gesture (MacNeilage 1998). Although the details of syllabification still vary substantially among languages (some languages tolerate much more syllable complexity than others), it is rare within a language that an entirely new, never-used syllable arises during phonological encoding. Some languages, such as Chinese or Japanese, make use of only a few hundred different syllables. When we talk for an hour, we produce some 15,000 syllable tokens. Hence, most syllables will be heavily overused in such a language. But that also holds for languages such as English or Dutch that have far more than 10,000 different syllables. Statistics show that speakers of these languages also produce most of their speech by means of only a few hundred different high-frequency syllables (data from Schiller, reported in Levelt, Roelofs, and Meyer 1999). It is likely, therefore, that in most cases the phonetic encoding of a syllable consists of accessing an overlearned articulatory gesture, a "gestural score" that specifies the sequence of articulatory targets (such as lip closing or making a glottal stop) to be realized in articulation. The repository of these syllabic gestural scores has been called the speaker's *syllabary* (Levelt 1992). In addition, phonetic encoding involves setting some free parameters for these gestures (such as force and rate), the gestural planning of very low-frequency syllables or new syllables outside the syllabary, the smoothing of syllabic junctures within a phonological word, and so on. The output of phonetic encoding is the articulatory or gestural score (see figure 4.1).

The final step in producing an utterance is *articulation*. The high-speed execution of gestural scores by the laryngeal and supralaryngeal articulatory musculature is the most complicated motor behavior we can produce. To generate some ten to fifteen speech sounds per second, the articulators (such as tongue tip, tongue body, velum, and lips) are simultaneously active in approaching their target positions; it is coarticulation that makes our astonishing speech rate possible (Liberman 1996). Articulation is, moreover, a sensorimotor event. Target positions can be approached in multiple ways (such as jaw vs. lip movement in lip closure). The articulators follow a least-effort solution, given the physical contingencies. The way a target position is going to be approached not only depends on the starting position of the relevant articulator (i.e., on the outcome of the previous gesture), but also on more external conditions, such as having food in the mouth or talking while resting the chin on the hand. Fast sensory feedback loops exist for the fine tuning of articulation.

Conceptual preparation, lexical selection, phonological code retrieval, phonological encoding, phonetic encoding, and articulation are the main stages in the generation of a spoken word. We have called these the *core processes*. The experimental evidence allows for rough estimations of the time windows in which these component processes operate (see Levelt et al. 1998). In fast picture naming, for instance, visual object recognition plus conceptual preparation takes about 150 msec, lexical selection another 125 msec, accessing the phonological code and the phonological encoding of a word again take about 125 msec, and phonetic encoding until the initiation of articulation lasts about 200 msec, for a total of some 600 msec.

As is the case for any complicated motor action, producing speech involves some degree of self-monitoring. We cannot help hearing our own voice while speaking, and when we attend to it, we may detect errors or other infelicities that may interfere with our intentions. We can then decide to stop and make repairs (Levelt 1983). There is good evidence for the assumption that we can also monitor the internal phonological score—that is, the incremental process of phonological syllabification (Wheeldon and Levelt 1995). This allows us to intercept potential trouble before it is given phonetic or articulatory shape. Both external and internal feedback loops (see figure 4.1) involve our normal speech understanding system (see McGuire, Silbersweig, and Frith 1996 for brain-imaging evidence).

4.2 An Analysis of Tasks Used in Brain-Imaging Studies of Word Production

Many different tasks have been used in brain-imaging studies of word production. Two of them, picture naming and verb/noun generation, involve all the core processes discussed in the previous section, but others, such as auditory word repetition, involve only the later stages of word production. To clarify the task structure involved in these different experimental methods, Indefrey and Levelt (2000) distinguished between core processes and so-called lead-in processes. Each task has a way of entering the word production mechanism. Picture naming, for example, is initiated through visual object recognition. That triggers the activation of one or more lexical concepts; from there the core processes take their further course. Here visual object recognition is the lead-in process. As another example, in pseudoword reading (that is, reading nonwords, such as *virsof*), the lead-in process is visual letter recognition and grapheme-to-phoneme conversion. That leads into the core process of phonological encoding—the speaker will do normal syllabification on the activated phoneme string (the example nonword will be syllabified as *vir-sof*, with stress on the first syllable). In this task, therefore, the initial core processes of conceptual preparation, lexical selection, and phonological code retrieval are not involved.[2]

For most tasks used in brain-imaging studies, the lead-in processes have been left unanalyzed. Earlier we gave an example of generating words from initial letters, but similar uncertainties exist for most other experimental tasks. A happy exception is the often-used task of picture naming. The lead-in process of visual object recognition is unproblematic. It is, moreover, an entirely natural lead-in process. Naming objects is a case of quite normal language use. Word reading is another natural case in our culture, and the word reading process is well understood. Other tasks, however, are far from natural. Widely used is the task of verb generation. Here the subject is visually presented with a noun, such as *hammer*, and instructed to produce a verb that expresses a use of the object (for instance, *hit*). The subject will probably imagine some action scene involving a hammer and then pick out the action for conceptual preparation, but this is a mere guess. In noun generation the subject is asked to generate exemplars of a semantic category, such as *tools*. Both tasks are so-called word-fluency tasks, and together we will label them *word generation*. For our analysis it is not essential to understand the lead-in process in much detail. It is necessary only to make a sophisticated guess about which of the core processes is the entry point for a given task. Despite the obscure lead-in process in verb generation, it presumably triggers conceptual preparation. In this respect verb generation is not different from picture naming, and the same holds for noun generation. The left side of figure 4.2 (also plate 1) presents our view of the lead-in processes and of their entry points into the core processes of word production. Picture naming and word generation (both verb and noun) enter at conceptual preparation. Generating from initial letter(s), which may involve the recognition of imagined visual words (see Friedman et al. 1998 for a recent task analysis), probably enters at the level of lexical selection (the subject must select one word rather than another). In word reading there will, normally, be activation of the word's phonological code. Though one cannot exclude the involvement of higher-level semantic processes in word reading, it certainly does not involve (normal) conceptually driven lexical selection. The word repetition task probably enters at the level of phonological encoding, although the phonological code is not necessarily retrieved. Pseudoword reading, as we have already mentioned, involves phonological encoding not based on a retrieved phonological code.

A final, major task variable in the literature is overt versus silent word production. We will assume that phonetic encoding and articulation are involved in overt word production tasks, but not, or much less so, in "silent" production tasks since one cannot exclude the possibility that an experimental subject engages in some "covert mumbling" when instructed to silently generate the target word.

This task analysis allows us to perform critical contrasts among functional brain-imaging data obtained with different word production tasks. For instance, the operation of phonological code retrieval is involved in picture naming, verb generation, generating from initial letters, and word reading, but not (or substantially less so) in pseudoword reading. Any brain region involved in all the former tasks but not in the latter is a potential site involved in phonological code retrieval.

4.3 A Componential Analysis of Cerebral Localizations: Some Main Findings

The full data analysis (Indefrey and Levelt 2000) involved fifty-eight different functional brain-imaging experiments in thirty-five studies of word production (see

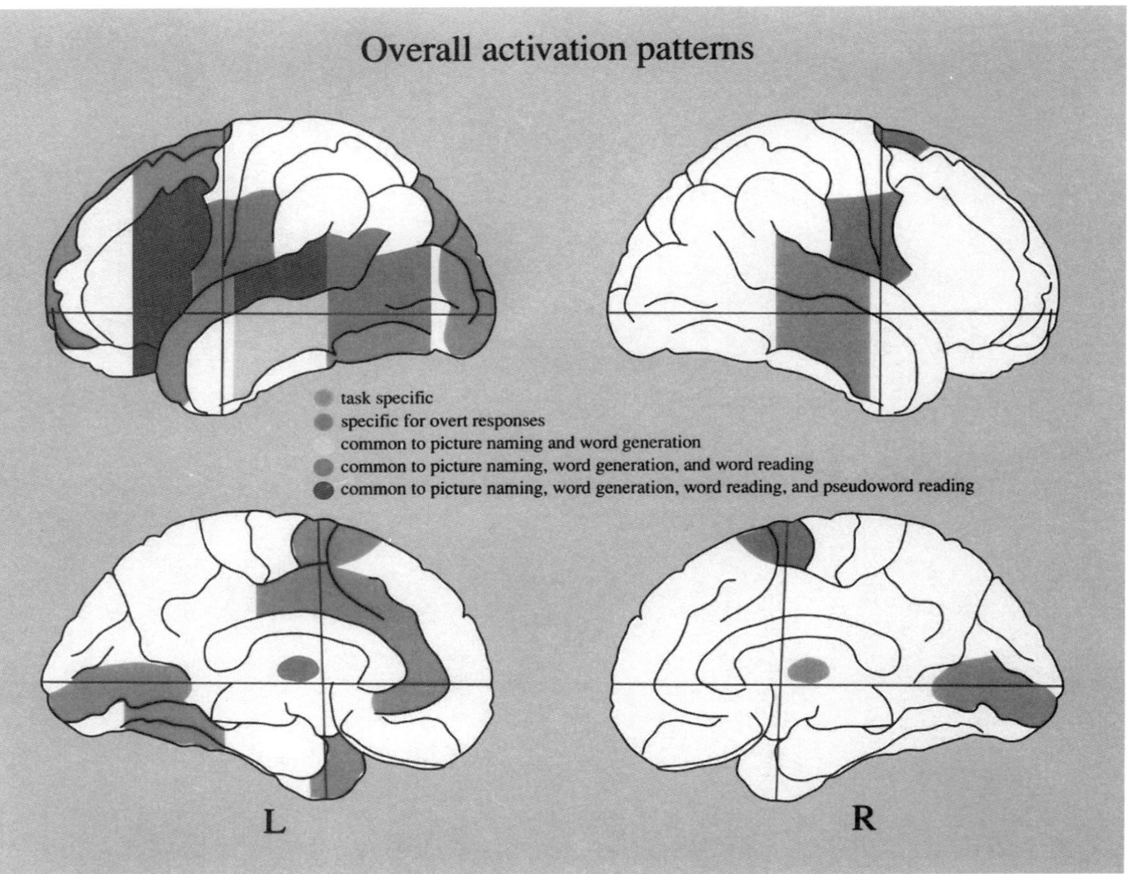

Figure 4.2
Overall left and right hemisphere activation patterns for various tasks in the meta-analysis. Pink, red, and blue colored regions (see plate 1) are involved with the core processes of word production.

Appendix), the majority of which were PET or fMRI studies. Our descriptive reference system for the coding of active loci in the brain was based on the stereotactic atlas of Talairach and Tournoux (1988). In terms of Talairach coordinates, we defined three domains in the frontal lobes—anterior ($y > 34$), posterior ($34 \geq y \geq 0$), and "motor" ($y < 0$); three domains in the temporal lobes—anterior ($y > -7$), mid ($-7 \geq y \geq -38$), and posterior ($y < -38$); three domains in the parietal lobes—"sensory" ($y > -23$), anterior ($-23 \geq y \geq -48$), and posterior ($y < -48$); and two domains in the occipital lobes—medial ($x \leq |25|$) and lateral ($x > |25|$). In most cases the reported activation data allowed for more fine-grained distinctions in terms of gyri and subcortical structures. Where possible, we also differentiated between anterior, mid, and posterior cingulum, medial and lateral cerebellum, as well as anterior and posterior insula. This gave us a total of 104 regions.

We also needed criteria to mark loci as "involved" in a particular set of critical experimental data. There were, on average, 8.8 activation sites reported per experiment. In other words, one could expect 1 in about 10 of the 104 possible loci to be active in a particular experiment. We expressed the agreement among studies about the activation of a particular brain region in terms of a binomial distribution. If, for any task contrast we made, the number of reports mentioning a particular active region exceeded a chance probability of 10%, we took the region to be "involved" in the critical component process.

In the first step of our analysis, we focused on distinguishing the core processes from the lead-in processes. The tasks of picture naming and of word generation involve the same core processes; they differ only in their lead-ins. Moreover, if word production is overt, both tasks involve *all* the core processes distinguished in the previous section. Hence, the activations shared in these two tasks should give us an initial picture of the brain regions involved in the core processes of word production. However, in many cases the studies used silent generation tasks, especially in word generation; hence, we risked losing the regions involved in phonetic encoding and articulation. To get the complete picture, we additionally opposed the overt and silent tasks, whatever they had been. The results of these contrasts are shown in figure 4.2 (plate 1).

The green-colored areas are involved in task-specific—that is, lead-in—processing. The nongreen areas are the ones involved in the core processes of word production. These areas are strictly left-lateralized, except for the sensorimotor areas specifically active in overt responding (marked in blue). The lateralized word-production network consists of Broca's area (the posterior inferior frontal gyrus), the midsuperior and middle temporal gyri, Wernicke's area (the posterior superior and middle temporal gyri), and the (left) thalamus.

The next step in the analysis was to partition this network in more detail. Beginning at the top component in figure 4.1 (conceptual preparation), we needed to contrast picture naming and word generation, on the one hand, with generation from initial letter(s) on the other hand. However, we could not reach criterion here because there were only two experiments with the initial letter task in the reported literature. Hence, we could only package conceptual preparation and lexical selection (henceforth *conceptually driven lexical selection*) together by opposing word reading to picture naming and verb generation. The distinguishing region here turned out to be the midsegment of the left middle temporal gyrus (dark pink in plate 1). Vandenberghe et al. (1996) indeed found this area to be part of a "common semantic system" involved in both word and object processing. However, in the concluding section of this chapter, we will argue that this is most probably a serious underestimation of the regions involved in conceptually driven lexical selection.

The stage of phonological code retrieval can be focused on by contrasting picture naming, word generation, and word reading with pseudoword reading, as discussed in the previous section. This contrast yields a clear result: the regions involved are Wernicke's area and the left thalamus. The finding that Wernicke's area is involved in phonological code retrieval is in excellent agreement with the results of an MEG study by Levelt et al. (1998) (see below).

Phonological encoding is the processing stage that all tasks, down to pseudoword reading (see figure 4.1) have in common. The regions most involved in all these tasks are the left posterior inferior frontal gyrus, including Broca's area and operculum, and the midsuperior temporal gyrus (both marked dark red in figure 4.2, plate 1). However, the small number of studies that used word generation from initial letters, word repetition, and pseudoword reading made it impossible to reach criterion in all cases. If the involvement of these regions can be reconfirmed in further research, the emerging picture for the phonological encoding network is that Wernicke's area provides access to lexical phonological codes (called *Wortvorstellungen* by Wernicke); they are transmitted to the midsuperior temporal lobe and, via the arcuate fasciculus, to Broca's area for further postlexical syllabification. Damage to the arcuate fasciculus indeed tends to block all speech output, except for a few recurring utterances (Nina Dronkers, University of California, Davis, personal communication). As will be argued later, the midsuperior temporal lobe may also be involved in a speaker's self-monitoring.

A comparison of all overt speech production tasks (without overt controls) to all silent tasks showed the bilateral involvement of sensorimotor areas (the blue regions in Figure 4.2, plate 1), and that is how it should be for the component processes of phonetic encoding and articulation. In addition, there was significant involvement of the left anterior superior temporal gyrus. This, however, only occurred in the picture-naming task; hence it would be wrong to say that this region is generally involved in overt word production. Similarly, the involvement of the right supplementary motor area (SMA) also reached our statistical criterion, but it was practically absent in picture naming tasks. Hence, we cannot claim general involvement in overt word production for this region either. Finally, both the left and right lateral and medial cerebellum are involved in the execution of overt word production tasks.

Turning now to the few published time course studies of word generation, we can use the time window estimates for the successive component processes involved in picture naming, presented above: roughly 150 msec for visual processing and conceptual preparation, 125 msec for lexical selection, another 125 msec for phonological encoding (including code retrieval), and some 200 msec for phonetic preparation and the initiation of articulation. Salmelin et al. (1994) and Levelt et al. (1998), both using MEG, found medial and increasingly lateral occipital activation corresponding to the first time window and extending into the second time window. In the study of picture naming by Levelt and associates, the time window for phonological encoding corresponded to a clustering of active dipole sources in Wernicke's area, which may signal the process of phonological code retrieval. The phonetic-articulatory time window, finally, corresponded to bilateral sensorimotor activation in the Salmelin et al. and Levelt et al. studies, but there was activation in other areas as well, in particular bilateral parietal in the Levelt et al. study. Preoperative subdural grid data by Crone et al. (1994) give information about the late time windows, after 300 ms postpicture onset. In picture-naming and overt word-repetition tasks, activation was measured in the left posterior and midtemporal lobes (there was no recording from the right hemisphere). Taken together, the timing data are consistent with the visual lead-in activation findings and the phonological encoding data from the PET and fMRI studies, but they are not yet very helpful in focusing on regions involved in conceptual and lemma processing.

4.4 Conclusions

The meta-analysis reported by Indefrey and Levelt (2000) and summarized in the present chapter is based on a detailed theory of lexical access in speaking, comprehensively reviewed in Levelt, Roelofs, and Meyer 1999. That theory was not on the minds of most of the research teams when they performed the experimental studies that we analyzed. On the contrary, their analyses of the experimental tasks used were in general quite minimal or ad hoc, mostly involving some interpretation of differences between experimental and control tasks as "semantic," "phonological," or the like. It is not at all self-evident that a post hoc analysis of the same experimental findings in terms of a different and more detailed processing model should yield any consistent result, but it does. This may plead for the processing model to start with, but it testifies as well to the quality and reliability of the reported experimental data.

Figure 4.3 (plate 2) summarizes the core findings of our meta-analysis. The network subserving the production of words is almost completely left-lateralized, exceptions being the bilateral sensorimotor regions involved in the phonetic encoding and/or

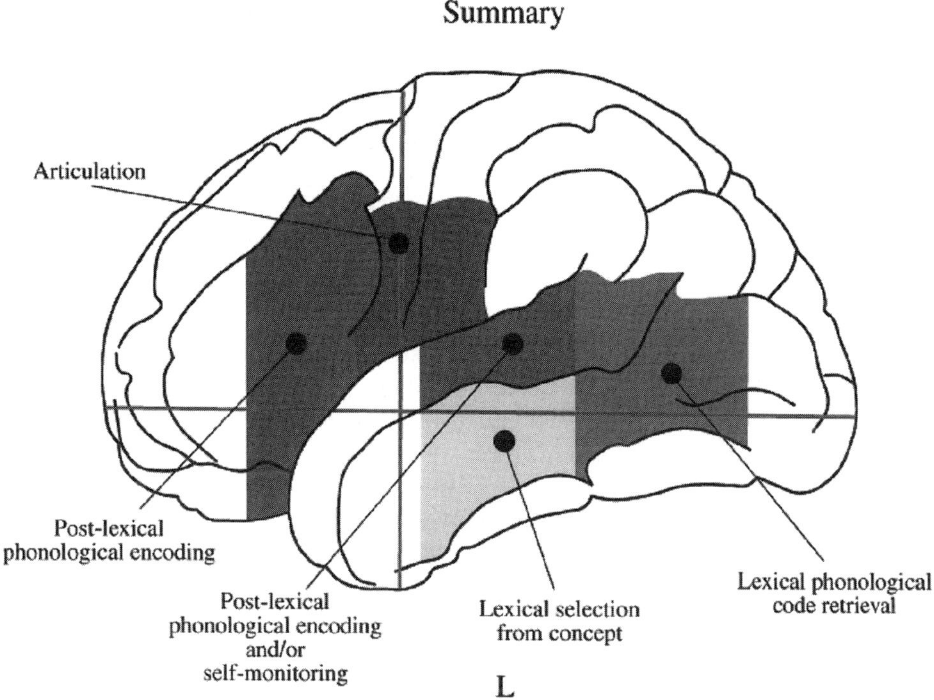

Figure 4.3
Summary of regions activated by various core processes in word production.

articulation of the target words and the bilateral cerebellar involvement in overt word production. The lead-in processes of different tasks can involve quite divergent cortical areas, such as the left prefrontal lobe in word generation or the occipital lobes in picture naming. However, the core processes of word generation appear to involve a stable network encompassing temporal and frontal lobe areas, sensorimotor areas, the left thalamus, and the cerebellum bilaterally. Under the statistical criteria we used, there is no evidence for the involvement of occipital lobes, parietal lobes, or prefrontal lobes in that basic network.

The processing theory provides a tentative interpretation of the regions involved in the network, as shown in figure 4.3 (plate 2). For the first steps in lexical access, conceptually driven lexical selection, the only area that met our criteria is the midpart of the middle temporal gyrus. Although we referred to independent evidence for an involvement of this area in semantic word processing, it is also likely that this will not be the full story. There is increasing evidence that the semantic processing involved in the generation of words from different semantic domains, such as tools, animals, or vegetables, at least partly involves different, category-specific brain regions (Damasio et al. 1996; Martin et al. 1996). Such brain regions will be obscured in our type of analysis.

The next processing step, retrieving a word's phonological code, appears to involve Wernicke's area. The convergence of evidence for this interpretation is encouraging. Not only do timing data from an MEG study support it, but there is also good evidence for Wernicke's area involvement in auditory word processing (Price et al. 1996). Further phonological encoding, such as rapid, incremental syllabification, involves Broca's and/or neighboring areas and the midsuperior temporal gyrus, according to our meta-analysis. The latter has not been noticed before as playing a part in phonological encoding, but the convergence of evidence is on first view substantial: the area was reported as active in thirty-eight out of fifty-seven relevant experimental word production studies that involved phonological encoding. However, care is necessary here. There is one other process, apart from phonological encoding, that is involved in all word production tasks: self-monitoring. If we are right in stipulating that self-monitoring implicates the speech comprehension system, one should expect to find midsuperior temporal lobe activation in most word production tasks, in accordance with the findings by McGuire, Silbersweig, and Frith (1996). In other words, in the present analysis we cannot really distinguish between a phonological encoding function of the superior temporal lobe and its potential role in the self-monitoring of the output of phonological encoding.

The meta-analysis indicates that phonetic encoding and articulation involve bilateral sensorimotor areas, a finding that confirms the reliability of our analysis procedure. Still, there may be more involved in phonetic encoding. If indeed overlearned motor programs, such as patterns of syllabic gestures, are activated during the execution of speech, one would expect the involvement of premotor areas (Rizolatti and Gentilucci 1988) and/or supplementary motor areas. Our gross division of three domains in the frontal lobes does not allow us to distinguish BA 6 from motor area BA 4, and often no more detail was presented in the individual studies either. Hence, the involvement of premotor cortex is, so far, not at all excluded.

If a post hoc application of a detailed processing model to data gathered from quite different perspectives already shows so much convergence, how much more can be achieved if the processing theory is used beforehand to guide the planning of functional brain-imaging studies of language?

Notes

1. A *lexical concept* is a concept for which a word exists in the target language.

2. There is evidence though that nonwords, whether spoken or written, do momentarily activate real words that are similar (see Norris and Wise 2000 for a warning of this kind). The printed pseudoword *virsof*, for instance, may to some extent activate a word such as *virtue*. Here we will assume that nontarget word activation will normally be of a lesser degree than target word activation.

References

Clark, E. V. 1997. Conceptual perspective and lexical choice in language acquisition. *Cognition* 64:309–343.

Clark, H. 1996. *Using language*. Cambridge, England: Cambridge University Press.

Crone, N. E., J. Hart, Jr., D. Boatman, R. P. Lesser, and B. Gordon. 1994. Regional cortical activation during language and related tasks identified by direct cortical electrical recording. Paper presented at the annual meeting of the Academy of Aphasia.

Damasio, H., T. J. Grabowski, D. Tranel, R. D. Hichwa, and A. R. Damasio. 1996. A neural basis for lexical retrieval. *Nature* 380:499–505.

Friedman, L., J. T. Kenny, A. L. Wise, D. Wu, T. A. Stuve, D. A. Miller, J. A. Jesberger, and J. S. Lewin. 1998. Brain activation during silent word generation evaluated with functional MRI. *Brain and Language* 64:231–256.

Indefrey, P., and W. J. M. Levelt. 2000. The neural correlates of language production. In *The new cognitive neurosciences* (2nd ed.), M. Gazzaniga, ed. Cambridge, Mass.: MIT Press.

Kempen, G. 1997. Grammatical performance in human sentence production and comprehension. Ms., University of Leiden.

Levelt, W. J. M. 1983. Monitoring and self-repair in speech. *Cognition* 14:41–104.

Levelt, W. J. M. 1989. *Speaking: From intention to articulation*. Cambridge, Mass.: MIT Press.

Levelt, W. J. M. 1992. Accessing words in speech production: Stages, processes, and representations. *Cognition* 42:1–22.

Levelt, W. J. M. 1996. Perspective taking and ellipsis in spatial descriptions. In *Language and space*, P. Bloom, M. A. Peterson, L. Nadel, and M. F. Garrett, eds., 77–107. Cambridge, Mass.: MIT Press.

Levelt, W. J. M. 1999. Language production: A blueprint of the speaker. In *Neurocognition of language*, C. Brown and P. Hagoort, eds. Oxford, England: Oxford University Press.

Levelt, W. J. M., P. Praamstra, A. S. Meyer, P. Helenius, and R. Salmelin. 1998. An MEG study of picture naming. *Journal of Cognitive Neuroscience* 10:553–567.

Levelt, W. J. M., A. Roelofs, and A. S. Meyer. 1999. A theory of lexical access in speech production. *Behavior and Brain Sciences* 22:1–37.

Liberman, A. 1996. *Speech: A special code*. Cambridge, Mass.: MIT Press.

MacNeilage, P. F. 1998. The frame/content theory of evolution of speech production. *Behavioral and Brain Sciences*, 21:499–511.

Martin, A., C. L. Wiggs, L. G. Ungerleider, and J. V. Haxby. 1996. Neural correlates of category-specific knowledge. *Nature* 379:649–652.

McGuire, P. K., D. A. Silbersweig, and C. D. Frith. 1996. Functional neuroanatomy of verbal self-monitoring. *Brain* 119:101–111.

Norris, D., and R. Wise. 2000. The study of prelexical and lexical processes in comprehension: Psycholinguistic and functional neuroimaging. In *The cognitive neurosciences* (2nd ed.), M. Gazzaniga, ed. Cambridge, Mass.: MIT Press.

Price, C. J., R. J. S. Wise, E. A. Warburton, C. J. Moore, D. Howard, K. Patterson, R. S. J. Frackowiak, and K. J. Friston. 1996. Hearing and saying: The functional neuro-anatomy of auditory word processing. *Brain* 119:919–931.

Rizolatti, G., and M. Gentilucci. 1988. Motor and visual-motor functions of the premotor cortex. In *Neurobiology of motor cortex*, P. Rakic and W. Singer, eds. Chichester, England: Wiley.

Roelofs, A. 1992. A spreading-activation theory of lemma retrieval in speaking. *Cognition* 42:107–142.

Salmelin, R., R. Hari, O. V. Lounasmaa, and M. Sams. 1994. Dynamics of brain activation during picture naming. *Nature* 368:463–465.

Talairach, J., and P. Tournoux. 1988. *Co-planar stereotaxic atlas of the human brain*. Stuttgart: Georg Thieme Verlag.

Vandenberghe, R., C. Price, R. Wise, O. Josephs, and R. S. J. Frackowiak. 1996. Functional anatomy of a common semantic system for words and pictures. *Nature* 383:254–256.

van Turennout, M., P. Hagoort, and C. M. Brown, 1998. Brain activity during speaking: From syntax to phonology in 40 milliseconds. *Science* 280:572–574.

Wheeldon, L. R., and W. J. M. Levelt. 1995. Monitoring the time course of phonological encoding. *Journal of Memory and Language* 34:311–334.

Appendix

Publications involved in the meta-analysis and their experimental word production tasks

Task	Publication	
Picture naming aloud	Ojemann 1983 *Beh. Brain. Sc. 2*:189–230	Ojemann et al. 1989 *J. Neurosurg. 71*:316–326
	Schäffler et al. 1993 *Brain 116*:695–715	Crone et al. 1994 *Paper Acad. Aphasia*
	Haglund et al. 1994 *Neurosurgery 34*:567–576	Salmelin et al. 1994 *Nature 368*:463–465
	Abdullaev and Melnichuk 1995 Techn. Rep. 95-09 U. Oregon	Bookheimer et al. 1995 *Hum. Brain Map. 3*:93–106
	Damasio et al. 1996 *Nature 380*:499–505	Levelt et al. (1998) *J. Cog. Neurosc. 10*:553–567
Picture naming silent	Bookheimer et al. 1995 *Hum. Brain Map. 3*:93–105	Martin et al. 1996 *Nature 379*:649–652
	Price, Moore, Humphreys et al. 1996 *Proc. R. Soc. Lond. B263*:1501–1507	
Word generation silent, verbs	Wise et al. 1991 *Brain 114*:1803–1817	Crivello et al. 1995 *Neuroimage 2*:253–263
	Poline et al. 1996 *Neuroimage 4*:34–54	Warburton et al. 1996 *Brain 119*:159–179
Word generation silent, nouns	Warburton et al. 1996 *Brain 119*:159–179	Paulesu et al. 1997 *NeuroReport 8*:2011–2016
Generation from initial letter(s)	Buckner et al. 1995 *J. Neurophysiol. 74*:2163–2173	Paulesu et al. 1997 *NeuroReport 8*:2011–2016

Appendix (continued)

Task	Publication	
Word reading aloud	Ojemann 1983 *Beh. Brain. Sc. 2*:189–230	Howard et al. 1992 *Brain 115*:1769–1782
	Sakurai et al. 1992 *NeuroReport 4*:327–330	Sakurai et al. 1993 *NeuroReport 3*:445–448
	Price et al. 1994 *Brain 117*:1255–1269	Bookheimer et al. 1995 *Hum. Brain Map. 3*:93–106
	Price, Moore, and Frackowiak 1996 *Neuroimage 3*:40–52	
	Gordon et al. 1997 W. Hulstijn (ed.) Speech Production. Elsevier	Herbster et al. 1997 *Hum.Brain Map. 5*:84–92
	Rumsey et al. 1997 *Brain 120*:739–759	
Word reading silent	Petersen et al. 1989 *J. Cog. Neurosc. 1*:153–170	Petersen et al. 1990 *Science 249*:1041–1044
	Bookheimer et al. 1995 *Hum. Brain Map. 3*:93–105	Menard et al. 1996 *Neuropsycholog 34*:185–194
	Price et al. 1996 *Neuroimage 3*:40–52	Beauregard et al. 1997 *J. Cog. Neurosci. 9*:441–461
	Hagoort et al. (submitted)	
Pseudoword reading aloud	Sakurai et al. 1993 *NeuroReport 4*:327–330	Indefrey et al. 1996 *Neuroimage 3*:S442
	Herbster et al. 1997 *Hum. Brain Map. 5*:84–92	Rumsey et al. 1997 *Brain 120*:739–759
Pseudoword reading silent	Petersen et al. 1990 *Science 249*:1041–1044	Fujimaki et al. 1996 Hashimoto (ed.) *Visualization*. Elsevier
	Hagoort et al. (submitted)	
Word repetition aloud	Petersen et al. 1989 *J. Cog. Neurosc. 1*:153–170	Howard et al. 1992 *Brain 115*:1769–1782
	Crone et al. 1994 *Paper Acad. Aphasia*	Price et al. 1996 *Brain 119*:919–931
	Gordon et al. 1997 W. Hulstijn (ed.) Speech Production. Elsevier	
Pseudoword repetition silent	Warburton et al. 1996 *Brain 119*:159–179	

Chapter 5

The Dependency Locality Theory: A Distance-Based Theory of Linguistic Complexity

Edward Gibson

A major issue in understanding how language is implemented in the brain involves understanding the use of language in language comprehension and production. However, before we look to the brain to see what areas are associated with language processing phenomena, it is necessary to have good psychological theories of the relevant behavioral phenomena. Recent results have suggested that constructing an interpretation for a sentence involves the moment-by-moment integration of a variety of different information sources, constrained by the available computational resources (see, e.g., Ford, Bresnan, and Kaplan 1982; MacDonald, Pearlmutter, and Seidenberg 1994; Trueswell, Tanenhaus, and Garnsey 1994; Trueswell 1996; Tyler and Marslen-Wilson 1977; McClelland, St. John, and Taraban 1989; Pearlmutter and MacDonald 1992; Crain and Steedman 1985; Altmann and Steedman, 1988; Ni, Crain, and Shankweiler 1996; see Gibson and Pearlmutter 1998 and Tanenhaus and Trueswell 1995 for summaries). This chapter presents evidence for one theory of resource use in sentence comprehension: the *dependency locality theory* (DLT). If the evidence for a theory such as this one accumulates, it will then make sense to look for neural correlates of the theory (see Kaan et al. 1998; Harris 1998, for some initial attempts to find event-related potential measurements of brain activity corresponding to the components of the DLT).

An important part of a theory of sentence comprehension is a theory of how sentence structures are assembled—sentence parsing—as words are input one at a time. Two important components of sentence parsing consume computational resources:

1. Performing structural integrations: connecting a word into the structure for the input thus far.
2. Keeping the structure in memory, which includes keeping track of incomplete dependencies.

The DLT is a theory of human computational resources in sentence parsing that relies on these two kinds of resource use. One of the key ideas underlying the theory is *locality*, such that the cost of integrating two elements (such as a head and a dependent, or a pronominal referent to its antecedent) depends on the distance between the two. This idea is elaborated extensively in section 5.3. The remainder of this chapter is organized as follows. First, some empirical observations regarding the processing difficulty associated with unambiguous structures are presented in section 5.1. It is argued that a computational resource theory needs to account for these empirical observations. Some earlier theories of computational resource use are then discussed in section 5.2. The DLT is presented in detail in section 5.3. It is shown that the DLT accounts for complexity effects in unambiguous structures as well as preferences in ambiguous structures. A summary and conclusions are provided in section 5.4.

5.1 Evidence for Computational Resource Constraints: Nesting Complexity

One way to investigate the constraints affecting sentence comprehension is to explore the factors responsible for processing complexity in unambiguous structures. A general class of structures that are complex independent of any ambiguity are *nested* (or *center-embedded*) structures. A syntactic category *A* is said to be nested within another category *B* if *B* contains *A*, a constituent to the left of *A*, and a constituent to the right of *A*. Increasing the number of nestings soon makes sentence structures unprocessable (Chomsky 1957, 1965; Yngve 1960; Chomsky and Miller 1963; Miller and Chomsky 1963; Miller and Isard 1964). For example, the sentences in (1) are increasingly complex:[1,2]

(1) a. The reporter disliked the editor.
   b. The reporter [$_{S'}$ who the senator attacked] disliked the editor.
   c. #The reporter [$_{S'}$ who the senator [$_{S'}$ who John met] attacked] disliked the editor.

In (1a), no lexical material intervenes between the subject noun phrase (NP) *the reporter* and the verb on which it depends, *disliked.* In (1b), the relative clause (RC) *who the senator attacked* occurs between the NP *the reporter* and the verb *disliked.* This RC is therefore nested between the NP and the verb. In (1c), a second RC is nested between the subject NP *the senator* and the verb *attacked* of the first RC. This RC, *who John met*, is therefore doubly nested. The resulting structure is so complex that it is unprocessable for most people.

The difficulty associated with processing nested structures is probably caused by the quantity of resources they require during their processing. First, note that there is no local ambiguity in (1c), so the processing difficulty associated with this sentence is not related to ambiguity confusions. Second, note that the difficulty in understanding (1c) is not due to lexical frequency or plausibility, because sentence (2) contains the same words and expresses the same ideas as (1c), yet (2) is much easier to understand:

(2) John met the senator [$_{S'}$ who attacked the reporter [$_{S'}$ who disliked the editor]].

The RCs in (2) are not nested as they are in (1c), so (2) is not difficult to understand.

Multiply nested structures are complex across different structures in all languages. For instance, the Japanese examples in (3) are increasingly nested and are correspondingly increasingly difficult to understand:

(3) a. Ani-ga imooto-o ijimeta.
older-brother-nom younger-sister-acc bullied
'My older brother bullied my younger sister.'

b. Bebiisitaa-ga [$_{S'}$ ani-ga imooto-o ijimeta to] itta.
babysitter-nom older-brother-nom younger-sister-acc bullied that said
'The babysitter said that my older brother bullied my younger sister.'

c. #Obasan-ga [$_{S'}$ bebiisitaa-ga [$_{S'}$ ani-ga imooto-o ijimeta to] itta to] omotteiru].
aunt-nom babysitter-nom older-brother-nom younger-sister-acc bullied that said that thinks
'My aunt thinks that the babysitter said that my older brother bullied my younger sister.'

In (3a), the object NP *imooto-o* 'sister-acc' is nested between the subject NP *ani-ga* 'brother-nom' and the verb *ijimeta* 'bullied'. In addition to this nesting, the clause *ani-ga imooto-o ijimeta to* 'that the brother bullies the sister' is nested between the subject NP *bebiisitaa-ga* 'babysitter-nom' and the verb *itta* 'said' in (3b), so this structure is more complex. In addition to the two nested relationships in (3b), in (3c) the complex clause *bebiisitaa-ga . . . itta* 'the babysitter said . . .' is nested between the subject NP *obasan-ga* 'aunt-nom' and the verb *omotteiru* 'thinks', making this sentence even more complex—so complex that people have great difficulty understanding it at all. A less nested version of (3c) is provided in (4):

(4) [$_{S'}$ Bebiisitaa-ga [$_{S'}$ ani-ga imooto-o ijimeta to] itta to] obasan-ga omotteiru.
babysitter-nom older-brother-nom younger-sister-acc bullied that said that aunt thinks
'My aunt thinks that the babysitter said that my older brother bullied my younger sister.'

Japanese allows objects to occur before subjects. By placing the clausal object *bebiisitaa-ga . . . itta* 'the babysitter said . . .' of the verb *omotteiru* 'thinks' at the front of the sentence, this clause is no longer nested between the subject NP *obasan-ga* 'aunt-nom' and the verb *omotteiru* 'thinks'. Sentence (4) is therefore easier to understand than (3c).[3]

5.2 Previous Theories of Nesting Complexity

One of the earliest theories of nesting difficulty is that difficulty is indexed by the maximal number of incomplete syntactic dependencies that the processor has to keep track of during the course of processing a sentence (for related proposals see Yngve 1960; Chomsky and Miller 1963; Miller and Chomsky 1963; Miller and Isard 1964; Bever 1970; Kimball 1973; Hakuta 1981; MacWhinney 1987; Abney and Johnson 1991; Gibson 1991; Pickering and Barry 1991; Lewis 1993; Stabler 1994).[4] This hypothesis accounts for the increasing complexity of (1a) through (1c) as follows. In (1a), there is at most one incomplete syntactic dependency in the processing of the sentence. For example, immediately after processing the NP *the reporter*, there is one incomplete syntactic dependency: the NP is dependent on a verb to follow. This dependency is satisfied on processing the next word, *disliked*. Sentence (1b) is more complex, however, because processing this sentence requires passing through a processing state with more incomplete dependencies. In particular, there are three incomplete dependencies at the point of processing *the senator* in (1b): (1) the NP *the reporter* is dependent on a verb to follow it; (2) the NP *the senator* is dependent on a different verb to follow; and (3) the pronoun *who* is dependent on a verb to follow (and this ends up being the same verb that *the senator* depends on). Sentence (1c) is even more complex because there are five incomplete dependencies at the point of processing *John*: the same three incomplete dependencies discussed previously for (1b), plus two more: (1) the NP *John* is dependent on another verb to follow, and (2) the pronoun *who* is dependent on a verb to follow. Thus (1c) is the most difficult to understand of the three.

Sentence (2) is much easier to understand than (1c) because there is at most one incomplete dependency during the course of processing (2), far fewer than the maximum number of incomplete dependencies incurred during the processing of (1c). For example, at the point of processing *the senator*, there are no incomplete dependencies: the input up to this point is *John met the senator*, which is a complete sentence. On processing *who*, there is one incomplete dependency, in that this pronoun is dependent on a verb to follow. The target verb arrives as the next word, however, so the complexity does not increase. The rest of the sentence is processed similarly, with never more than one incomplete dependency. The Japanese nesting effects are accounted for similarly under the incomplete dependency hypothesis.

An extension of the incomplete dependency hypothesis is that complexity is indexed by the maximal number of incomplete dependencies of the same kind (Lewis 1993, 1996; Stabler 1994), where two syntactic dependencies are the same if the same case (such as nominative case for the subject of a verb, and accusative case for the object of a verb, and so on) is assigned in the relationship. According to this hypothesis, different kinds of incomplete syntactic dependencies do not interfere with one another, but similar incomplete syntactic dependencies simultaneously present at a processing state are difficult for the processor to keep track of. This extension of the incomplete dependency hypothesis is motivated by a variety of empirical observations regarding syntactic complexity (Lewis 1993, 1996; Stabler 1994).

According to the incomplete similar dependency hypothesis, the incomplete nominative and accusative case-assignment relationships at the point of processing the object NP *imooto-o* 'sister-acc' in (3a) do not interfere with one another. Thus the maximum complexity of processing (3a) is only one incomplete dependency, because there is never more than one incomplete syntactic dependency of the same kind at any processing state. On the other hand, in (3b), there are two incomplete nominative case assignment relationships at the point of processing the NP *ani-ga*, 'brother-nom', leading to a maximal complexity of two incomplete dependencies for this sentence structure. Sentence (3c) is even more complex under this hypothesis, because there are three incomplete nominative case-assignment relationships at the point of processing the most embedded subject *ani-ga* 'brother-nom'.

The incomplete similar dependency hypothesis also accounts for the English complexity contrasts observed earlier in a similar way. The maximal complexity of (1a) is one incomplete dependency, because there is at most one incomplete dependency of one kind at any point in the processing of this sentence. The maximal complexity of (1b) is two incomplete dependencies, because there are at most two incomplete dependencies of the same kind in the processing of this sentence: at the point of processing the embedded subject *the senator*, there are two incomplete dependencies involving nominative case-assignment. The maximal complexity of (1c) is three incomplete dependencies, because at the point of processing the most embedded subject *John*, there are three incomplete dependencies involving nominative case assignment.

5.2.1 Problems with Previous Theories of Nesting Complexity

These theories of nesting complexity reveal a number of empirical problems, one of which I will illustrate here. I will discuss other problems with the incomplete dependency approaches when I present evidence for the DLT. The problem for the incomplete dependency theories that I will concentrate on here is the lack of complexity of the examples in (5):

(5) a. A book [that some Italian [that I have never heard of] wrote] will be published soon by MIT Press. (Frank 1992)
b. The reporter who everyone that I met trusts said the president won't resign yet. (Bever 1974)

Sentences (5a) and (5b) are structurally similar to (1c) but much easier to understand.

(1) c. #The reporter [who the senator [who John met] attacked] disliked the editor.

All three examples contain an RC nested within an RC nested within the main clause of the sentence. For example, in (5a), the RC *that some Italian ... wrote* is nested between the subject NP *a book* and the VP *will be published*. And the RC *that I have never heard of* is further nested between the subject *some Italian* and the verb *wrote* of the outer RC. But (5a) and (5b) are much easier to understand than (1c).

There is an important difference between (5a) and (5b) on the one hand and (1c) on the other: (5a) and (5b) contain a pronoun (e.g., *I*, *you*) as the subject of the most embedded RC: *some Italian that I have never heard of* in (5a) and *everyone that I met* in (5b), whereas the most embedded subject is a proper name in (1c): *the senator who John met*. When the most embedded subject of nested RC structures is a pronoun, the structures are much easier to process (Bever 1970; Kac 1981).

Warren and Gibson (1999, also discussed in Gibson 1998) performed a questionnaire study evaluating whether this generalization was true. In this study, participants were asked to rate sentences for their perceived difficulty on a scale from 1 to 5, where 1 indicated a sentence that was easy to understand and 5 indicated a sentence that was difficult to understand. Warren and Gibson compared sentences like (1c) to sentences that differed minimally from (1c) by replacing the most embedded subject by a first- or second-person pronoun, as in (6), in which the proper name *John* is replaced with the pronoun *I*:

(6) The reporter [who the senator [who I met] attacked] disliked the editor].

A third condition was also compared, in which the most deeply embedded subject was replaced by an NP having the form of a definite description, such as *the professor*:

(7) The reporter [who the senator [who the professor met] attacked] disliked the editor].

The results of the questionnaire are displayed in the graph in figure 5.1. As can be seen from the graph, the structures with the embedded pronouns were rated significantly easier to understand than the other two kinds of structures. This effect was robust in both the participant and item analyses.

Complexity theories that rely on incomplete dependencies do not predict the observed complexity difference. Changing the content of the most embedded subject NP to a pronoun does not change the maximal number of incomplete syntactic dependencies in the structures. For example, there are maximally five incomplete syntactic dependencies in processing (1c), at the point of processing the most embedded subject *John*. If the most embedded subject is a pronoun, such as *I* in (6), the maximal number of incomplete dependencies is still five. Similarly, if only incomplete nominative case assignments are counted, there is the same maximal complexity in both (1c) and (6)—three in each—because the pronoun *I* takes part in the same kind of syntactic dependency relationship as *John*. As a result, these theories predict no dif-

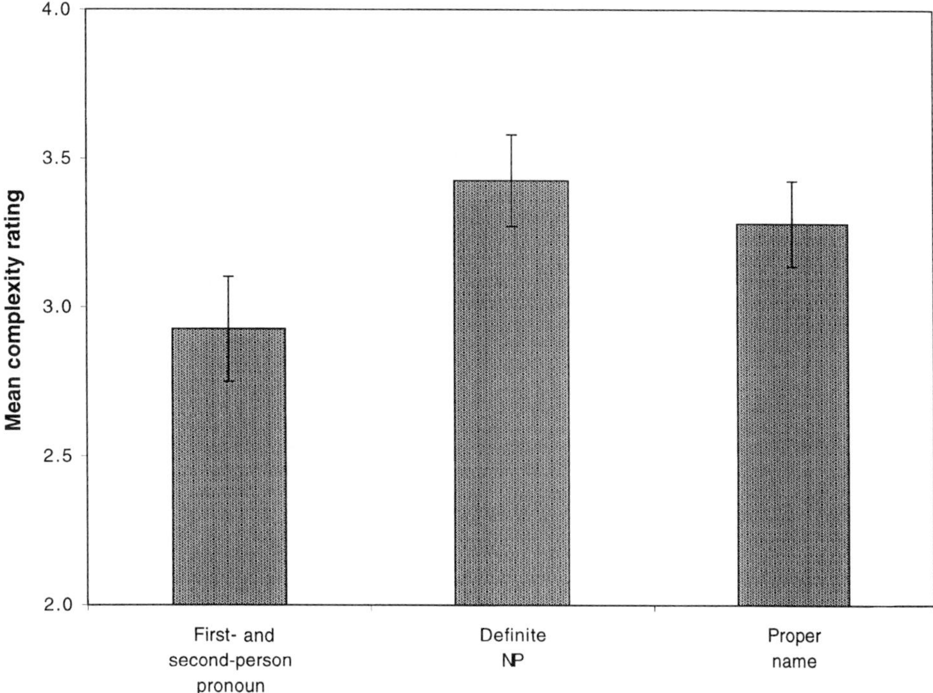

Figure 5.1
Complexity ratings for nested structures containing different kinds of NPs in the most embedded subject position (from Warren and Gibson 1999). The scale that participants used went from 1 (easy to understand) to 5 (hard to understand).

ference between (1c) and (6), but there is a large complexity difference between the two.

5.3 The Dependency Locality Theory

As a result of problems such as the one just exemplified, Gibson (1998) proposed a new theory of the use of computational resources in sentence comprehension: the *syntactic prediction locality theory* (SPLT). A variant of the SPLT—the *dependency locality theory* (DLT)—was also presented in Gibson (1998), along with some preliminary conceptual evidence in favor of the DLT over the SPLT. In addition, Gibson and Ko (1998) present empirical evidence from reading time studies supporting the DLT over the SPLT. Consequently, I will consider only the DLT here. There are two key insights in the DLT:

1. Resources are required for *two* aspects of language comprehension: (1) *storage* of the structure built thus far (as in earlier theories) and (2) *integration* of the current word into the structure built thus far. The integration aspect of resource use in sentence comprehension has been ignored in most resource theories preceding the DLT (and SPLT). The claim that both storage and integration consume resources is closely related to claims about resource use in other cognitive domains. In these domains, working memory resources are assumed to have both storage and processing/integration components (see Baddeley 1990; Just and Carpenter 1992; Anderson 1994; Lewis 1996).
2. The structural integration complexity depends on the *distance* or *locality* between the two elements being integrated (see other distance-based theories of linguistic complexity: Wanner and Maratsos 1978; Joshi 1990; Rambow and Joshi 1994; Hawkins 1990, 1994).

It turns out that many resource complexity effects can be explained using integration cost alone. As a result, I will first discuss the integration component of the DLT. I will then show how this component of the theory accounts for a number of complexity effects. Next, I will introduce the storage cost component of the theory.

5.3.1 Integration Cost

Following Gibson (1991), I will assume that maximal projections corresponding to the lexical entries for a newly input word *w* are constructed, with the speed of access dependent on the frequency of the relevant lexical entry (MacDonald, Pearlmutter, and Seidenberg 1994; Trueswell, Tanenhaus, and Garnsey 1994). Each of these maximal projections XP includes maximal projections of syntactic predictions for all the possible syntactic categories that can immediately follow *w* as the next word in a grammatical sentence. There are a number of components to the process of integrating XP and its semantic and discourse meaning into the discourse and syntactic structure(s) built thus far. First, there is a *structural integration* component, such that XP's syntactic category is matched with a syntactic expectation in the syntactic structure already built. This syntactic attachment will involve a head-dependent relationship between some category in XP (possibly the head *w*) and some projection of a head in the structure. The structural integration process also involves linking pronouns to their appropriate antecedents.

Following structural integration, there are also processes that interpret the resulting structural attachments (see Frazier 1978 for arguments that structural attachments precede contextual plausibility evaluations; see McElree and Griffith 1995 for evidence that this is the case). In particular, there is a process of discourse integration (e.g., constructing or accessing a discourse referent in the discourse model; see Kamp 1981 and Heim 1982) and one of evaluating the plausibility of the resultant discourse structure(s) in the current context, two processes that may run in tandem (or may be two parts of one more complex process). In this chapter, I will concentrate on the processes of structural integration and discourse processing.

It has been established the discourse processing literature that the difficulty of processing an NP depends on the accessibility of the referent of the NP in the discourse (Haviland and Clark 1974; Haliday and Hasan 1976; Garrod and Sanford 1977, 1982; see Garrod and Sanford 1994 for a summary). The less accessible the referent of an NP is in the discourse, the more resources are required to find or construct it (Warren and Gibson 1999). Focused entities or individuals, which are usually referred to with pronouns, are highly accessible, so they require a small quantity of resources to access. Nonfocused entities or individuals in the discourse require more resources to access. Such NPs are usually referred to using proper names and definite descriptions. Elements new to the discourse, which are usually introduced using indefinite NPs, require the most resources because they must be constructed in the discourse model. I will follow Gibson (1998) in assuming a simplified version of discourse-processing cost such that only the processing of new discourse referents consumes resources. A discourse referent is an entity that has a spatiotemporal location so that it can later be referred to with an anaphoric expression, such as a pronoun for NPs, or tense on a verb for events (Webber 1988). In particular, it is assumed that processing the head noun of an NP that refers to a new discourse object consumes substantial resources, and processing the head verb of a VP that refers to a new discourse event (also a discourse referent) consumes substantial resources, but processing other words does not consume substantial resources in the discourse processing component of structure building. This discourse-processing assumption is a simplification of Warren and Gibson's (1999) hypothesis, in that it only distinguishes costs for old and new referents, but no finer-grained distinctions are made according to accessibility.

As noted, it is assumed that the process of structural integration depends on the distance between the heads of the two projections being integrated together. The computational motivation for this hypothesis is that integrating a newly input maximal projection, XP, headed by h_2, with a previous syntactic category headed by h_1 (as in figure 5.2) involves retrieving aspects of h_1 from memory. In an activation-based framework, this process involves reactivating h_1 to a target threshold of activation. Because of the limited quantity of activation in the system, h_1's activation will decay as intervening words are processed and integrated into the structure for the input. Thus, the difficulty of the structural integration depends on the complexity of all aspects of the integrations that took place in the interim since h_1 was last highly activated. That is, the difficulty of the structural integration depends on the complexity of the structural integrations in the interim, as well as on the discourse integrations and the plausibility evaluations in the interim.

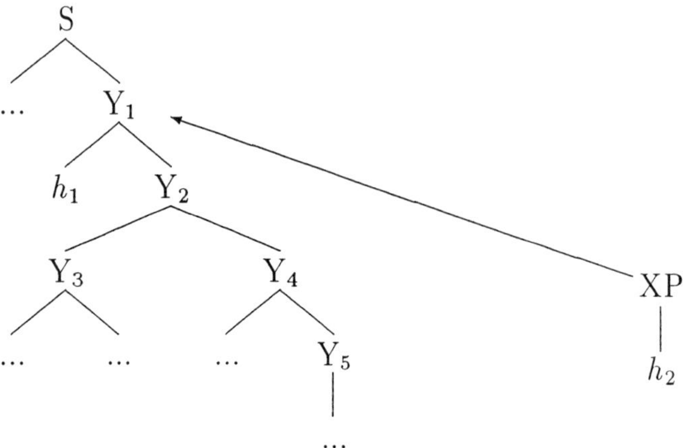

Figure 5.2
Structural integration of a maximal projection XP of a newly input head h_2 to an attachment site headed by a head h_1 in the structure for the input so far. Depending on the type of syntactic attachment and on the syntactic assumption, the structural integration may involve adjunction of a node in the structure built thus far.

In principle, this distance-based structural integration cost might be quantified in many ways. For simplicity, I will initially concentrate on the cost associated with building new discourse referents in the intervening region. (See Warren and Gibson 1999 for evidence for the more general proposal that discourse accessibility—not simply new vs. old referents—affects the distance-based structural integration cost.) Thus I will ignore the structural difficulty and contextual plausibility of the intervening integrations in computing the distance-based difficulty of a structural integration. To work out the specific predictions of the structural integration cost proposal, it is necessary to have a hypothesis about the relationship between the number of new discourse referents processed and the resulting structural integration cost. The structural integration cost apparently rises with the initial few intervening new discourse referents but then heads toward a maximal cost (Gibson 1998). For simplicity, however, I will assume a linear relationship between the number of new discourse referents and structural integration cost, such that one *energy unit* (EU) is expended for each new discourse referent in the intervening region. My assumptions about discourse processing and structural integration cost are summarized as follows:

(8) *DLT simplified discourse processing cost* (the cost associated with accessing or constructing the discourse structure for the maximal projection of the input word head h_2)
1 energy unit (EU) is consumed if h_2 is the head of a new discourse referent;
0 EUs otherwise.

(9) *DLT structural integration cost*
The structural integration cost associated with connecting the syntactic structure for a newly input head h_2 to a projection of a head h_1 that is part of the current structure for the input is dependent on the complexity of the computations that took place between h_1 and h_2. For simplicity, it is assumed that 1 EU is consumed for each new discourse referent in the intervening region.

To see how these assumptions apply, consider an example in which both h_1 and h_2 head phrases indicating discourse referents that were introduced by h_1 and h_2. Furthermore, suppose that two other discourse referents were introduced between h_1 and h_2. The cost of building the new discourse structure and connecting the phrase structure for h_2 to the phrase headed by h_1 would be 3 EUs, corresponding to 1 EU for constructing the new discourse referent, and 2 EUs for the structural integration cost, corresponding to the two intervening discourse referent heads.

In summary, the comprehension difficulty at a word in a sentence (e.g., as measured by reading times) is assumed to be determined by a combination of the following factors: (1) the frequency of the lexical item being integrated, (2) the structural integration cost at that word, (3) the storage cost at that word, (4) the contextual plausibility of the resulting structure, and (5) the discourse complexity of the resulting structure. In addition, there may also be some reanalysis difficulty, if the current word is not compatible with the most highly ranked structure built thus far (Gibson, Babyonyshev, and Kaan 1998). Furthermore, it is assumed that the overall intuitive complexity of a sentence depends to a large degree on the maximum intuitive complexity incurred at any processing state during the processing of a sentence. In the examples to be considered later, there are minimal lexical frequency and contextual plausibility differences throughout the processing of the sentences being compared, and there are no temporary ambiguities leading to reanalysis. So we may focus on structural integration, discourse complexity, and storage costs as the main contributors to complexity differences. I will initially consider the effect of structural integration and discourse complexity alone, ignoring storage cost. This is also an oversimplification, but the predicted patterns are similar when storage cost is also considered.

5.3.2 Accounting for Nesting Complexity Effects within the DLT

Consider the complexity contrast between the singly nested RC structure in (1b) and the doubly nested RC structure in (1c).

(1) b. The reporter who the senator attacked disliked the editor.
c. The reporter who the senator who John met attacked disliked the editor.

The maximal discourse and structural integration cost incurred during the processing of (1b) occurs at the point of processing *attacked*. At this point, one discourse referent is introduced—the event referent for the verb *attacked*—and three structural integrations take place:

1. The verb *attacked* is integrated as the verb for the subject NP *the senator*. No new discourse referents intervene. As a result, this integration step is cost free according to the simplified integration cost assumptions above.
2. An empty category to be coindexed with the RC pronoun *who* is integrated as the object of *attacked*. The attachment step is local, with no new discourse referents intervening.
3. The object-position empty category is coindexed with the preceding RC pronoun *who*. Two discourse referents were introduced in the interim—the NP *the senator* and the event referent *attacked*—leading to an integration cost of 2 EUs for this step.

The discourse and structural integration cost at *attacked* is therefore 3 EUs: 1 EU for the construction of the new discourse referent, and 2 EUs for the structural integrations. The discourse and structural integration cost at the following word *disliked* is also 3 EUs, corresponding to 1 EU for the construction of the event referent indicated by the verb *disliked*, and a structural integration cost of 2 EUs corresponding to the two new discourse referents—*the senator* and *attacked*—that separate the verb *disliked* and the subject NP *the reporter*, to which this verb connects. The total integration cost of 3 EUs, occurring at the verb *attacked* and at the verb *disliked*, is greater than at any other point in processing this sentence structure.

Now consider the doubly nested RC structure in (1c). The points of maximal total integration cost in this sentence also occur at the points of processing the verbs *attacked* and *disliked*, but the costs at these points are much higher here than in the singly embedded RC example in (1b). In particular, the total integration cost at *attacked* in (1c) is 7 EUs, corresponding to:

1. 1 EU for the construction of the event referent indicated by the tensed verb *attacked*
2. 2 EUs for the structural integration of the verb *attacked* to its subject NP *the senator*, corresponding to two discourse referents—*John* and *met*—that were introduced in the interim
3. 0 EUs for the integration of an empty category as object of the verb *attacked*
4. 4 EUs for the structural integration coindexing the object empty category with the preceding RC pronoun *who*, EUs because four new discourse referents—*the senator*, *John*, *met*, and *attacked*—separate the empty category and its coindexed pronoun

The maximal total integration cost in the doubly nested structure in (1c) is therefore substantially greater than that for the singly nested structure in (1b). Thus, according to the DLT, the cause of the processing difficulty associated with nesting complexity is simply that too many long distance structural integration steps take place at the same point in processing a nested structure.

It should be emphasized that aspects of the DLT have been oversimplified up to this point. Importantly, the structural integration cost function is not actually linear, so that a single long structural integration will never be as complex as multiple shorter integrations taking place at the same processing state. The nonlinearity of the cost function must be kept in mind when considering predictions of the DLT with respect to other linguistic structures. In addition, the distance function assumed thus far increments its cost for new discourse referents alone. Processing other kinds of elements also probably causes measurable increments in structural integration cost. Finally, the storage cost at a processing state also affects the processing load at that state. Despite these oversimplifications, the explanations provided by the DLT for nesting complexity effects are essentially the same when a more complete theory is considered. For example, although storage cost is important to account for some sentence processing effects (some of which will be discussed later), it is not critical for the comparisons just discussed, because the storage costs are the same at the locations that were compared (which will be verifiable below, once the storage cost component of the DLT is discussed).

In addition to accounting for general nesting complexity differences, the DLT accounts for the relative lack of difficulty associated with processing doubly nested structures like (6), in which the most embedded subject is a pronoun:

(6) The reporter who the senator who I met attacked disliked the editor.

Because referents for first- and second-person pronouns are already present in the current discourse, integrating across them consumes fewer resources than integrating across new discourse referents, according to the discourse-based DLT structural integration cost hypothesis. The point of maximal integration cost in (6) occurs at the point of processing the second verb *attacked*, just an in (1c), discussed earlier. However, the structural integration steps are less costly at this point in (6) than in (1c), because fewer new discourse referents are crossed in the integration steps in (6).[5] The distance-based DLT therefore provides a straightforward account of the observed contrast—a contrast not accounted for by earlier theories.

The DLT also explains a number of other nesting complexity contrasts not accounted for by earlier theories. For example, it accounts for the contrast between (1) embedding an RC within a complement clause (CC) of a noun and (2) the reverse embedding consisting of a CC within an RC:

(10) a. *Complement clause, then relative clause* (CC/RC)
The fact that the employee who the manager hired stole office supplies worried the executive.

b. *Relative clause, then complement clause* (RC/CC)
#The executive who the fact that the employee stole office supplies worried hired the manager.

The CC/RC embedding is much easier to understand than the RC/CC embedding (Cowper 1976; Gibson 1991, 1998; Gibson and Thomas 1998). The DLT integration hypothesis accounts for the CC/RC versus RC/CC contrast straightforwardly. The points of maximal integration cost in both structures occur at the verbs in each. In the CC/RC structure, the total integration cost for the most embedded verb *hired* is 3 EUs. The total integration cost for the verb *stole* is also 3 EUs, and the cost for the matrix verb *worried* is 6 EUs. In the RC/CC structure the total integration cost for the most embedded verb *stole* is only 1 EU, and the total integration cost at the matrix verb *hired* is 6 EUs, as in the CC/RC structure. It is at the point of processing the second verb *worried* in the RC/CC structure that the maximal integration cost occurs. The total integration cost at this point is 9 EUs, more than at any point in the CC/RC structure. The RC/CC structure is therefore more difficult to process than the CC/RC structure.

Another interesting nesting contrast accounted for by the DLT is that adding an extra new discourse referent at a nested location in a sentence leads to increased complexity. For example, (11b) is more complex than (11a) (Gibson and Nakatani 1998):

(11) a. The possibility that the administrator who the nurse supervised lost the medical reports didn't bother the intern from the maternity ward.
b. The possibility that the administrator who the nurse from the maternity ward supervised lost the medical reports didn't bother the intern.

In (11b) the prepositional phrase (PP) *from the maternity ward* is in a nested position, modifying the most embedded subject *the nurse*, whereas the same PP is in a nonnested position in (11a). According to the DLT, the points of highest integration cost in (11a) and (11b) are at the three verbal regions: *supervised*, *lost*, and *didn't bother*. These integration steps are all harder in (11b) than in (11a) because an extra new discourse referent intervenes in each case, and the contrast is accounted for.

5.3.3 Comparing DLT Integration Costs to Comprehension Times in Simple Relative Clause Structures

Although the DLT was initially developed to account for complexity effects in complex structures such as (1c) and (6), it accounts for processing effects in simple structures as well. One well-established complexity phenomenon to be explained by a computational resource theory is the greater complexity of an object-extracted RC as compared with a subject-extracted RC in a subject-verb-object language like English:

(12) *Subject extraction*
The reporter who sent the photographer to the editor hoped for a good story.

(13) *Object extraction*
The reporter who the photographer sent to the editor hoped for a good story.

In (12), the relative pronoun *who* is extracted from the subject position of the RC, whereas the same pronoun is extracted from the object position in (13). The object extraction is more complex by a number of measures, including phoneme monitoring, online lexical decision, reading times, and response accuracy to probe questions (Holmes 1973; Hakes, Evans, and Brannon 1976; Wanner and Maratsos 1978; Holmes and O'Regan 1981; Ford 1983; Waters, Caplan, and Hildebrandt 1987; King and Just 1991). In addition, the volume of blood flow in the brain is greater in language areas for object extractions than for subject extractions (Stromswold et al. 1996; Just et al. 1996), and aphasic stroke patients cannot reliably answer comprehension questions about object-extracted RCs, although they perform well on subject-extracted RCs (Caramazza and Zurif 1976; Caplan and Futter 1986; Grodzinsky 1989; Hickok, Zurif, and Canseco-Gonzalez 1993).

The DLT accounts for reading-time effects in these RC structures. Let us compare the integration costs predicted by the DLT at each word in (13) and (12) to actual reading times for participants in a self-paced reading experiment performed by Gibson and Ko (1998). The hypothesis is that DLT integration cost predicts reading times, when other factors such as temporary ambiguity, word length, and word frequency are controlled for. Again, this is an oversimplification even within the DLT, because reading times will also be affected by storage costs. But as long as storage costs are small, this simplification suffices. The word-by-word predictions of the DLT for the object-extracted RC structure in (13) are presented in table 5.1.

The DLT integration cost predictions for the object-extracted RC can be summarized as follows. Reading times are predicted to be fast for the first five words—*the reporter who the photographer*—in the object-extracted RC in (13), then slow on the embedded verb *sent*. Reading times should speed up again on the prepositional phrase *to the editor*, then slow down on the main verb of the sentence *hoped*, then speed up again on the final words *for a good story*.

A comparison between these predicted integration costs and actual reading times is presented in figure 5.3, based on data from thirty-two participants and sixteen items in a self-paced word-by-word reading experiment conducted by Gibson and Ko (1998). In this reading task, participants read sentences on a computer screen, at their own pace. At the beginning of a trial, a sentence is displayed on the screen with all nonspace characters replaced by dashes. When the participant presses the space bar, the first word of the sentence is displayed, replacing the corresponding dashes. When the participant presses the space bar a second time, the first word reverts to dashes,

Table 5.1
Word-by-word predictions of the DLT for the object-extracted RC structure in (13)

	Input word													
Cost type	The	reporter	who	the	photographer	sent	to	the	editor	hoped	for	a	good	story
New discourse referent	0	1	0	0	1	1	0	0	1	1	0	0	0	1
Structural integration	0	0	0	0	0	2	0	0	0	3	0	0	0	0
Total	0	1	0	0	1	3	0	0	1	4	0	0	0	1

Table 5.2
Word-by-word predictions of the DLT for the subject-extracted RC structure in (12)

	Input word													
Cost type	The	reporter	who	sent	the	photographer	to	the	editor	hoped	for	a	good	story
New discourse referent	0	1	0	1	0	1	0	0	1	1	0	0	0	1
Structural integration	0	0	0	0	0	0	0	0	0	3	0	0	0	0
Total	0	1	0	1	0	1	0	0	1	4	0	0	0	1

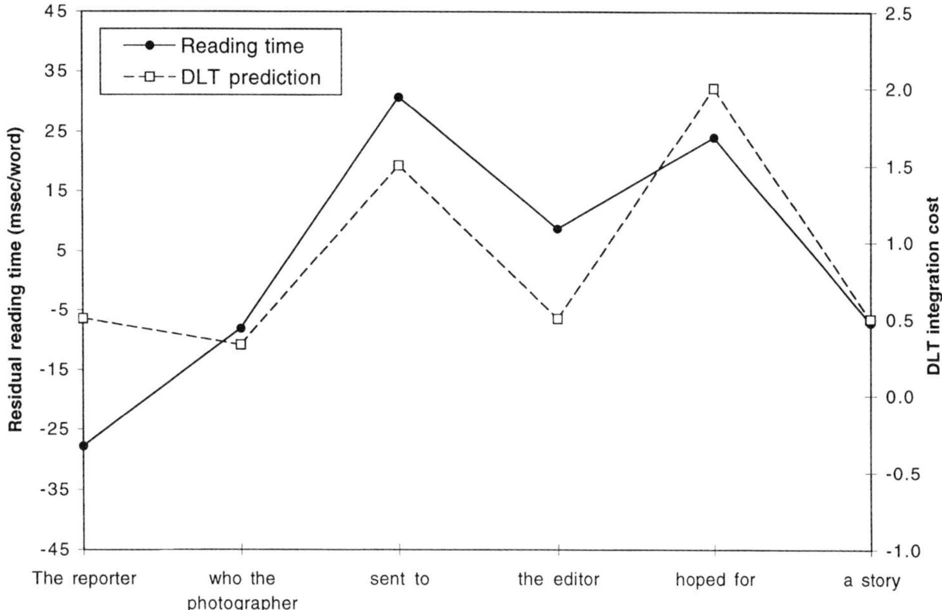

Figure 5.3
A comparison between residual reading times and locality-based integration costs in an object-extracted RC structure.

and the second word is displayed in place of the appropriate dashes. Each subsequent press of the space bar reveals the next word and removes the previous word. The computer records the time between each button-press, which represents the reading time for each word.

The reading-time data in the figure represent reading times normalized for length for each individual participant, computed by subtracting from raw reading times each participant's predicted time to read words of the same length, calculated by a linear regression equation across all sentences in the experiment (Ferreira and Clifton 1986). Thus a typical word will be read at 0 ms of normalized reading time (*residual reading time*), whereas words read quickly will have negative residual reading times, and words read slowly will have positive residual reading times. To reduce noise, the words are grouped in two- and three-word regions, and the average residual reading times are provided for each region. Because there is a reading-time spillover in self-paced reading, such that slow reading times are often reflected one or two words after a point of high complexity, locations of high predicted DLT integration cost were grouped with the following word. Other groupings were made according to constituent groupings in the remainder of the sentences. The reading times and DLT integration cost predictions are closely correlated for the object-extracted RC ($r = 0.79$, $r^2 = 0.63$, $F(1,4) = 6.85$, $p < 0.06$).

The word-by-word predictions of the DLT for the subject-extracted RC structure in (12) are presented in table 5.2.

The integration costs for this construction are the same as for the object extraction, except on the embedded verb *sent*. In the subject extraction, the cost of integrating the embedded verb *sent* is 1 EU, because although it indicates a new discourse referent, this is a local structural integration. Thus, in contrast to the object-extracted RC, reading times should be fast all the way through the subject-extracted RC until the main verb of the sentence—*hoped*—is encountered, at which point reading times should slow down. Reading times should then speed up again after this.

A comparison between the predicted integration costs and actual reading times for the subject-extracted RC structure is presented in figure 5.4, based on data from Gibson and Ko's (1998) self-paced reading experiment. As for the object-extracted RC structure, the reading times and DLT integration cost predictions are also closely correlated for the subject-extracted RC structure ($r = 0.77$, $r^2 = 0.60$, $F(1,4) = 5.99$, $p < 0.08$). Combining the subject- and object-extracted RC data yields a significant

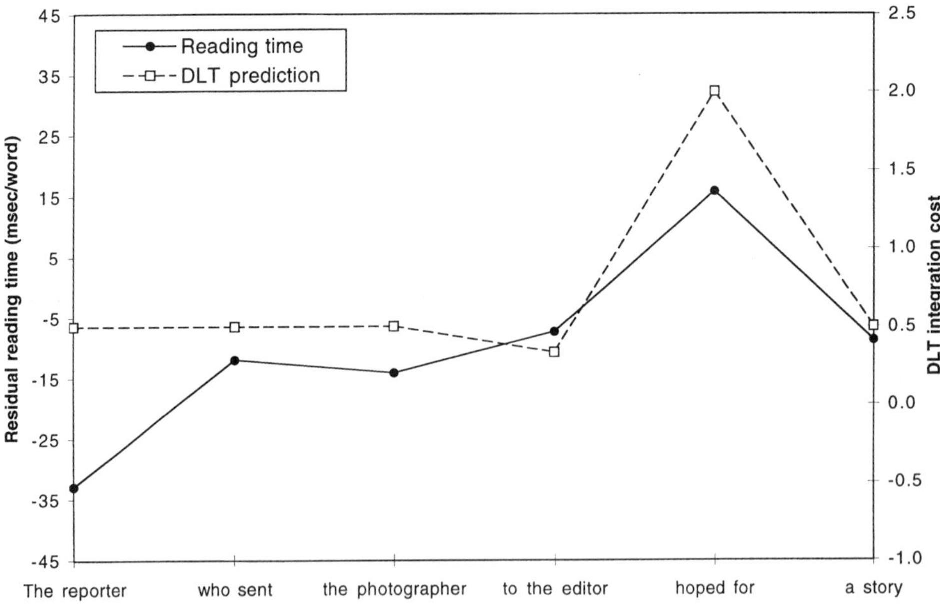

Figure 5.4
A comparison between residual reading times and locality-based integration costs in a subject-extracted RC structure.

correlation between reading times and DLT predictions, accounting for almost 60% of the variance in the RTs ($r = 0.77$, $r^2 = 0.59$, $F(1,4) = 14.7$, $p < 0.005$). Related reading-time data are provided by King and Just (1991), as well as in another experiment performed by Gibson and Ko (1998) and reported in Gibson (1998).

5.3.4 Crosslinguistic Support for the DLT

The evidence provided thus far in support of the DLT integration cost hypothesis has all come from the processing of English. However, the claims being made are about the nature of computational resource use in human language processing more generally, not just in English. Evidence from the processing of other languages is therefore crucial to the enterprise. Some Japanese evidence in support of the DLT is provided by Babyonyshev and Gibson (1999). They had participants rate the processing difficulty of a number of different structures, including the following two:

(14) Obasan-wa [bebiisitaa-ga [ani-ga naita] to itta] to omotteiru.
aunt-top babysitter-nom older-brother-nom cried that said that thinks
My aunt thinks that the babysitter said that my older brother cried.

(15) Obasan-wa [bebiisitaa-ga [ani-ga imooto-o ijimeta] to
aunt-top babysitter-nom older-brother-nom younger-sister-acc bullied that
itta] to omotteiru.
said that thinks
My aunt thinks that the babysitter said that my older brother bullied my younger sister.

Both (14) and (15) are doubly nested clausal structures. The difference between the two is that the most embedded clause in (14) is intransitive, containing a subject and a verb (*ani-ga naita* 'brother cried'), whereas the most embedded clause in (15) is transitive, containing a subject, an object, and a verb (*ani-ga imooto-o ijimeta* 'brother bullied sister'). The inclusion of the extra object NP, a new discourse referent, increases the distances between the subjects and the verbs for all three verbs, just as adding the prepositional phrase did so for the English examples discussed earlier (Gibson and Nakatani 1998). Thus the DLT predicts larger structural integration costs on each of the verbs, and correspondingly worse complexity ratings for the transitive structure in (15). The results from Babyonyshev and Gibson's (1999) difficulty rating experiment confirmed this prediction: the transitive structures were rated as significantly harder to understand than the intransitive structures.

Babyonyshev and Gibson present further evidence in support of the DLT from the processing of other Japanese constructions. Other crosslinguistic evidence relevant to the processing of unambiguous constructions is provided by Bach, Brown, and Marslen-Wilson (1986), who investigated nesting complexity in Dutch and German.

(See Gibson 1998 for a demonstration that this evidence supports the DLT. Much additional crosslinguistic support of the DLT with respect to ambiguity resolution is also described in Gibson 1998. Languages for which some evidence is described there include Spanish, German, Dutch, and Finnish.)

5.3.5 The DLT Storage Cost Component

I have concentrated on the integration cost component of the DLT so far. There is a second component of the theory: the storage cost component. According to the storage cost component, each syntactic head required to complete the current input string as a grammatical sentence is associated with a storage cost.[6] Under most syntactic theories (e.g., Bresnan 1982; Chomsky 1981, 1995; Pollard and Sag 1994) the minimal number of syntactic head categories in an English sentence is two: a noun for the subject and a verb for the predicate. The DLT storage cost hypothesis is given in (16):

(16) *DLT storage cost*
1 memory unit (MU) is associated with each syntactic head required to complete the current input as a grammatical sentence.

Consider (16) with respect to the object-extracted RC structure in (17):

(17)

	Input word								
	The	reporter	who	the	senator	attacked	disliked	the	editor
Storage cost (in MUs)	2	1	3	4	3	1	1	1	0

At the point of processing the sentence-initial determiner *the*, two syntactic heads are needed to form a grammatical sentence: a noun and a verb. There is therefore a cost of 2 MUs at this point. After processing *reporter*, only one head is needed to complete a grammatical sentence: a verb. The storage cost is therefore 1 MU here. When the pronoun *who* is processed, the rest of an RC must follow, in addition to the main verb of the sentence. The RC requires two more heads: a verb, and an empty category position in the RC to be associated with the RC pronoun *who*. Thus the total storage cost at this point is 3 MUs. For example, the sentence could be completed as *The reporter who slept left*. In this continuation, the three heads that are needed at the point of processing *who* end up being (1) the verb *slept*; (2) an empty category in subject position of this verb, which refers to the same individual as *who*; and (3) the verb *left*.

After processing the second instance of *the* (following *who*), four heads are needed to make a grammatical sentence: two verbs, an empty category position in the RC to be associated with the RC pronoun *who*, and noun for the determiner *the*. The noun *senator* satisfies the last of these requirements, leaving a cost of 3 MUs at this point. The verb *attacked* then satisfies the prediction for a verb in the RC, and an empty category can also be connected at this point, licensed in the object position of the verb *attacked*. The storage cost at *attacked* is therefore only 1 MU, corresponding to the prediction of the main verb. The main verb *disliked* is encountered next, satisfying this prediction. However, this verb requires an NP object to its right, resulting in a cost of 1 MU. The determiner *the* does not satisfy the prediction for a noun, but it does not add any additional predictions either, so the storage cost remains at 1 MU here. Finally, the noun *editor* is attached at the noun object of the verb *disliked*, completing a grammatical sentence. There is therefore no storage cost on completion of the sentence.

Now that the storage and integration cost components of the DLT have been specified, it is necessary to say how the two parts of the theory interrelate to provide a theory of comprehension times and intuitive complexity. The set of assumptions made by Gibson (1998) with respect to this issue are as follows: (1) integrations and storage access the same pool of resources (Just and Carpenter 1992; see Caplan and Waters 1999); (2) there is a fixed capacity of resources in the resource pool; and (3) each predicted syntactic head takes up a fixed quantity of resources. As a result, the more resources that are required in storage, the slower integrations occur.

It is also possible that storage costs might not all consume a fixed quantity of resources. Alternatively, fewer resources might by used for each additional syntactic prediction stored as more predictions are stored. For example, 1 storage unit might be used to store one prediction, but only 1.5 units to store two predictions, and only 1.75 units for three. The result of such a system might be that, as more predictions are stored, some are stored less well. Consequently, the likelihood that all predictions will be recalled may decrease as more are stored.

There are of course many other possibilities for the relationship between storage and integration cost. Currently, there is no empirical data that decides among these possibilities. We will therefore not make a commitment here, beyond assuming that larger quantities of either storage or integration cost cause slower integration times, and that intuitive complexity is determined by the maximal integration time in the parse of a sentence.

5.3.6 Applying the DLT to Ambiguity Resolution

The evidence put forward thus far in support of the DLT has come from the processing of unambiguous structures. This section considers some predictions that the DLT makes when used as part of a metric in ambiguity resolution. The DLT ambiguity resolution claim is given in (18):

(18) *Ambiguity resolution hypothesis*

In choosing among ambiguous structures, two of the factors that the processor uses to evaluate its choices are DLT storage and structural integration cost (in addition to informational constraints, such as lexical frequencies, plausibility, and context).

Consider the ambiguity resolution hypothesis with respect to an ambiguous example like (19):

(19) The bartender told the detective that the suspect left the country yesterday.

The adverb *yesterday* can be linked to either the local verb *left* or to the more distant verb *told*. There is no memory cost difference between the two resultant structures, but there is a structural integration cost difference: the attachment to *left* crosses only one new discourse referent, whereas the attachment to *told* crosses four new discourse referents. Thus the local integration to *left* is strongly preferred. (For earlier accounts of locality preferences in ambiguity resolution, see Kimball 1973; Frazier and Fodor 1978; Gibson 1991; Stevenson 1994; Gibson et al. 1996.[7] See Gibson 1998 for discussion of further evidence of locality preferences in ambiguity resolution.)

Consider now the DLT ambiguity resolution hypothesis with respect to the ambiguity in (20):

(20) The evidence examined by the lawyer turned out to be unreliable.

There is a temporary ambiguity at the word *examined* between a past-tense main verb (MV) interpretation and a past-participle reduced relative (RR) interpretation. The past-tense and the past-participle readings are roughly equally frequent in the Brown corpus (Francis and Kučera 1982). Plausibility strongly favors the RR structure, because it is plausible for evidence to be examined, but it is not plausible for evidence to examine something (Ferreira and Clifton 1986; Trueswell, Tanenhaus, and Garnsey 1994). There is no structural integration cost difference between the two potential attachments, because both are local. There is potentially a small memory cost difference between the two, favoring the MV structure. In particular, one syntactic head is needed to complete the MV structure as a grammatical sentence: a noun in the object position of the transitive verb *examined*. One or possibly two syntactic heads are needed to complete the RR structure as a grammatical sentence: (1) the main verb of the sentence, and possibly (2) a modifier for the reduced relative clause, because single-word reduced relative clauses are not very acceptable. Thus the DLT memory costs are either balanced for this ambiguity or slightly favoring the MV structure. Weighing all the applicable factors together, the RR structure is preferred, primarily because of the large plausibility difference (Trueswell, Tanenhaus, and Garnsey 1994).

In contrast to the ambiguity resolution hypothesis proposed here, in which resource use is a factor, recent lexicalist "constraint-based" processing theories claim that ambiguity resolution is determined exclusively by lexical frequencies and plausibility (MacDonald, Pearlmutter, and Seidenberg 1994; Trueswell, Tanenhaus, and Garnsey 1994), with no effect of resource use. Evidence for this claim comes from a number of reading-time studies of a few types of English temporary ambiguities, including the MV/RR ambiguity. However, the ambiguities on which this claim is based are all similar to the MV/RR ambiguity in that there is minimal or no resource use difference between the potential structures in the temporary ambiguities in question. It is therefore dubious to conclude that resource use plays no role in ambiguity resolution based on these ambiguities, because resource use does not differ very much in these cases.[8]

To test the resource use hypothesis, it is necessary to compare the resolution of an ambiguity with a small resource complexity difference with the resolution of ambiguities with larger resource complexity differences, while controlling for lexical frequency and plausibility. Gibson, Grodner, and Tunstall (1997) did exactly this by exploring the MV/RR structure embedded within a relative clause, as in (21):

(21) The witness who the evidence examined by the lawyer implicated seemed to be very nervous.

The items were constructed using Trueswell, Tanenhaus, and Garnsey's MV/RR items as a base, so that plausibility factors highly favored the RR interpretation of the ambiguous verb *examined*. However, syntactic complexity as measured by the DLT storage cost strongly favors the MV reading in this variant of the MV/RR ambiguity. In particular, only one syntactic head is required to complete the implausible MV structure as a grammatical sentence: the main verb of the sentence. In contrast, three or four syntactic heads are needed to complete the RR structure grammatically: (1) the main verb of the sentence, (2) a verb for the relative clause, (3) an empty NP to be associated with the RC pronoun *who*, and possibly (4) an adverbial modifier for the single-word reduced relative clause. The storage cost difference between the two structures is therefore two or three syntactic heads, two more than in the MV/RR ambiguities explored earlier. This difference is much larger than in any of the ambiguities that motivated the lexically based ambiguity resolution hypothesis.[9] If the DLT storage cost is being used in ambiguity resolution online, people should have more difficulty following the RR reading of the verb *examined* in (21) than they will in a control case like (20). To test this hypothesis, Gibson and colleagues compared the reading times of sentences like (21) to closely related examples like (23a), with a small storage complexity difference between the MV and RR readings. They also tested unambiguous control sentences for each type of structure, as in (22) and (23b) respectively.

(22) *Large storage cost difference, unambiguous control*
The witness who the evidence that was examined by the lawyer implicated seemed to be very nervous.

(23) a. *Small storage cost difference, ambiguous*
The witness thought that the evidence examined by the lawyer implicated his next-door neighbor.
b. *Small storage cost difference, unambiguous*
The witness thought that the evidence that was examined by the lawyer implicated his next-door neighbor.

As in the simple MV/RR ambiguities in (20), the storage complexity at the point of processing *examined* in (23a) is one syntactic prediction for the MV structure and one or two syntactic predictions for the RR structure, resulting in a smaller storage cost difference for this MV/RR structure.

The participants' residual reading times for each of these conditions are plotted in figure 5.5. The first result of interest to the DLT is that reading times for the region *the evidence examined by the lawyer* were significantly faster in the small storage cost conditions than in the large storage cost conditions. Although the same structural integrations are being performed in all these conditions, there is a larger syntactic storage load in the large storage conditions than in the small storage conditions, leading to longer reading times in these conditions, as predicted.

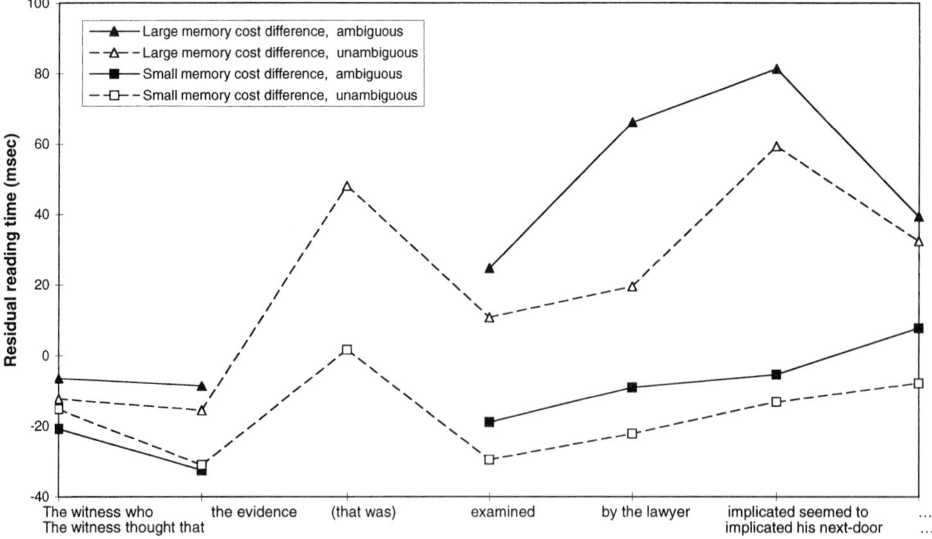

Figure 5.5
Residual reading times for sixty subjects taking part in a self-paced, word-by-word, moving-window reading experiment involving four conditions that crossed DLT storage complexity difference (high storage complexity difference, low storage complexity difference) with ambiguity (ambiguous, unambiguous).

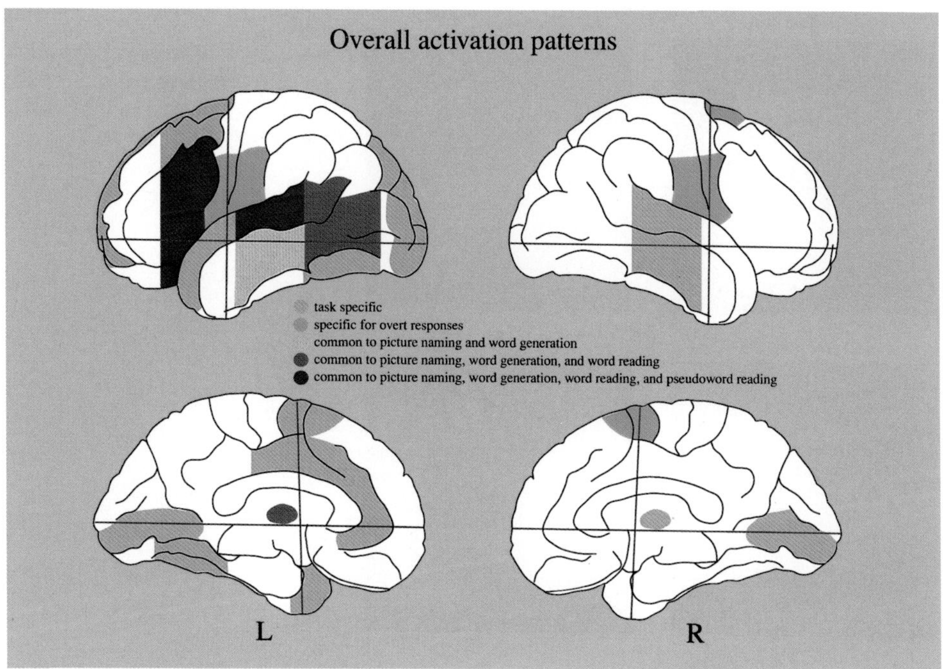

Plate 1
Overall left and right hemisphere activation patterns for various tasks in the meta-analysis. Pink, red, and blue colored regions are involved with the core processes of word production.

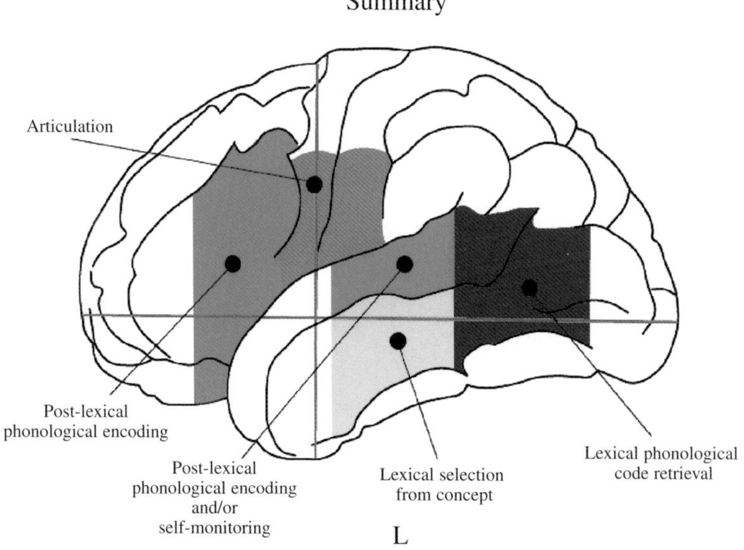

Plate 2
Summary of regions activated by various core processes in word production.

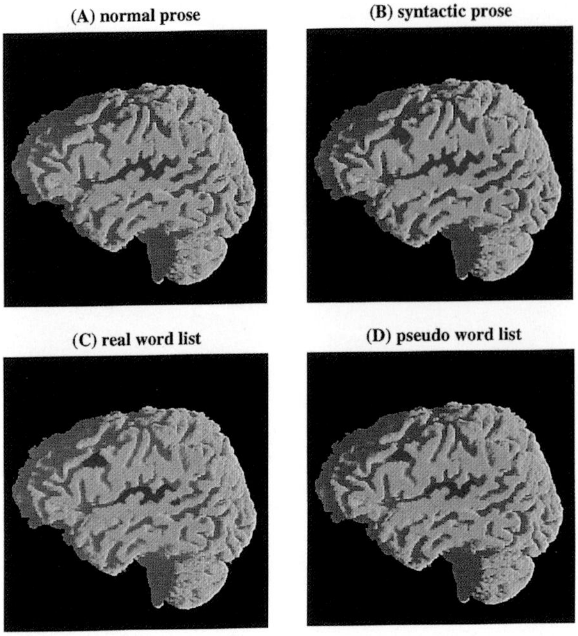

(A) normal prose
(B) syntactic prose
(C) real word list
(D) pseudo word list

Plate 3
Significant clusters of activation for each condition in the left hemisphere, as indicated by fMRI illustrated in the sagittal view.

(A) normal prose
(B) syntactic prose
(C) real word list
(D) pseudo word list

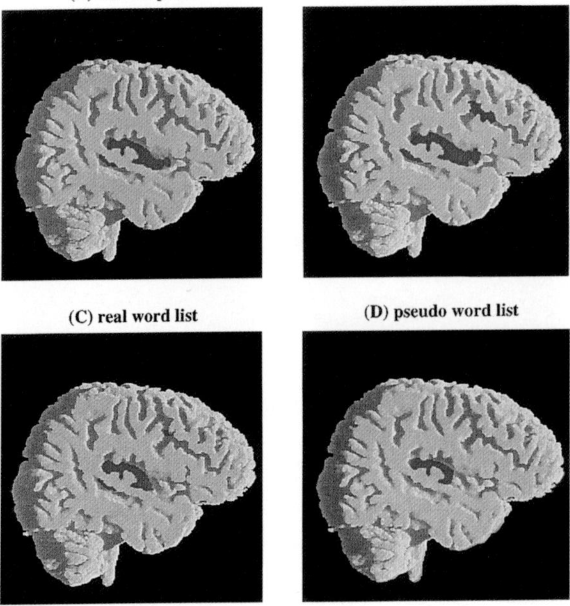

Plate 4
Siginificant clusters of activation for each condition in the right hemisphere, as indicated by fMRI illustrated in the sagittal view.

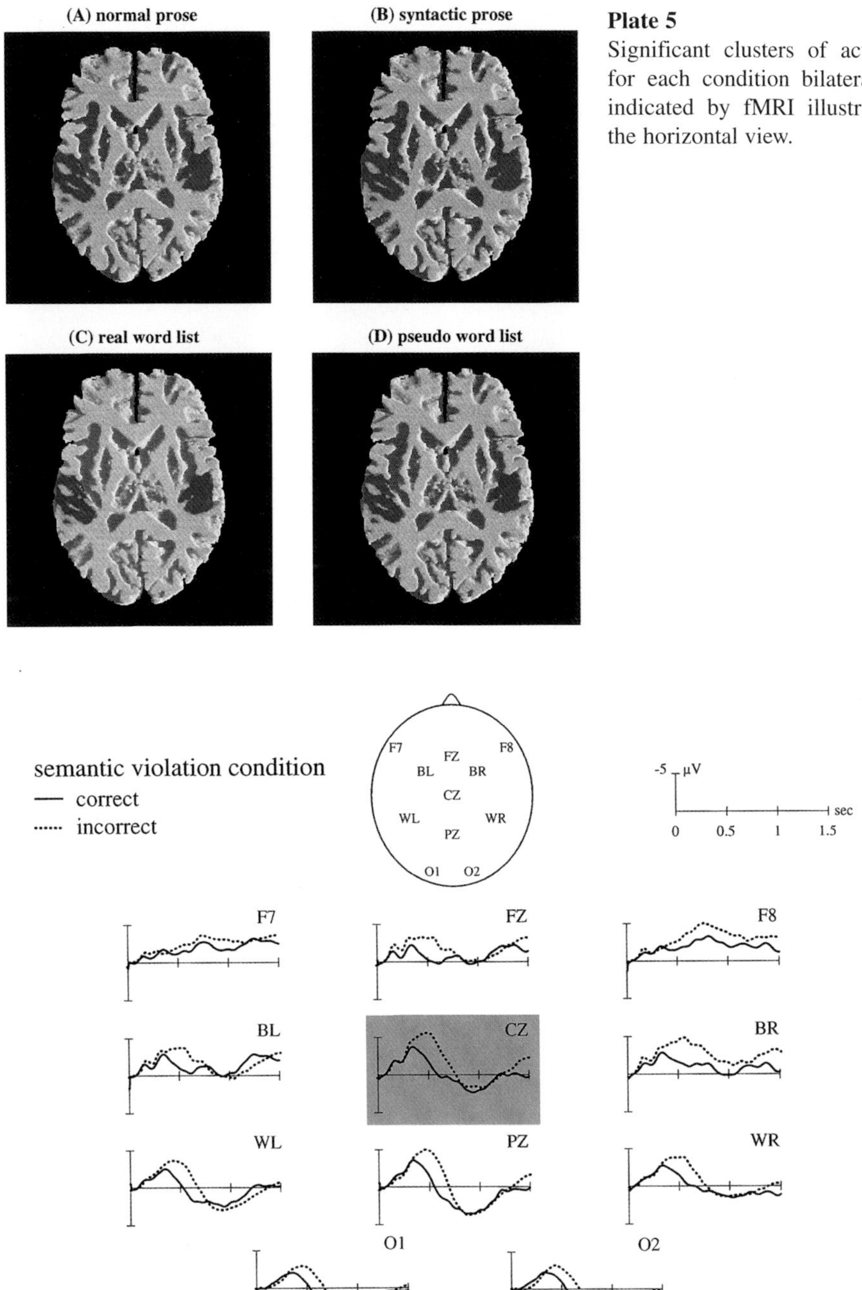

Plate 5

Significant clusters of activation for each condition bilaterally, as indicated by fMRI illustrated in the horizontal view.

Plate 6

Average of event-related potentials for the correct and the semantically incorrect condition. Vertical line indicates onset of the critical word.

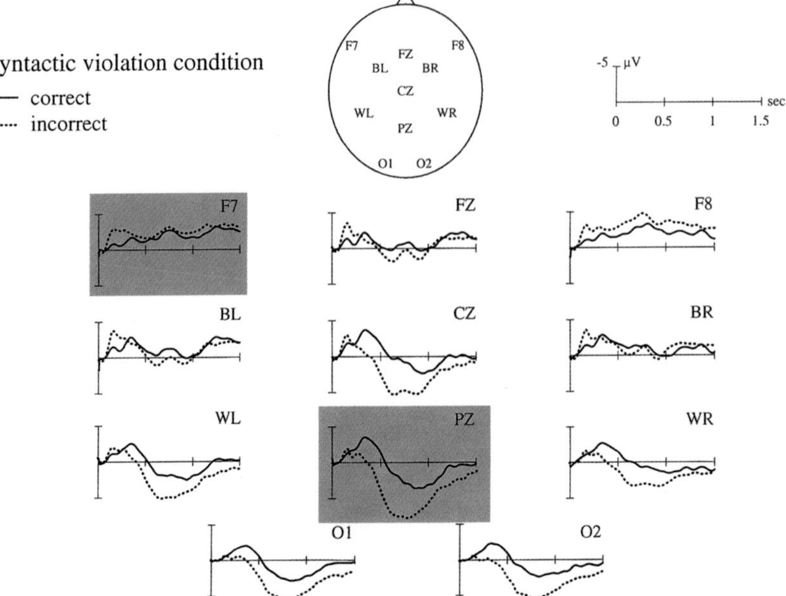

Plate 7
Average of event-related potentials for the correct and the syntactically incorrect condition. Vertical line indicates onset of the critical word.

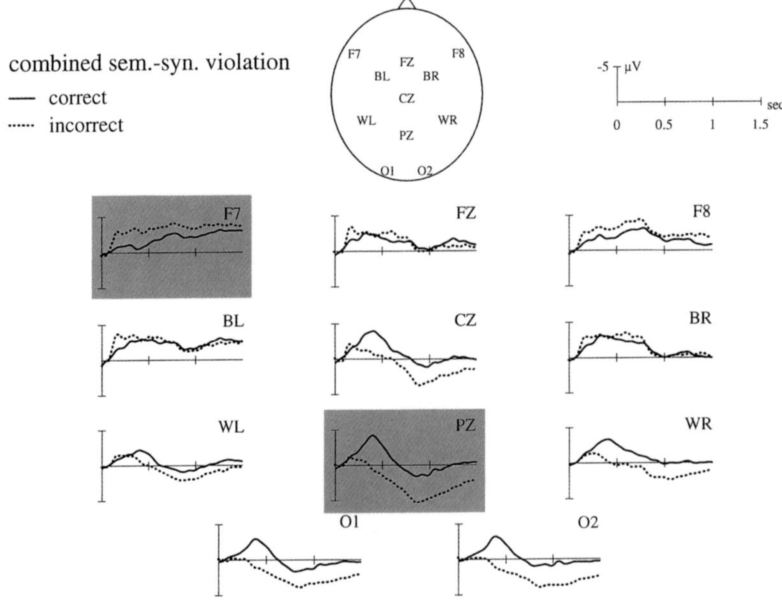

Plate 8
Average of event-related potentials for the correct and the combined violation condition. Vertical line indicates onset of the critical word.

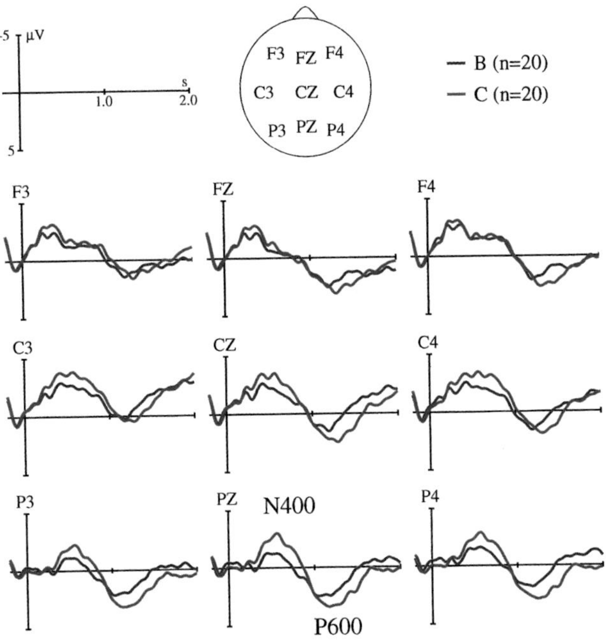

Plate 9

Average of even-related potentials for the critical verb in B, i.e., sentences with appropriate pause (14), and in C, i.e., sentences with inappropriate pause (15).

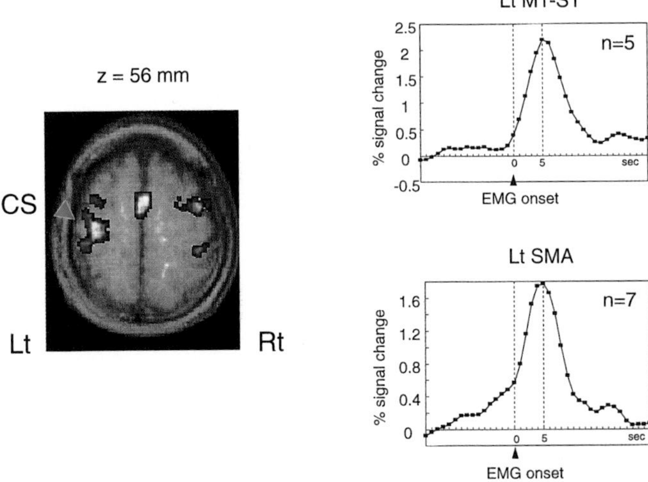

Plate 10

Activated areas (*left*) and the time course of their activation (*right*) with respect to self-initiated extension of the right wrist in the left primary sensorimotor area (Lt M1-S1, average of five trials) and the left supplementary motor area (Lt SMA, average of seven trials), studied by movement-associated fMRI in a single subject. The triangle in the left figure indicates the central sulcus (CS). The activity starts in SMAs earlier than in the contralateral M1-S1. (Studied by K. Toma, unpublished data.)

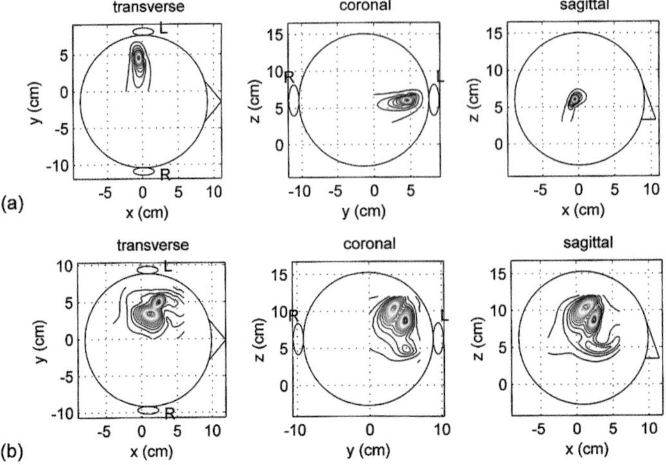

Plate 11

(*a*) Results of applying the time-domain MUSIC algorithm to the auditory response shown in figure 10.3a. (*b*) Results of applying the time-domain MUSIC algorithm to the somatosensory response shown in figure 10.3b. The localizer in equation (14) was calculated in a three-dimensional volume in the left hemisphere with a 0.5-cm interval. The maximum-intensity projections onto the transverse, coronal, and sagittal planes are shown. Each contour shows the relative value of the localizer, and locations where the localizer reaches a peak are considered to be the source locations. The circles depicting a human head represent approximate location of the subject's scalp surface. The letters *L* and *R* indicate the left and the right hemispheres, respectively.

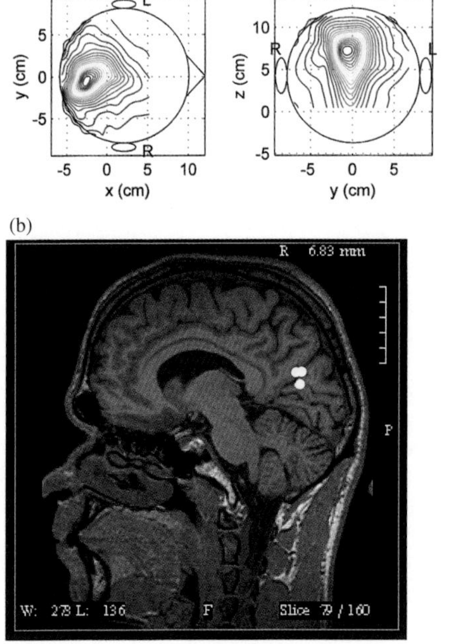

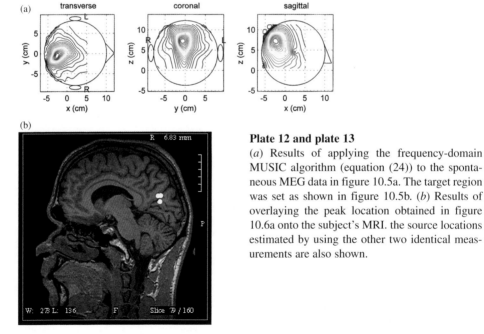

Plate 12 and plate 13

(*a*) Results of applying the frequency-domain MUSIC algorithm (equation (24)) to the spontaneous MEG data in figure 10.5a. The target region was set as shown in figure 10.5b. (*b*) Results of overlaying the peak location obtained in figure 10.6a onto the subject's MRI. the source locations estimated by using the other two identical measurements are also shown.

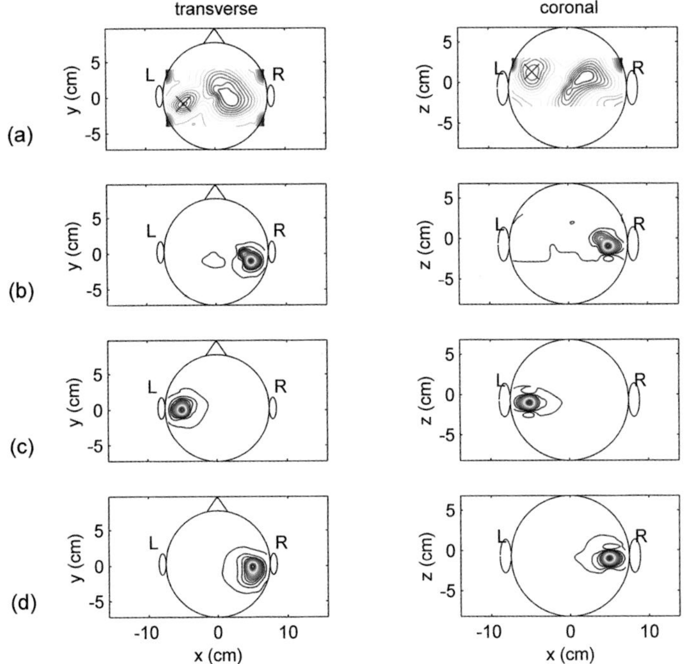

Plate 14
(*a*) Results of applying the single-source MUSIC algorithm (equation (14)) to the data shown in figure 10.7. (*b*)-(*d*) Results of applying the two-source MUSIC algorithm (equation (17)). The cross mark in (*a*) indicates the position at which one source was fixed to obtain the results in (*b*). Results in (*c*) and (*d*) were obtained by fixing one source at which the localizer reached its maximum in the results in (*b*) and (*c*), respectively.

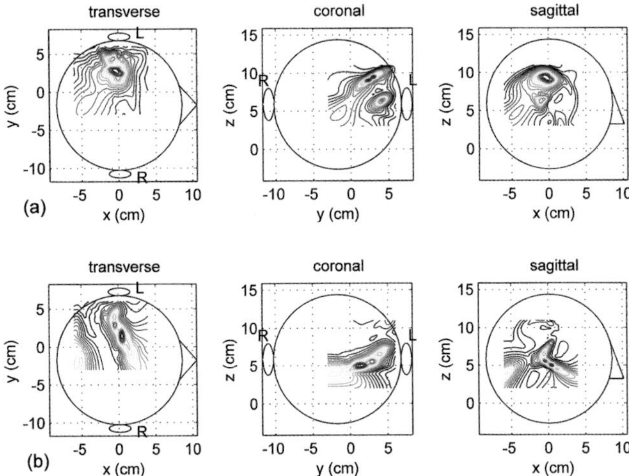

Plate 15
Results of applying the conventional localizer in equation (14). Results are shown for the evoked responses to (*a*) /dae/ and (*b*) /tae/ (reproduced from [18]).

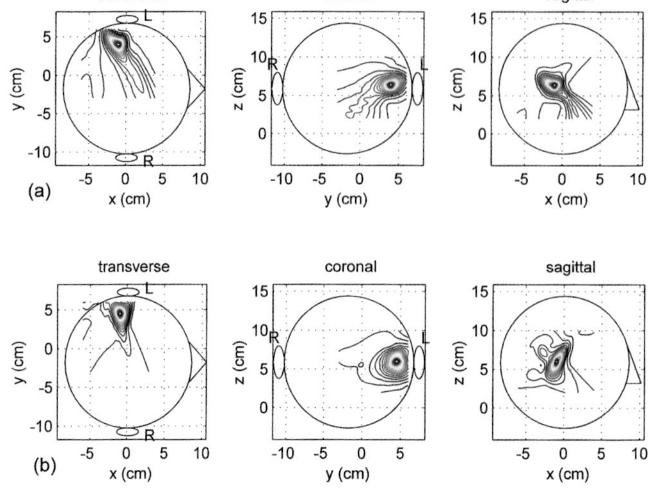

Plate 16
Results of applying the prewhitened localizer in equation (31). Results are for the evoked responses to (*a*) /dae/ and (*b*) /tae/ (reproduced from [18]).

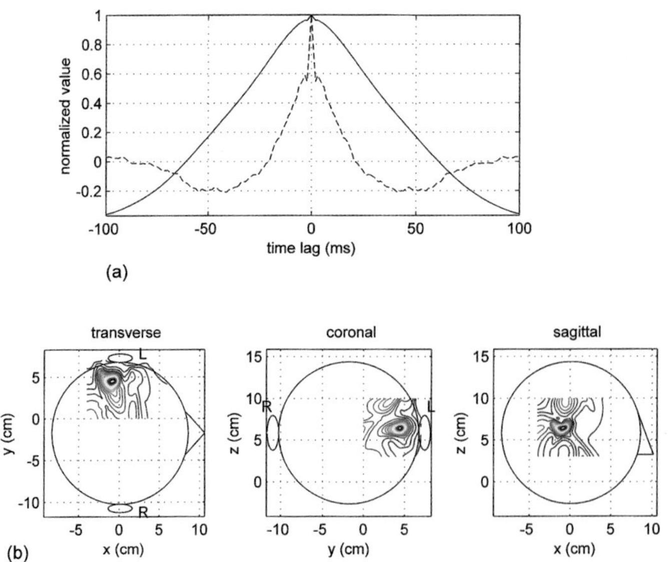

Plate 17
(*a*) Temporal autocorrelation function of the auditory-evoked response elicited by the speech sound /dae/. The autocorrelation function was averaged over channels. The solid line indicates the autocorrelation obtained from the poststimulus part, and the broken line indicates the autocorrelation obtained from the prestimulus part. (*b*) Results of applying the method described in section 10.4.3. Five covariance matrices $\boldsymbol{R}_b(\tau)$ with τ = 6, 12, 18, 24, and 30 msec were used to estimate the noise subspace.

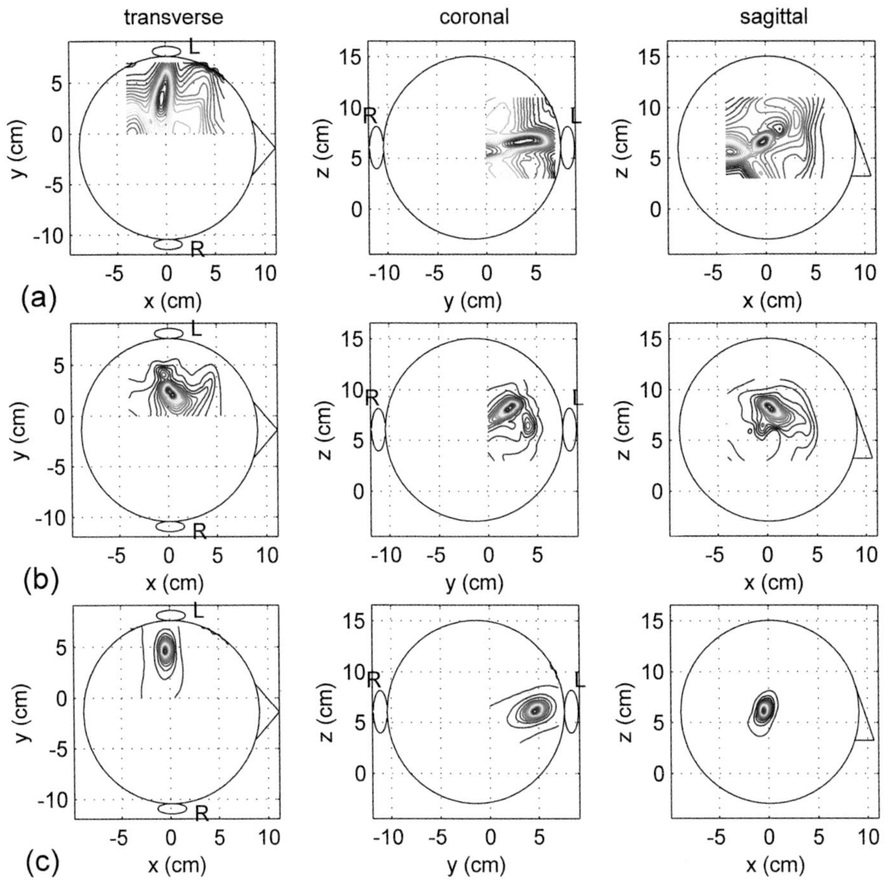

Plate 18

(*a*) Results of applying the conventional MUSIC algorithm to the averaged data containing the artificial time jitter. (*b*) Results of applying the conventional MUSIC algorithm to raw-epoch data. (*c*) Results of applying the prewhitening MUSIC algorithm to raw-epoch data (reproduced from [24]).

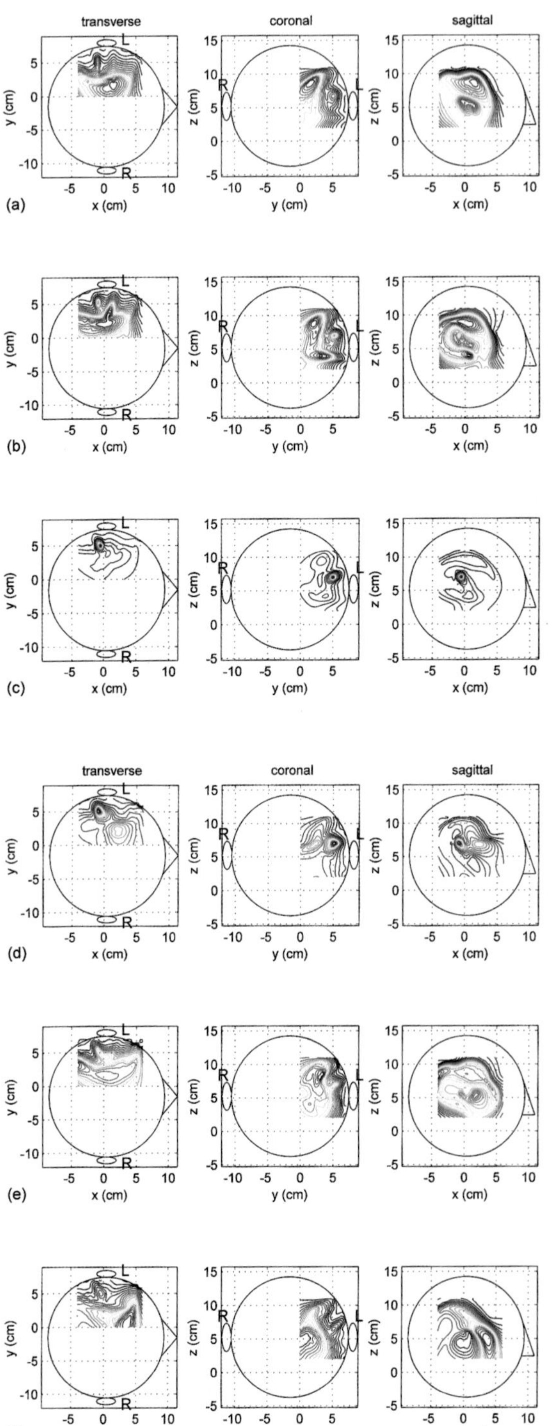

Plate 19

The results of applying the waveform-based subtraction method. The data portion between 0 and 200 msec was selected from the auditory-button-press data and the portion between t_s and t_s +200 msec was selected from the self-paced button-press data. Results for (*a*) $t_s = -10$, (*b*) $t_s = -30$, (*c*) $t_s = -50$, (*d*) $t_s = -70$, (*e*) $t_s = -90$, and (*f*) $t_s = -110$ msec (reproduced from [20]).

Plate 20

(*plate 19 continued*)

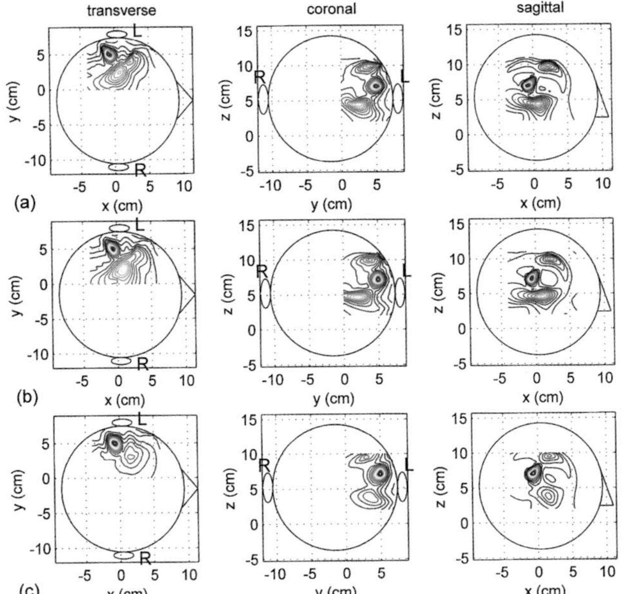

Plate 21
The results of applying the covariance-difference analysis. the data portion between 0 and 200 msec was selected from the auditory-button-press data and the portion between t_s and $t_s + 200$ msec was selected from the self-paced button-press data. Results for (*a*) $t_s = -10$, (*b*) $t_s = -30$, (*c*) $t_s = -50$, (*d*) $t_s = -70$, (*e*) $t_s = -90$, and (*f*) $t_s = -110$ msec (reproduced from [20]).

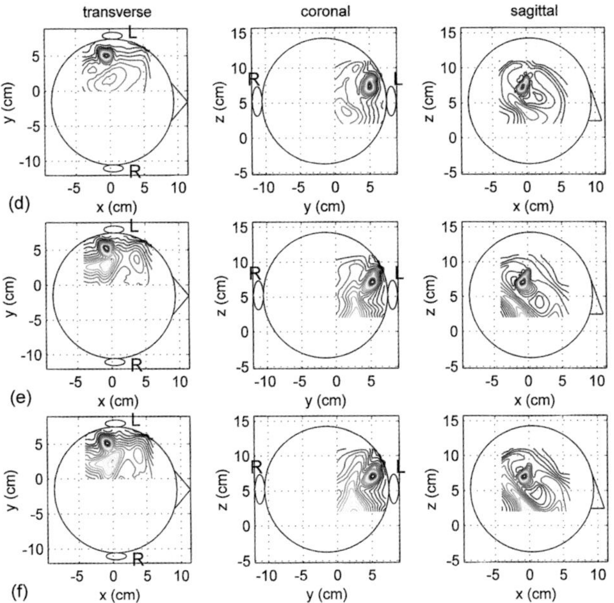

Plate 22
(*plate 21 continued*)

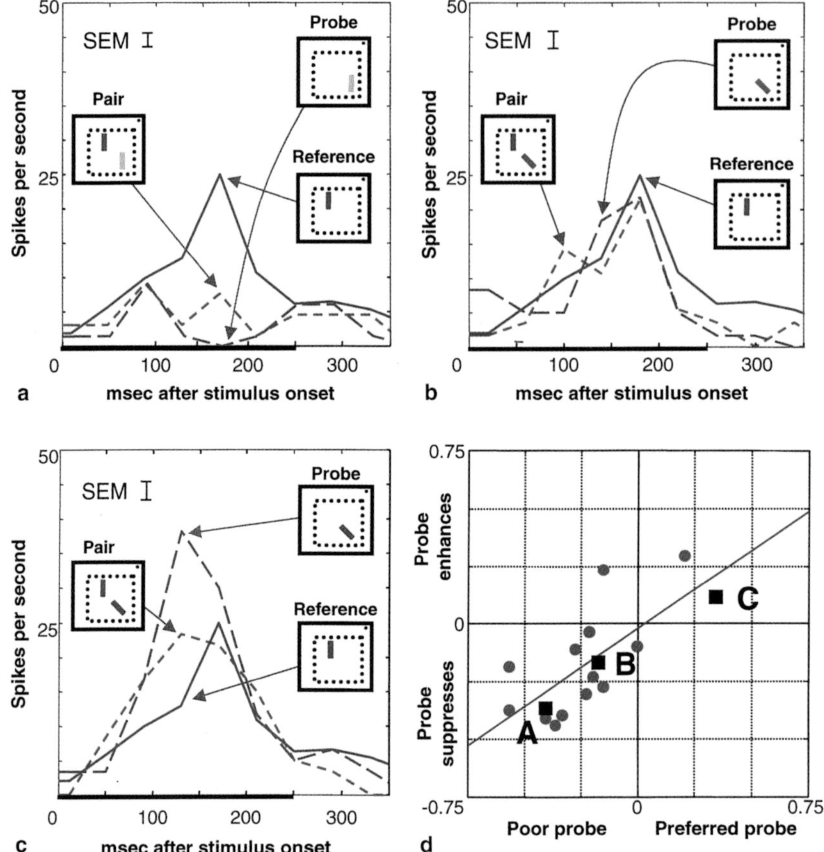

Plate 23

In the absence of attention, stimuli compete to control neuronal responses. The response of a single V4 neuron to the reference, a probe, and the corresponding pair is shown for three probes in each of panels a, b, and c. The horizontal axis shows time (in msec) from stimulus onset, and the thick horizontal bar indicates stimulus duration. The vertical bar in the upper left-hand corner shows the standard error of the mean (SEM) of the response of this neuron, averaged over the three stimulus conditions for each panel. The blue line that is constant across all three panels shows the response to the reference stimulus, which was a vertical green bar. (*a*) The green line indicates the response to a vertical yellow probe that drove the cell at a low average rate. The response to the pair, indicated by a red line, was strongly suppressed by the probe stimulus. (*b*) A 45° blue bar probe, which elicited a response similar to the response to the reference stimulus, caused little or no change in the cell's response. (*c*) A 45° green bar probe, which elicited a response larger than the response to the reference stimulus, increased the cell's response. (*d*) Indices of selectivity (horizontal axis) and sensory interaction (vertical axis) for all sixteen probe stimuli. The indices corresponding to each of the probes illustrated in panels a, b, and c are indicated by squares and are labeled in panel d. A negative selectivity index (indicating that the response to the probe was less than the response to the reference stimulus was typically paired with a negative sensory interaction index (indicating that the addition of the poor probe suppressed the response of the cell). Nonselective reference-probe pairs showed little or no sensory interactions. Preferred probes increased the response to the reference stimulus.

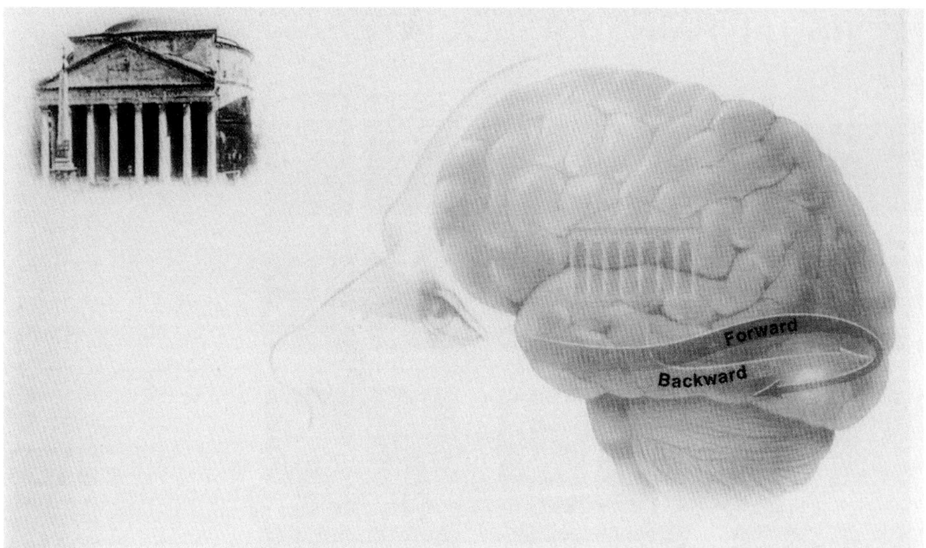

Plate 24
Visual perception mainly relies on the forward, bottom-up flow of information. Image retrieval or imagery experience, in contrast, highlights the backward projections as an anatomical substrate of top-down mental operations. If an imagery task requires reconstruction of the detailed local geometry of the image (as in counting the columns in a memory of the Pantheon), backward signals from higher-order representations might reach topographically organized visual areas. This illustration does not indicate that mental images are actual pictures in the brain; obviously we cannot assume a homunculus in the brain that looks at the images. Adapted from Miyashita 1995; artwork by K. Sutliff.

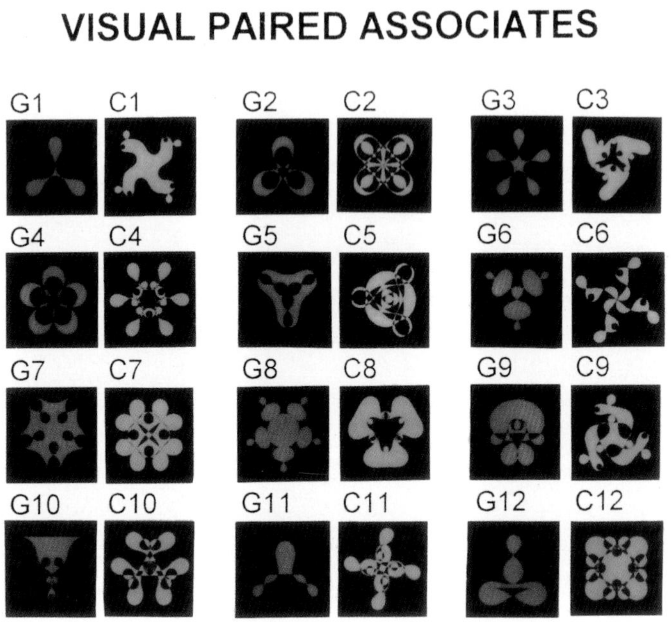

VISUAL PAIRED ASSOCIATES

G1 C1 G2 C2 G3 C3
G4 C4 G5 C5 G6 C6
G7 C7 G8 C8 G9 C9
G10 C10 G11 C11 G12 C12

Plate 25
Image-retrieval task for monkeys. The pair-association with color switch (PACS) task uses twelve pairs of colored pictures. When one member of each pair is shown, trained monkeys can retrieve and choose the other member of the paired associates. The first pair consists of the picture G1 (green) and picture C1 (cyan), the second pair consists of G2 and C2, and so on.

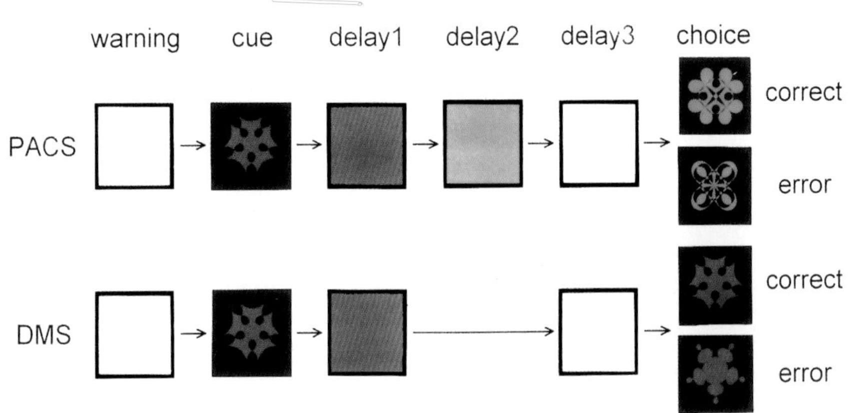

Plate 26
Sequence of events in the image-retrieval task. Both PACS trials and DMS trials use the same color stimuli shown in figure 12.2 (plate 25). In each trial of the task, a cue stimulus is presented, and then the monkey is rewarded when he or she chooses the correct stimulus. The correct stimulus is the paired associate of the cue in PACS trials and the cue itself in DMS trials. PACS trials and DMS trials were given randomly. Event sequence is the following: warning, gray square for fixation (1 sec in both trials); cue, one of twenty-four colored pictures (0.5 sec); delay period 1, fixation square that has the same color as the cue picture (2 sec in PACS trials, 5 sec in the DMS trials); delay period 2, fixation square that has the same color as the paired associate of the cue picture (3 sec in PACS trials); delay period 3, fixation gray square (1 sec in both trials); choice, a choice of two stimuli (1.2 sec in both trials).

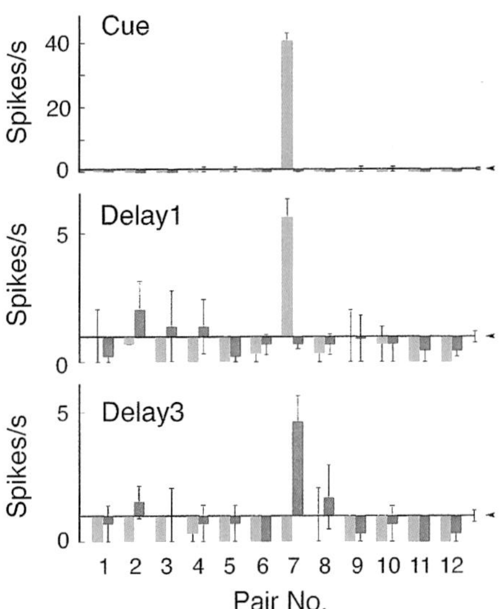

Plate 27
Stimulus selectivity of the inferotemporal neuron (the same as that in figure 12.4) is shown in different task periods (top, cue period; middle, delay period 1; bottom, delay period 3). The ordinate shows the mean discharge rate in each task period after the presentation of a cue stimulus; cue stimuli are labeled *Pair no.* on the abscissa (green histogram bar in no. 1: G1, cyan/blue histogram bar in no. 1: C1, and so on). This neuron selectively responded to the cue stimulus G7 during the cue period. Note that the cue stimulus C7 does not elicit any response during the cue period and delay period 1 in this neuron, but during delay periods 2 and 3 the same neuron suddenly became active.

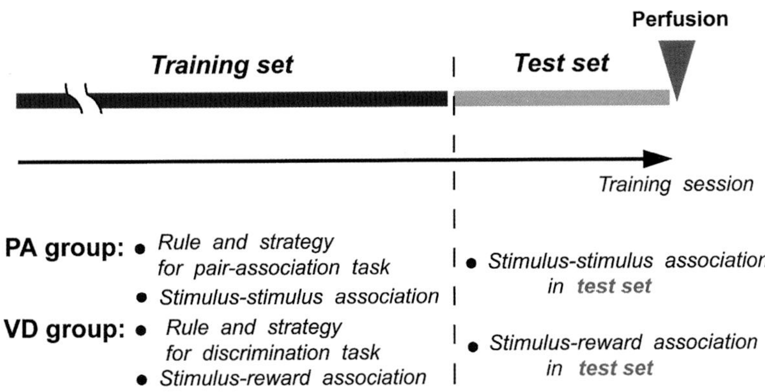

Plate 28
Experimental design to detect learning-induced activation of molecular markers in monkeys. To detect the expression of gene specifically related to the paired associated learning, two different control procedures were introduced. First, the monkeys learned the rule and task strategy during the learning of the *training-set* stimuli, and then the expression of molecular markers was detected during the learning of the *test-set* stimuli. Second, the expression during paired associated learning was compared with that during visual discrimination learning. The paired associated learning and visual discrimination learning used the same visual stimuli, same motor responses, and same number of rewards.

A

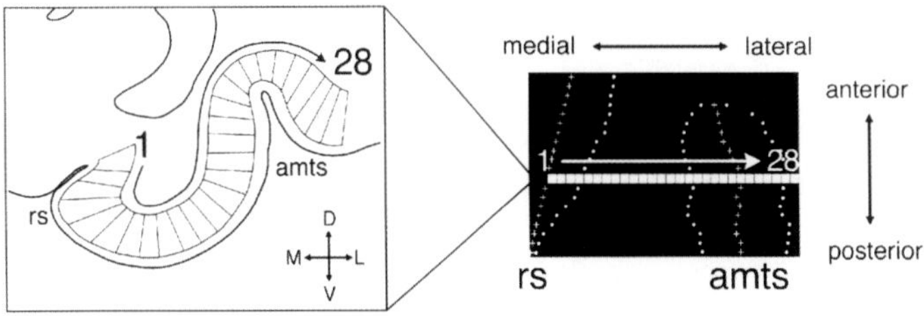

B

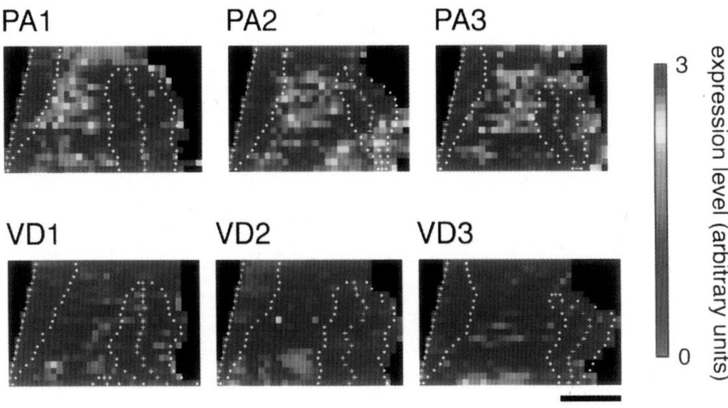

Plate 29

Two-dimensional unfolded maps of the monkey temporal cortex indicating ZIF268 expression levels. (*A*) Line drawing of twenty-eight radial, segmented areas in a coronal section through the right medioventral temporal cortex (left). The cortical area in each section was subdivided into a number of radial segments. To display the spatial distribution of ZIF268 expression levels, the segmented areas were reconstructed as a two-dimensional unfolded map (right). The fundus and lip of a sulcus are outlined by white crosses and dots, respectively. Serial sections were aligned along the fundus of the rhinal sulcus, rs (rhinal sulcus); amts (anterior middle temporal sulcus); D, L, V, M =dorsal, lateral, ventral, medial. (*B*) The expression levels of ZIF268 in the temporal cortex of individual monkeys. The density of reaction products of ZIF268 immunostaining in the segments is indicated on the unfolded maps (similar to the right panel in A) in pseudocolor representation. The maps from monkeys with visual pair-association learning (PA1–PA3) and visual discrimination learning (VD1–VD3) are shown in the upper panels and lower panels, respectively. The values are normalized so that the mean density of the reaction products of all segments from all six monkeys is 1.0 (Okuno and Miyashita 1996). The boundaries of cortical areas were indicated by gray dots. Scale bar, 10 mm (Okuno and Miyashita 1996).

Second, the experimental participants read the disambiguating prepositional phrase more slowly in the ambiguous large storage condition than in the disambiguated large storage condition, as predicted by the DLT applied to ambiguity resolution. Crucially, there was also a significant interaction of storage cost difference (large, small) and ambiguity (ambiguous, unambiguous) in the disambiguating PP, such that the reanalysis effect was significantly larger in the large storage conditions than in the small storage conditions (where there was a numerical but nonsignificant difference in reading times). This pattern of results is consistent with the hypothesis that people initially follow the main-verb reading in (21), because of its much lower syntactic complexity and in spite of its implausibility. On the other hand, people use the plausibility information to perform the disambiguation in (23a), because the syntactic complexity does not strongly favor either interpretation. Thus syntactic storage cost complexity as measured by the DLT appears to be an independent factor involved in ambiguity resolution that is not reducible to frequency and plausibility.

5.4 Summary and Conclusions

A theory of linguistic complexity has been proposed here that associates (1) increasing structural integration cost with the distance of attachment, and (2) storage cost with predicted syntactic categories. This theory—the dependency locality theory—provides a unified theory of a large array of disparate processing phenomena, including the following:

1. Online reading times of subject- and object-extracted relative clauses
2. The complexity of doubly nested relative clause constructions
3. The greater complexity of embedding a sentential complement within a relative clause than the reverse embedding in both English and Japanese
4. The lower complexity of multiply embedded structures with pronominals in the most embedded subject position in both English and Japanese
5. The high complexity of certain two-clause constructions
6. The greater complexity of nesting clauses with more arguments in Japanese
7. Ambiguity effects—syntactic complexity effects independent of plausibility and frequency
8. Numerous other effects not discussed here (see Gibson 1998), including:
a. Heaviness effects (Bever 1970; Hawkins 1990, 1994; Wasow 1997)
b. The greater complexity of center-embedded constructions as compared with cross-serial constructions (Bach, Brown, and Marslen-Wilson 1986)
c. Gap-positing preferences in temporarily ambiguous structures
d. Argument-attachment preferences in temporarily ambiguous structures

Understanding how the language comprehension mechanism uses computational resources will continue to be a fundamental area of computational psycholinguistic research in the coming years, as it has been over the past forty years.

Notes

I would like to thank the participants at the conference in addition to the following people for helpful comments on earlier drafts of this work: Dan Grodner, Carson Schütze, and Tessa Warren. Any remaining errors are my own. Funding for some of the work reported here was provided by NSF grant SBR-9729037 "Empirical Investigations of Locality Effects in Linguistic Complexity" and by the MIT/JST joint international Mind Articulation Project.

1. Although the phrase structure hypotheses implicit here are standard across most syntactic theories (Chomsky 1981, 1995; Bresnan 1982; Pollard and Sag 1994), some of the assumptions are less universally accepted. For example, the inventory of categories and their relationship to one another are debatable (Pollard and Sag 1994; Chomsky 1995; Steedman 1996), as is the implicit claim that there exist empty-category positions mediating long distance dependencies (Pickering and Barry 1991; Steedman 1996). The specific assumptions made with respect to these controversial issues are for convenience only, so that we have a consistent notation to discuss sentence meaning.

2. Sentences that cause extreme processing difficulty are prefixed with the symbol #.

3. One factor that can contribute to the processing complexity of nested structures but that is orthogonal to the factors to be investigated here is semantic similarity. Center-embedded RC structures like (1c) are easier to comprehend if the NPs come from distinct semantic classes and if the roles assigned by the following verbs are also compatible with distinct semantic classes, so that it is easy to guess who is doing what to whom (Stolz 1967; Schlesinger 1968; King and Just 1991). For example, (i) is easier to comprehend than (1c) (Stolz 1967):

(i) ?#The vase that the maid that the agency hired dropped on the floor broke into a hundred pieces.

Although semantic-role disambiguation improves the acceptability of these kinds of structures, a complexity theory based on semantic role interference alone is insufficient to explain many complexity effects. For example, although (i) is easier to comprehend than (1c), it is still very complex, and this complexity needs to be accounted for. Furthermore, including an additional pragmatically distinguishable nested RC makes the structure virtually unprocessable, similar to or more complex than (1c):

(ii) #The vase that the maid that the agency that the lawyer represented hired dropped on the floor broke into a hundred pieces.

Hence factors other than semantic similarity or interference are responsible for the complexity of nested structures like (ii).

4. A class of models of nesting complexity that will not be discussed here are connectionist models (e.g., Kempen and Vosse 1989; Elman 1991; Weckerly and Elman 1992; Miikkulainen 1996; Christiansen and Chater 1999). The goal for these models is to have the complexity phenomena fall out from the architecture of the processor. This kind of model, with a basis in neural architecture, may eventually provide an architectural explanation of the approach proposed here. However, because these types of models are still quite novel, they have not yet been applied to a wide range of phenomena across languages.

5. The maximal integration cost for (6) is 5 EUs, as compared to 7 EUs for (1c).

6. This hypothesis is very similar to the incomplete dependency hypothesis outlined in section 5.2. There is currently no empirical evidence relevant to deciding between indexing storage cost difficulty in terms of predicted categories or incomplete dependencies: either hypothesis suffices for the data that we know of thus far. Experiments are being run that will help decide between these and other possibilities.

7. Factors other than locality also affect modifier attachment preferences crosslinguistically. See Cuetos and Mitchell 1988; Frazier and Clifton 1996; Gibson et al. 1996; Gibson, Pearlmutter, and Torrens 1999; and Hemforth, Konieczny, and Scheepers, forthcoming, for evidence and theories about what other factors affect modifier attachment preferences.

8. To be fair, MacDonald and colleagues' and Trueswell and associates' claims center around demonstrating that a particular structure-based ambiguity resolution hypothesis, Minimal Attachment (Frazier 1978), is incorrect. They are less explicit about ruling out other possible syntactic complexity metrics.

9. It should be noted that although storage cost favors the MV structure in this ambiguity, structural integration cost actually favors the RR structure, because there is an extra integration between the object position of *examined* and the pronoun *who* in the MV structure. Gibson (1998) proposes that, in conflicts between minimizing storage and minimizing structural integration cost, storage cost is minimized. The motivation for this assumption is that storage cost is effectively potential structural integration cost—structural integration cost that will be expended later—and processing additional material cannot lower this cost, only increase it, leading to larger structural integration costs downstream. Thus by minimizing storage cost, the parser minimizes structural integration costs over the course of the sentence.

References

Abney, S. P., and M. Johnson. 1991. Memory requirements and local ambiguities of parsing strategies. *Journal of Psycholinguistic Research* 20:233–250.

Altmann, G., and M. Steedman. 1988. Interaction with context during human sentence processing. *Cognition* 30:191–238.

Anderson, J. R. 1994. *Learning and memory*. New York: Wiley.

Babyonyshev, M., and E. Gibson. 1999. The complexity of nested structures in Japanese. *Language* 75:423–450.

Bach, E., C. Brown, and W. Marslen-Wilson. 1986. Crossed and nested dependencies in German and Dutch: A psycholinguistic study. *Language and Cognitive Processes* 1:249–262.

Baddeley, A. 1990. *Human memory*. Needham Heights, Mass.: Allyn and Bacon.

Bever, T. G. 1970. The cognitive basis for linguistic structures. In *Cognition and the development of language*, ed. J. R. Hayes, 279–362. New York: Wiley.

Bever, T. G. 1974. The ascent of the specious, or there's a lot we don't know about mirrors. In *Explaining linguistic phenomena*, ed. D. Cohen, 173–200. Washington, D.C.: Hemisphere.

Bresnan, J. 1982. *The mental representation of grammatical relations*. Cambridge, Mass.: MIT Press.

Caplan, D., and C. Futter. 1986. Assignment of thematic roles by an agrammatic aphasic patient. *Brain and Language* 27:117–135.

Caplan D., and G. S. Waters. 1999. Verbal working memory and sentence comprehension. *Behavioral and Brain Sciences* 22:77–126.

Caramazza, A., and E. Zurif. 1976. Dissociation of algorithmic and heuristic processes in sentence comprehension: Evidence from aphasia. *Brain and Language* 3:572–582.

Chomsky, N. 1957. *Syntactic structures*. The Hague: Mouton.

Chomsky, N. 1965. *Aspects of the theory of syntax*. Cambridge, Mass.: MIT Press.

Chomsky, N. 1981. *Lectures on government and binding*. Dordrecht: Foris.

Chomsky, N. 1995. *The minimalist program*. Cambridge, Mass.: MIT Press.

Chomsky, N., and G. A. Miller. 1963. Introduction to the formal analysis of natural languages. In *Handbook of mathematical psychology*, vol. 2, ed. R. D. Luce, R. R. Bush, and E. Galanter, 269–321. New York: Wiley.

Christiansen, M. H., and N. Chater. 1999. Toward a connectionist model of recursion in human linguistic performance. *Cognitive Science* 23:157–205.

Cowper, E. A. 1976. Constraints on sentence complexity: A model for syntactic processing. Ph.D. dissertation, Brown University, Providence, R.I.

Crain, S., and M. Steedman. 1985. On not being led up the garden path: The use of context by the psychological parser. In *Natural language processing: Psychological, computational, and theoretical perspectives*, ed. D. Dowty, L. Karttunen, and A. Zwicky, 320–358. Cambridge, England: Cambridge University Press.

Cuetos, F., and D. C. Mitchell. 1988. Cross-linguistic differences in parsing: Restrictions on the use of the late closure strategy in Spanish. *Cognition* 30:73–105.

Elman, J. L. 1991. Distributed representations, simple recurrent networks, and grammatical structure. *Machine Learning* 7:195–225.

Ferreira, F., and C. Clifton, Jr. 1986. The independence of syntactic processing. *Journal of Memory and Language* 25:348–368.

Ford, M. 1983. A method for obtaining measures of local parsing complexity throughout sentences. *Journal of Verbal Learning and Verbal Behavior* 22:203–218.

Ford, M., J. Bresnan, and R. Kaplan 1982. A competence-based theory of syntactic closure. In *The mental representation of grammatical relations*, ed. J. Bresnan, 727–796. Cambridge, Mass.: MIT Press.

Francis, W. N., and H. Kučera. 1982. *Frequency analysis of English usage: Lexicon and grammar*. Boston: Houghton Mifflin.

Frank, R. 1992. Syntactic locality and tree-adjoining grammar: Grammatical, acquisition, and processing perspectives. Ph.D. dissertation, University of Pennsylvania, Philadelphia.

Frazier, L. 1978. On comprehending sentences: Syntactic parsing strategies. Ph.D. dissertation, University of Connecticut, Storrs.

Frazier, L., and C. Clifton, Jr. 1996. *Construal*. Cambridge, Mass.: MIT Press.

Frazier, L., and J. D. Fodor. 1978. The Sausage Machine: A new two-stage parsing model. *Cognition* 6:291–325.

Garrod, S., and A. J. Sanford. 1977. Interpreting anaphoric relations: The integration of semantic information while reading. *Journal of Verbal Learning and Verbal Behavior* 16:77–90.

Garrod, S. C., and A. J. Sanford. 1982. The mental representation of discourse in a focused memory system: Implications for the interpretation of anaphoric noun phrases. *Journal of Semantics* 1:21–41.

Garrod, S. C., and A. J. Sanford. 1994. Resolving sentences in a discourse context: How discourse representation affects language understanding. In *Handbook of psycholinguistics*, ed. M. A. Gernsbacher, 675–698. San Diego: Academic Press.

Gibson, E. 1991. A computational theory of human linguistic processing: Memory limitations and processing breakdown. Ph.D. dissertation, Carnegie Mellon University, Pittsburgh.

Gibson, E. 1998. Linguistic complexity: Locality of syntactic dependencies. *Cognition* 68:1–76.

Gibson, E., M. Babyonyshev, and E. Kaan. 1998. Sentence reanalysis: Generalized incremental processing within a parallel processing framework. Poster presented at the Eleventh CUNY Sentence Processing Conference, Rutgers, N.J.

Gibson, E., D. Grodner, and S. Tunstall. 1997. Evidence for a syntactic complexity metric in ambiguity resolution independent of lexical effects. Poster presented at the Tenth CUNY Sentence Processing Conference, Santa Monica, Calif.

Gibson, E., and K. Ko. 1998. An integration-based theory of computational resources in sentence comprehension. Paper presented at the Fourth Architectures and Mechanisms in Language Processing Conference, University of Freiburg, Germany.

Gibson, E., and K. Nakatani. 1998. The lexical and locality basis for linguistic complexity. Ms., MIT, Cambridge, Mass.

Gibson, E., and N. Pearlmutter. 1998. Constraints on sentence comprehension. *Trends in Cognitive Science* 2:262–268.

Gibson, E., N. Pearlmutter, E. Canseco-Gonzales, and G. Hickok. 1996. Recency preference in the human sentence processing mechanism. *Cognition* 59:23–59.

Gibson, E., N. Pearlmutter, and V. Torrens, V. 1999. Recency and lexical preferences in Spanish. *Memory and Cognition* 27:603–611.

Gibson, E., and J. Thomas. 1998. The complexity of English nested structures. Ms., MIT, Cambridge, Mass.

Grodzinsky, Y. 1989. Agrammatic comprehension of relative clauses. *Brain and Language* 31:480–499.

Hakes, B., J. Evans, and L. Brannon. 1976. Understanding sentences with relative clauses. *Memory and Cognition* 4:283–296.

Hakuta, K. 1981. Grammatical description versus configurational arrangement in language acquisition: The case of relative clauses in Japanese. *Cognition* 9:197–236.

Haliday, M. A. K., and R. Hasan. 1976. *Cohesion in English*. London: Longman.

Harris, A. 1998. Electrophysiological indices of syntactic processing difficulty. Ph.D. dissertation, MIT, Cambridge, Mass.

Haviland, S. E., and H. H. Clark. 1974. What's new? Acquiring new information as a process in comprehension. *Journal of Verbal Learning and Verbal Behavior* 13:512–521.

Hawkins, J. A. 1990. A parsing theory of word order universals. *Linguistic Inquiry* 21:223–262.

Hawkins, J. A. 1994. *A performance theory of order and constituency*. Cambridge, England: Cambridge University Press.

Heim, I. 1982. The semantics of definite and indefinite noun phrases. Ph.D. dissertation, University of Massachusetts, Amherst.

Hemforth, B., L. Konieczny, and C. Scheepers. Forthcoming. Syntactic attachment and anaphor resolution: Two sides of relative clause attachment. In *Architectures and mechanisms for language processing*, ed. M. Crocker, M. Pickering, and C. Clifton, Jr. Cambridge, England: Cambridge University Press.

Hickok, G., E. Zurif, and E. Canseco-Gonzalez. 1993. Structural description of agrammatic comprehension. *Brain and Language* 45:371–395.

Holmes, V. 1973. Order of main and subordinate clauses in sentence perception. *Journal of Verbal Learning and Verbal Behavior* 12:285–293.

Holmes, V. M., and J. K. O'Regan. 1981. Eye fixation patterns during the reading of relative clause sentences. *Journal of Verbal Learning and Verbal Behavior* 20:417–430.

Joshi, A. K. 1990. Processing crossed and nested dependencies: An automaton perspective on the psycholinguistic results. *Language and Cognitive Processes* 5:1–27.

Just, M. A., and P. A. Carpenter. 1992. A capacity theory of comprehension: Individual differences in working memory. *Psychological Review* 99:122–149.

Kaan, E., A. Harris, E. Gibson, and P. Holcomb. 1998. The P600 as an index of syntactic integration difficulty. Paper presented at the Fourth Architectures and Mechanisms in Language Processing Conference, University of Freiburg, Germany.

Kac, M. B. 1981. Center-embedding revisited. In *Proceedings of the Third Annual Conference of the Cognitive Science Society*, 123–124. Hillsdale, N.J.: Erlbaum.

Kamp, H. 1981. A theory of truth and semantic representations. In *Formal methods in the study of language*, ed. J. Groenendijk, T. M. V. Janssen, and M. Stokhof. Amsterdam: Mathematisch Centrum.

Kempen, G., and T. Vosse. 1989. Incremental syntactic tree formation in human sentence processing: A cognitive architecture based on activation decay and simulated annealing. *Connection Science* 1:273–290.

Kimball, J. 1973. Seven principles of surface structure parsing in natural language. *Cognition* 2:15–47.

King, J., and M. A. Just. 1991. Individual differences in syntactic processing: The role of working memory. *Journal of Memory and Language* 30:580–602.

Lewis, R. 1993. An architecturally-based theory of human sentence comprehension. Ph.D. dissertation, Carnegie Mellon University, Pittsburgh.

Lewis, R. 1996. A theory of grammatical but unacceptable embeddings. *Journal of Psycholinguistic Research* 25:93–116.

MacDonald, M. 1997. Lexical representations and sentence processing: An introduction. *Language and Cognitive Processes* 12:121–136.

MacDonald, M., N. Pearlmutter, and M. Seidenberg. 1994. The lexical nature of syntactic ambiguity resolution. *Psychological Review* 101:676–703.

MacWhinney, B. 1987. The Competition Model. In *Mechanisms of language acquisition*, ed. B. MacWhinney, 249–308. Hillsdale, N.J.: Erlbaum.

McClelland, J. L., M. St. John, and R. Taraban. 1989. Sentence comprehension: A parallel distributed processing approach. *Language and Cognitive Processes* 4:SI287–335.

McElree, B., and T. Griffith. 1995. Syntactic and thematic processing in sentence comprehension: Evidence for a temporal dissociation. *Journal of Experimental Psychology: Learning Memory, and Cognition* 21:134–157.

Miikkulainen, R. 1996. Subsymbolic case-role analysis of sentences with embedded clauses. *Cognitive Science* 20:47–73.

Miller, G. A., and N. Chomsky. 1963. Finitary models of language users. In *Handbook of mathematical psychology*, vol. 2, ed. R. D. Luce, R. R. Bush, and E. Galanter, 419–491. New York: Wiley.

Miller, G. A., and S. Isard. 1964. Free recall of self-embedded English sentences. *Information and Control* 7:292–303.

Ni, W., S. Crain, and D. Shankweiler. 1996. Sidestepping garden-paths: Assessing the contributions of syntax, semantics, and plausibility in resolving ambiguities. *Language and Cognitive Processes* 11:283–334.

Pearlmutter, N., and M. MacDonald. 1992. Plausibility and syntactic ambiguity resolution. *Proceedings of the Fourteenth Conference of the Cognitive Science Society*, 498–503. Hillsdale, N.J.: Erlbaum.

Pickering, M., and G. Barry. 1991. Sentence processing without empty categories. *Language and Cognitive Processes* 6:229–259.

Pollard, C., and I. A. Sag. 1994. *Head-driven phrase structure grammar*. Chicago: University of Chicago Press.

Rambow, O., and A. Joshi. 1994. A processing model for free word-order languages. In *Perspectives on sentence processing*, ed. C. Clifton Jr., L. Frazier, and K. Rayner, 267–301. Hillsdale, N.J.: Erlbaum.

Schlesinger, I. M. 1968. *Sentence structure and the reading process*. The Hague: Mouton.

Stabler, E. P. 1994. The finite connectivity of linguistic structures. In *Perspectives in sentence processing*, ed. C. Clifton, Jr., L. Frazier, and K. Rayner, 303–336. Hillsdale, N.J.: Erlbaum.

Steedman, M. 1996. *Surface structure and interpretation*. Cambridge, Mass.: MIT Press.

Stevenson, S. 1994. Competition and recency in a hybrid network model of syntactic disambiguation. *Journal of Psycholinguistic Research* 23:295–322.

Stolz, W. S. 1967. A study of the ability to decode grammatically novel sentences. *Journal of Verbal Learning and Verbal Behavior* 6:867–873.

Stromswold, K., D. Caplan, N. Alpert, and S. Rauch. 1996. Localization of syntactic comprehension by positron emission tomography. *Brain and Language* 52:452–473.

Tanenhaus, M. K., and J. C. Trueswell. 1995. Sentence comprehension. In *Speech, Language, and Communication*, ed. J. Miller and P. Eimas, 217–262. San Diego: Academic Press.

Trueswell, J. C. 1996. The role of lexical frequency in syntactic ambiguity resolution. *Journal of Memory and Language* 35:566–585.

Trueswell, J. C., M. K. Tanenhaus. and S. M. Garnsey. 1994. Semantic influences on parsing: Use of thematic role information in syntactic disambiguation. *Journal of Memory and Language* 33:285–318.

Tyler, L. K., and W. D. Marslen-Wilson. 1977. The on-line effects of semantic context on syntactic processing. *Journal of Verbal Learning and Verbal Behavior* 16:683–692.

Wanner, E., and M. Maratsos. 1978. An ATN approach in comprehension. In *Linguistic theory and psychological reality*, ed. M. Halle, J. Bresnan, and G. Miller, 119–161. Cambridge, Mass.: MIT Press.

Warren, T., and E. Gibson. 1999. The effects of discourse status on intuitive complexity: Implications for quantifying distance in a locality-based theory of linguistic complexity. Poster presented at the Twelfth CUNY Sentence Processing Conference, CUNY, New York.

Wasow, T. 1997. Remarks on grammatical weight. *Language Variation and Change* 9:81–105.

Waters, G. S., D. Caplan, and N. Hildebrandt. 1987. Working memory and written sentence comprehension. In *Attention and performance*, vol. 12: *The psychology of reading*, ed. M. Coltheart, 531–555. Hillsdale, N.J.: Erlbaum.

Webber, B. L. 1988. Tense as discourse anaphor. *Computational Linguistics* 14:61–73.

Weckerly, J., and J. L. Elman. 1992. A PDP approach to processing center-embedded sentences. In *Proceedings of the Fourteenth Annual Conference of the Cognitive Science Society*, 414–419. Hillsdale, N.J.: Erlbaum.

Yngve, V. H. 1960. A model and an hypothesis for language structure. *Proceedings of the American Philosophical Society* 104:444–466.

Chapter 6

The Neuronal Dynamics of Auditory Language Comprehension

Angela D. Friederici

We have known for more than a century that specific brain areas in the dominant left hemisphere support language processing. The early functional neuroanatomy was based on lesion studies. It is only in the last decade that functional neuroimaging methods such as positron emission tomography (PET) and functional magnetic resonance tomography (fMRT) have become available, providing information about the brain-behavior relationship in the intact brain. Although quite essential for an adequate description of the biological basis of language, information concerning *where* in the brain language processes take place cannot be sufficient, since language processing unfolds in time. Therefore, it appears that an adequate description must include information about the temporal parameters of language processes. Ideally these two information types—the neurotopography and the temporal dynamics of the neuronal processes underlying language—will merge into a picture that not only identifies the specific components of the neuronal network responsible for language processes but, moreover, specifies how and when these components interact in time.

The present chapter is an attempt to draw such a picture for the domain of language comprehension. First, I will briefly describe competing psycholinguistic models of language comprehension. Second, I will identify the particular brain regions involved in language comprehension as revealed by functional imaging and try to specify their particular function in this multifaceted process. Third, I will describe the temporal coordination of the brain activity as revealed by neurophysiological measures providing a high temporal resolution. It will become obvious that a fine-grained temporal structure of syntactic and semantic processes underlies the human capacity to understand spoken language online.

From psycholinguistic models of language comprehension it is clear that language processing requires the activation of phonological, syntactic, and semantic information. All models agree that these different types of information are processed by different cognitive subcomponents during comprehension. They disagree, however, with respect to when these different types of information interact in time (see Frauenfelder and Tyler 1987). Two extreme positions can be identified. One position is associated with the so-called serial or syntax-first models, which hold that the parser initially builds up a syntactic structure independent of lexical-semantic information (e.g., Frazier 1987a, 1987b; Gorrell 1995). According to this type of model, semantic aspects only come into play at a later stage—that is, when thematic role assignment takes place. As long as the thematic representation is compatible with the initial syntactic structure, comprehension is directly achieved. If not, the parser has to pass through a revision stage adjusting the initial structure (e.g., Fodor and Inoue 1998). The alternative position is associated with so-called interactive models. Although differing to some degree in their detail, interactive models hold that structural and semantic information interact during comprehension at any point in time (Marslen-Wilson and Tyler 1980; McClelland, St. John, and Taraban 1989; MacDonald, Just, and Carpenter 1992; Bates et al. 1996). The issue of whether syntactic and semantic information interact immediately or late in the comprehension process still appears unresolved in the behavioral literature. Additional evidence concerning the temporal structure of language processing and the possible interaction of different types of information, however, comes from electrophysiological studies using event-related potential (ERP) measures, which allow one to register the brain's activity as input is encountered. These ERP measures, in contrast to behavioral measures, do not register the result of a process, but are able to monitor the process as it develops in time. Thus ERPs make it possible to temporally segregate different subprocesses. Additional parameters of the ERP such as spatial distribution and polarity can also help to distinguish different subprocesses.

But before turning to the temporal aspects of the brain's activity during language comprehension, we will consider the particular brain structures involved. A spatial segregation of the different cognitive subprocesses constituing language comprehension will certainly add to the evidence for the functional independence of these subprocesses.

6.1 Functional Neuroanatomy as Revealed by Brain Imaging

The *phonological subsystem* of the auditory processing system has been localized in temporal as well as frontal brain regions by a number of PET and fMRI studies, mostly using tasks with single-word presentation. It was shown that the superior temporal gyrus of the left and the right hemisphere is responsible for the perceptual analysis of speech signals. These brain regions are active when participants listen to language stimuli passively (Petersen et al. 1988; Wise et al. 1991; Zatorre et al. 1992). This finding is supported by recent fMRI studies (Binder et al. 1994, for word listening; Schlosser et al. 1998, for sentence listening). The posterior region of the left superior temporal gyrus and the adjacent planum temporale is specifically involved in auditory language comprehension (Petersen et al. 1989; Zatorre et al. 1996), since this region is not active when processing simple tones (Lauter et al. 1985; Zatorre et al. 1992) or when discriminating tones (Démonet et al. 1992, 1994).

Not only are these temporal areas involved; PET studies indicate an involvement of left inferior frontal regions in phonetic processing. Activation of Broca's area is reported to be most evident when the task requires a detailed analysis of phonetic units or phonetic sequences (Démonet et al. 1992; Zatorre et al. 1996). An inspection of the particular activation foci in the available studies seems to indicate that phonetic and phonological processing occurs in the superior-dorsal part of Brodmann area (BA44) adjacent to BA6, but not in the inferior-ventral part of BA44, classically called Broca's area. This observation suggests a functional distinction between the superior-dorsal and the inferior part of BA44. It was proposed that the superior-dorsal part is primarily involved in processing of phonetic sequences, whereas the inferior part is primarily involved in processing syntactic sequences (Friederici 1998b; also see below).

The evaluation of the *semantic subsystem* has initially focused on visual word presentation. A number of studies are investigating various aspects of semantic processing. Early studies primarily used a combined comprehension-production task—that is, the word-generation task. In this task subjects are required to name a word semantically associated with a presented word (Petersen et al. 1989; Buckner et al. 1995; Wise et al. 1991). When using this paradigm without controlling for the production aspect, activation was found in left BA45/46 and in BA44 (for a review of brain-imaging studies on production, see chapter 4). When, one extracts the particular activation responsible for the processing of semantic information during perception, however, left BA47 is identified as the relevant area (Martin et al. 1995, 1996; Fiez 1997). This area seems active whenever strategic aspects of semantic processing are required. Processing semantic information while passively listening, in contrast, primarily activates the temporal region BA22/42, mostly bilaterally (Petersen et al. 1989, 1990; Frith et al. 1991).

The *syntactic subsystem* so far has only been investigated in a few PET and fMRI studies, mostly on reading. In a PET study, Stromswold et al. (1996) registered participants' brain activation while they read English subject and object relative clause sentences. They reported a selective activation of the pars opercularis in the left third frontal convolution (BA44) as a function of syntactic complexity. This result was replicated in a more recent PET study using the same material (Caplan, Alpert, and Waters 1998). In an fMRI study Just and colleagues (Just et al. 1996) also investigated the reading of English subject and object relative clause sentences. As in the PET studies, they found maximal activation in the left third frontal convolution (BA44 and BA45), but additional activation in the left Wernicke's area as well as some activation in the homotopic areas in the right hemisphere. Activation in BA44 and BA45 was also found to be specially related to syntactic processing in reading complex Japanese sentences (Inui et al. 1998). In contrast, a PET study comparing the auditory processing of syntactically structured sentences containing pseudowords with unstructured lists of pseudowords in French did not identify Broca's area as being responsible for syntactic processes, but rather the left and right temporal pole (Mazoyer et al. 1993).

In the following I will present a most recent fMRI study from our laboratory that aimed to identify the phonological, semantic, and syntactic subsystems by directly comparing the processing of different types of auditory language input within the same subjects (Friederici, Meyer, and von Cramon, forthcoming). In contrast to the studies just discussed, in which different sentence types were presented in homogeneous blocks, we used an event-related fMRI design in which different auditory stimulus types were presented in a pseudorandomized order.

The stimuli were of four different types: (1) normal sentences (hereafter called *normal prose*), (2) syntactically correct sentences with all function words and grammatical morphemes intact, but in which content words were replaced by pseudowords (hereafter called *syntactic prose*), (3) unstructured lists of content words (hereafter called *real-word lists*), and (4) unstructured lists of phonologically legal pseudowords (hereafter called *pseudoword lists*).

(1) The hungry cat hunts the quick mouse.

(2) The slonky clat wunts the reappy rosel.

(3) The cook storm cat velocity hole glory.

(4) The storf rool mong recelant laft apine.

(These examples are English adaptations of German sentences and word lists applied in the present study.)

These four conditions should allow the identification of the neuronal network involved in auditory language processing and the particular function of the areas identified.

Subjects were required to listen to these types of input and to judge whether the input had a syntactic structure and whether it contained real content words. Stimuli were presented in an unpredictable—that is, pseudorandomized—order. Eight scans were taken from each subject using a 3-Tesla fMRI.

The results from eighteen subjects indicate that the patterns of activation vary as a function of the type of auditory language input (see figures 6.1 and 6.2, plates 3 and 4). As expected, all auditory stimulus types caused activation in Heschl's gyri and the planum temporale bilaterally. By comparing the sentence versus the word list conditions we found particular regions to be more strongly engaged in sentence processing (normal prose and syntactic prose) than in the processing of word lists (real words and pseudowords). These regions are the posterior portion of the superior temporal

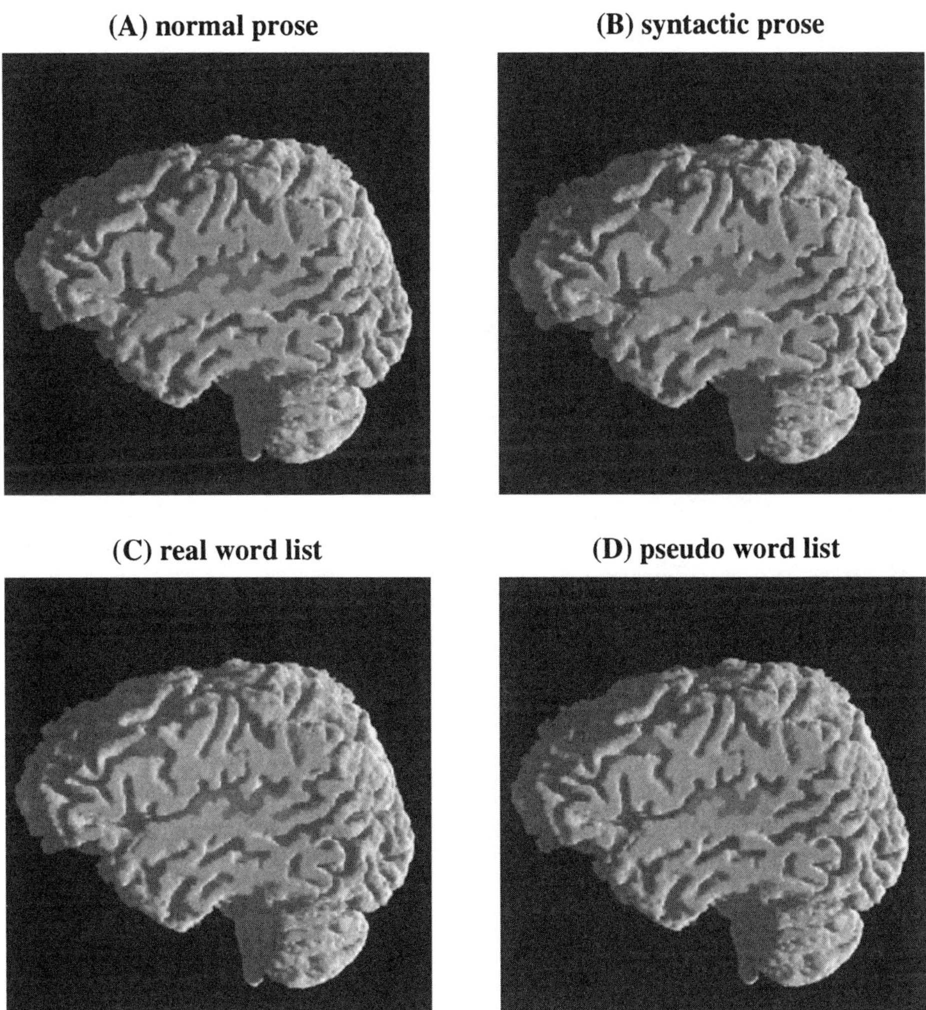

Figure 6.1
Significant clusters of activation for each condition in the left hemisphere, as indicated by fMRI illustrated in the sagittal view.

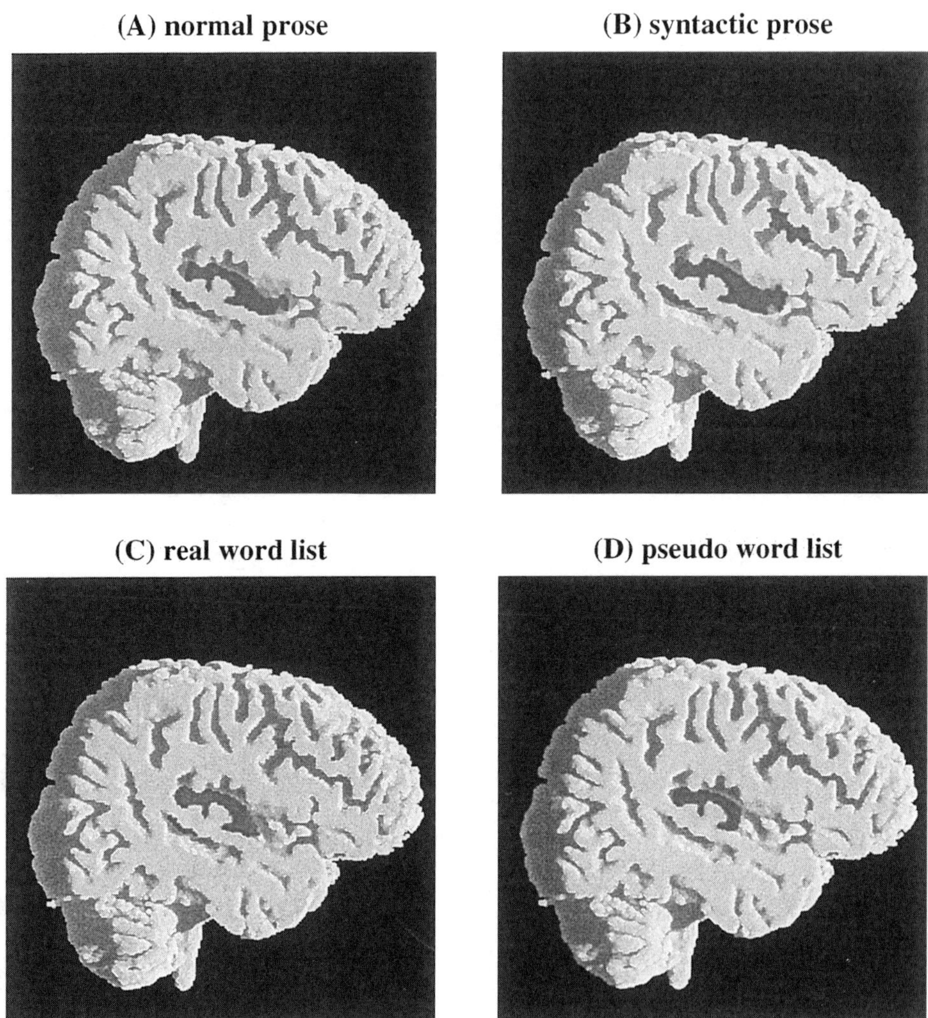

Figure 6.2
Significant clusters of activation for each condition in the right hemisphere, as indicated by fMRI illustrated in the sagittal view.

gyrus bilaterally and a cortical area at the midportion of the superior temporal sulcus in the right hemisphere, and furthermore, the banks of the left posterior ascending ramus of the sylvian fissure (planum parietale). In addition, a considerable increase in blood flow occurred in the thalamus bilaterally, in the two prose conditions but not in the word-list conditions. Interestingly, normal prose showed generally less activation than syntactic prose (see figure 6.3, plate 5). Processing of the latter was correlated with additional activation in the deep left frontal operculum, in the cortex lining the junction of the inferior precentral sulcus and the inferior frontal sulcus bilaterally, as well as in the ascending branch of the left intraparietal sulcus unilaterally.

For word lists, independent of whether they consisted of pseudowords or real words, the activation in the left as well as in the right superior temporal gyrus was reduced compared to the two prose conditions. Both types of word lists activate the cortex lining the junction of the left inferior precentral sulcus and the inferior frontal sulcus. The two types of word lists, however, could be differentiated from each other by an additional activation in the cortex lining the junction of the left inferior precentral sulcus and the inferior frontal sulcus in the right hemisphere observed for real words, but not for pseudowords.

Thus the cerebral network subserving auditory sentence processing includes the left temporal and inferior frontal cortex as well as its right hemisphere homotopic regions. Systematic comparisons between the different conditions allow a functional specification of particular brain areas associated with language comprehension. The processing of *phonological information* is correlated with significant activation in the primary auditory cortices and in the posterior segment of the superior temporal gyrus bilaterally, including the planum temporale. In addition, a small part of the cortex at the junction of the inferior precentral sulcus and the inferior frontal sulcus in the left hemisphere seems involved in phonological processing. Processing of *semantic information* in this study was correlated with an additional small activation focus in the right superior-dorsal part of Broca's area. Processing of *syntactic information* during auditory sentence comprehension was reflected by a considerable increase of the hemodynamic response in the superior temporal gyrus bilaterally extending to its midportion, and further with a specific activation in the deep portion of the left frontal operculum, near the pars triangularis in the Broca's area.[1] Interestingly, the left frontal operculum was only significantly activated during syntactic prose, but not during normal prose. This might suggest that processing of normal speech occurs automatically, without requiring additional cerebral resources of the left frontal operculum. Additional resources associated with activation in the left inferior frontal region, however, may be required when complex sentences are to be read (Just et al. 1996; Stromswold et al. 1996; Caplan, Alpert, and Waters 1998), or when syntactic processing is required in the presence of pseudowords.

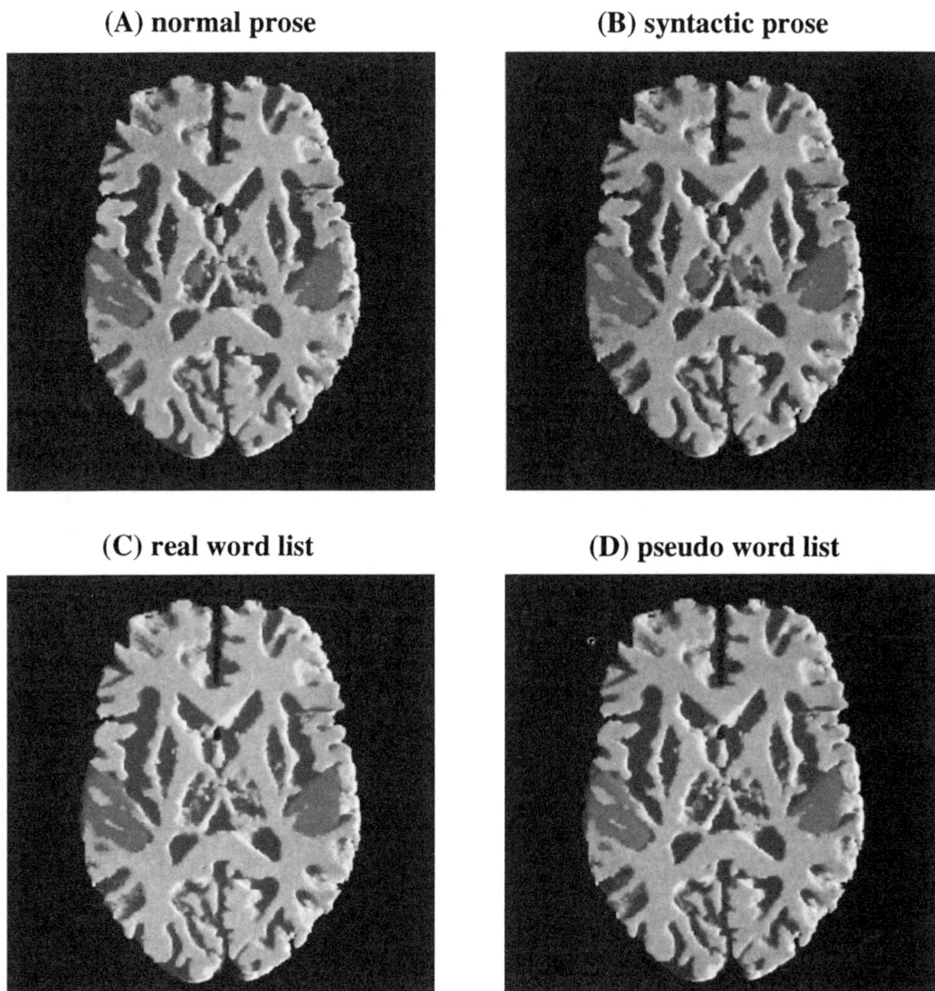

Figure 6.3
Significant clusters of activation for each condition bilaterally, as indicated by fMRI illustrated in the horizontal view.

6.2 Functional Neurochronometry as Revealed by Electrophysiology

Research concerning the electrophysiological markers of language processing provides quite a number of studies looking at different aspects of language processing. Auditory perception and *phonological* processes have been investigated using electroencephalographic (EEG) and magnetoencephalographic (MEG) measures. The early acoustic processes are reflected by the N100/P200 complex in the ERP. These components vary as a function of stimulus intensity, presentation rate, and attention (Näätänen and Picton 1987). Phonological processes as investigated by EEG and MEG experiments at the consonant-vowel level indicate that primary auditory processes are supported by the posterior part of the primary auditory cortices, whereas language-specific processes also involve the superior part of the left temporal lobe. This conclusion is based on the finding that the M100, the magnetic counterpart of the electric N100, in response to passive listening is localized in these areas (Kuriki and Murase 1989; Poeppel et al. 1996). When phoneme discrimination is required there is an asymmetrical activation with a dominance in the left hemisphere (Poeppel et al. 1996). For further details, see chapter 2.

The early ERP research on word and sentence processing generally used a visual presentation mode. In all sentence processing studies, sentences were presented visually without exception in a word-by-word manner with pauses up to 800 msec between words. The influential study by Kutas and Hillyard (1980, 1983) had identified a specific ERP component for the processing of *semantic* information. This component is a negativity peaking about 400 msec after the onset of a word whose semantic integration into the prior context is either impossible or difficult. With reference to its polarity and temporal characteristics, this component is called N400. The component is usually broadly distributed over the posterior part of both sides of the skull, slightly lateralized to the right hemisphere. A review of all the studies of the N400 is beyond the scope of this chapter (for a review, see Van Petten 1995). Here it may suffice to mention that the N400 was observed in a number of different languages; it was found for semantically anomalous words in word context as well as in sentence context; and, moreover, it was identified in the visual as well as in the auditory domain. Functionally the N400 is taken as a general marker of semantic processing (Kutas and Hillyard 1980, 1983). More recently, its function has been specified as reflecting lexical-semantic integration in particular, rather than processes of lexical access or semantic processes in general (Chwilla, Brown, and Hagoort 1995).

With respect to *syntactic* processes two ERP components have been identified: a left anterior negativity and a late positivity. These two components are taken to reflect different stages of syntactic processing, an early phase of initial structure building and a later phase of secondary processes including reanalysis and repair (Friederici 1995). An early left anterior negativity (ELAN) between 100 and 200 msec is observed in response to phrase structure violations realized as word-category errors (Neville et al. 1991; Friederici, Pfeifer, and Hahne 1993). A left anterior negativity (LAN) between 300 and 500 msec has been registered in response to morphosyntactic violations (Coulson, King, and Kutas 1998; Gunter, Stowe, and Mulder 1997; Penke et al. 1997; Münte, Matzke, and Johannes 1997), as well as in response to verb argument violations (Rösler et al. 1993). While these negativities are only evoked by outright violations, a centro-parietal positivity around 600 msec, labeled P600, is observed both with the processing of garden-path sentences (Osterhout and Holcomb 1992, 1993; Friederici et al. 1998) and with outright syntactic violations (following the left anterior negativity) (Gunter, Stowe, and Mulder 1997; Coulson, King, and Kutas 1998; Hahne and Friederici 1999a).

The combined language-related ERP findings have led to the proposal that there are three processing stages during language comprehension (Friederici 1995): (1) In an early stage of first-pass parsing, the initial structure is built on the basis of categorical information (see also Frazier 1987a, 1987b). This first-pass parsing stage is reflected by the ELAN (100–200 msec) observable for word-category violations. (2) During the second stage (300–500 msec), lexical information is processed: violations concerning the word's meaning are reflected in the N400. This holds true for violations concerning the semantic relation between lexical elements—that is, between nouns or between a particular verb and a noun (e.g., selectional restriction violation). Violations concerning the syntactic agreement relation between lexical elements (e.g., case violation and agreement violation) indicated by semantically uninterpretable morphology (Chomsky 1995), in contrast, appear to be reflected in a LAN.[2] (3) The third stage is correlated with the late positivity. This P600 component appears to reflect a stage of secondary processes during which garden-path sentences are revised and incorrect sentences are repaired.

The discussion concerning the particular functional identity of the P600 is still ongoing. While some authors view the P600, also called *Syntactic Positive Shift* (Hagoort, Brown, and Groothusen 1993), as the primary reflection of syntactic processes (Osterhout and Holcomb 1992; Hagoort, Brown, and Groothusen 1993), others take it to reflect secondary syntactic processing (Friederici, Pfeifer, and Hahne 1993; Friederici 1995; Münte, Matzke, and Johannes 1997), and some take the P600 as an index for syntactic integration difficulty in general (Kaan, Harris, and Holcomb 2000). The last notion implies not that the difficulty may not be determined by purely structural factors, but that it may possibly also be mediated by discourse and thematic factors (Gibson 1998).

6.2.1 When Syntax Meets Semantics[3]

All ERP studies evaluated the interaction by completely crossing semantic and syntactic factors. Thus, in each of the studies there were four conditions: a correct condition, as well as a condition in which the critical word violated the context with respect to either semantic aspects, syntactic aspects, or both. While semantic violations were either realized as selectional restriction violations or as a variation in semantic expectancy (cloze probability) in these studies, they differed systematically in how the syntactic violation was realized. Two visual studies realized the syntactic violation as a morphosyntactic error, whereas one visual and one auditory study realized the syntactic violation as a word-category error violating phrase structure.

The two studies that investigate the interaction of a morphosyntactic violation (gender agreement) and a semantic variable (Gunter, Friederici, and Schriefers 1998 2000; Hagoort and Brown 1997) come to different conclusions. Hagoort and Brown (1997) found an additive effect for the N400 in the critical double violation condition. The results of Gunter, Friederici, and Schriefers (1998, 2000), in contrast, show an N400 as a function of the (semantic) cloze probability independent of the gender agreement violation, and a left anterior negativity between 300 and 500 msec as a function of gender agreement violation independent of the semantic variable. A P600 varied as a function of both the gender agreement violation and the cloze probability. The findings from the latter study seem to indicate that morphosyntactic and semantic aspects are processed independently and in parallel around 400 msec, and that the two types of information do interact only during a later stage.

The following two studies investigated the interaction between a phrase structure violation and a semantic violation (Friederici, Steinhauer, and Frisch 1999; Hahne and Friederici 1998). Here only the latter study will be presented, since the former was conducted in the visual domain. Details of the former are available in Friederici, Steinhauer, and Frisch 1999.

The auditory experiment (Hahne and Friederici 1998) comprised four conditions: (5) correct sentences, (6) sentences containing a selectional restriction violation, (7) sentences containing a phrase structure violation, and (8) sentences containing a double violation.

(5) Das Baby wurde *gefüttert.*
the baby was fed

(6) *Das Lineal wurde *gefüttert.*
the ruler was fed

(7) *Die Gans wurde im *gefüttert.*[4]
the goose was in the fed

(8) *Die Burg wurde im *gefüttert.*
the castle was in the fed

Subjects listened to sentences of these types in pseudorandomized order. After each sentence they were required to indicate the sentence's grammaticality with respect to syntax and meaning. ERPs were recorded from nineteen electrodes.

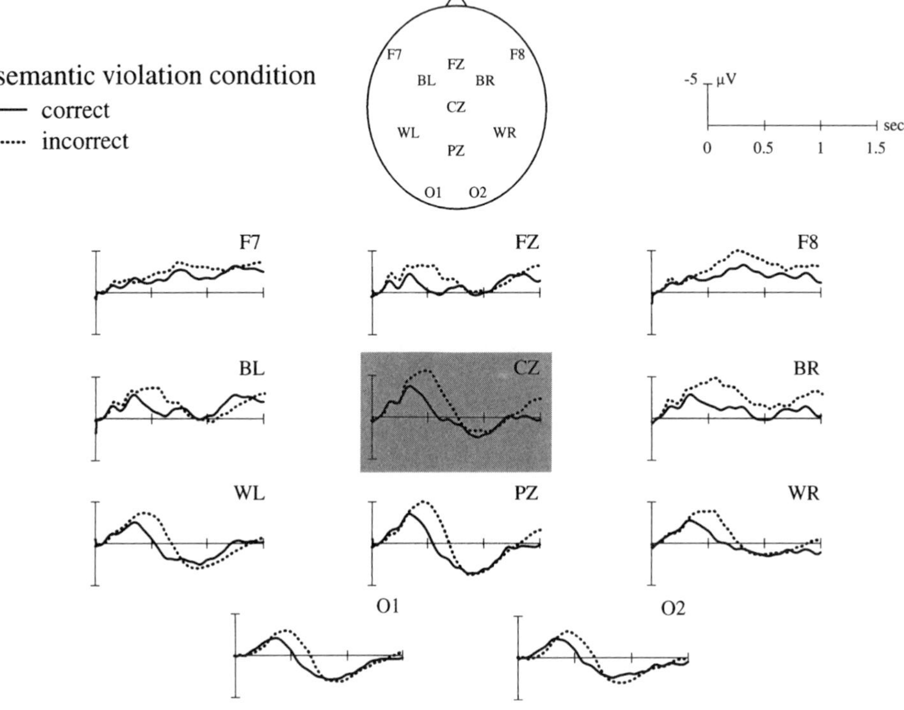

Figure 6.4
Average of event-related potentials for the correct and the semantically incorrect condition. Vertical line indicates onset of the critical word.

The ERP patterns for each violation condition compared to the correct condition were as follows. For the semantic condition we found the expected N400 component (see figure 6.4, plate 6). For the syntactic condition we observed a biphasic early negativity–late positivity pattern (see figure 6.5, plate 7), replicating earlier results (Friederici, Pfeifer, and Hahne 1993). For the double violation condition we found an early left anterior negativity and a P600, but no N400 (see figure 6.6, plate 8). These findings seem to suggest that a phrase structure violation detected early, as indicated by the early left anterior negativity, can block lexical integration processes usually reflected by the N400. From these data we can conclude that phrase structure building processes, based on categorical information, can precede lexical-semantic integration processes as proposed by syntax-first models.

With respect to the psycholinguistic discussion of whether semantic and syntactic information interact, the ERP study by Gunter, Friederici, and Schriefers (1998, 2000) indicates that these two information types interact during a late stage in the comprehension process as reflected in the P600. In the early stage there appear to be

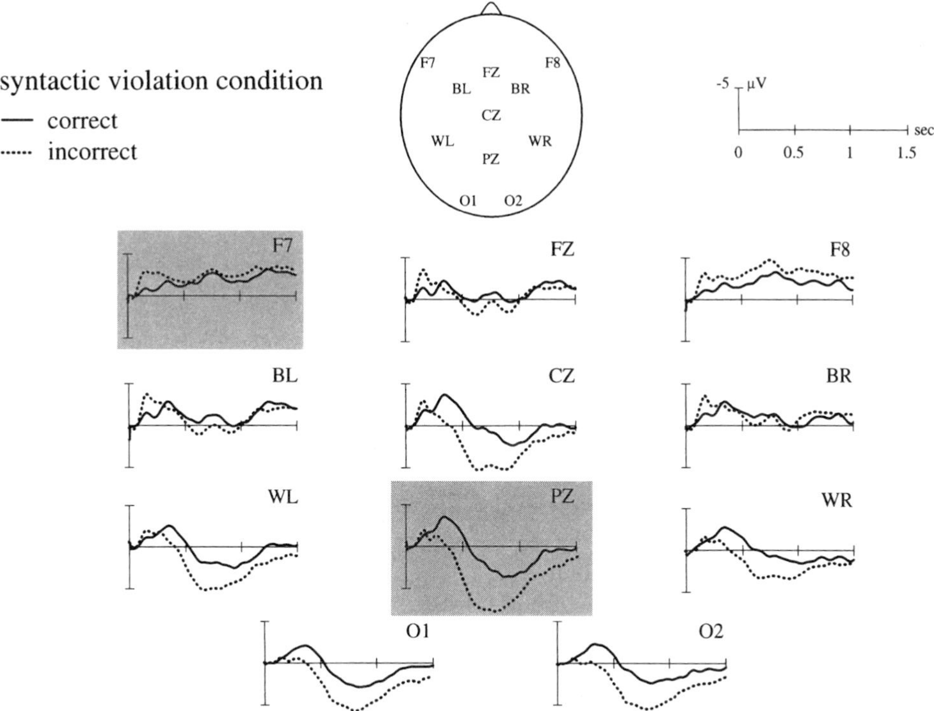

Figure 6.5
Average of event-related potentials for the correct and the syntactically incorrect condition. Vertical line indicates onset of the critical word.

two phases, a very early phase during which only categorical information is processed (100–200 msec) and a later phase during which lexical-semantic and morphosyntactic information are active. Gender information and meaning information seem to be processed in parallel, as indicated by the independence of the LAN effect from the semantic variable and the independence of the N400 effect (Gunter, Friederici, and Schriefers 1998, 2000). However, it appears that categorical information available early from morphosyntactic markers can influence meaning processing, though not vice versa. The available ERP data show that lexical-semantic integration may be blocked if it is not licensed by phrase structure rules (Friederici, Steinhauer, and Frisch 1999; Hahne and Friederici 1998). This latter finding supports serial syntax-first models that restrict the first-pass parse to phrase structure building on the basis of categorical information. Other types of syntactic information are processed in parallel but independent from meaning, providing evidence for parallel models. The interaction of semantic and syntactic information during a late processing stage

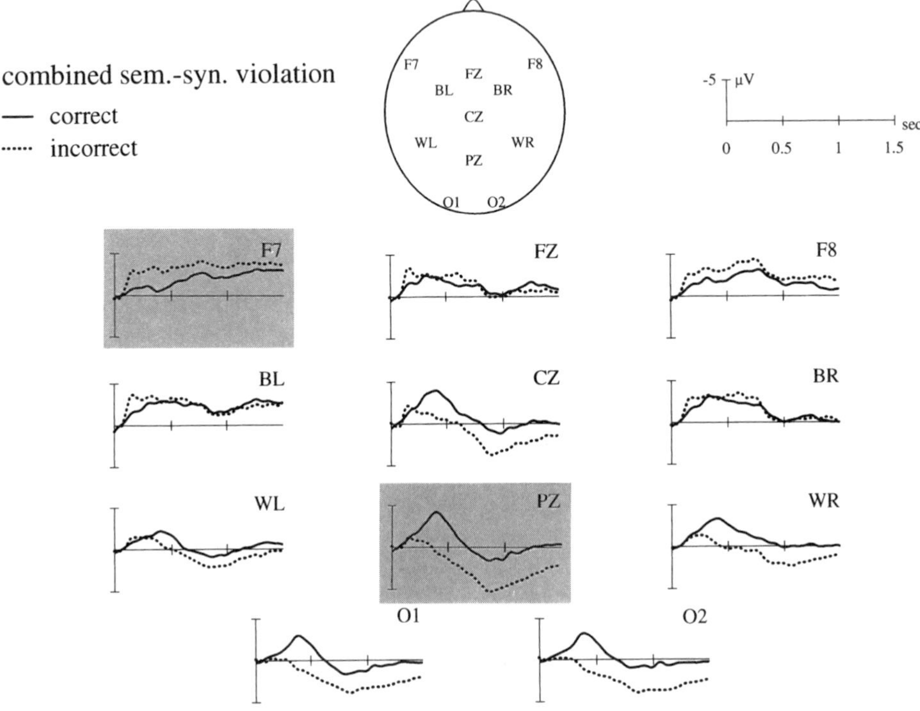

Figure 6.6
Average of event-related potentials for the correct and the combined violation condition. Vertical line indicates onset of the critical word.

may be responsible for behavioral findings supporting highly interactive models. Thus these data demonstrate that an adequate model of language comprehension may gain from the neurochronometry of the processes involved.

6.2.2 When Syntax Meets Prosody

Most language comprehension models do not consider auditory processing of language in particular. However, reaction-time studies suggest that prosodic information available in the auditory input can influence syntactic processing quite substantially (Marslen-Wilson et al. 1992; Warren, Grabe, and Nolan 1995). The question that arises is at what stage prosodic information comes into play. Because prosodic information is available early during auditory language comprehension, it may already affect syntactic processing at an early stage.

We investigated this question in a study that used sentences with phrase structure violations realized as word-category errors, similar to the violations in the previous study, and crossed this violation type with an inappropriate intonational pattern—that is, stress on the word preceding the word-category error (Jescheniak, Hahne, and Friederici 1998).

Crossing these variables resulted in four different sentence types: sentences that were syntactically and prosodically correct, as in (5); sentences that were syntactically incorrect but prosodically appropriate, as in (7); sentences that were syntactically correct but with an inappropriately stressed preposition (indicated by capital letters), as in (11); and sentences with a double violation (12), containing a phrase structure error at the word *fed* that was preceded by an inappropriately stressed preposition.

(11) *Die Gans wurde IM Stall *gefüttert.*
the goose was IN THE barn *fed*

(12) *Die Gans wurde IM *gefüttert.*
the goose was IN THE *fed*

Interestingly, for sentences like (11) no ELAN was observed, in contrast to that found for the prosodically correct but ungrammatical counterpart (7). This seems to suggest that prosodic information such as word stress can influence first-pass parsing processes, or can at least influence those involved in the detection categorical violations.

In an ERP experiment in which we presented correct but temporally structurally ambiguous sentences, we were able to show the early influence of prosodic information on normal phrase structure building processes (Steinhauer, Alter, and Friederici 1999).

The German sentences (13) and (14) are structurally ambiguous up to the second verb, which disambiguates the structure indicating whether *Anna* is the object of the first verb (13) or the second verb (14).

(13) [Peter verspricht Anna zu arbeiten]$_{IP1}$ [und . . .]
Peter promises Anna to work and . . .

(14) [Peter verspricht]$_{IP1}$ [Anna zu entlasten]$_{IP2}$ [und . . .]
Peter promises Anna to support and . . .
'Peter promises to support Anna.'

When looking at the bracketing of the intonational phrases (IPs), the prosodic differences between these two sentence types become obvious: there is an additional intonational phrase boundary in (14) prosodically realized by the insertion of a pause after the first verb.

In our experiment a similar pause was inserted in the original sentence type (13), to test whether this inappropriate prosodic information misguides the early syntactic

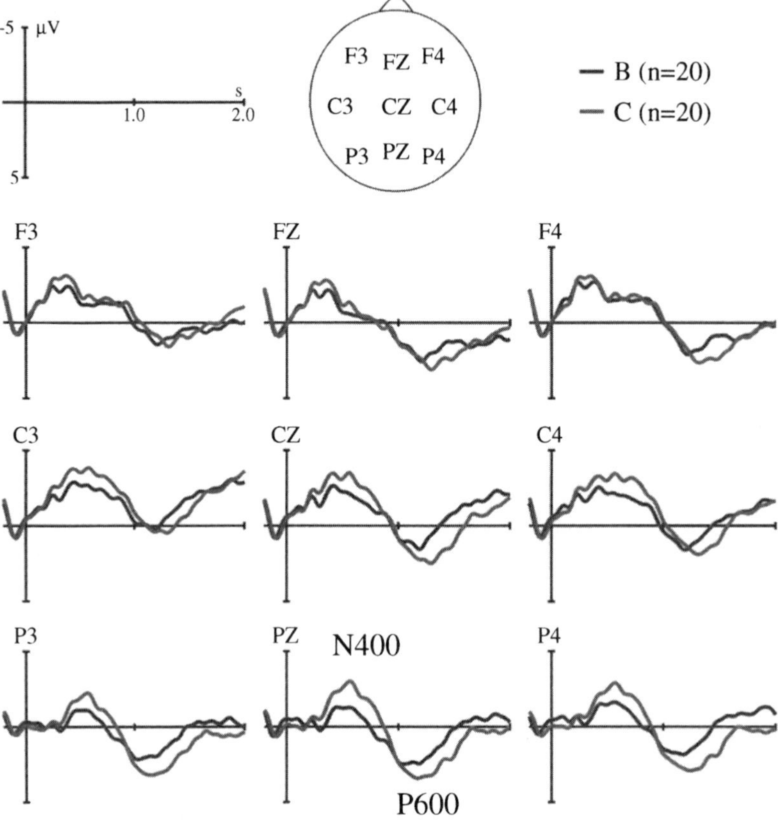

Figure 6.7
Average of event-related potentials for the critical verb in B, i.e., sentences with appropriate pause (14) and in C, i.e., sentences with inappropriate pause (15).

parse. If so, we expect an ERP effect at the disambiguating second verb (*arbeiten*) in sentence type (15).

(15) *[Peter verspricht]$_{IP1}$ [Anna zu arbeiten]$_{IP2}$ [und . . .]$_{IP3}$
Peter promises Anna to work and . . .

Comparing the verb in the sentence with correct prosody (14) and in sentence (15) with an inappropriately inserted pause after the first verb, we observed an N400 effect followed by a P600 (see figure 6.7, plate 9). This pattern indicates that subjects indeed misparsed sentence (15) with the inappropriate prosodic information, expecting a transitive verb. Thus, when encountering the intransitive verb, the system first signals the unexpected verb (N400) and than reanalyzes the initial parse (P600). This finding clearly indicates that prosodic information can influence the initial syntactic parse. Psycholinguistic models dealing with auditory language comprehension will have to take this into consideration.

6.2.3 A Tentative Model

A tentative model of the neuronal dynamics of auditory language comprehension can be sketched as follows.[5] When processing speech, the system already receives early structural information through prosody. The bracketing provided by prosodic information does not entirely map onto syntactic bracketing, but the overlap is large and ERP data show that the prosodic structure is dominant during the initial parsing stage. The tight link between prosodic and syntactic structure allows a very fast initial parse (Steinhauer, Alter, and Friederici 1999; Jescheniak, Hahne, and Friederici 1998). Word-category information is soon available to build the local phrase structure (Friederici, Pfeifer, and Hahne 1993; Hahne and Friederici 1998, 1999). This early syntactic processing is independent of lexical-semantic information (Hahne and Friederici 1998). Lexical-semantic information only comes into play when thematic roles are assigned. If initial syntactic structure and thematic structure map well, comprehension has taken place adequately; if not, the system has to revise the previously built structures either through a syntactically licensed reanalysis (Friederici 1998a) or through a thematically guided repair process (Gunter, Friederici, and Schriefers 1998, 2000).

6.3 A Final Note: How Can the Neuronal Activity and the Hemodynamic Response Meet?

The ultimate goal of the neurocognitive approach to language is to bring together information concerning the location of the neuronal network supporting the human ability to comprehend (and produce) language and information about how the different subcomponents of the network are temporally organized. The relation between the neuronal activity measured by EEG or MEG and the hemodynamic response as registered by PET or fMRI is still not well understood. Also, the direct coupling between the particular neurophysiological and hemodynamic data is not obvious. For example, the relation between the N400 and the brain areas held responsible for semantic processing is far from clear. Using intracranial electrophysiological measures, the neuronal generators of the N400 have been localized within the anterior medial part of the temporal lobe bilaterally (Nobre, Allison, and McCarthy 1994). Although the scalp distribution of the N400 is compatible with fMRI studies reporting bilateral activation in the superior temporal gyrus and the superior temporal sulcus for semantic processing during listening (e.g., Démonet et al. 1992; Binder et al. 1994), the relation between the activation in the left frontal gyrus registered by

PET and fMRI and the distribution of the N400 component in the ERP is still unclear. One possible explanation for the less obvious relation between PET/fMRI and ERP results in this case may be that processes correlated with frontal activation are not part of the processing reflected in the N400. This is not unlikely, because the activation in the left frontal gyrus has been correlated with strategic semantic processes in particular (e.g., Fiez 1997).

When trying to combine brain-imaging data and electrophysiological findings with respect to syntactic processing, we can only speculate that the processes concerning phrase structure rules reflected in the early left anterior negativity are supported by the brain area identified as the left frontal operculum in fMRI studies. Future research will have to resolve the direct relation between the hemodynamic and the neurophysiological response in general, and for language processes in particular.

Notes

I thank Anja Hahne and Martin Meyer for helpful comments on the manuscript.

1. Note that prosodic information supporting bracketing of language input is also available in the stimulus. Experiments to disentangle prosodic and syntactic parsing in the fMRI are currently being carried out.

2. This hierarchy in the availability of categorical and semantic information may be dependent on when during the input the different types of information become available. For example, in morphologically rich languages, word category may only be marked by the suffix and is thus only available late during auditory language perception. The results of Friederici, Hahne, and Mecklinger (1996) indicate that the "early left anterior negativity" is registered later when measured from the word onset for words that mark their word category information in a suffix. When measured from the word-category decision point, however, the latency of the left anterior negativity again falls in the "early" time window. Therefore, the differentiation between processes reflected by the ELAN and those reflected by the LAN implies a hierarchy in the availability of different information types with categorical information being available earlier than the rest.

3. Note that the title of this section is borrowed from a paper by Gunter, Stowe, and Mulder (1997).

4. The phrase structure violation is due to the fact that the word following the preposition is a verb, although the preposition (concatenated with the article: *in* + *dem* becomes *im*) obligatorily requires a noun before the sentence final verb.

5. Here I refer to the data presented in this chapter. Reference to work from other laboratories was provided in the previous sections.

References

Bates, E., A. Devescovi, A. Hernandez, and L. Pizzamiglio. 1996. Gender priming in Italian. *Perception and Psychophysics* 58(7):992–1004.

Binder, J. R., S. M. Rao, T. A. Hammeke, F. Z. Yetkin, A. Jesmanówicz, P. A. Bandettini, E. C. Wong, L. D. Estkowski, M. D. Goldstein, V. M. Haughton, and J. S. Hyde. 1994.

Functional magnetic resonance imaging of human auditory cortex. *Annals of Neurology* 35:662–672.

Buckner, R. L., S. E. Petersen, J. G. Ojemann, F. M. Miezin, L. R. Squire, and M. E. Raichle. 1995. Functional anatomic studies of explicit and implicit memory retrieval tasks. *Journal of Neurosciences* 15:12–29.

Caplan, D., N. Alpert, and G. Waters. 1998. Effects of syntactic structure and propositional number on patterns of regional cerebral blood flow. *Journal of Cognitive Neuroscience* 10(4):541–552.

Chomsky, N. 1995. *The minimalist program.* Cambridge, Mass.: MIT Press.

Chwilla, D. J., C. M. Brown, and P. Hagoort. 1995. The N400 as a function of the level of processing. *Psychophysiology* 32:274–285.

Coulson, S., J. W. King, and M. Kutas. 1998. Expect the unexpected: Event-related brain response to morphosyntactic violations. *Language and Cognitive Processes* 13:21–58.

Démonet, J.-F., F. Chollet, S. Ramsay, D. Cardebat, J.-L. Nespoulous, R. Wise, A. Rascol, and R. Frackowiak. 1992. The anatomy of phonological and semantic processing in normal subjects. *Brain* 115:1753–1768.

Démonet, J.-F., C. Price, R. Wise, and R. S. J. Frackowiak. 1994. A PET study of cognitive strategies in normal subjects during language tasks: Influence of phonetic ambiguity and sequence processing on phoneme monitoring. *Brain* 117:671–682.

Fiez, J. A. 1997. Phonology, semantics, and the role of the left inferior prefrontal cortex. *Human Brain Mapping* 5:79–83.

Fodor, J. D., and A. Inoue. 1998. Attach anyway. In *Reanalysis in sentence processing*, ed. F. Ferreira and J. D. Fodor. Dordrecht: Kluwer Academic Publishers.

Frauenfelder, U. H., and L. K. Tyler. 1987. The process of spoken word recognition: An introduction. *Cognition* 25:1–20.

Frazier, L. 1987a. Sentence processing: A tutorial review. In *Attention and performance XII*, ed. M. Coltheart, 559–586. Hillsdale, N.J.: Erlbaum.

Frazier, L. 1987b. Theories of sentence processing. In *Modularity in knowledge representation and natural-language processing*, ed. J. Garfield, 291–307. Cambridge, Mass.: MIT Press.

Friederici, A. D. 1995. The time course of syntactic activation during language processing: A model based on neuropsychological and neurophysiological data. *Brain and Language* 50:259–281.

Friederici, A. D. 1998a. Diagnosis and reanalysis: Two processing steps the brain may differentiate. In *Reanalysis in sentence processing*, ed. F. Ferreira and J. D. Fodor, 177–200. Dordrecht: Kluwer.

Friederici, A. D. 1998b. The neurobiology of language comprehension. In *Language comprehension: A biological approach*, ed. A. D. Friederici, 263–301. Berlin: Springer.

Friederici, A. D., A. Hahne, and A. Mecklinger. 1996. The temporal structure of syntactic parsing: Early and late event-related brain potential effects elicited by syntactic anomalies. *Journal of Experimental Psychology: Learning, Memory, and Cognition* 22:1219–1248.

Friederici, A. D., M. Meyer, and D. Y. von Cramon. Forthcoming. Auditory language comprehension: An event-related fMRI study on the processing of syntactic and lexical information. *Brain and Language.*

Friederici, A. D., E. Pfeifer, and A. Hahne. 1993. Event-related brain potentials during natural speech processing: Effects of semantic, morphological, and syntactic violations. *Cognitive Brain Research* 1:183–192.

Friederici, A. D., K. Steinhauer, and S. Frisch. 1999. Lexical integration: Sequential effects of syntactic and semantic information. *Memory and Cognition* 27:438–453.

Friederici, A. D., K. Steinhauer, A. Mecklinger, and M. Meyer. 1998. Working memory constraints on syntactic ambiguity resolution as revealed by electrical brain responses. *Biological Psychology* 47:193–221.

Frith, C. D., K. J. Friston, P. F. Liddle, and R. S. J. Frackowiak. 1991. A PET study of word finding. *Neuropsychologia* 29:1137–1148.

Gibson, E. 1998. Linguistic complexity: Locality of syntactic dependencies. *Cognition* 68: 1–76.

Gorrell, P. 1995. *Syntax and parsing*. Cambridge, England: Cambridge University Press.

Gunter, T. C., A. D. Friederici, and H. Schriefers. 1998. Gender violations, semantic expectancy, and ERPs. Poster presented at the Twelfth International Conference on Event-Related Potentials of the Brain, Boston.

Gunter, T. C., A. D. Friederici, and H. Schriefers. 2000. Syntactic gender and semantic expectancy: ERPs reveal early autonomy and late interaction. *Journal of Cognitive Neuroscience* 12:520–541.

Gunter, T. C., L. A. Stowe, and G. Mulder. 1997. When syntax meets semantics. *Psychophysiology* 34:660–676.

Hagoort, P., and C. Brown. 1997. When syntax and semantics meet. Poster presented at the Fourth Annual Meeting of the Cognitive Neuroscience Society, Boston.

Hagoort, P., C. Brown, and J. Groothusen. 1993. The syntactic positive shift as an ERP-measure of syntactic processing. *Language and Cognitive Processes* 8:439–483.

Hahne, A., and A. D. Friederici. 1998. ERP-evidence for autonomous first-pass parsing processes in auditory language comprehension. *Journal of Cognitive Neuroscience*, Suppl., 125.

Hahne, A., and A. D. Friederici. 1999. Electrophysiological evidence for two steps in syntactic analysis: Early automatic and late controlled processes. *Journal of Cognitive Neuroscience* 11:193–204.

Inui, T., Y. Otsu, S. Tanaka, T. Okada, S. Nishizawa, and J. Konishi. 1998. A functional MRI analysis of comprehension processes of Japanese sentences. *NeuroReport* 9:3325–3328.

Jescheniak, J. D., A. Hahne, and A. D. Friederici. 1998. Brain activity patterns suggest prosodic influences on syntactic parsing in the comprehension of spoken sentences. *Music Perception* 16:55–62.

Just, M. A., P. A. Carpenter, T. A. Keller, W. F. Eddy, and K. R. Thulborn. 1996. Brain activation modulated by sentence comprehension. *Science* 274:114–116.

Kaan, E., A. Harris, and P. Holcomb. 2000. The P600 as an index of syntactic integration difficulty. *Language and Cognitive Processes* 15:159–201.

Kuriki, S., and M. Murase. 1989. Neuromagnetic study of the auditory responses in right and left hemispheres of the human brain evoked by pure tones and speech sounds. *Experimental Brain Research* 77:127–134.

Kutas, M., and S. A. Hillyard. 1980. Reading senseless sentences: Brain potentials reflect semantic incongruity. *Science* 207:203–205.

Kutas, M., and S. A. Hillyard. 1983. Event-related brain potentials to grammatical errors and semantic anomalies. *Memory and Cognition* 11:539–550.

Lauter, J. L., P. Herschovitch, C. Formby, and M. E. Raichle. 1985. Tonotopic organization in the human auditory cortex revealed by position emission tomography. *Hearing Research* 20:199–205.

MacDonald, M. A., M. A. Just, and P. A. Carpenter. 1992. Working memory constraints on the processing of syntactic ambiguity resolution. *Cognitive Psychology* 24:56–98.

Marslen-Wilson, W., and L. K. Tyler. 1980. The temporal structure of spoken language understanding. *Cognition* 8:1–71.

Marslen-Wilson, W., L. K. Tyler, P. Warren, P. Grenier, and C. S. Lee. 1992. Prosodic effects in minimal attachment. *Quarterly Journal of Experimental Psychology* 45A:73–87.

Martin, A., J. V. Haxby, F. M. Lalonde, C. L. Wiggs, and L. G. Ungerleider. 1995. Discrete cortical regions associated with knowledge of color and knowledge of action. *Science* 270:102–105.

Martin, A., C. L. Wiggs, L. G. Ungerleider, and J. V. Haxby. 1996. Neural correlates of category-specific knowledge. *Nature* 379:649–652.

Mazoyer, B. M., N. Tzourio, V. Frak, A. Syrota, N. Murayama, O. Levrier, G. Salamon, S. Dehaene, L. Cohen, and J. Mehler. 1993. The cortical representation of speech. *Journal of Cognitive Neuroscience* 5:467–479.

McClelland, J. L., M. St. John, and R. Taraban. 1989. Sentence comprehension: A parallel distributed processing approach. *Language and Cognitive Processes* 4:287–335.

Münte, T. F., M. Matzke, and S. Johannes. 1997. Brain activity associated with syntactic incongruencies in words and pseudo-words. *Journal of Cognitive Neuroscience* 9:318–329.

Näätänen, R., and T. Picton. 1987. The N1 wave of the human electric and magnetic response to sound: A review and an analysis of the component structure. *Psychophysiology* 24:375–425.

Neville, H. J., J. Nicol, A. Barss, K. Forster, and M. Garrett. 1991. Syntactically based sentence processing classes: Evidence from event-related brain potentials. *Journal of Cognitive Neuroscience* 3:155–170.

Nobre, A. C., T. Allison, and G. McCarthy. 1994. Word recognition in the human inferior temporal lobe. *Nature* 372:260–263.

Osterhout, L., and P. J. Holcomb. 1992. Event-related brain potentials elicited by syntactic anomaly. *Journal of Memory and Language* 31:785–804.

Osterhout, L., and P. J. Holcomb. 1993. Event-related potentials and syntactic anomaly: Evidence of anomaly detection during the perception of continuous speech. *Language and Cognitive Processes* 8:413–437.

Penke, M., H. Weyerts, M. Gross, E. Zander, T. F. Münte, and A. Clahsen. 1997. How the brain processes complex words: An ERP-study of German verb inflections. *Cognitive Brain Research* 6:37–52.

Petersen, S. E., P. T. Fox, M. I. Posner, M. A. Mintum, and M. E. Raichle. 1988. Positron emission tomographic studies of the cortical anomaly of single-word processing. *Nature* 331:585–589.

Petersen, S. E., P. T. Fox, M. I. Posner, M. A. Mintum, and M. E. Raichle. 1989. Positron emission tomographic studies of the processing of single words. *Journal of Cognitive Neuroscience* 1:153–170.

Petersen, S. E., P. T. Fox, A. Z. Snyder, and M. E. Raichle. 1990. Activation of extrastriate and frontal cortical areas by visual words and word-like stimuli. *Science* 249:1041–1044.

Poeppel, D., E. Yellin, C. Phillips, T. P. L. Roberts, H. A. Rowley, K. Wexler, and A. Marantz. 1996. Task-induced asymmetry of the auditory evoked M100 neuromagnetic field elicited by speech sounds. *Cognitive Brain Research* 4:231–242.

Rösler, F., A. D. Friederici, P. Pütz, and A. Hahne. 1993. Event-related brain potentials while encountering semantic and syntactic constraint violations. *Journal of Cognitive Neuroscience* 5:345–362.

Schlosser, M. J., N. Aoyagi, R. K. Fulbright, J. C. Gore, and G. McCarthy. 1998. Functional MRI studies of auditory comprehension. *Human Brain Mapping* 6:1–13.

Steinhauer, K., K. Alter, and A. D. Friederici. 1999. Brain potentials indicate immediate use of prosodic cues in natural speech processing. *Nature Neuroscience* 2:191–196.

Stromswold, K., D. Caplan, N. Alpert, and S. Rauch. 1996. Localization of syntactic comprehension by positron emission tomography. *Brain and Language* 52:452–473.

Van Petten, C. 1995. Words and sentences: Event-related brain potential measures. *Psychophysiology* 32:511–525.

Warren, P., E. Grabe, and F. Nolan. 1995. Prosody, phonology, and parsing in closure ambiguities. *Language and Cognitive Processes* 10:457–486.

Wise, R., F. Chollet, U. Hadar, K. J. Friston, E. Hoffner, and R. S. J. Frackowiak. 1991. Distribution of cortical networks involved in word comprehension and word retrieval. *Brain* 114:1803–1817.

Zatorre, R. J., A. C. Evans, E. Meyer, and A. Gjedde. 1992. Lateralization of phonetic and pitch discrimination in speech processing. *Science* 256:846–849.

Zatorre, R. J., E. Meyer, A. Gjedde, and A. C. Evans. 1996. PET studies of phonetic processing of speech: Review, replication, and reanalysis. In M. Raichle and P. S. Goldman-Rakic (eds.), Special issue: Cortical imaging—microscope of the mind. *Cerebral Cortex* 6(1), R3–R4:21–30.

Chapter 7

Neural Control of Cognition and Language

Masao Ito

The principle of control systems has primarily been developed for designing machines, but since Wiener (1961) pointed out its importance in terms of cybernetics, it has given us useful insights into the functions of living beings. The brain is composed of innumerable neurons interconnected through synapses, both excitatory and inhibitory, including some that exhibit plasticity such as long-term potentiation and depression (LTP and LTD, respectively). Elaborate neuronal networks thus constructed are connected to sensory and effector organs, thereby forming various neural systems such as the sensory, motor, and emotion systems. The principle of control systems has commonly been applied to relatively simple problems of movement control, but this chapter will extend this principle to cognition and language. This standpoint seems to be effective, particularly for explaining recently revealed roles of the cerebellum not only in movement but also in cognition and language.

7.1 The Central Nervous System as the Control System

The entire central nervous system can be viewed as consisting of two different types of systems, the functional and the regulatory (Ito 1997, 1998b) (figure 7.1). In lower vertebrates such as fish, amphibians, and reptiles, three major functional neural systems are incorporated in the brainstem and spinal cord, systems (1) for reflexes, (2) for compound movements such as locomotion and saccadic eye movements, and (3) for innate behaviors such as food and water intake, aggression, or reproduction. In birds and lower mammals, the cerebral cortex is evolved and performs (4) sensorimotor functions such as sensation-driven voluntary movements, while in primates the association cortex is expanded and is capable of (5) higher-order cognitive functions such as thought. These five functional systems are integrated with the four major regulatory systems: (a) the sleep-wakefulness center in the brainstem for recovery, (b) the cerebellum for adaptiveness, (c) the basal ganglia for stability, and (d) the limbic system for purposefulness. Each regulatory system assists each of the five functional systems in a unique, characteristic manner, as will be shown for the cerebellum.

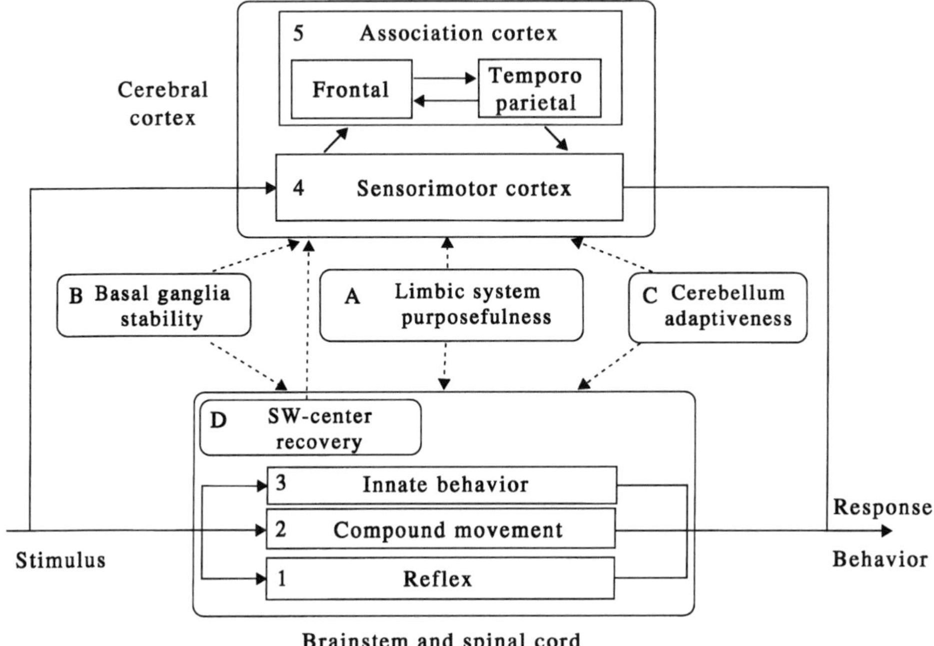

Figure 7.1
Hierarchical control system structure of the central nervous system

The general structure of a control system, consisting of a controller, its accessory apparatus, and a control object (figure 7.2a), can be applied to the functional systems. Reflexes constitute a typical control system with their center in the spinal cord or brainstem as the controller and an effector, namely muscles or glands, as the control object (figure 7.2b). Compound movement systems include a central pattern generator connected to the controller (figure 7.2c). The controller for innate behavior systems includes generators of complex behavioral patterns located in or around the hypothalamus (figure 7.2d). In sensation-driven voluntary movements, the cerebral cortex acts as the controller, while a segmental neuronal pool in the spinal cord connected to the musculoskeletal system in a limb constitutes the control object (figure 7.3a). The cerebral cortex contains the sensory and perisensory cortex for elaborate information processing and the premotor cortex for programming complex movements, and based on the activities of these cortical areas as accessory apparatus, the motor cortex eventually generates motor command signals. In "thought" effected by the association cortex, the frontal association areas appear to play roles as the controller with the temporoparietal association areas probably containing the control objects (figure 7.3b). These control objects could be images, ideas, or concepts for-

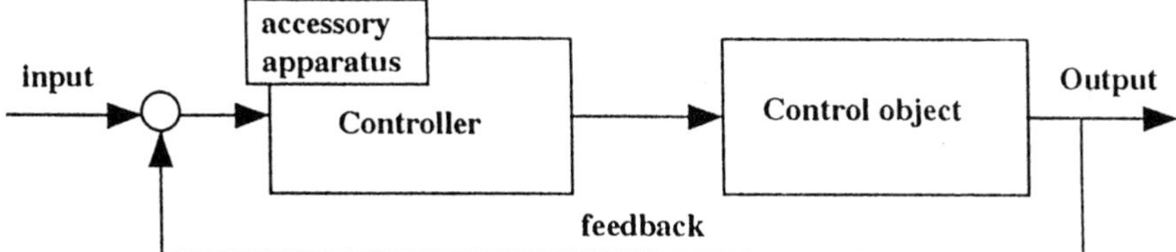

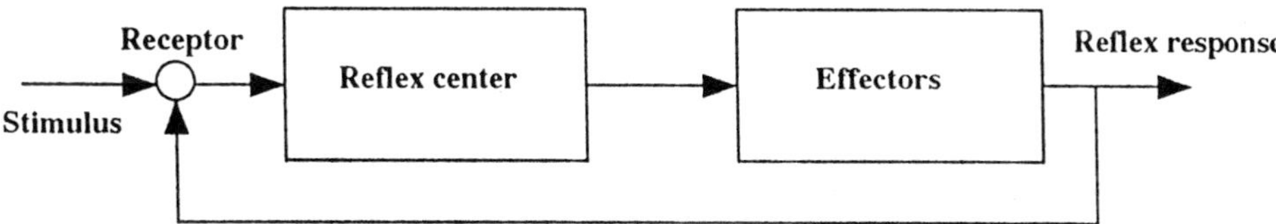

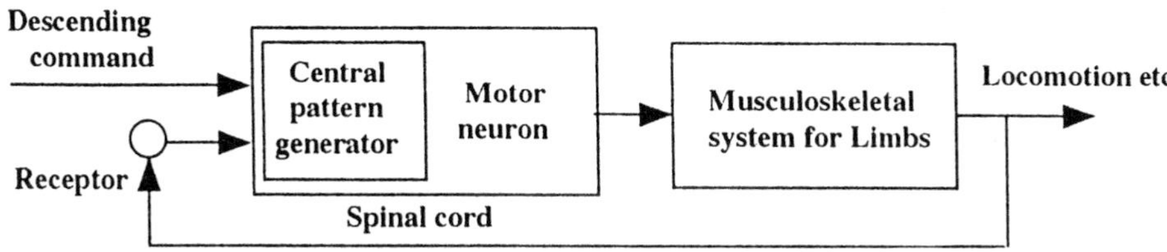

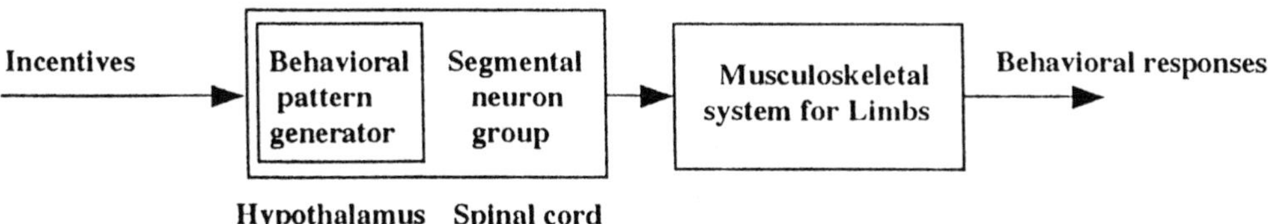

Figure 7.2
Control system structures of subcortical neural systems

A Voluntary movement

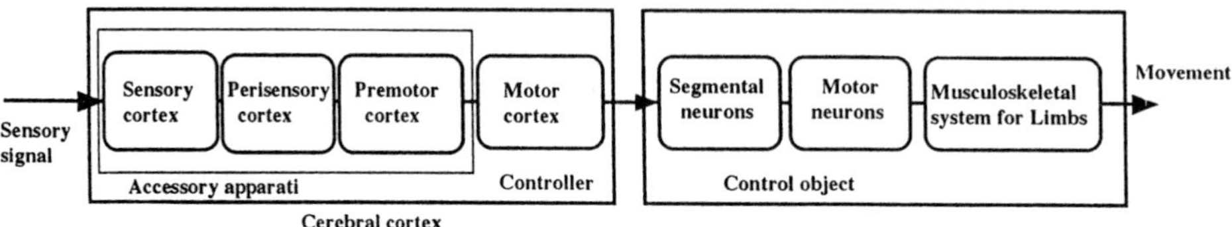

B Thought

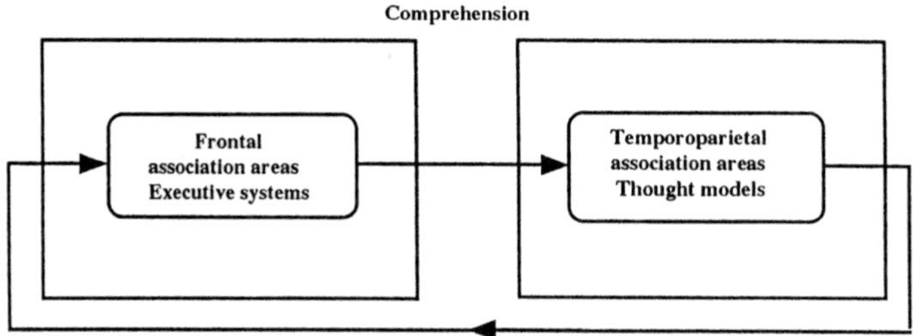

Figure 7.3
Control system structures of cortical systems

mulated through a number of association steps from sensory signals and eventually represented in the temporoparietal areas. They will collectively be called *thought models*. Since the frontal association areas are large, it is presently difficult to precisely locate the postulated controller role in them. Currently, the executive attentional system, which is informed about the processes taking place within the organization and which exercises some control over the system, is assumed to include the anterior cingulate gyrus (Posner 1994). Working memory functions are assigned to the lateral frontal association areas (Goldman-Rakic 1997). Very recently, however, the role in shifting attention from one category of stimulus attributes to another has been located in human inferior frontal areas (Konishi et al. 1998).

The classic model of language organization (figure 7.4a) is analogous to that for voluntary limb movements (figure 7.3a). When one speaks in response to heard voices, the cerebral cortex acts as the controller, while segmental and motor neurons in the medulla and cervical cord and the orofacial and laryngeal muscles effecting movements of the lips, tongue, and vocal cord innervated by them constitute the control object. The motor command sent by the motor cortex to the control object is generated by activities in the auditory cortex and in Wernicke's and Broca's areas. The process of inner hearing may be executed through feedback connections from

A Hearing-speech

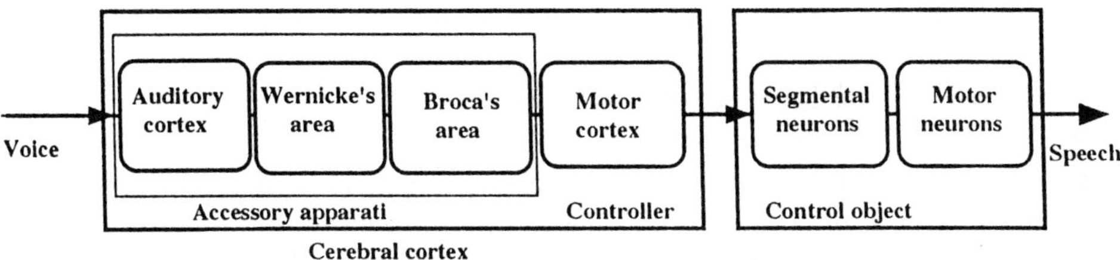

B Verbal thought

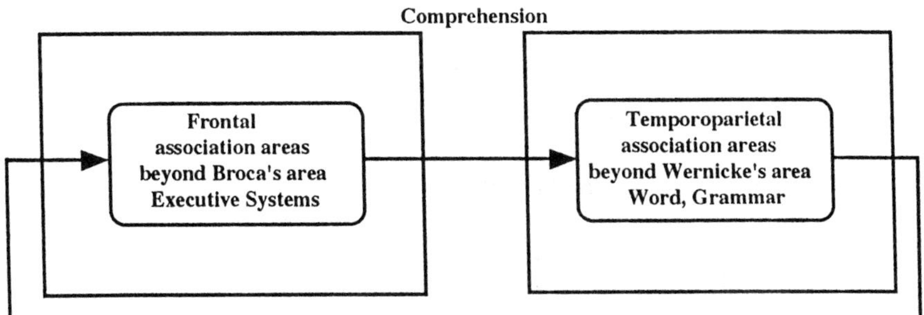

Figure 7.4
Control system structures of language systems

Broca's area to Wernicke's area. The neural system for verbal thought is likewise conceived (figure 7.4b) by analogy with the association cortex functions for thought in general (figure 7.3b).

Note that reflexes, compound movements, innate behaviors, and sensation-triggered voluntary movements are all executed in close association with the external world. The inputs are stimuli received from the external world and the outputs are responses directed toward the external world. In contrast, the association cortex operates within the cerebral loop formed between the frontal and temporoparietal areas; this is the brain structure presumed to execute mental activities without direct linkage with the external world. Special attention must be paid to the prominent contrast between the sensory cortex as part of the controller in sensorimotor functions (figure 7.3a) and the temporoparietal areas as the control object in thought functions (figure 7.4b). The development of projections from the frontal association areas to the temporoparietal areas seems to be an important evolutionary step.

There, the bottom-up mechanism of the brain based on its interactions with the external world is changed to top-down mechanisms using the connections of the frontal association areas to the internal world formed in the temporoparietal areas.

7.2 Mechanisms and Roles of the Cerebellum

The cerebellum has a remarkably uniform structure and can be assumed to be composed of adaptive units called *cerebellar corticonuclear microcomplexes*, or more simply *microcomplexes*, which change their input-output relationships through a process of learning driven by error signals (figure 7.5). A type of synaptic plasticity called *long-term depression* (LTD) is the major mechanism underlying this error-driven learning process (Ito 1993, 1998a). In LTD, when error signals conveyed by climbing fibers collide with input signals conveyed by mossy fibers at the parallel

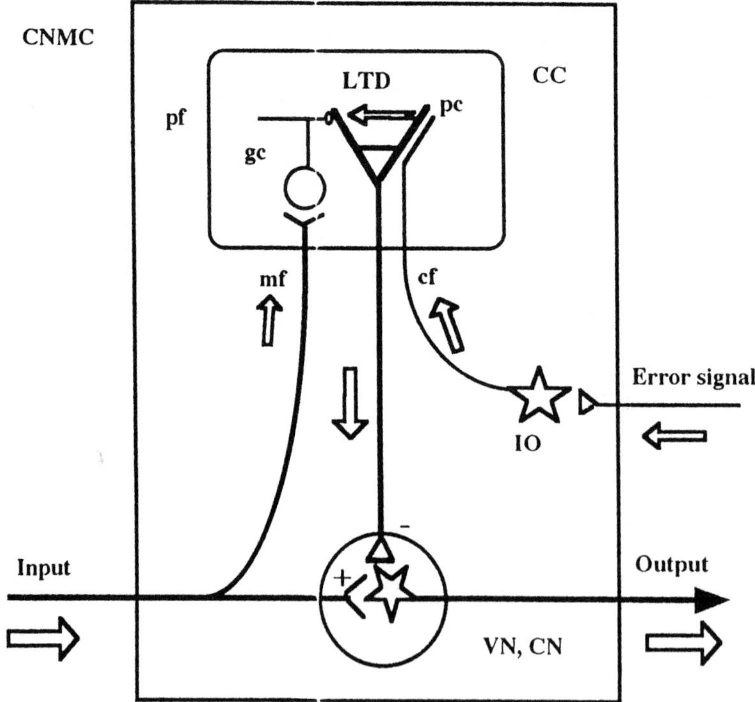

Figure 7.5
Cerebellar corticonuclear microcomplex (CNMC). CC-cerebellar cortex, pf-parallel fiber, gc-granule cell, pc-Purkinje cell, cf-climbing fiber, mf-mossy fiber, IO-inferior olive, VN-vestibular nucleus, CN-cerebellar nucleus.

fiber-Purkinje cell synapses, the transmission efficacy at these synapses is persistently depressed. The inhibitory output of Purkinje cells on cerebellar nuclear neurons is thus modified so that the relationship between mossy fiber inputs and nuclear outputs is persistently changed.

In neural systems for reflexes, for compound movements, and probably also for innate behaviors, a microcomplex is connected to the controller, enabling adaptive control in the neural system (figure 7.6a). For example, when an animal's locomotion on a treadmill is perturbed by a sudden change of speed of one limb, the locomotion initially becomes irregular, but the cerebellar microcomplex connected to the locomotion system acts to modify parameters of locomotion by referring to the errors forwarded to it through spinocerebellar pathways so that stable locomotion is restored (Yanagihara and Kondo 1996; Ito et al. 1998).

The cerebellum, however, appears to be involved in the sensorimotor or association cortex functions in a different manner, namely, by provision of internal models for control in the following way. Consider a microcomplex that is fed by input signals common to a system to be copied and that is detecting discrepancies of outputs as error signals (figure 7.6b). When the error signals are fed to the cerebellar unit to induce self-reorganization of its neuronal networks, the signal transfer characteristics of the microcomplex will be modified to minimize the error signals until the microcomplex becomes a model having signal transfer characteristics identical to those of the system to be copied.

The loop connection between the cerebral motor area and the paravermal cortex of the cerebellum appears to provide such a model for voluntary motor control (Ito 1984). When the motor cortex sends command signals to the musculoskeletal system of a limb to perform a voluntary movement, the same signals may be sent to the cerebellar model of the musculoskeletal system, the output of which is relayed back to the motor cortex (figure 7.7). Thus, a voluntary movement can be performed without using the external sensory feedback monitoring the actual movement, and can instead rely on internal feedback through a model in the cerebellum. This control system operation explains why movement exercise increases skill: a cerebellar model of a musculoskeletal system is formed during repeated exercise. It also explains dysmetria, a typical cerebellar symptom: while a healthy person can point to his or her nose with a fingertip accurately even with closed eyes, a patient with cerebellar disease becomes unable to do so, apparently due to the absence of a cerebellar model for the finger-to-nose pointing movement.

If the musculoskeletal system is represented by the orofacial and laryngeal muscle system for lip, tongue, and vocal cord, and the motor cortex by the cerebral cortex including auditory cortex and Wernicke's and Broca's areas, figure 7.8 represents the similar involvement of the cerebellum in the hearing/speech control.

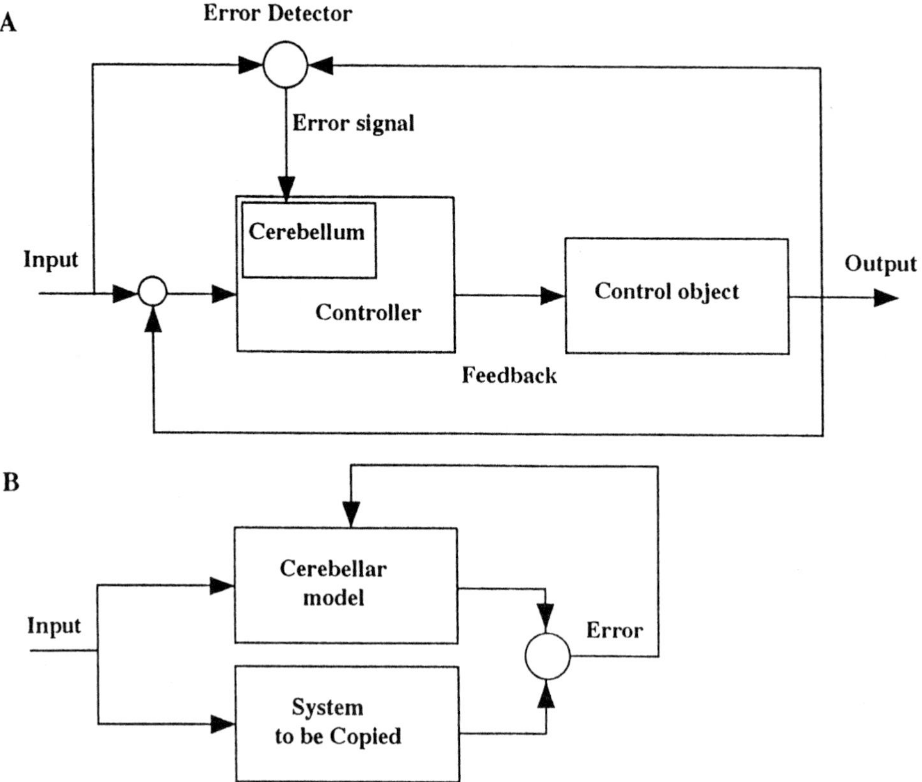

Figure 7.6
Two different uses of CNMC: (*a*) as an accessory apparatus for adaptive control; (*b*) for forming a model copying a system.

The existence of close mutual anatomical connections between the association cortex and the cerebellar hemisphere has been established (Middleton and Strich 1998; Schmahmann 1996). A microcomplex may therefore be connected to the cerebral loop as a copy of the thought model in the temporoparietal areas (figure 7.9). If the microcomplex has an equivalent property in terms of signal transmission to the thought model, the thought may be conducted by the frontal areas acting on the microcomplex rather than on the thought model in the temporoparietal areas. The benefit of this operation is that the control can be effected without the conscious effort needed for exploring the temporoparietal areas. If the thought model is verbal in nature, consisting of words and grammar, figure 7.9 represents a possible control scheme for verbal thought.

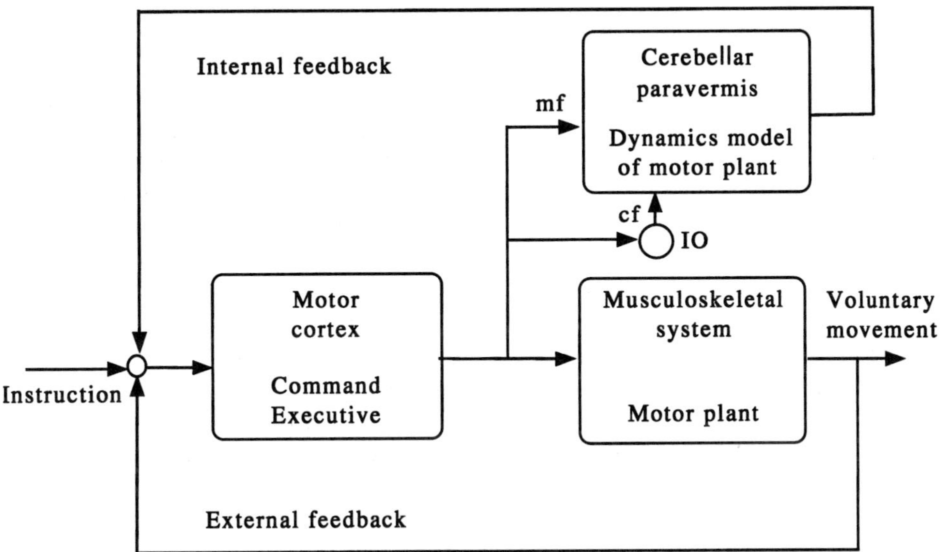

Figure 7.7
Cerebellar-aided dynamic model control of voluntary movements. A hypothetical block diagram.

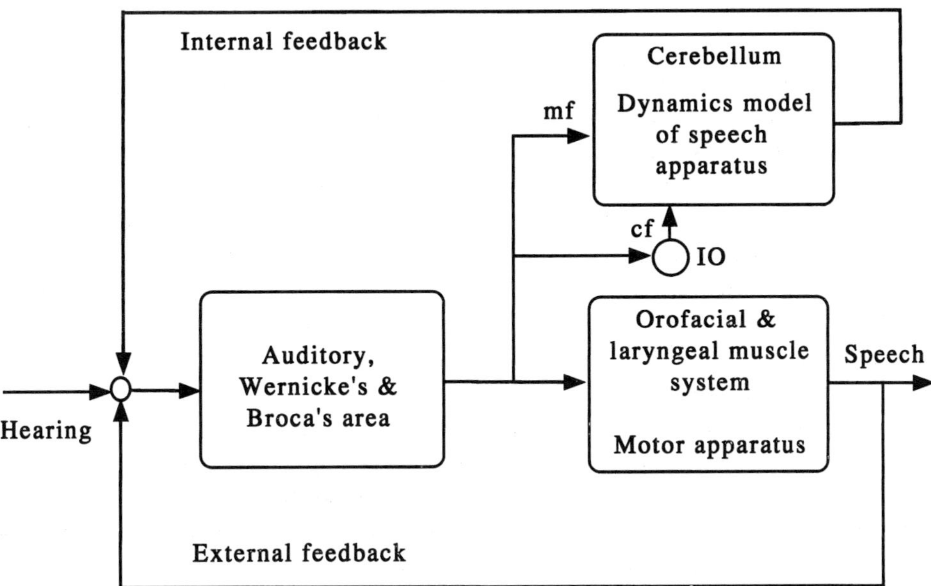

Figure 7.8
Cerebellar-aided dynamic model control of speech production. A hypothetical block diagram.

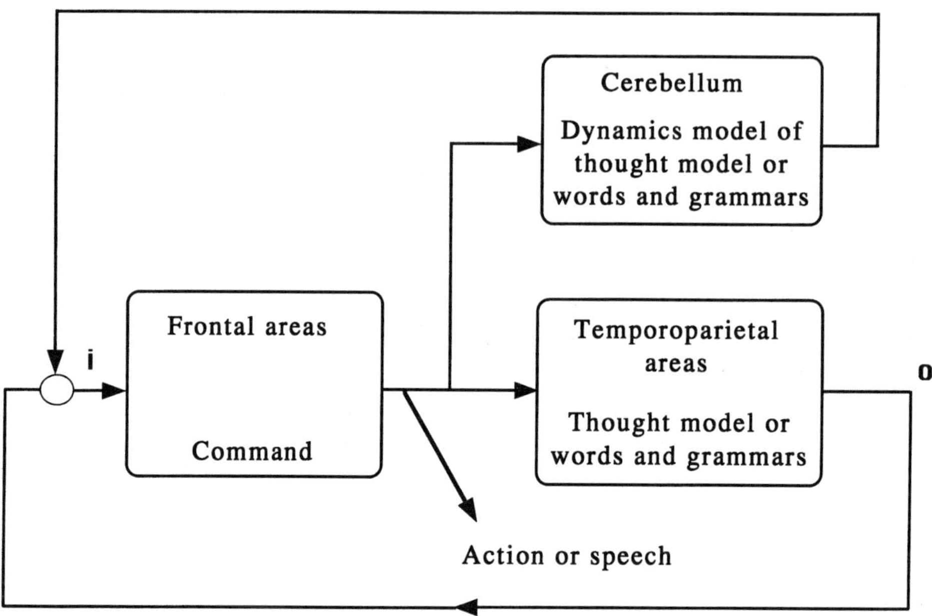

Figure 7.9
Cerebellar control with copy (analogous to the dynamics model in figure 7.8) of nonverbal or verbal thought model.

Cerebrocerebellar connections do not always form a loop, and the cerebellar hemisphere is often connected in parallel to the cerebral cortex. Kawato, Furukawa, and Suzuki (1987) proposed that the cerebellum forms a model of the controller instead of the control object (for recent references, see Wolpert, Mial, and Kawato 1998). In this scheme, the microcomplex inserted in parallel to the frontal areas should have signal transferring properties reciprocally equal to those of the thought model, either verbal or nonverbal, in the temporoparietal areas (figure 7.10). The benefit of this operation would be that the thought process can be conducted without conscious attention.

A fundamental assumption for the present argument is that, from the viewpoint of control systems, mental activities are analogous to movements. In the same way that we move our arms and legs, we move images, concepts, and ideas in our mind. The objects to be controlled are very different in cases of movement and thought, but the control system principles could be identical for both. The same control system principles are thus applied to problems of both movement and thought (Ito 1993).

In motor control, a dynamics or an inverse dynamics of a control object can precisely be defined as a function of its movement. It has recently been reported that

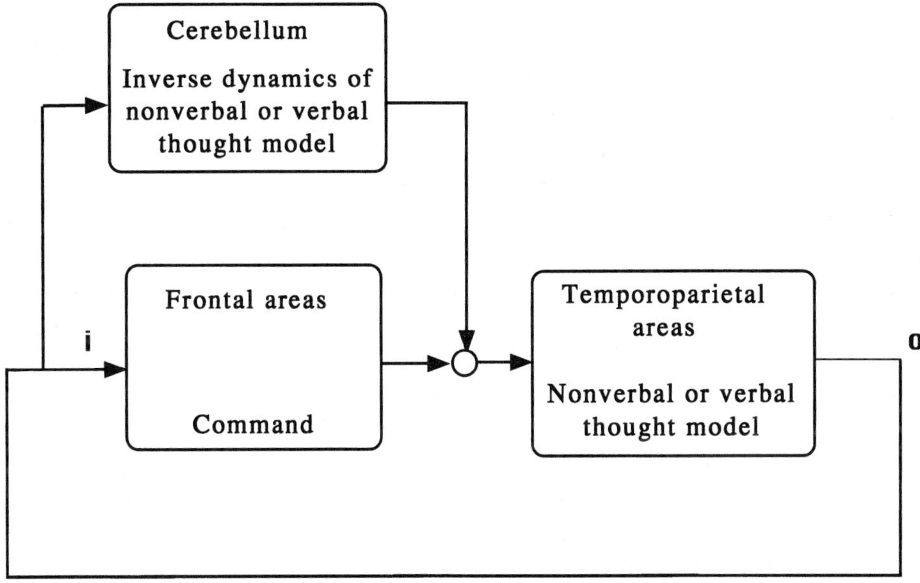

Figure 7.10
Cerebellar control with inverse model of nonverbal or verbal thought model. Note that inverse dynamics implies an analogy to motor control.

Purkinje cell activity in the ventral paraflocculus during ocular movements elicited by movement of the whole visual field indeed represents the inverse dynamics of eyeballs (Shidara et al. 1995). However, it is as yet unclear how properties of nonverbal or verbal thought models can be defined in a manner similar to the dynamics or inverse dynamics of the musculoskeletal system.

7.3 Evidence for Cerebellar Roles in Cognition and Language

Lesions of the cerebellum elicit a symptom called *ataxic dysarthria*, a disturbance in the muscular control of speech (see Gordon 1996). Ataxic dysarthria is characterized by slurred speech with abnormal rhythm due to defective functioning of the cerebellar paravermis. This condition suggests a control system for speech in which the cerebral cortex, including Broca's area and motor cortex, acts as the controller. The speech apparatus, including the orofacial and laryngeal muscle systems, serves as the control object (figure 7.8), with the cerebellar paravermis providing an internal model of the control object.

Roles of the cerebellum in cognitive functions are suggested by deficits induced by cerebellar lesions in cognitive planning, in practice-related learning and error detection, in judging time intervals, in rapidly shifting attention between sensory modalities, and in cognitive operations in three-dimensional space (Schmahmann and Sherman 1997; Akshoomoff, Courchesne, and Townsend 1997). Recent brain-imaging studies support this view of the cerebellum (Allen et al. 1997).

For verbal thought, the left frontal association areas appear to act as the controller—primarily the inferior and middle frontal gyri but also including the medial surface of the hemisphere, extending beyond the classical Broca's area in the posterior inferior frontal gyrus. Thought models encoding language as control objects are likely represented in the left temporoparietal areas extending beyond the classical Wernicke's area in the posterior superior temporal gyrus to the surrounding middle and inferior temporal gyri and the angular gyrus, as suggested by recent functional MRI studies (see Binder 1997).

Language comprehension is believed to involve the left frontal association areas. Manipulation by the left frontal association areas of language-encoding thought models in the temporoparietal areas would be a neural correlate of language comprehension. The right cerebellar hemisphere could be involved in language functions, since cerebellar lesions cause language disorders nonmotor in nature. In a typical case of a patient with cerebellar lesions, Silveri, Leggio, and Molinari (1994) reported agrammatic speech, consisting of omission of freestanding grammatical morphemes and production of infinitive forms in place of inflected forms. A deficit of error detection in word finding and in learning arbitrary associations between words and an impairment of verbal associative learning have also been reported to result from cerebellar lesions (Fiez et al. 1992). Riva's (1998) case report of a viral cerebellitis patient presenting with language disorders suggests that the cerebellum is involved in the processing and programming of verbal and sequential functions.

The right cerebellar hemisphere is activated during reading, verb generation, and other semantic tasks such as word-stem completion, and naming actions in response to line drawings, as well as rhyme and synonym production (Raichle et al. 1994; Klein et al. 1995). Activation of these areas is, however, attenuated during practiced verb generation, and is replaced by activation of the automatic system including areas of the sylvian-insular cortex bilaterally (Raichle et al. 1994; Passingham 1997).

7.4 Comments

To uncover the neural mechanism underlying language function is still a very difficult task in the field of neuroscience. One particular reason for this difficulty is the fact that language is uniquely human, so that invasive techniques that are effectively used in animal experiments cannot be applied. Nevertheless, localization of language-related areas in the cerebral cortex has been well established, and we have clearly defined the brain regions to be targeted for neuroscientific approaches. While noninvasive brain imaging provides a novel approach for demonstrating activities in the language-related areas, recording from individual neurons has only occasionally been successful. Apparently, lack of technology for analyzing neural events at the cellular level is a bottleneck in the neuroscientific study of language.

The principle of control systems described in this chapter seems a promising approach for understanding the evolution of the brain architecture for language functions. An important possibility derived from the present considerations is that at a certain stage of evolution, the frontal areas that originally were recipients of sensory signals were converted into senders of command signals to the temporoparietal cortex. The original bottom-up mechanism processing stimuli from the external world thus changed to a top-down mechanism acting on the internal world, leading to the emergence and development of the cognitive function of thought in primates.

The control system structure for language function analogous to the more primitive sensorimotor and nonverbal thought functions suggests common neural mechanisms for these functions. The uniqueness of nonverbal thought appears to lie in the mechanism of formation of thought models in the neuronal networks of the temporoparietal areas. The uniqueness of verbal thought must also lie in the mechanism of formation of verbal thought models, namely words and grammar, in the neuronal networks of the temporoparietal areas. These mechanisms should be a target for future neuroscientific research on language function.

References

Akshoomoff, N. A., E. Courchesne, and J. Townsend. 1997. Attention coordination and anticipation control. In *The cerebellum and cognition*, ed. J. D. Schmahmann. San Diego: Academic Press. (*International Review of Neurobiology* 41, 575–598.)

Allen, G., R. B. Buxton, E. C. Wong, and E. Courchesne. 1997. Attentional activation of the cerebellum independent of motor involvement. *Science* 275, 1940–1943.

Binder, J. R. 1997. Neuroanatomy of language processing studied with functional MRI. *Clinical Neurosciences* 4, 87–94.

Fiez, J. A., S. E. Petersen, M. K. Cheney, and M. E. Raichle. 1992. Impaired non-motor learning and error detection associated with cerebellar damage. *Brain* 115, 155–178.

Fiez J. A., and M. E. Raichle. 1998. Linguistic processing. In *The cerebellum and cognition*, ed. J. D. Schmahmann. San Diego: Academic Press. (*International Review of Neurobiology* 41, 233–254.)

Goldman-Rakic, P. 1997. Neurobiology: Space and time in the mental universe. *Nature* 386, 559–560.

Gordon, N. 1996. Speech, language, and the cerebellum. *European Journal of Disorders of Communication* 31, 359–367.

Ito, M. 1984. *The cerebellum and neural control.* New York: Raven Press.

Ito, M. 1993. Movement and thought: Identical control mechanisms by the cerebellum. *Trends in Neuroscience* 16, 448–450.

Ito, M. 1997. Cerebellar microcomplexes. In *The cerebellum and cognition*, ed. J. D. Schmahmann. San Diego: Academic Press. (*International Review of Neurobiology* 41, 475–487.)

Ito, M. 1998a. Cerebellar learning in the vestibulo-ocular reflex. *Trends in Cognitive Sciences* 2, 313–321.

Ito, M. 1998b. Consciousness from the viewpoint of the structural-functional relationships of the brain. *International Journal of Psychology* 33, 191–197.

Ito, S., H. Yuasa, Z.-W. Luo, M. Ito, and D. Yanagihara. 1998. A mathematical model of adaptive behavior in quadruped locomotion. *Biological Cybernetics* 78, 337–347.

Kawato, M., K. Furukawa, and R. Suzuki, 1987. A hierarchical neuronal network model for control and learning of voluntary movement. *Biological Cybernetics* 57, 169–185.

Klein, D., B. Milner, R. Zatorre, E. Meyer, and A. C. Evans. 1995. The neural substrates underlying word generation: A bilingual functional-imaging study. *Proceedings of the National Academy of Sciences of the USA*, 92, 2899–2903.

Konoshi, S., K. Nakajima, I. Uchida, M. Kameyama, K. Nakahara, K. Sekihara, and Y. Miyashita. 1998. Transient activation of inferior prefrontal cortex during cognitive set shifting. *Nature Neuroscience* 1, 60–84.

Middleton, F. A., and P. L. Strich. 1998. Cerebellar output: Motor and cognitive channels. *Trends in Cognitive Sciences* 2.

Passingham, R. E. 1997. Attention to action. In *The cerebellum and cognition*, ed. J. D. Schmahmann. San Diego: Academic Press. (*International Review of Neurobiology* 41, 131–143.)

Posner, M. I. 1994. Attention: The mechanisms of consciousness. *Proceedings of the National Academy of Sciences of the USA* 91, 7398–7403.

Raichle, M. E., J. A. Fiez, T. O. Videen, A. M. K. MacLeod, J. V. Pardo, P. T. Fox, and S. E. Petersen. 1994. Practice-related changes in human brain functional anatomy during nonmotor learning. *Cerebral Cortex* 4, 8–26.

Riva, D. 1998. The cerebellar contribution to language and sequential functions: Evidence from a child with cerebellitis. *Cortex* 34, 279–287.

Schmahmann, J. D. 1996. From movement to thought: Anatomic substrates of the cerebellar contribution to cognitive processing. *Human Brain Mapping* 4, 174–198.

Schmahmann, J. D., and J. C. Sherman. 1997. Cerebellar cognitive affective syndrome. In *The cerebellum and cognition*, ed. J. D. Schmahmann. San Diego: Academic Press. (*International Review of Neurobiology* 41, 433–440.)

Shidara, M., M. Kawano, H. Gomi, and M. Kawato. 1995. Inverse-dynamic encoding of eye movements by Purkinje cells in the cerebellum. *Nature* 365, 50–52.

Silveri, M. C., M. G. Leggio, and M. Molinari. 1994. The cerebellum contributes to linguistic production: A case of agrammatic speech following a right cerebellar lesion. *Neurology* 44, 2047–2050.

Wiener, N. 1961. *Cybernetics.* 2nd ed. Cambridge, Mass.: MIT Press.

Wolpert, D. M., R. C. Mial, and M. Kawato. 1998. Internal models in the cerebellum. *Trends in Cognitive Sciences* 2, 338–347.

Yanagihara, D., and I. Kondo. 1996. Nitric oxide plays a key role in adaptive control of locomotion in cats. *Proceedings of the National Academy of Sciences of the USA* 93, 13292–13297.

Part II

Image and the Brain

Chapter 8

Imaging Neuroscience: System-Level Studies of the Physiology and Anatomy of Human Cognition

Richard S. J. Frackowiak

This chapter will address the issue of how noninvasive brain-monitoring techniques can be applied to investigate the functional anatomy of the human brain. The visual system will be used as an illustrative paradigm. Within that system, the notion of investigating functional specialization will be developed for the early perceptual regions and pathways. For example, experiments using perceptual illusions and perceptual ambiguity in normal subjects, coupled with studies in patients with specific visual deficits, will be used to illustrate principles. The advantages and disadvantages of the available techniques—PET, fMRI, EEG—will be discussed by reference to their use. The interaction between perception and attention and the relevance to visual learning will be used to illustrate how integrative brain mechanisms can be studied. The notion of functional and effective connectivity and different ways of demonstrating and quantifying interregional interactions in distributed systems will be dealt with and the implications for further study discussed.

Why do we know so little about the functional architecture of the human brain in comparison with other organs of the body? This is a legitimate and somewhat puzzling question, but the answer is almost mundane. The brain, like these other organs, apparently homogeneous in composition, at least to the naked eye, is much less readily accessible in life. The average brain weighs approximately 1.4 kg and is contained within an impenetrable skull. Removal of pieces of tissue during life for examination by histoanatomical and electrophysiological techniques in normal people is ethically unacceptable. The science of brain function has, therefore, largely depended on inferences made from observations of abnormal behavior in life and correlations with postmortem lesions. Though remarkably fruitful over the last 120 years in generating hypotheses about how the brain is functionally organized, there is a problem with this approach. Conclusions depend on an assumption that the brain is composed of functionally discrete modules that can be removed, leaving behind the remaining parts of the brain with their functions relatively undisturbed. This assumption is now known to be a simplification. The damaged brain, like the learning normal brain, can adapt. For example, patients with paralysis due to strokes may show spontaneous recovery of function for many months following a lesion (Chollet et al. 1991). Additionally, brain areas may contribute differentially to different behaviors or in different contexts.

The development of noninvasive techniques for monitoring human brain function in life have revolutionized our methods for gathering data about how the human brain is functionally organized. The history of these methods starts in 1972 with the manufacture of the first CT scanning machines. These scanners used x-rays to generate images of the anatomy of the brain with remarkable clarity. Techniques depending on magnetic resonance technology now supersede x-ray CT by providing greater contrast between the various tissues of the brain with no exposure to radiation, and they are completely noninvasive.

The basic principles of reconstruction tomography pioneered by Godfrey Hounsfield and Allan Cormack were rapidly applied to the detection of radioactive trace molecules in the body. The resultant images of the functional architecture of the brain can be coregistered with anatomical scans to provide a long-awaited means of functionally examining the normal human brain in life.

Enormous advances in the performance of these various techniques have occurred, and other procedures now complement them (Toga and Mazziotta 1996). This chapter will review some of these techniques and indicate the type of knowledge being obtained. At present, changes in brain activity associated with pure thought, emotion, and cognitive processes are measurable. The collected data convey new information about how our organ of cognition is functionally organized.

8.1 Imaging Neuroscience

The aim of functional neuroimaging is to describe the functional organization of the human brain at the level of large neuronal groupings, networks, and systems. The systems level of description addresses how integrated brain functions are embodied in the physical structure of the brain. Important areas of inquiry include how sensory input is mapped onto the human sensory cortices and how complex sensory representations are built up; how interactions between sensory and motor representations occur during sense-guided motor output; how cognitive functions, such as memory, language, and emotion are organized; and what the role of consciousness in human behavior is.

Early sensory input and final motor output are arranged in multiple topographically organized maps. For example, the frontal eye fields lie caudally behind the sulcus principalis in Brodmann area (BA) 8 in primates but in the premotor area (BA6) in human brain (Anderson et al. 1994). The functional homologies between nonhuman primate and human brains are unclear and discrepancies are increasingly found. These results question how far information about the system-level organization of the brain can be transposed from one primate species to another. Another example is afforded by the massive and unique development of the frontal and parietal lobes coincident with the evolution of language in the human brain. We still know very little of the functional specialization of different regions in the frontal and parietal lobes of humans. Their elucidation promises further insights into the organization of peculiarly human cognitive behaviors.

The brain is organized at various levels in both temporal and spatial domains. Neurons, neuronal groupings, modules, and larger-scale functionally homogeneous or cooperative neuronal populations are different spatial levels of brain organization. Electrical activities with periodicities of milliseconds, hundreds of milliseconds, or seconds all occur in the brain. For example, the action potential, the evoked potential, the readiness potential, and the delta wave during EEG are examples of different temporal levels of organization. Modern noninvasive imaging techniques are bringing such levels of organization within the range of measurement, and hence they provide a means for systematic analysis of the spatial and temporal functional architecture of the human brain.

Brain mapping consists of the characterization of local physiological changes in the brain associated with selective working of perceptual, motor, or cognitive systems. Brain mapping is causing a revolution in the fields of psychology and neuropsychology that is no less dramatic than that caused in neuropathology and neuroanatomy by structural scanning with CT or MRI.

8.2 Anatomical Studies

The anatomical arrangement of living human brain tissues can be reconstructed by capitalizing on their differential ability to attenuate x-rays directed through them (computerized tomography or CT scanning). Magnetic resonance imaging (MRI) can also be used to generate a variety of structural images of the brain without using ionizing radiation. The variety of information that can be obtained with MRI, the greater contrast between gray matter, white matter, and cerebrospinal fluid in MR as opposed to CT scans, and the lack of dependence on ionizing radiation, make this the method of choice for describing macroscopic human neuroanatomy.

8.3 Functional Studies

8.3.1 Positron Emission Tomography

Positron emission tomography (PET) is a very sensitive functional imaging method based on the detection of trace quantities of ionizing radiation. Positron emitting isotopes are used to tag trace amounts of substances of biological interest. The regional distribution of radioactivity recorded by scanning from the brain after tracer administration gives information about the functional variable being traced. In the instance of functional activation studies, the variable of interest is perfusion, where *perfusion* is defined as nutrient-tissue blood flow, and the most common tracer used is water, which is most conveniently tagged with positron-emitting oxygen-15 (^{15}O). Oxygen-15 has a short half-life of 2.1 min and with modern equipment can be used to scan the whole brain of a subject a dozen or more times in one scanning session, with safe and acceptable radiation exposure (Frackowiak et al. 1997).

The temporal and spatial resolution of functional images obtained with PET are both limited. Integration of signals over tens of seconds is necessary to generate images with an optimal spatial resolution of approximately $3 \times 3 \times 3$ mm. Practically, the resolution is often worse (typically a sphere with diameter 8–16 mm). Discrimination of much closer foci of functional activation is achieved by recording multiple scans under different scanning conditions. There are also methods for mapping the distribution of random, short-lived (1 sec or less) brain events. However, even in ideal circumstances, events with transient, millisecond-range time constants cannot be demonstrated with PET.

8.3.2 Functional Magnetic Resonance Imaging

Functional MRI (fMRI) is an adaptation of MRI that records changes in successive images that are related to tissue function. It depends on special MRI scanner hardware configurations, appropriate magnet characteristics, and choice of data acquisition and reconstruction parameters. There are a number of methods of scanning, often designated by acronyms, the more important of which are described in the following paragraphs.

fMRI can be performed with intravascular injections of contrast material (Belliveau et al. 1991). The attraction of the method is that it is based on well established physiological principles. Nondiffusible injected contrast material traverses the vessels of the brain, resulting in a signal determined by local blood volume. Changes in relative blood volume occur and can be monitored during cerebral activation. The method is currently limited by the load of intravenous contrast material that can be safely administered to a human subject, and by the speed with which it is cleared from the bloodstream. A new method for labeling inflowing blood magnetically, eschewing the need for contrast material, renders this technique totally noninvasive (EPISTAR). A disadvantage of EPISTAR is that, at present, a single or at most a few slices of the brain can be imaged at a time, necessitating a priori selection of areas to study (Edelman et al. 1994).

Another totally noninvasive fMRI method that is brain oxygen–level dependent—the BOLD method—produces images that reflect changes in a number of activity-dependent variables that alter the local magnetic properties of brain tissue and hence produce recordable signals (Ogawa et al. 1990; Kwong et al. 1992). These variables include local changes of blood volume, perfusion, and the amounts of oxyhemoglobin and hemoglobin in the draining blood. Equivalent brain activity tends to produce smaller changes in image intensity with BOLD fMRI than with PET, but with better signal-to-noise characteristics.

BOLD fMRI scanning can be done with very fast image acquisition (50 msec a slice with a recovery time in that slice of about 700 msec before another image can be recorded from it) called *echoplanar imaging* or EPI (Schmitt, Stehling, and Turner 1998). Changes in a behavioral or physiological state induced during scanning can be conveniently yoked to changes in image signal by repeated, fast imaging of the whole brain in sequentially acquired slices. Unfortunately, the BOLD signal has a long half-life of several seconds. It is this fact, rather than the rapidity with which scans can be recorded, that limits the temporal resolution of the method. A technique for recording event-related images has been developed that depends on characterizing the evoked hemodynamic response function (HRF). The method is formally analogous to event-related potential recordings from the brain, except that a long interval must elapse between repetitions of stimuli to prevent contamination between HRFs from successive stimuli (Josephs, Turner, and Friston 1997). Outstanding issues limiting the usefulness of fMRI include artifacts in brain regions, such as the inferior frontal cortex, that lie close to bone-air interfaces, and movement-related image distortions that are difficult to avoid in ill patients.

8.4 Mapping Transient Cerebral Events

Mapping and analysis of short time-course brain events and of short time-constant temporospatial correlations of activity in different cerebral regions requires techniques such as magnetoencephalography (MEG) and electroencephalography (EEG), both of which record and can be used to map spontaneous brain activity (Hari 1996; Rugg and Coles 1995). The sampling of brain activity by these methods is limited physically by the number of electrodes that can be attached to the scalp or magnetic sensors that can be arranged around the head. This undersampling contributes to the so-called inverse problem, which means that it is mathematically impossible to find a single and unique solution for the number and sites of origin of active brain areas responsible for any pattern of electrical activity recorded from the scalp (Scherg and Von Cramon 1986). Information from other areas of neuroscience may make one solution more biologically plausible than others, though this is by no means guaranteed. It is compounded in MEG by the fact that signals are only detected from cortex that lies perpendicular to the scalp surface. EEG signals, on the other hand, suffer from dispersion and attenuation by the scalp and skull, so that the cortex lying closest to the skull contributes most to the recordings. Brain activity is recorded with difficulty from deep structures with either method.

One way of increasing the significance of detected electrical activity is provided by event-related potential (ERP) mapping (Rugg and Coles 1995). A cognitive or physiological task of interest is repeated, and recording of evoked activity is time-locked to the stimulus or response in some defined way. The records are averaged to maximize relevant signal relative to underlying measurement noise and then mapped. Only recently has the prospect been explored of constraining the localization of sources of electrical or magnetic activity by spatially more accurate functional techniques, such as PET or fMRI.

8.4.1 What Is Being Mapped?

In a series of experiments on the rat sensory system and with pharmacological manipulation of the hypothalamopituitary axis, Sokoloff and his group have shown that local synaptic activity is reflected by local glucose consumption (Sokoloff 1984). Activity-dependent glucose uptake is therefore localized at the projection sites of activated neurons rather than in the vicinity of their cell bodies. It is not absolutely clear what the coupling mechanisms are, nor what is the contribution, if any, of local glial metabolism to the changes of glucose uptake associated with synaptic activity. The mathematical relationship between metabolism and the number of impulses crossing a synapse is also unknown.

Energy is consumed by the activity of both excitatory and inhibitory synapses. Electrophysiological excitation and inhibition should not be confused with cerebral activation and deactivation defined by changes in cerebral energy metabolism. An inhibitory synapse will consume energy (activation), but will also lead to inhibition of activity in target neurons, which will, therefore, show reduced synaptic activity at their projection site. A local area of brain may contain afferent excitatory synapses from distant sites, as well as populations of inhibitory and excitatory local interneurons. The resultant local change of energy metabolism is a sum of the activity in all these synaptic populations. The changes of local energy metabolism recorded noninvasively are therefore complex and represent the net synaptic activity at a site in the brain.

8.4.2 Sensory Maps

Our sensory world is dependent on sensory signals that are mapped onto the primary sensory areas of the brain. A noninvasive description of these maps and of the early stages of sensory processing in the human brain has been directed by knowledge obtained in the monkey and by observations in brain-damaged humans. The visual system has been extensively studied by functional neuroimaging and will be used here to illustrate principles underlying investigation of sensory processing.

A categorical comparison of the distribution of brain activity during passive exposure to a visual stimulus and a control state provides an example of the simplest type of experimental design (Zeki et al. 1991). In the case of early sensory processing this approach is relatively free of assumptions; with more complex cognitive functions a simple categorical approach is prone to errors of interpretation, as will be discussed later.

8.4.3 Visual Maps

In the human visual system, the retinotopic organization of the primary visual cortex (V1) has been confirmed with functional imaging by scanning during stimulation at various eccentricities from the fixation point (Fox et al. 1987). The results confirm the well-known representation of a quadrantic visual field in the opposite hemisphere and quadrant of the calcarine cortex. Foveal fixation is represented at the occipital pole, often spreading onto the lateral cortex. Peripheral vision is represented more rostrally in the calcarine cortex. Relatively new computerized methods that render the cortex as a flattened map facilitate calculation of retinal distances that subtend different angles in visual space (magnification factors).

The human prestriate occipital cortex contains area V5, associated with human visual motion perception (Watson et al. 1993). Activity in V5, on the lateral surface of the brain, is augmented by attentional mechanisms and can be partially attenuated by divided attention tasks. Attention alters the V5 response to any moving stimulus. Accurate coregistration of functional images with anatomical MRI scans shows that the position of V5 is quite variable among normal individuals, reflecting the variable anatomy of the occipital pole in the normal human population. However, there is a constant relationship of V5 to two human sulci, the ascending limb of the inferior temporal sulcus and the inferior occipital sulcus. This finding establishes an invariant principle about the structural and functional organization of this part of the human brain (Watson et al. 1993).

Human color perception, in the sense of perceiving an object as being the same color whatever the ambient light, is associated with activation of the fusiform and adjacent parts of the lingual gyri (Lueck et al. 1989). The human occipital visual cortex is therefore divided into functionally specialized regions. There is a precise correlation of the position of V4 with the position of lesions that lead to the syndrome of achromatopsia. There is also a description in the clinical literature of a patient with lesions to both occipitotemporal convexities encompassing area V5 and a grossly disturbed perception of visual movement, rendering her dyskinetopsic (Shipp et al. 1994).

Another approach to functional mapping of the early visual areas is by using retinotopically organized stimuli and capitalizing on the fact that borders between functional areas can be discriminated by the sequential representations of vertical and horizontal visual meridians (Tootell et al. 1996). This approach has been especially successful using fMRI and computerized brain-flattening techniques. The position of human area V3 has also been defined by meridian experiments (Shipp et al. 1995). Functional and retinotopic stimuli give very similar results about the visual cortex, even if sometimes confusions of nomenclature are introduced as a result of using the different approaches (Hadjikhani et al. 1998; Zeki et al. 1998). Much remains to be done in mapping the human visual extrastriate cortex. For example, areas as yet unmapped require functional attribution, and evolutionary developments in the organization of the human, compared to the monkey, visual cortex need investigation.

The role of the extrastriate areas can also be examined in patients with lesions to the visual system. There are minor visual pathways, in comparison to the optic radiation, that reach extrastriate areas directly from the retina, bypassing the primary visual cortex. Activity in V5 without activation of V1 has been shown in a patient with total destruction of the primary visual cortex documented by anatomical MRI and a dense hemianopia (Barbur et al. 1993). The patient is sufficiently aware of residual but degraded motion vision in his otherwise blind hemifield to be able, when tested, to describe its direction and presence verbally, without error. This observation leads to the first and rather interesting conclusion that in humans, functionally relevant visual signals reach the specialized extrastriate cortex directly and presumably, therefore, may modulate activity reaching V5 by the classical route through V1. Second, the perception of visual motion (albeit a degraded form of perception) is, at least in part, a property of activity in a specialized area alone, divorced from other, earlier components of the visual processing pathways. There is an added implication that signals from V5 can, in these abnormal circumstances, be propagated to and "inform" function in extravisual areas of the brain, such as those associated with language.

Processing of visual signals beyond the extrastriate cortex has been explored in humans in terms of pathways, anatomically defined in nonhuman primates, that are thought to deal with recognition of object position or with knowledge of its identity (Haxby et al. 1994). Such ideas have echos in the human neurological syndromes of simultagnosia (part of Balint's syndrome) and visual object agnosia found in stroke patients with lesions to posterior parietal and posterior temporal regions respectively. A third pathway, associated with visual object-guided action, has been demonstrated in humans with tasks involving reaching for and drawing of objects in different positions of space. These activities result in activation of the ventral posterior parietal lobes. The definition of further specializations is more than probable in the human brain, in which integration of visual signals with various aspects of behavior occurs at multiple anatomical levels (Zeki 1993). Each specialized area has reciprocal connections with other multiply dispersed areas and draws on signals from these areas as the behavioral contingencies demand.

8.4.4 Motor Maps

Mapping of simple movements about joints has confirmed a degree of somatotopic organization in humans, with sites of maximal activation lying along the motor strip in a pattern illustrated by Penfield's homunculus (Colebatch et al. 1991). The activated areas tend to overlap in extent, but the centers of mass of the activations are clearly separated along the central sulcus. Somatotopy, with the arm represented in a dorsoventral axis and the shoulder lying ventralmost, is also present in supplementary motor areas on the mesial surface of the cortex.

Multiple motor representations can be demonstrated in the human brain by selection of appropriate behavioral conditions during scanning (Fink et al. 1997). Activations have been found at sites in the insula, in the ventral and dorsal premotor cortex, in the primary motor and sensory cortices, in the rostralmost parts of the dorsolateral parietal cortex, and in at least three sites on the mesial cortex in the anterior and posterior SMA and in the dorsal and ventral cingulate cortex. There is preliminary evidence that some if not all of these areas are somatotopically organized into maps, with separate peaks in each activation cluster for movements of different body parts. This finding has implications with respect to any potential for reorganization and restitution of lost function that might follow brain injury.

Extensive activation of motor-related areas is found when self-selected actions are made, without instruction or spatial constraint. In addition to the motor areas already described, there is activation of both dorsolateral prefrontal cortices, areas of the mesial frontal cortex extending down to the level of the genu of the corpus callosum and into the frontal pole, and areas of the lateral and mesial parietal cortex including inferior as well as superior parietal lobules (Deiber et al. 1991). Activations of the basal structures, especially putamen and thalamus, are most evident when movements are self-paced or when a constant rather than a phasic force is exerted, or when a stimulus-response association is made or accessed (Dettmers et al. 1996). There are also major activations of the cerebellar hemisphere ipsilateral to a moving limb and of the cerebellar vermis.

8.5 Motor Imagery

Imagining a movement can help improve performance, a fact well known by musicians and athletes and sometimes used by physiotherapists. Cerebral activity associated with imagined actions surrounds areas that are associated solely with motor execution. Making a movement activates motor imagery areas and additional regions associated specifically with movement execution (Stephan et al. 1995). There is functional specialization in component areas of this widespread motor system. The posterior supplementary motor area (pSMA) can be subdivided functionally into distinct rostral and caudal parts. The rostral pSMA is activated with imagined movement, and the more caudoventral pSMA is additionally activated by movement execution. The cingulate functions in a similar rostrocaudally distributed manner. These facts suggest a possible anatomical and functional basis for disorders of the conceptualization of action (apraxias).

Preparing to make a movement or attending to automated movements produces prominent activations in the dorsolateral prefrontal cortex, anterior SMA, and anterior cingulate cortex (Jueptner, Frith, et al. 1997; Jueptner, Stephan, et al. 1997). The role of the prefrontal cortex in the initiation and selection of movements is substantial. Controversy exists about the nature of this contribution, especially in view of data suggesting a role for the same area in working memory. Loading short-term memory beyond the span of working memory activates DLPFC. Intrinsically generated compared to extrinsically specified movements specifically activate DLPFC and the anterior cingulate cortex. There are failures of activation of the cingulate cortex and DLPFC in diseases characterized by poverty of spontaneous action such as Parkinson's disease and depression with motor retardation. These abnormalities can be reversed, with amelioration of symptoms, by dopaminergic drugs (Jenkins et al. 1992).

8.6 Integrating Intention and Action

Extrinsically specified movements are accompanied by significantly greater activation of the motor cortex than those that are intrinsically generated. The same applies to extrinsically specified and internally generated word lists when language tasks are examined (Frith et al. 1991). DLPFC is activated in the left, language-dominant hemisphere by internally generated language tasks, and this activation is accompanied by significant deactivation of the superior temporal cortex, including primary auditory and auditory association areas. In an extrinsically specified task there is prominent activation of the same temporal regions. These observations suggest an interaction between DLPFC, which initiates a movement or a verbal response, and the relevant modality-specific cortex that executes it. It also indicates a difference in cortical activity between actions that are internally generated and those that are responses to stimuli in the environment. Such distinctions may be relevant to diseases that include among possible symptoms a misattribution of actions or thoughts —for example, feelings of alien control in schizophrenia, the alien-hand syndrome of corticobasal degeneration, and delusions in states of impaired awareness. In general, multiple scans recorded in time under different but related task conditions are required for investigation of spatiotemporal correlations of cognitively associated brain activity. Grave neurological disorders such as schizophrenia that have few if any associated structural abnormalities detectable in life may well turn out to be functional disorders in the sense that they turn out to be due to abnormalities of cortical connectivity (Dolan et al. 1995).

8.7 Changes in Brain Activity Associated with Task Difficulty

Graded cognitive tasks are often associated with graded responses. Parametric scanning depends on recording task parameters and correlating them with scan data, thus identifying regions in which the magnitude of activation is a function of task. Task difficulty may itself be varied. For example, activity in the visual cortex increases with rising flash frequency, reaches a maximum, then falls off at frequencies that become difficult to discriminate perceptually (Fox and Raichle 1985). The perception of pitch can be tested with pure tones of different frequency, and the resulting activations form a tonotopic map in the transverse temporal gyrus (Hari 1996).

At a more cognitive level, activity increases linearly with the number of words heard per unit time in the primary auditory cortex, to which the auditory apparatus projects (Price et al. 1992). The posterior temporal (Wernicke's) area, to which the auditory cortex projects, shows a different response with such stimuli. Activation is found as soon as words are heard, but no further change in local brain activity occurs across a range of word frequencies. The conversion of a time-dependent response in the primary auditory cortex to one in which activity is invariant at different word presentation rates suggests a possible mechanism for integration of frequency-determined neural activity into a form that signals phonological identity. Breakdown of this system may be a basis for the expressive aphasia encountered with damage to Wernicke's area.

Similarly, activity in the primary motor cortex and associated regions of the "executive" motor system increases exponentially with rate of repetitive movement or amount of constant force exerted (Dettmers et al. 1995). There are no such exponential changes in other motor-related areas associated with the initiation or sequencing of movements.

8.8 Are Cognitive Processes Independent?

A direct comparison of brain scans in different behavioral states is not always appropriate for the study of cognition because such a strategy assumes that interactions between brain areas and activity in them can be regarded as additive (or subtractive). Simple sensory stimulation is often associated with correlated activity in the primary sensory areas of the brain. Such correlations between activity and strength of stimulation are often linear. However, when sensory signals are distributed among brain areas for the purposes of generating or modifying behavior, the evoked activations are rarely simply correlated with the amount of sensory input (Friston et al. 1996). There are two principal reasons. Sensory signals may drive activity of a region (bottom-up activation). On the other hand the response to a volley of sensory signals in a brain region may be altered by modulatory influences from other brain areas (Frackowiak et al. 1997; Friston et al. 1997). These areas may be setting a behavioral context, mediating the degree of attention, or reflecting how well a behavior has been learned. Such context-modifying signals will interact with the sensory volley in a nonlinear manner. We have developed methods of image analysis that take into account these complex, higher-order interactions between brain regions. They search for nonlinear responses and context-sensitive modulation of activity in brain regions. These methods have suggested ways of examining the cerebral basis of attention, expectation, and the like and how these functions exert their modifying effects on behavior.

Certain brain processes can be activated by tasks despite the absence of explicit instructions designed to engage them. When subjects are explicitly asked to read and to attend to the orthographic features of words rather than to their meaning, the whole language network comprising a large number of anterior and posterior brain regions is activated. Many of these regions are known, from other studies, to activate with a variety of language-related functions, including the appreciation of meaning. Such obligatory activation, in the absence of explicit instruction or conscious effort, also questions an approach to functional brain imaging that depends solely on a categorical comparison of scans in different behavioral states (Price, Wise, and Frackowiak 1996).

Many functional neuroimaging experiments depend on self-reporting by subjects. This fact is sometimes used to suggest that the data thus obtained are "soft." Introspection and the reporting of observations or actions is an intimate part of everyday existence, even in the sphere of science. Introspection has been used to investigate human brain functions with the clinicopathological lesion method for over a century. The repeated demonstration of consistent patterns of brain activation during specified mental activity provides objective measurements that are difficult to refute. Such measurements bring the investigation of thought, consciousness, emotion, and similar brain functions into the realm of "hard" scientific inquiry.

8.9 Attention Results in Altered Patterns of Neuronal Activation

Behaviorally, repetitive task performance results in habituation and adaptation effects. The physiological correlates of such general psychological mechanisms are interesting in relation to attention. For example, in a task consisting of verb generation to target nouns, responses to novel categories of target produce activation in a distributed network that includes the prefrontal cortex and a number of other language-related areas. If such a task is repeated until the responses are overlearned, the pattern of activation is attenuated and resembles that obtained with the simple repetition of words (Raichle et al. 1994). This result indicates that response selection has become automatic—that is, the subject no longer has to attend to what he or she is doing. Introduction of new noun targets leads to a return to the original pattern of activation, concomittant with the reengagement of attentional mechanisms.

Motor skill learning can be measured during repetitive performance of a manual dexterity task. One such task involves following a rapidly rotating target with a handheld stylus (Grafton et al. 1992). Measures of accuracy at different speeds can be recorded, and improved performance manifests itself as greater accuracy and longer time on target. Such improvement correlates with increased activity in the primary and supplementary motor cortices. Activation of the brain during performance of such tasks can be modified for two reasons. First, improved performance will result in greater motor activity due simply to improved performance. Second, modifications of activity may occur due to the acquisition of a new motor skill (or memory of a motor action). A proper interpretation of the imaging result therefore depends on a realization that performance and skillfulness are separate, but confoundable, attributes of a motor act. When a motor task is performed repeatedly to the same performance criterion, eliminating any performance confound, then progressive attenuation of activity in the premotor cortex and cerebellum occurs as the task becomes automatic (Friston et al. 1992).

When scanning is performed during learning of a novel sequence of key presses (such as in learning a piano piece) with error feedback via an auditory signal, greater activation occurs in the right premotor area during naive, attentive performance than when the sequence has been overlearned (Jueptner, Stephan, et al. 1997). Conversely, activity in the supplementary motor cortex is greater in the automatic than in a naive state. The visual and language-associated cortices show less activity than usual in the naive learning condition that engages attention than when the task is overlearned. When a task is novel and requires considerable attentional resources, there appear to be mechanisms for large-scale deactivation of perceptual systems that are not engaged by the task. When a task becomes overlearned, attentional needs decline and activity in nonengaged sensory areas returns to normal relative to activity in the remainder of the brain.

Paying attention to stimuli is a general psychological mechanism that generates different patterns of activity depending on which attentional process is engaged. Selective sensory attention results in augmentation of activity in specialized, modality-specific areas relevant to the percept to which attention is directed (Corbetta et al. 1991). This mechanism was discovered in experiments on the visual system. A divided attention task involving categorization of colored ellipses of different orientations presented at various rates has been used to identify areas in which activity is dependent on the amount of attention required. Difficult compared to easy categorization tasks activate frontal regions. Selective attention to object attributes of increasing difficulty results in two types of modulation of activation in the inferior temporal cortex. The relationship between task difficulty and activity changes so that there is greater activation for equivalent rates of visual object presentation when attention is engaged. The source of this modification of the stimulus-response relationship appears to be in the frontal cortex because activity here is entirely independent of object attributes (Rees, Frackowiak, and Frith 1997). It only depends on the engagement of attention, whatever the task difficulty. In addition, a change in the baseline, unstimulated activity occurs in the same inferior temporal cortex when the visual task generates an expectation of increased attentional requirements. These two mechanisms can be considered analogous to changes in gain in the object-recognition system or to changes in its offset. This example shows that brain mapping presently has the ability to provide information about integrative brain mechanisms in addition to data localizing brain activity to functionally specialized areas.

8.10 Synthesis and Conclusions

The field of functional brain mapping is in a state of rapid technical development. New methods are being added to those already available for gathering data about the human brain noninvasively. The data derived from the different mapping modalities are often complementary, but there is much to be done to exploit the differential strengths of these methods (ffytche et al. 1995). Advances in electrophysiology promise a much-needed improvement in temporal resolution. Uniquely human complex brain functions require functional assignment to distributed networks of brain areas. Cognitive processes require definition in physiological and anatomical terms. Measurement of the strength of functional connection between large populations of neurons in brain areas should help establish quantitative relationships and principles of brain function. In turn, these interregional relationships may be amenable to investigation using simultaneous multiple-electrode recordings from a number of distributed brain areas in nonhuman primates. The hope is that judicious and hypothesis-led use of the panoply of available methods will bridge the gap of understanding between molecular and synaptic neural mechanisms and the integration of these mechanisms into large-scale functional brain systems.

Note

The author is supported by the Wellcome Trust as a Principal Research Fellow.

References

Anderson, T. J., I. H. Jenkins, D. J. Brooks, M. Hawken, R. S. J. Frackowiak, and C. Kennard. 1994. Cortical control of saccades and fixation in man: A PET study. *Brain* 117:1073–1084.

Barbur, J. L., J. D. G. Watson, R. S. J. Frackowiak, and S. Zeki. 1993. Conscious visual perception without V1. *Brain* 116:1293–1302.

Belliveau, J. W., D. N. Kennedy, R. C. McKinstry, B. R. Buchbinder, R. M. Weisskoff, M. S. Cohen, J. M. Vevea, T. J. Brady, and B. R. Rosen. 1991. Functional mapping of the human visual cortex using magnetic resonance imaging. *Science* 254:716–719.

Chollet, F., V. DiPiero, R. J. S. Wise, D. J. Brooks, R. J. Dolan, and R. S. J. Frackowiak. 1991. The functional anatomy of motor recovery after ischaemic stroke in man. *Annals of Neurology* 29:63–71.

Colebatch, J. G., M. P. Deiber, R. E. Passingham, K. J. Friston, and R. S. J. Frackowiak. 1991. Regional cerebral blood flow during voluntary arm and hand movements in human subjects. *Journal of Neurophysiology* 65:1392–1401.

Corbetta, M., F. M. Miezin, S. Dobmeyer, G. L. Shulman, and S. E. Petersen. 1991. Selective and divided attention during visual discriminations of shape, color, and speed: Functional anatomy by positron emission tomography. *Joural of Neuroscience* 11:2383–2402.

Deiber, M. P., R. E. Passingham, J. G. Colebatch, K. J. Friston, P. D. Nixon, and R. S. J. Frackowiak. 1991. Cortical areas and the selection of movement: A study with PET. *Experimental Brain Research* 84:392–402.

Dettmers, C., G. R. Fink, R. N. Lemon, K. M. Stephan, R. E. Passingham, D. Silbersweig, A. Holmes, M. C. Ridding, D. J. Brooks, and R. S. J. Frackowiak. 1995. Relation between cerebral activity and force in the motor areas of the human brain. *Journal of Neurophysiology* 74:802–815.

Dettmers, C., R. N. Lemon, K. M. Stephan, G. R. Fink, and R. S. J. Frackowiak. 1996. Cerebral activation during the exertion of sustained static force in man. *NeuroReport* 7:2103–2110.

Dolan, R. J., P. Fletcher, C. D. Frith, K. J. Friston, R. S. J. Frackowiak, and P. M. Grasby. 1995. Dopaminergic modulation of impaired cognitive activation in the anterior cingulate cortex in schizophrenia. *Nature* 378:180–182.

Edelman, R. R., B. Siewert, D. G. Darby, V. Thangaraj, A. C. Nobre, M. M. Mesulam, and S. Warach. 1994. Qualitative mapping of cerebral blood flow and functional localization with echo-planar MR imaging and signal targetting with alternating radio-frequency. *Radiology* 192:513–520.

ffytche, D. H., C. Guy, and S. Zeki. 1995. The parallel visual motion inputs into areas V1 and V5 of human cerebral cortex. *Brain* 118:1375–1394.

Fink, G. R., R. S. J. Frackowiak, U. Pietrzyk, and R. E. Passingham. 1997. Multiple non-primary motor areas in the human cortex. *Journal of Neurophysiology* 77:2164–2174.

Fox, P. T., F. M. Miezin, J. M. Allman, D. E. Van Essen, and M. E. Raichle. 1987. Retinotopic organisation of human visual cortex mapped with positron emission tomography. *Journal of Neuroscience* 7:913–922.

Fox, P. T., and M. E. Raichle. 1985. Stimulus rate determines regional brain blood flow in striate cortex. *Annals of Neurology* 17:303–305.

Frackowiak, R. S. J., K. J. Friston, C. D. Frith, R. J. Dolan, and J. C. Mazziotta. 1997. *Human brain function*. San Diego: Academic Press.

Friston, K. J., C. Buechel, G. R. Fink, J. Morris, E. Rolls, and R. J. Dolan. 1997. Psychophysiological and modulatory interactions in neuroimaging. *NeuroImage* 6:218–229.

Friston, K. J., C. D. Frith, R. D. Passingham, P. F. Liddle, and R. S. J. Frackowiak. 1992. Motor practice and neurophysiological adaptation in the cerebellum: A PET study. *Proceedings of the Royal Society of London: Biological Sciences* 243:223–228.

Friston, K. J., C. J. Price, P. Fletcher, C. Moore, R. S. J. Frackowiak, and R. J. Dolan. 1996. The trouble with cognitive subtraction. *NeuroImage* 4:97–104.

Frith, C. D., K. J. Friston, P. F. Liddle, and R. S. J. Frackowiak. 1991. Willed action and the prefrontal cortex in man. *Proceedings of the Royal Society of London: Biological Sciences* 244:241–246.

Grafton, S., J. C. Mazziotta, S. Presty, K. J. Friston, R. S. J. Frackowiak, and M. E. Phelps. 1992. Functional anatomy of human procedural learning determined with regional cerebral blood flow and PET. *Journal of Neuroscience* 12:2542–2548.

Hadjikhani, N., A. K. Liu, A. M. Dale, P. Cavanagh, and R. B. H. Tootell. 1998. Retinotopy and colour sensitivity in human visual cortical area V8. *Nature Neuroscience* 1:235–241.

Hari, R. 1996. MEG in the study of human cortical functions. *Electroencephalography and Clinical Neurophysiology* (Suppl.) 47:47–54.

Haxby, J. V., B. Horwitz, L. G. Ungerleider, J. M. Maisog, P. Pietrini, and C. L. Grady. 1994. The functional organisation of human extrastriate cortex: A PET rCBF study of selective attention to faces and locations. *Journal of Neuroscience* 14:6336–6353.

Jenkins, I. H., W. Fernandez, E. D. Playford, A. J. Lees, R. S. J. Frackowiak, R. E. Passingham, and D. J. Brooks. 1992. Impaired activation of the supplementary motor area in Parkinson's disease is reversed when akinesia is treated with apomorphine. *Annals of Neurology* 32:749–757.

Josephs, O., R. Turner, and K. Friston. 1997. Event related fMRI. *Human Brain Mapping* 5:243–248.

Jueptner, M., C. D. Frith, D. J. Brooks, R. S. J. Frackowiak, and R. E. Passingham. 1997. Anatomy of motor learning, 2: Subcortical structures and learning by trial and error. *Journal of Neurophysiology* 77:1325–1337.

Jueptner, M., K. M. Stephan, C. D. Frith, D. J. Brooks, R. S. J. Frackowiak, and R. E. Passingham. 1997. Anatomy of motor learning, 1: Frontal cortex and attention to action. *Journal of Neurophysiology* 77:1313–1324.

Kwong, K. K., J. W. Belliveau, D. A. Chesler, I. E. Goldberg, R. M. Weisskoff, B. P. Poncelet, D. N. Kennedy, B. E. Hoppel, M. S. Cohen, R. Turner, H. Cheng, T. J. Brady, and B. R. Rosen. 1992. Dynamic magnetic resonance imaging of human brain activity during primary sensory stimulation. *Proceedings of the National Academy of Sciences of the USA* 89:5675–5679.

Lueck, C. J., S. Zeki, K. J. Friston, M. P. Deiber, P. Cope, V. J. Cunningham, A. A. Lammertsma, C. Kennard, and R. S. J. Frackowiak. 1989. The colour centre in the cerebral cortex of man. *Nature* 340:386–389.

Ogawa, S., T. M. Lee, A. R. Kay, and D. W. Tank. 1990. Brain magnetic resonance imaging with contrast dependent on blood oxygenation. *Proceedings of the National Academy of Sciences of the USA* 87:9868–9872.

Price, C., R. J. S. Wise, and R. S. J. Frackowiak. 1996. Demonstration of implicit processing of visually presented words and pseudowords. *Cerebral Cortex* 6:62–70.

Price, C., R. J. S. Wise, S. Ramsay, K. J. Friston, D. Howard, K. Patterson, and R. S. J. Frackowiak. 1992. Regional response differences within the human auditory cortex when listening to words. *Neuroscience Letters* 146:179–182.

Raichle, M. E., J. A. Fiez, T. O. Videen, A. K. MacLeod, J. V Pardo, P. T. Fox, and S. E. Petersen. 1994. Practice-related changes in human brain functional anatomy during non-motor learning. *Cerebral Cortex* 4:8–26.

Rees, G., R. S. J. Frackowiak, and C. D. Frith. 1997. Two modulatory effects of attention that mediate object categorization in human cortex. *Science* 275:835–838.

Rugg, M. D., and M. G. H. Coles. 1995. *Electrophysiology of mind: Event related brain potentials and cognition*. Oxford, England: Oxford University Press.

Scherg, M., and D. Von Cramon. 1986. Evoked dipole source potentials of the human auditory cortex. *Electroencephalography and Clinical Neurophysiology* 65:344–346.

Schmitt, F., M. K. Stehling, and R. Turner. 1998. *Echo-planar imaging: Theory, technique and application*. Berlin: Springer-Verlag.

Shipp, S., B. M. de Jong, J. Zihl, R. S. J. Frackowiak, and S. Zeki. 1994. The brain activity related to residual motion vision in a patient with bilateral lesions of V5. *Brain* 117:1023–1038.

Shipp, S., J. D. G. Watson, R. S. J. Frackowiak, and S. Zeki. 1995. Retinotopic maps in human prestriate visual cortex: The demarcation of areas V2 and V3. *NeuroImage* 2:125–132.

Sokoloff, L. 1984. *Metabolic probes of central nervous system activity in experimental animals and man*. Sunderland, Mass.: Sinauer Associates.

Stephan, K. M., G. R. Fink, R. E. Passingham, D. Silbersweig, A. Ceballos Baumann, C. D. Frith, and R. S. J. Frackowiak. 1995. Imagining the execution of movements: Functional anatomy of the mental representation of upper extremity movements in healthy subjects. *Journal of Neurophysiology* 73:373–386.

Toga, A. W., and J. C. Mazziotta. 1996. *Brain mapping: The methods*. San Diego: Academic Press.

Tootell, R. B., A. M. Dale, M. I. Sereno, and R. Malach. 1996. New images from human visual cortex. *Trends in Neurosciences* 19:481–489.

Watson, J. D. G., R. Myers, R. S. J. Frackowiak, J. V. Hajnal, R. P. Woods, J. C. Mazziotta, S. Shipp, and S. Zeki. 1993. Area V5 of the human brain: Evidence from a combined study using positron emission tomography and magnetic resonance imaging. *Cerebral Cortex* 3:79–94.

Zeki, S. 1993. A theory of multi-stage integration in the visual cortex. In *A vision of the brain*. Oxford, England: Blackwell Scientific.

Zeki, S., D. J. McKeefry, A. Bartels, and R. S. Frackowiak. 1998. Has a new colour area been discovered? *Nature Neuroscience* 1:335–336.

Zeki, S., D. J. McKeefry, A. Bartels, and R. S. J. Frackowiak. 1991. A direct demonstration of functional specialization in human visual cortex. *Journal of Neuroscience* 11:641–649.

Chapter 9

Central Control of Voluntary Movement as Studied by Multidisciplinary Noninvasive Approaches

Hiroshi Shibasaki

Self-initiated movements are commonly associated with increased activation in the contralateral primary sensorimotor area (M1-S1), the bilateral supplementary motor areas (SMAs), the contralateral basal ganglia, and the ipsilateral cerebellar hemisphere—activation revealed as an increase in the regional cerebral blood flow (rCBF) when studied by positron emission tomography (PET). Complex sequential movements show a greater activation especially in the SMAs and the ipsilateral M1-S1 compared with simple repetitive movements. The rCBF study by PET, however, does not provide precise temporal information with respect to the actual time of movement, but scalp-recorded electrical potentials (EEGs) averaged time-locked to the movement onset give supplementary information as to the timing in the order of milliseconds. The movement-related cortical potentials appear in SMAs and M1-S1 about 2 sec before the movement onset, first bilaterally and later more contralaterally with somatotopic organization. Magnetoencephalography (MEG) provides more accurate spatial information than EEG, but it can detect only the current flow tangentially oriented with respect to the head surface. The most recently developed technique of functional magnetic resonance imaging (fMRI) has much better temporal resolution than PET, although still in the order of seconds. Based on the results of studies of self-initiated movements using all these noninvasive techniques, it is suggested that the "will to move" might involve at least the mesial frontal lobes, including the rostral SMA and the conventional SMA (SMA proper).

Self-initiated termination of muscle contraction shows surprisingly similar results to self-initiated muscle contraction in terms of both the activated brain structures and their time evolution with respect to the movement. It is therefore postulated that the "will to stop movement" might involve the same cortical structures as the "will to move," although there might be differences at the neuronal level.

Movement involving the whole body, like walking, cannot be studied by PET, fMRI, or MEG, because the subject's head has to be fixed in these techniques. Single photon emission computed tomography (SPECT) in a split-dose method using a radiotracer of long half-life can be applied to this kind of study. In our study, gait was associated with increased rCBF in the bilateral SMAs, the part of M1-S1 corresponding to the lower limbs and trunk, the precuneus, and the cerebellum. In patients with Parkinson's disease, smaller activation was seen in the left SMA, left anterior cingulate gyrus, and cerebellar hemispheres as compared with age-matched controls. To elucidate the mechanism underlying the marked improvement of gait initiation by visual stimuli ("paradoxical" gait) in Parkinson patients, the effects of transverse versus parallel lines were compared. In both Parkinson and control groups, the posterior parietal cortex and cerebellar hemispheres showed greater activation with the transverse lines compared with the parallel lines. In the Parkinson group, the right lateral premotor cortex showed enhanced activation by the transverse lines to a significantly greater degree than in the control group, suggesting that the ventral premotor area, as a part of the central network engaged in the visuomotor control, plays an essential role in the paradoxical gait initiated by transverse lines.

Thus, the central control of voluntary movements in humans can be studied by using a multidisciplinary noninvasive approach, and it is extremely important to understand and make the best of the different characteristics of each technique, depending on the specific purpose of each study.

9.1 Use of a Multidisciplinary Noninvasive Approach for the Study of Human Brain Functions

The noninvasive techniques that have become available to study human brain functions are based on either electrophysiological or neuroimaging principles. Electrophysiological techniques include electroencephalography (EEG), magnetoencephalography (MEG), and transcranial magnetic stimulation (TMS). Neuroimaging techniques in the narrow sense consist of positron emission tomography (PET), single photon emission computed tomography (SPECT), and functional magnetic resonance imaging (fMRI). All these techniques have different characteristics, which need to be taken into account in order to answer questions about "where in the brain and when" the function of interest takes place. First of all, the electrophysiological techniques can study only cortical functions, and thus do not directly help in the study of subcortical functions such as those of the basal ganglia, cerebellum, and thalamus. Analysis of task-related EEG fields or task-related change of background activities provides us with the precise temporal information with respect to an event in the order of milliseconds, but spatial information is limited unless special source-localization techniques are adopted (for example, see Shindo et al., 1998). MEG, by contrast, can provide us with more accurate information both in time and space. The disadvantages of MEG, however, are its expense and its inability to record a current source that is radially oriented with respect to the head surface. Theoretically, MEG can only record current flow directed tangentially to the head surface, such as the one situated in the cortical sulcus, while EEG can record a mixture of radially and tangentially oriented current sources—although the former more than the latter. Cortical rhythms recorded by either EEG or MEG from multiple sites during certain tasks can be subjected to further analysis in order to study the functional coupling among different cortical areas (Gerloff, Richard, et al. 1998).

In TMS, a brief high-current pulse passed through a coil of wire induces a magnetic field, which then creates an electric current in the brain. Since this electric current transiently activates or reversibly inactivates the underlying neural structures, this technique has been applied to the study of various cortical functions and their plastic changes (Cohen et al. 1998). TMS is much less expensive than most other noninvasive techniques and is easy to use repeatedly both on normal subjects and on patients.

The biggest advantage of the neuroimaging techniques PET and fMRI is that they allow us to study the whole brain, including the deep subcortical structures such as the cerebellum, basal ganglia, and thalamus. PET usually utilizes O15-labeled water as a radiotracer for the activation studies, which has a half-life of about 2 min. The radiotracer is first injected intravenously, and during the following 1.5 to 2 min the brain's radioactivity is scanned by the PET camera while the subjects are performing the required tasks on the scanner bed. Although it gives relatively accurate spatial information, the resulting increase of regional cerebral blood flow (rCBF) is due to overall activation occurring throughout the scanning period, which provides very limited time information for the specific event. One of the disadvantages of PET is the limited number of sessions allowed for a particular experiment, to avoid excessive exposure of the subject to radioisotopes. Furthermore, it is usually necessary to calculate the functional areas common to all or the majority of the subjects studied by using, for example, statistical parametric mapping (SPM).

SPECT is much less expensive than PET, but since it uses a radiotracer of longer half-life, it is impossible to repeat the sessions or to do the control studies usually essential in this kind of research. However, Fukuyama et al. (1996, 1997) have taken advantage of the characteristics of SPECT to study the brain regions related to movements involving the whole body, such as walking and urination, as described later in this chapter.

At present fMRI is the technique most commonly used to study human brain functions. This technique is entirely noninvasive, so that it is possible to carry out as many sessions as required by an experiment, and it has a better time resolution than PET, although it is still limited to the order of seconds. Besides being able to study steady-state activation during a series of tasks, it is now possible to study the sequential activity changes time-locked to specific events (event-associated fMRI), as described later.

In this chapter, the central control mechanisms of voluntary movement will be discussed based on comparison of the results obtained by using these different noninvasive methods.

9.2 Where in the Brain, and When, Does the Will to Move Occur?

Voluntary movements are largely divided into two types: self-initiated movements and stimulus- or cue-triggered movements. When brain functions associated with self-initiated movements are studied by PET, using ^{15}O labeled water as a radiotracer, the obtained image is the result of overall activation occurring throughout the scanning time, usually 1.5 to 2 min. In our study, simple repetition of self-paced finger movements was associated with increased rCBF markedly in the contralateral sensorimotor cortex (M1-S1) with clear somatotopic organization, and moderately in supplementary motor areas (SMAs) as well as in the contralateral cingulate gyrus and putamen (Shibasaki et al. 1993). In complex sequential finger movements, in addition to activation in the above regions, rCBF was increased markedly in the SMAs and the contralateral premotor area, and moderately in the ipsilateral M1-S1 and cerebellum (Shibasaki et al. 1993). Comparison of the mean rCBF increase against the resting condition between the simple and complex movements revealed a greater increase during the complex task in the SMAs and the ipsilateral M1-S1. In support of this particular finding, the later component of the scalp-recorded, slow negative EEG shifts preceding voluntary movement (NS′) was larger in the sequential extension of the middle followed by index finger than in the simultaneous extension of those two fingers at the midline vertex and bilateral precentral regions. This result suggested the greater activation of SMAs and bilateral M1-S1 in the complex sequential movement than in the simple simultaneous movement (Kitamura et al. 1993). This is an example in which the neuroimaging and EEG data confirm one another in terms of spatial information, and in which the latter technique supplements the former in terms of temporal information.

Among the neuroimaging techniques in the narrow sense, fMRI provides us with the best temporal information. The movement-associated signal increase of fMRI was seen in SMAs starting several seconds before the actual muscle contraction (figure 9.1, plate 10) (Toma et al. 1999). It was followed by a similar signal increase in the hand area of the precentral gyrus (most likely the primary motor cortex or M1) contralateral to the moving hand, which started about 3 sec before the muscle contraction. In this kind of movement-associated fMRI study, the finger movement had to be carried out at an extremely slow pace—once every 30 sec or even more slowly. This is due to the fact that the hemodynamic change reflected as an fMRI signal change is supposed to peak at least several seconds after the corresponding event. Therefore, the remarkably early onset of the movement preparation, as

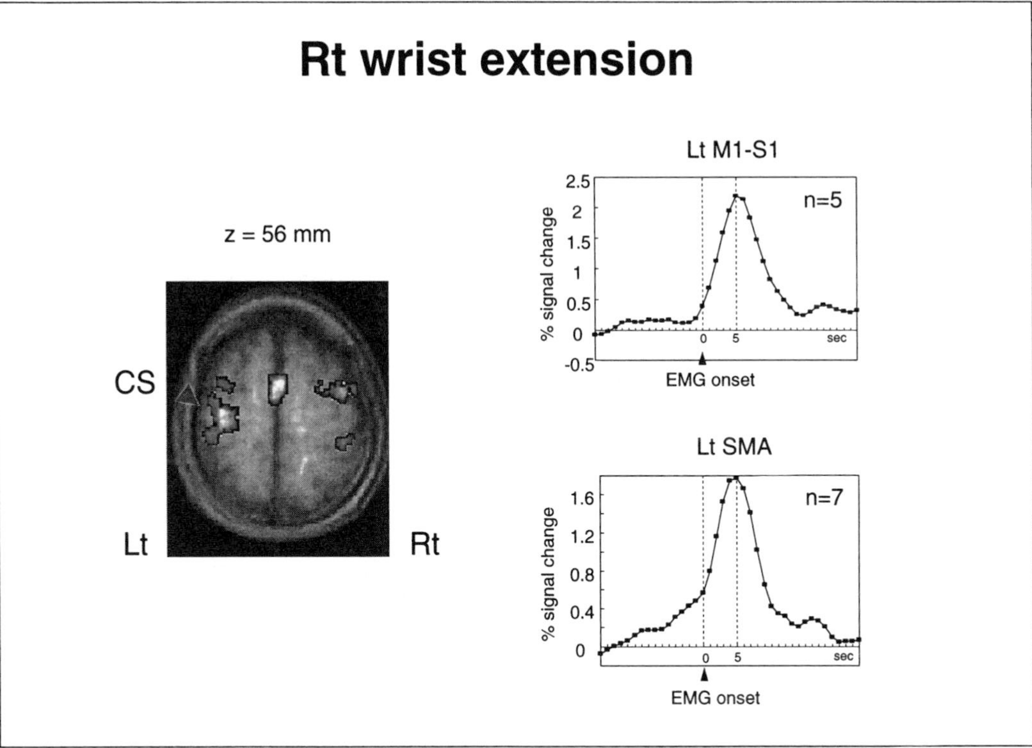

Figure 9.1
Activated areas (*left*) and the time course of their activation (*right*) with respect to self-initiated extension of the right wrist in the left primary sensorimotor area (Lt M1-S1, average of five trials) and the left supplementary motor area (Lt SMA, average of seven trials), studied by movement-associated fMRI in a single subject. The triangle in the left figure indicates the central sulcus (CS). The activity starts in SMAs earlier than in the contralateral M1-S1. (Studied by K. Toma, unpublished data.)

observed in the fMRI study, might be due to this extremely long intertrial interval. At any rate, this finding suggests that before the self-paced movement the SMAs are activated earlier than the M1.

EEG and MEG studies give us more accurate information on the time relationship between brain response and actual event or task as compared with neuroimaging studies. Self-initiated, simple finger movement is preceded by a surface-negative EEG potential shift starting about 2 sec before the movement onset. These premovement potentials can be recorded by back averaging the EEGs with respect to the movement onset, which is usually defined as the beginning of the electromyographic (EMG) discharge associated with the movement (Kornhuber and Deecke 1965). When those potentials are recorded from electrodes placed on the head surface, the initial slope (Bereitschaftspotential or readiness potential, BP) is maximal at the midline central area regardless of the site of movement, and symmetrically and widely distributed over the head (Kornhuber and Deecke 1965; Shibasaki et al. 1980; Shibasaki 1993). The later, steeper slope called *negative slope* (NS′) is maximal at the central region contralateral to the movement in case of hand movement and at the midline central region in case of foot movement (Shibasaki et al. 1980, 1981). These potentials can be recorded from subdural electrodes placed on the surface of the cerebral cortex while patients with medically intractable partial epilepsy are evaluated before surgical treatment to identify the precise epileptogenic focus and also the physiological functions of adjacent cortical areas. From such subdural electrodes, BP is recorded from the mesial aspect of frontal lobes and a restricted area of the lateral precentral gyrus (hand area of M1), both bilaterally but somatotopically corresponding to the site of movement (Neshige, Lüders, and Shibasaki 1988; Ikeda et al. 1992). NS′ is recorded also from bilateral mesial frontal lobes, much larger on the contralateral side, and from the somatotopically corresponding area of the contralateral M1.

In the human mesial frontal lobes, two distinct areas can be recognized based on the results of electric stimulation as well as recording of BP/NS′. One is the conventional SMAs or SMA proper that show somatotopic organization, though not as distinctly as M1. The other is a relatively small area located just rostral to the SMA proper (rostral SMA), which shows no somatotopy by either electric stimulation or recording of BP/NS' (Yazawa et al. 1998). These findings suggest that, at least in these three motor areas—rostral SMA, SMA proper, and M1—an excitatory postsynaptic potential (EPSP) increasingly occurs from 2 sec prior to the movement onset, first bilaterally and later mainly contralaterally, with somatotopic organization at least in the SMA proper and M1.

MEG has an advantage over EEG in spatial resolution because, unlike EEG, MEG is not influenced by differences in electric conductivity of structures surrounding the cerebral cortex, such as cerebrospinal fluid, the skull, and subcutaneous tissues. As described earlier, a big disadvantage of MEG is that it can record only the current flow that is oriented tangentially to the head surface, while EEG can record both radially and tangentially oriented current flow. This fact, however, means that, once a certain activity is recorded by MEG, it certainly reflects a sulcal activity arising from a tangentially oriented generator source. In fact, when premovement slow shifts are recorded by MEG, the magnetic field corresponding to BP appears much later than the electric field, and it is much more contralaterally predominant as compared with the BP (figure 9.2). These findings can be explained by postulating that in the early phase of the motor preparatory period, in addition to SMAs, the crown of the

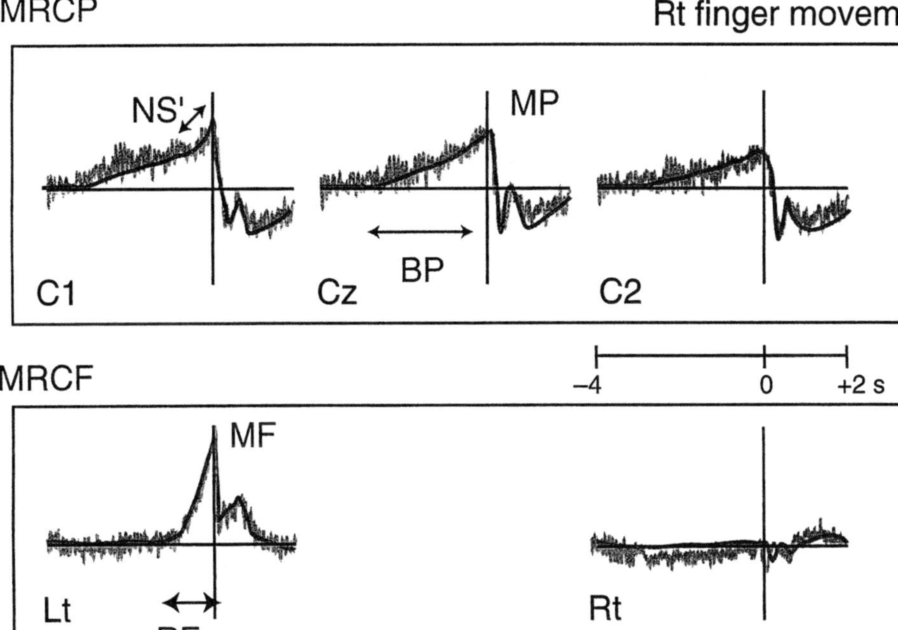

Figure 9.2
Movement-related cortical potentials (MRCP) and magnetic fields (MRCF) simultaneously recorded in a single subject. Self-paced right-finger movement. EEG (MRCP) starts earlier than MEG with bilaterally symmetric distribution at least initially, and MEG (MRCF) appears later in the premovement period with clear contralateral predominance. (Recorded by T. Nagamine.)

precentral gyrus is bilaterally activated, thus producing the midline maximum and bilaterally symmetric EEG potentials (MRCP). Later the anterior bank of the contralateral central sulcus becomes strongly active, joining the previously active areas and producing a mainly contralateral MEG field (MRCF).

Reduction in the amount of rhythmic cortical oscillations of certain frequency bands in association with certain events or tasks (called *event-related desynchronization* (Pfurtscheller 1988)) is known to reflect an aspect of neuronal activation in the underlying cortical area, and here again, MEG provides better materials for this analysis than EEG due to its higher spatial resolution. Localization of event-related desynchronization can be studied, for example, by rectifying the activities passed through a narrow bandpass filter and averaging the obtained data with respect to the task (temporal spectral evolution) (Salmelin and Hari 1994). In our study employing self-initiated finger movement, the task-related MEG desynchronization was seen in the hand areas of the bilateral, but more predominantly contralateral, precentral gyrus, starting 2–3 sec before the movement onset (Nagamine et al. 1996). By the currently available MEG recording, however, it is impossible to clearly identify the rhythmic activity generated from SMAs. This is most likely due to the relatively deep location of the SMAs with respect to the head surface.

In the experimental paradigms investigating motor control mechanisms, the repetition rate of movements is an important factor. Sadato et al. (1996) reported that the slower repetition rate of movement is associated with a greater rCBF increase in the SMAs than the faster rate is, with the opposite pattern being observed in M1-S1. For movement-related cortical EEG or MEG activities employing the fast repetition rate, the early component cannot be identified because of the short intertrial intervals, while only the activities immediately preceding or following each movement can be analyzed (Gerloff et al. 1997; Gerloff, Uenishi, et al. 1998). These steady-state movement-related magnetic fields allowed us to identify the activity immediately preceding the onset of finger movement occurring in the contralateral precentral gyrus and the activity immediately following it in the contralateral postcentral gyrus (Gerloff, Uenishi, et al. 1998).

The question as to "where in the brain and when the will to move occurs" has not been completely solved yet. However, all these noninvasive studies suggest that, among cortical structures, the nonprimary motor areas—especially the rostral SMA and the SMA proper—are the most likely site of motor initiation.

9.3 Where in the Brain, and When, Does the Will to Stop Movement Occur?

The existence of negative motor areas was suggested by clinical observation, such as spontaneous or stimulus-induced negative myoclonus of cortical origin (Shibasaki et al. 1994; Shibasaki 1995), and inhibition of movement by electric or magnetic stimulation of certain areas of the motor cortices (Lüders et al. 1995; Wassermann et al. 1993). Based on these findings, we investigated the cortical mechanism of voluntary muscle relaxation (termination of muscle contraction) by using various noninvasive methods, including the recording of BP/NS′ (Terada et al. 1995), analysis of magnetic fields as well as changes of the rhythmic MEG oscillations in association with the muscle relaxation, and the movement-associated fMRI (Toma et al. 1999). All these data showed an activation pattern quite similar in terms of both space and time to that observed in association with the ordinary movement caused by voluntary muscle contraction. It is therefore suggested that the "will to stop movement" might involve the same cortical structures as the "will to move," although the differences in the precise mechanisms at the neuronal level remain to be discovered.

9.4 Central Control of Gait and Its Abnormality in Parkinson's Disease

On clinical grounds, observation of various movement disorders often provides us with a clue to the understanding of mechanisms underlying the central motor control and its disorders in humans.

In a movie based on a novel by Oliver Sacks, a patient with Parkinsonism showed difficulty in moving his hands quickly by his own free will, but he could catch a ball in his hands when it was suddenly thrown to him. Moreover, patients with Parkinson's disease often find it difficult to walk on a flat floor, whereas they find it much easier to climb upstairs. In a hospital situation, if a line or a series of lines is shown transversely in front of such patients, they can easily start walking by stepping across the lines. These phenomena are called *kinésie paradoxale* or paradoxical movement, and suggest a strong influence of visual input on gait initiation. Several theories have been put forward to explain these phenomena. For example, Glickstein and Stein (1991) postulated that the pathways relaying visual stimuli may bypass the damaged basal ganglia and allow an intact cerebellar circuit to be used for visuomotor control, but the underlying mechanisms have remained unsolved.

Before addressing the question as to which structures in the brain are involved in the improvement of gait initiation by visual input, we first studied the possible mechanisms behind Parkinsonian patients' difficulty in initiating gait. Obviously a movement like gait cannot be investigated using PET, fMRI, or MEG, because it is essential to fix the subject's head in order to use these techniques. Therefore, we took advantage of SPECT to study whole-body movements like walking. After intravenous injection of 99mTc-labeled HMPAO, the subject walked on a floor for about 15 min and then lay down on the scanner bed for a 20-min measurement of rCBF. For a control condition, the subject stayed in the supine position on the bed for 30 min, and then a larger dose of the same radiotracer was administered, followed by a second scanning. This split-dose method allowed us to calculate the blood-flow increase due to walking as against the resting condition (Fukuyama et al. 1996, 1997).

By using the above technique, we compared the Parkinson's patients with age-matched healthy subjects as the control. In both groups, when the walking condition was compared with the rest condition, significant rCBF increases were observed in the bilateral SMAs, the part of M1-S1 corresponding to the lower extremities and trunk regions, precuneus, and cerebellum. In between-group analysis, the Parkinson's patients showed smaller rCBF increases in the left SMA, left anterior cingulate gyrus, and cerebellar hemispheres as compared with the control subjects (Hanakawa et al. 1999).

To elucidate the mechanism underlying the improvement of gait initiation by visual stimulus in Parkinson's patients, we compared the effects on the SPECT-rCBF of

Enhanced Activation in Parkinson
(Transverse vs Parallel Lines)

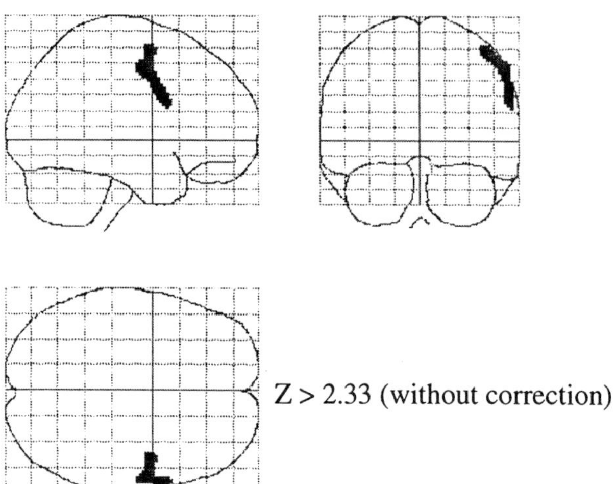

Figure 9.3
Enhanced activation in the right lateral premotor cortex by transverse lines in Parkinson's disease in SPECT-rCBF study. This area showed enhanced activation by showing the transversely oriented lines as against the parallel lines to a significantly greater extent in patients with Parkinson's disease as compared with age-matched control subjects. (Modified from Hanakawa et al. 1999.)

lines drawn transversely versus lines drawn parallel with respect to the direction of walking in the patients and age-matched controls. The subjects walked on a treadmill moving at a constant speed. Behaviorally, the cadence (the number of steps per minute) in the Parkinson's group significantly decreased (normalized) in the transversely placed line condition as compared with the parallel-line condition.

The areas showing larger increase of rCBF in the transversely placed line compared to the parallel-line condition included the posterior parietal cortex and cerebellar hemispheres in both Parkinson's patients and the control subjects. In the Parkinson group, the right lateral premotor cortex showed enhanced activation by the transverse lines to a significantly greater degree than in the control group (figure 9.3) (Hanakawa et al. 1999). In monkeys, the premotor cortex was shown to be important especially for visually guided movements (Mushiake, Inase, and Tanji 1991). Therefore, these findings suggest that the ventral premotor area, as a part of the central network engaged in the visuomotor control, plays an essential role in paradoxical movement in Parkinson's disease.

9.5 Conclusion

As we have shown, the central control of voluntary movements in humans can be studied by using a multidisciplinary noninvasive approach, and it is extremely important to understand and make the best of the different characteristics of the individual techniques, depending on the specific purpose of each study.

References

Cohen, G. C., Ziemann, U., Chen, R., Classen, J., Hallett, M., Gerloff, C., and Butefisch, C. 1998. Studies of neuroplasticity with transcranial magnetic stimulation. *Journal of Clinical Neurophysiology* 15:305–324.

Fukuyama, H., Matsuzaki, S., Ouchi, Y., Yamauchi, H., Nagahama, Y., Kimura, J., and Shibasaki, H. 1996. Neural control of micturition in man examined with single photon emission computed tomography using 99mTc-HMPAO. *NeuroReport* 7:3009–3012.

Fukuyama, H., Ouchi, Y., Matsuzaki, S., Nagahama, Y., Yamauchi, H., Ogawa, M., Kimura, J., and Shibasaki, H. 1997. Brain functional activity during gait in normal subjects: A SPECT study. *Neuroscience Letters* 228:183–186.

Gerloff, C., Richard, J., Hadley, J., Schulman, A. E., Honda, M., and Hallett, M. 1998. Functional coupling and regional activation of human cortical motor areas during simple, internally paced and externally paced finger movements. *Brain* 121:1513–1531.

Gerloff, C., Toro, C., Uenishi, N., Cohen, L. G., Leocani, L., and Hallett, M. 1997. Steady-state movement-related cortical potentials: A new approach to assessing cortical activity associated with fast repetitive finger movements. *Electroencephalography and Clinical Neurophysiology* 102:106–113.

Gerloff, C., Uenishi, N., Nagamine, T., Kunieda, T., Hallett, M., and Shibasaki, H. 1998. Cortical activation during fast repetitive finger movements in humans: Steady-state movement-related magnetic fields and their cortical generators. *Electroencephalography and Clinical Neurophysiology* 109:444–453.

Glickstein, M., and Stein, J. 1991. Paradoxical movement in Parkinson's disease. *Trends in Neurosciences* 14:480–482.

Hanakawa, T., Katsumi, Y., Fukuyama, H., Hayashi, T., Honda, M., Kimura, J., and Shibasaki, H. 1999. Mechanisms underlying gait disturbances in Parkinson's disease. A single photon emission computed tomography study. *Brain* 122:1271–1282.

Hanakawa, T., Fukuyama, H., Katsumi, Y., Honda, M., and Shibasaki, H. 1999. Enhanced lateral premotor activity during paradoxical gait in Parkinson's disease. *Annals of Neurology* 45:329–336.

Ikeda, A., Lüders, H. O., Burgess, R. C., and Shibasaki, H. 1992. Movement-related potentials recorded from supplementary motor area and primary motor area: Role of supplementary motor area in voluntary movements. *Brain* 115:1017–1043.

Kitamura, J., Shibasaki, H., Takagi, A., Nabeshima, H., and Yamaguchi, A. 1993. Enhanced negative slope of cortical potentials before sequential as compared with simultaneous extensions of two fingers. *Electroencephalography and Clinical Neurophysiology* 86:176–182.

Kornhuber, H. H., and L. Deecke. 1965. Hirnpotentialänderungen bei Willkürbewegungen und passiven Bewegungen des Menschen: Bereitschaftspotential und reafferente Potentiale. *Pflügers Archivum der gesamte Physiologie* 294:1–17.

Lüders, H. O., Dinner, D. S., Morris, H. H., Wyllie E., and Comair, Y. G. 1995. Cortical electrical stimulation in humans: The negative motor areas. *Advances in Neurology* 67:115–129.

Mushiake, H., Inase, M., and Tanji, J. 1991. Neuronal activity in the primate premotor, supplementary, and precentral motor cortex during visually guided and internally determined sequential movements. *Journal of Neurophysiology* 66:705–718.

Nagamine, T., Kajola, M., Salmelin, R., Shibasaki, H., and Hari, R. 1996. Movement-related slow cortical magnetic fields and changes of spontaneous MEG- and EEG-brain rhythms. *Electroencephalography and Clinical Neurophysiology* 99:274–286.

Neshige, R., Lüders, H., and Shibasaki, H. 1988. Recording of movement-related potentials from scalp and cortex in man. *Brain* 111:719–736.

Pfurtscheller, G. 1988. Mapping of event-related desynchronization and type of derivation. *Electroencephalography and Clinical Neurophysiology* 70:190–193.

Sadato, N., Ibanez, V., Deiber, M.-P., Campbell, G., Leonardo, M., and Hallett, M. 1996. Frequency-dependent changes of regional cerebral blood flow during finger movements. *Journal of Cerebral Blood Flow and Metabolism* 16:23–33.

Salmelin, R., and R. Hari. 1994. Spatiotemporal characteristics of sensorimotor neuromagnetic rhythms related to thumb movement. *Neuroscience* 60:537–550.

Shibasaki, H. 1993. Movement-related cortical potentials. In Halliday A. (ed.), *Evoked potentials in clinical testing*, 2nd ed., 523–537. Edinburgh: Churchill Livingstone.

Shibasaki, H. 1995. Pathophysiology of negative myoclonus and asterixis. *Advances in Neurology* 67:199–209.

Shibasaki, H., Barrett, G., Halliday, E., and Halliday, A. M. 1980. Components of the movement-related cortical potential and their scalp topography. *Electroencephalography and Clinical Neurophysiology* 49:213–226.

Shibasaki, H., Barrett, G., Halliday, E., and Halliday, A. M. 1981. Cortical potentials associated with voluntary foot movement in man. *Electroencephalography and Clinical Neurophysiology* 52:507–516.

Shibasaki, H., Sadato, N., Lyshkow, H., Yonekura, Y., Honda, M., Nagamine, T., Suwazono, S., Magata, Y., Ikeda, A., Miyazaki, M., Fukuyama, H., Asato, R., and Konishi, J. 1993. Both primary motor cortex and supplementary motor area play an important role in complex finger movement. *Brain* 116:1387–1398.

Shibasaki, H., Ikeda, A., Nagamine, T., Mima, T., Terada, K., Nishitani, N., Kanda, M., Takano, S., Hanazono, T., Kohara, N., Kaji, R., and Kimura, J. 1994. Cortical reflex negative myoclonus. *Brain* 117:477–486.

Shindo, K., Ikeda, A., Musha, T., Terada, K., Fukuyama, H., Taki, W., Kimura, J., and Shibasaki, H. 1998. Clinical usefulness of the diploe tracing method for localizing interictal spikes in partial epilepsy. *Epilepsia* 39:371–379.

Terada, K., Ikeda, A., Nagamine, T., and Shibasaki, H. 1995. Movement-related cortical potentials associated with voluntary muscle relaxation. *Electroencephalography and Clinical Neurophysiology* 95:335–345.

Toma, K., Honda, M., Hanakawa, T., Okada, T., Fukuyama, H., Ikeda, A., Nishizawa, S., Konishi, J., and Shibasaki, H. 1999. Activities of the primary and supplementary motor areas increase in preparation and execution of voluntary muscle relaxation: An event-related fMRI study. *Journal of Neuroscience* 19:3527–3534.

Wassermann, E. M., Pascual-Leone, A., Valls-Sole, J., Toro, C., Cohen, L. G., and Hallett, M. 1993. Topography of the inhibitory and excitatory responses to transcranial magnetic stimulation in a hand muscle. *Electroencephalography and Clinical Neurophysiology* 89:424–433.

Yazawa, S., Ikeda, A., Kunieda, T., Mima, T., Nagamine, T., Ohara, S., Terada, K., Taki, W., Kimura, J., and Shibasaki, H. 1998. Human supplementary motor area is active in preparation for both voluntary muscle relaxation and contraction: Subdural recording of Bereitschaftspotential. *Neuroscience Letters* 244:145–148.

Chapter 10

Neuromagnetic Inverse Modeling: Application of Eigenstructure-Based Approaches to Extracting Cortical Activities from MEG Data

Kensuke Sekihara, David Poeppel, Alec Marantz, and Yasushi Miyashita

Neuron activity in a human brain induces bioelectric currents, which generate a weak magnetic field that can be detected by a superconducting quantum interference device (SQUID) magnetometer on a scalp surface [1]. The aim of neuromagnetic imaging is to visualize these activities and thus provide functional information about brain dynamics. One major problem here is to develop an efficient algorithm to estimate the neural-current distributions from measured magnetic fields. Because neural-current distributions are inherently three dimensional, this estimation is basically underdetermined.

To avoid this problem, the neural-current distribution is often modeled by using highly localized current sources. That is, the three-dimensional current distribution is modeled by several discrete sources, and their locations and magnitudes are estimated from multichannel neuromagnetic recordings. The model introduced here is called the *equivalent current dipole* (ECD) [2]. The ECD model is physiologically plausible to some extent [1], and some neuromagnetic data such as those from primary-sensory responses can be well explained by the existence of a single ECD or multiple ECDs.

The problem of estimating discrete sources from measurements conducted by an array of sensors is a common problem in a wide variety of signal-processing fields [3, 4]. For instance, estimating the direction of arrival of wavefronts generated by multiple discrete signals is an important problem in radar, sonar, electronic surveillance, and seismic exploration. This problem has therefore been an active research topic for the last two decades in the signal-processing community, and many methods have been proposed to solve this problem.

Among these methods, eigenstructure-based methods have attracted much attention after Schmidt's pioneering work on the multiple signal classification (MUSIC) algorithm [5, 6]. Compared with the conventional maximum-likelihood-based method, MUSIC can provide overwhelming computational simplicity in that the source can be localized by a single-source search, regardless of the number of sources. The mathematical structure of the neuromagnetic inverse problem is similar to that in the direction-of-arrival estimation of narrowband signals received by an array of antennas with diverse polarizations. Eigenstructure-based methods such as the MUSIC algorithm can therefore successfully be applied to solve the neuromagnetic inverse problem [7].

This chapter reviews some applications of the eigenstructure-based approach for solving the neuromagnetic inverse problem. Section 10.1 introduces the mathematical notations and briefly describes the conventional maximum-likelihood method. Section 10.2 presents the basic principle of the eigenstructure-based methods from the point of view of their interesting geometric interpretations. Section 10.3 formulates the MEG-MUSIC algorithm. Here, not only the conventional time-domain formulation but also the frequency-domain formulation are presented. Section 10.4 focuses on the problem of interference rejection. Brain activities not only generate a magnetic field signal associated with the task of interest but also generate interferences, and such interferences often cause deteriorating influence on the final source estimation of the signal. Thus, interference rejection is one major problem when we deal with real-life MEG data. Section 10.5 presents the results of applying the several MUSIC-based methods described in the preceding sections to various types of MEG data.

Throughout this chapter, plain italics indicate scalars, lowercase boldface italics indicate vectors, and uppercase boldface italics indicate matrices. The superscript T indicates the matrix transpose, and the superscript $*$ indicates the complex conjugate for a scalar variable and the conjugate transpose for a matrix. The eigenvalues are numbered in decreasing order.

10.1 Neuromagnetic Inverse Problem

10.1.1 Definitions

Let us define the magnetic field measured by the mth detector coil at time t as $b_m(t)$, and a column vector $\boldsymbol{b}(t) = [b_1(t), b_2(t), \ldots, b_M(t)]^{\mathrm{T}}$ as a set of measured data where M is the total number of detector coils. A total of P current sources are assumed to generate the neuromagnetic field, and the locations of these sources are denoted as $\boldsymbol{x}_1, \boldsymbol{x}_2, \ldots, \boldsymbol{x}_P$. The magnitude of the pth source at time t is defined as $s_p(t)$, and the source magnitude vector is defined as $\boldsymbol{s}(t) = [s_1(t), s_2(t), \ldots, s_P(t)]^{\mathrm{T}}$. The orientation of the pth source is defined as its normal vector $\boldsymbol{\eta}_p = (\eta_p^x, \eta_p^y, \eta_p^z)^{\mathrm{T}}$, where $\|\boldsymbol{\eta}_p\| = 1$. We define a $3P \times P$ matrix that expresses the orientations of all P sources as $\boldsymbol{\Psi}$ such that

$$\boldsymbol{\Psi} = \begin{bmatrix} \boldsymbol{\eta}_1 & 0 & \cdots & 0 \\ 0 & \boldsymbol{\eta}_2 & \cdot & \vdots \\ \vdots & \cdot & \ddots & 0 \\ 0 & \cdots & 0 & \boldsymbol{\eta}_P \end{bmatrix}$$

We assume that the orientation of each source is time independent unless otherwise noted. This assumption is plausible to some extent because the source orientation is, in principle, determined by the anatomical structure of a brain, which does not change in time.

The lead field vector for the θ (which is equal to x, y, or z) component of the source at $\boldsymbol{x}$ is defined as

$$\boldsymbol{l}^{\theta}(\boldsymbol{x}) = [l_1^{\theta}(\boldsymbol{x}), l_2^{\theta}(\boldsymbol{x}), \ldots, l_M^{\theta}(\boldsymbol{x})]^{\mathrm{T}} \tag{1}$$

Here, $l_m^{\theta}(\boldsymbol{x})$ expresses the mth sensor output induced by the unit-magnitude source located at $\boldsymbol{x}$ and directed in the θ direction. We define the lead-field matrix for the location at $\boldsymbol{x}$ as

$$\boldsymbol{L}(\boldsymbol{x}) = [\boldsymbol{l}^{x}(\boldsymbol{x}), \boldsymbol{l}^{y}(\boldsymbol{x}), \boldsymbol{l}^{z}(\boldsymbol{x})] \tag{2}$$

which represents the sensitivity of the sensor array at $\boldsymbol{x}$. We also define, for later use, the lead-field vector for a location $\boldsymbol{x}$ and an orientation $\boldsymbol{\eta}$ as $\boldsymbol{l}(\boldsymbol{\eta}, \boldsymbol{x})$, which is given by $\boldsymbol{l}(\boldsymbol{\eta}, \boldsymbol{x}) = \boldsymbol{L}(\boldsymbol{x})\boldsymbol{\eta}$. The composite lead field matrix for the entire set of P sources is defined as

$$\boldsymbol{L}_c = [\boldsymbol{L}(\boldsymbol{x}_1), \boldsymbol{L}(\boldsymbol{x}_2), \ldots, \boldsymbol{L}(\boldsymbol{x}_P)] \tag{3}$$

Note that when the source locations are unknown, the composite lead-field matrix is unknown. The relationship between $\boldsymbol{b}(t)$ and $\boldsymbol{s}(t)$ is expressed as

$$\boldsymbol{b}(t) = (\boldsymbol{L}_c\boldsymbol{\Psi})\boldsymbol{s}(t) + \boldsymbol{n}(t) \tag{4}$$

where $\boldsymbol{n}(t)$ is the additive noise. The MEG inverse problem is that of estimating source locations $\boldsymbol{x}_1, \ldots, \boldsymbol{x}_P$ and source activity $\boldsymbol{s}(t) = [s_1(t), \ldots, s_P(t)]^{\mathrm{T}}$ from measurement $\boldsymbol{b}(t)$.

10.1.2 Maximum-Likelihood Solution

The conventional way of estimating the source locations is based on the maximum-likelihood principle. Namely, we minimize the least-squares cost function,

$$\mathscr{F} = \langle \|\boldsymbol{b}(t) - \hat{\boldsymbol{L}}_c\hat{\boldsymbol{s}}(t)\|^2 \rangle \tag{5}$$

where the estimates of $\boldsymbol{L}_c$ and $\boldsymbol{s}(t)$ are denoted as $\hat{\boldsymbol{L}}_c$ and $\hat{\boldsymbol{s}}(t)$, respectively, and $\langle\cdot\rangle$ indicates the ensemble average, which can be replaced by the time average in practice. Following the standard procedure for this kind of problem [8], we separate the linear parameter $\boldsymbol{s}(t)$ from the source locations, which are the nonlinear parameters, by substituting $\hat{\boldsymbol{s}}(t) = (\hat{\boldsymbol{L}}_c^{\mathrm{T}}\hat{\boldsymbol{L}}_c)^{-1}\hat{\boldsymbol{L}}_c^{\mathrm{T}}\boldsymbol{b}(t)$ into equation (5). Denoting the unit matrix as $\boldsymbol{I}$, the resulting least-squares cost function is

$$\mathscr{F} = \langle \|(\boldsymbol{I} - \hat{\boldsymbol{L}}_c(\hat{\boldsymbol{L}}_c^{\mathrm{T}}\hat{\boldsymbol{L}}_c)^{-1}\hat{\boldsymbol{L}}_c^{\mathrm{T}})\boldsymbol{b}(t)\|^2 \rangle = \langle \|\boldsymbol{\Pi}_L^{\perp}\boldsymbol{b}(t)\|^2 \rangle = \boldsymbol{\Pi}_L^{\perp}\boldsymbol{R}_b(\boldsymbol{\Pi}_L^{\perp})^{\mathrm{T}} \tag{6}$$

where $\boldsymbol{R}_b$ is the measurement covariance matrix defined by $\boldsymbol{R}_b = \langle \boldsymbol{b}(t)\boldsymbol{b}^{\mathrm{T}}(t) \rangle$. In equation (6), $\mathbf{\Pi}_L^\perp$ is defined as $\mathbf{\Pi}_L^\perp = \mathbf{I} - \hat{\mathbf{L}}_c(\hat{\mathbf{L}}_c^{\mathrm{T}}\hat{\mathbf{L}}_c)^{-1}\hat{\mathbf{L}}_c^{\mathrm{T}}$ and is called the *projection operator* that projects a vector onto the space orthogonal to the column space of $\hat{\mathbf{L}}_c$.

The right-hand side of equation (6) contains only the locations of the sources as unknown parameters, and the optimum estimate for the source locations can be obtained by minimizing this cost function. In the conventional procedure, however, this estimation requires a $3P$ dimensional search, where P is the number of sources. Generally, for such a highly multidimensional search, there is no guarantee of obtaining the correct solution, and we need to set the initial estimate as close to the true solution as possible to avoid convergence to a false solution.

10.2 Principle of the Eigenstructure-Based Approach

This section presents the basic principles of the eigenstructure-based approach from the point of view of its geometrical interpretation. We particularly focus on the MUSIC algorithm, which can perform source localization by using only a three-dimensional search, regardless of the number of sources. To explain the basic principle, let us assume a very simple situation: only two sources exist at $\mathbf{x}_1$ and $\mathbf{x}_2$ with known fixed orientations. The magnitudes for these sources are denoted as $s_1(t)$ and $s_2(t)$. Omitting the orientation terms, the composite lead-field matrix can be expressed as $\mathbf{L}_c = [\mathbf{l}(\mathbf{x}_1), \mathbf{l}(\mathbf{x}_2)] = [\mathbf{l}_1, \mathbf{l}_2]$, where $\mathbf{l}_1 = \mathbf{l}(\mathbf{x}_1)$ and $\mathbf{l}_2 = \mathbf{l}(\mathbf{x}_2)$. Thus, neglecting the additive noise, the basic relationship in equation (4) is simplified to

$$\mathbf{b}(t) = \mathbf{L}_c\mathbf{s}(t) = s_1(t)\mathbf{l}_1 + s_2(t)\mathbf{l}_2 \tag{7}$$

Note that $\mathbf{l}_1$ and $\mathbf{l}_2$ are vectors in the M-dimensional real vector space $\mathbb{R}^M$. It can be understood from equation (7) that measurement $\mathbf{b}(t)$ exists in a space spanned by $\mathbf{l}_1$ and $\mathbf{l}_2$, namely, in the column space of $\mathbf{L}_c$. This column space is therefore called the *signal subspace*, and its orthogonal complement is called the *noise subspace*.

Let us define the three-dimensional space where sources can exist as the source space Θ. The lead-field vector $\mathbf{l}(\mathbf{x})$ represents a single point in $\mathbb{R}^M$. Thus, when $\mathbf{x}$ is varied over Θ, the vector $\mathbf{l}(\mathbf{x})$ traces a trajectory in $\mathbb{R}^M$. This trajectory is expressed as

$$\mathscr{L} = \{\mathbf{l}(\mathbf{x}) : \mathbf{x} \in \Theta\} \tag{8}$$

This $\mathscr{L}$ is referred to as the *array manifold.* The signal subspace and the array manifold are conceptually illustrated in figure 10.1, where the dimension M is set at three, the signal subspace is represented by a two-dimensional plane, and the array manifold is represented by a curve winding through $\mathbb{R}^3$.

The key factor in understanding how the MUSIC algorithm works is that the array manifold intersects the signal subspace at the true source locations $\mathbf{x}_1$ and $\mathbf{x}_2$, as depicted in figure 10.1. The source locations can therefore be estimated by calculating

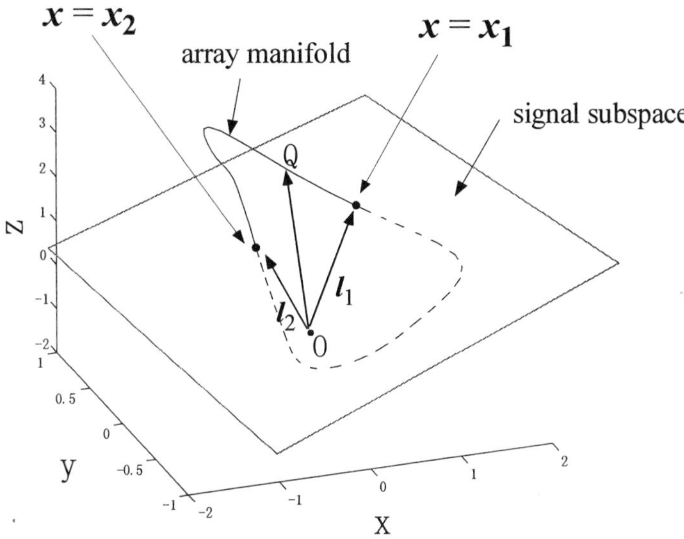

Figure 10.1
Conceptual view of the array manifold and signal subspace when the number of sensors is three ($M = 3$) and the number of the sources is two. The signal subspace is a plane, and the array manifold is a curve winding through the three-dimensional vector space $\mathbb{R}^3$. The uppercase letter Q represents an arbitrary point in the array manifold, and the letter O represents the origin.

the distance between a point in the array manifold and the signal subspace, and by choosing source locations with that distance equal to zero. In practice, since we do not know the source locations, the signal subspace should be estimated from the measured data. Let us define the eigenvectors of the sample covariance matrix of the measured data $\boldsymbol{R}_b$ as $\{\boldsymbol{e}_1, \ldots, \boldsymbol{e}_M\}$. Among the M eigenvalues of $\boldsymbol{R}_b$, the P largest eigenvalues come from the signal and $M - P$ eigenvalues from the noise. Then, the maximum likelihood estimate of the signal subspace is known to be the span of the signal-level eigenvectors $\{\boldsymbol{e}_1, \ldots, \boldsymbol{e}_P\}$ [9]. Likewise, the maximum likelihood estimate of the noise subspace is known to be the span of the noise-level eigenvectors $\{\boldsymbol{e}_{P+1}, \ldots, \boldsymbol{e}_M\}$. Therefore, it can easily be shown that equation (14) in the next section exactly calculates (the inverse of) the distance between the signal subspace and a specific point in the array manifold.

So far, we have assumed that the source covariance matrix $\boldsymbol{R}_s$ is a full-rank matrix. However, if highly correlated sources exist, this assumption no longer holds, and the source locations cannot be estimated by simply calculating the above-mentioned distance. This correlated source case is illustrated in figure 10.2. Here, the signal subspace is no longer a plane but a line indicated by an arrow. In this figure, (a) shows the case where the points Q and Q′ are not equal to the source locations and

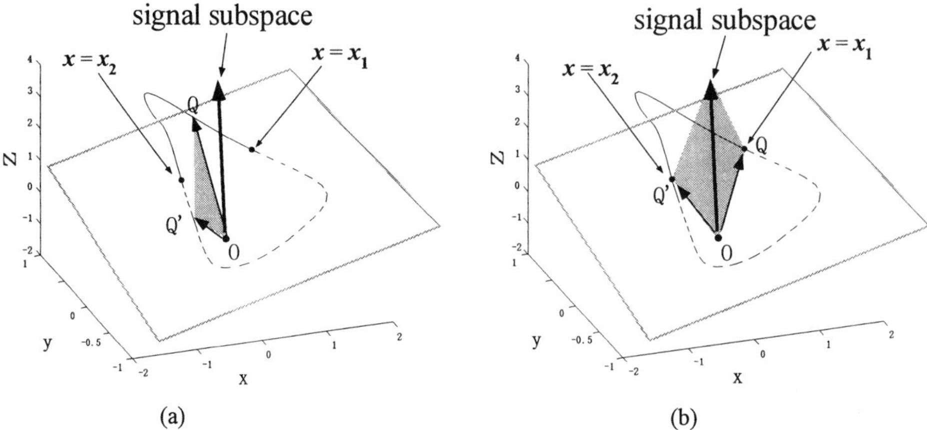

Figure 10.2
Conceptual view of the array manifold and signal subspace when the two sources are coherent. The letters Q and Q' are arbitrary points in the array manifold. (*a*) The case where the signal subspace is not contained in the plane spanned by the vectors $\overrightarrow{OQ}$ and $\overrightarrow{OQ'}$. (*b*) The signal subspace is contained in the plane spanned by the vectors $\overrightarrow{OQ}$ and $\overrightarrow{OQ'}$. The points Q and Q' correspond to the true source locations in this case.

(b) shows the case where Q and Q′ are equal to the source locations. As shown in the figure, the source locations can be obtained by finding the locations $\boldsymbol{x}_1$ and $\boldsymbol{x}_2$ at which the span of the vectors $\boldsymbol{l}(\boldsymbol{x}_1)$ and $\boldsymbol{l}(\boldsymbol{x}_2)$ includes the degenerated signal subspace. This is the basic principle of the multisource MUSIC algorithm [5].

10.3 Formulation of the MEG-MUSIC Algorithm

10.3.1 Time-Domain Implementation

In the preceding section, we presented a basic idea behind the eigenstructure-based source localization methods. Here, we present a detailed formulation of the MEG MUSIC algorithm. Using equation (4), we get the relationship

$$\langle \boldsymbol{b}(t)\boldsymbol{b}^{\mathrm{T}}(t)\rangle = (\boldsymbol{L}_c\boldsymbol{\Psi})\langle \boldsymbol{s}(t)\boldsymbol{s}^{\mathrm{T}}(t)\rangle(\boldsymbol{\Psi}^{\mathrm{T}}\boldsymbol{L}_c^{\mathrm{T}}) + \langle \boldsymbol{n}(t)\boldsymbol{n}^{\mathrm{T}}(t)\rangle \tag{9}$$

where it is assumed that the noise is uncorrelated with the signal. It is also assumed that the noise in the measured data is white Gaussian noise with variance σ^2, so we have $\langle \boldsymbol{n}(t)\boldsymbol{n}^{\mathrm{T}}(t)\rangle = \sigma^2\boldsymbol{I}$. We use the measurement covariance matrix $\boldsymbol{R}_b = \langle \boldsymbol{b}(t)\boldsymbol{b}^{\mathrm{T}}(t)\rangle$ and define the covariance matrix of the source activities as $\boldsymbol{R}_s$—that is, $\boldsymbol{R}_s = \langle \boldsymbol{s}(t)\boldsymbol{s}^{\mathrm{T}}(t)\rangle$. Thus, we get the basic relationship between these covariance matrices,

$$\boldsymbol{R}_b = (\boldsymbol{L}_c\boldsymbol{\Psi})\boldsymbol{R}_s(\boldsymbol{\Psi}^{\mathrm{T}}\boldsymbol{L}_c^{\mathrm{T}}) + \sigma^2\boldsymbol{I} \tag{10}$$

Unless the source activities are perfectly correlated with each other, the rank of $\boldsymbol{R}_s$ is equal to the number of sources P. Therefore, $\boldsymbol{R}_b$ has P eigenvalues greater than σ^2 and $M - P$ eigenvalues equal to σ^2. Let us define the matrices $\boldsymbol{E}_S$ and $\boldsymbol{E}_N$ as $\boldsymbol{E}_S = [\boldsymbol{e}_1, \ldots, \boldsymbol{e}_P]$ and $\boldsymbol{E}_N = [\boldsymbol{e}_{P+1}, \ldots, \boldsymbol{e}_M]$, where $\{\boldsymbol{e}_j\}$ with $j = 1, 2, \ldots, M$ are the eigenvectors of $\boldsymbol{R}_b$.

To estimate the locations of the sources, the MUSIC algorithm takes advantage of the fact that the lead field vector at each $\boldsymbol{x}_p$ is orthogonal to the noise-level eigenvectors. This can be understood by first considering

$$(\boldsymbol{R}_b - \sigma^2 \boldsymbol{I})\boldsymbol{e}_j = (\boldsymbol{L}_c \boldsymbol{\Psi})\boldsymbol{R}_s(\boldsymbol{\Psi}^{\mathrm{T}} \boldsymbol{L}_c^{\mathrm{T}})\boldsymbol{e}_j = 0 \qquad \text{for } j = P+1, \ldots, M \tag{11}$$

Since $\boldsymbol{L}_c \boldsymbol{\Psi}$ is a full column-rank matrix, and we assume that $\boldsymbol{R}_s$ is a full-rank matrix, the above equation results in

$$(\boldsymbol{\Psi}^{\mathrm{T}} \boldsymbol{L}_c^{\mathrm{T}})\boldsymbol{e}_j = 0 \qquad \text{for } j = P+1, \ldots, M \tag{12}$$

This implies that the lead-field matrix with the correct source orientation at the true source location is orthogonal to any $\boldsymbol{e}_j$, where $j = P+1, \ldots, M$—that is, it is orthogonal to the noise subspace. The source locations can thus be obtained by checking the orthogonality between the lead-field vector $\boldsymbol{l}(\boldsymbol{\eta}, \boldsymbol{x})$ $(= \boldsymbol{L}(\boldsymbol{x})\boldsymbol{\eta})$ and the noise subspace projector $\boldsymbol{E}_N \boldsymbol{E}_N^{\mathrm{T}}$.

In practice, some kind of measure to evaluate this orthogonality is needed to implement the MUSIC algorithm; this orthogonality measure is often called the *MUSIC localizer*. For such a localizer, we can use [10]

$$J(\boldsymbol{x}) = \max_{\eta} \left(\frac{\boldsymbol{l}(\boldsymbol{\eta}, \boldsymbol{x})^{\mathrm{T}} \boldsymbol{l}(\boldsymbol{\eta}, \boldsymbol{x})}{\boldsymbol{l}(\boldsymbol{\eta}, \boldsymbol{x})^{\mathrm{T}} \boldsymbol{E}_N \boldsymbol{E}_N^{\mathrm{T}} \boldsymbol{l}(\boldsymbol{\eta}, \boldsymbol{x})} \right) \tag{13}$$

This maximization problem can be solved by using the generalized-eigenproblem formulation, namely,

$$J(\boldsymbol{x}) = 1/\lambda_{min}[\boldsymbol{L}^{\mathrm{T}}(\boldsymbol{x})\boldsymbol{E}_N \boldsymbol{E}_N^{\mathrm{T}} \boldsymbol{L}(\boldsymbol{x}), \boldsymbol{L}^{\mathrm{T}}(\boldsymbol{x})\boldsymbol{L}(\boldsymbol{x})] \tag{14}$$

where $\lambda_{min}[\,\cdot\,,\,\cdot\,]$ indicates the minimum generalized eigenvalue of the matrix pair. This MUSIC localizer is calculated in the source space, and the locations where the localizer reaches a peak are chosen as the source locations.

Equation (14) was obtained under the assumption that sources do not change their orientations. It is worth noting that when this assumption does not hold and the source orientations change, this localizing function can still be used to detect source locations. In such cases, instead of equation (10), we have the relationship

$$\boldsymbol{R}_b = \boldsymbol{L}_c \boldsymbol{R}_{\Psi s} \boldsymbol{L}_c^{\mathrm{T}} + \sigma^2 \boldsymbol{I} \tag{15}$$

Here, we define $\boldsymbol{R}_{\Psi s}$ as $\boldsymbol{R}_{\Psi s} = \langle \boldsymbol{\Psi}(t)\boldsymbol{s}(t)\boldsymbol{s}^{\mathrm{T}}(t)\boldsymbol{\Psi}^{\mathrm{T}}(t) \rangle$. Therefore, assuming that the matrix $\boldsymbol{R}_{\Psi s}$ is a full-rank matrix, we also obtain the relationship

$$\boldsymbol{L}_c^{\mathrm{T}}\boldsymbol{e}_j = 0 \qquad \text{for } j = P+1, \ldots, M \tag{16}$$

Since the source locations that satisfy equation (16) also satisfy equation (12), the localizer in equation (14) is still effective even when the source orientations are time dependent.

If highly correlated sources exist, the source-covariance matrix $\boldsymbol{R}_s$ is no longer a full-rank matrix and the orthogonality relationship in equation (12) or (16) does not hold. This fact has already been pointed out in section 10.2, where the multisource MUSIC algorithm was introduced to handle this source correlation problem. Defining $\boldsymbol{L}_2(\boldsymbol{x}_1, \boldsymbol{x}_2)$ as

$$\boldsymbol{L}_2(\boldsymbol{x}_1, \boldsymbol{x}_2) = [\boldsymbol{L}(\boldsymbol{x}_1), \boldsymbol{L}(\boldsymbol{x}_2)] = [\boldsymbol{l}^x(\boldsymbol{x}_1), \boldsymbol{l}^y(\boldsymbol{x}_1), \boldsymbol{l}^z(\boldsymbol{x}_1), \boldsymbol{l}^x(\boldsymbol{x}_2), \boldsymbol{l}^y(\boldsymbol{x}_2), \boldsymbol{l}^z(\boldsymbol{x}_2)]$$

the localizer to implement the two-source MUSIC algorithm can be expressed as

$$J(\boldsymbol{x}_1, \boldsymbol{x}_2) = 1/\lambda_{min}[\boldsymbol{L}_2^{\mathrm{T}}(\boldsymbol{x}_1, \boldsymbol{x}_2)\boldsymbol{E}_N\boldsymbol{E}_N^{\mathrm{T}}\boldsymbol{L}_2(\boldsymbol{x}_1, \boldsymbol{x}_2), \boldsymbol{L}_2^{\mathrm{T}}(\boldsymbol{x}_1, \boldsymbol{x}_2)\boldsymbol{L}_2(\boldsymbol{x}_1, \boldsymbol{x}_2)] \tag{17}$$

We show in section 10.5.3 that this source-correlation problem occurs when we try to simultaneously detect the auditory cortices in both hemispheres by using whole-head measurements. We also show that the two-source localizer in equation (17) is effective for such a case.

10.3.2 Frequency-Domain Implementation

The MUSIC source localization can also be implemented in the frequency domain [11]. Let us denote the Fourier transform of $\boldsymbol{b}(t)$, $\boldsymbol{s}(t)$, and $\boldsymbol{n}(t)$ as $g_b(f)$, $g_s(f)$, and $g_n(f)$, respectively. Then, the Fourier transform of equation (4) gives

$$g_b(f) = (\boldsymbol{L}_c\boldsymbol{\Psi})g_s(f) + g_n(f) \tag{18}$$

Let us also define the cross-spectral matrices $\boldsymbol{G}_b(f)$, $\boldsymbol{G}_s(f)$, and $\boldsymbol{G}_n(f)$ such that $\boldsymbol{G}_b(f) = \langle g_b(f)\boldsymbol{g}_b^*(f)\rangle$, $\boldsymbol{G}_s(f) = \langle g_s(f)\boldsymbol{g}_s^*(f)\rangle$, and $\boldsymbol{G}_n(f) = \langle g_n(f)\boldsymbol{g}_n^*(f)\rangle$. We assume that the noise is white Gaussian and that $\boldsymbol{G}_n(f) = \sigma_D^2\boldsymbol{I}$, where σ_D^2 is the noise power density. From equation (18), the relationship between the cross–power spectrum matrices,

$$\boldsymbol{G}_b(f) = (\boldsymbol{L}_c\boldsymbol{\Psi})\boldsymbol{G}_s(f)(\boldsymbol{\Psi}^{\mathrm{T}}\boldsymbol{L}_c^{\mathrm{T}}) + \sigma_D^2\boldsymbol{I} \tag{19}$$

is obtained. We further assume that the frequency range from f_1 to f_2 contains the signal of interest. Denoting

$$\boldsymbol{\Gamma}_b = \int_{f_1}^{f_2} \boldsymbol{G}_b(f)\,df \qquad \text{and} \qquad \boldsymbol{\Gamma}_s = \int_{f_1}^{f_2} \boldsymbol{G}_s(f)\,df \tag{20}$$

we have

$$\boldsymbol{\Gamma}_b = (\boldsymbol{L}_c\boldsymbol{\Psi})\boldsymbol{\Gamma}_s(\boldsymbol{\Psi}^{\mathrm{T}}\boldsymbol{L}_c^{\mathrm{T}}) + \sigma_f^2\boldsymbol{I} \tag{21}$$

where $\sigma_f^2 = \sigma_D^2(f_2 - f_1)$.

Let us denote the jth eigenvector of $\boldsymbol{\Gamma}_b$ as $\boldsymbol{v}_j$ and assume that, among total M eigenvalues of $\boldsymbol{\Gamma}_b$, P' largest eigenvalues arise from the signal. We have

$$(\boldsymbol{\Gamma}_b - \sigma^2 \boldsymbol{I})\boldsymbol{v}_j = (\boldsymbol{L}_c \boldsymbol{\Psi})\boldsymbol{\Gamma}_s(\boldsymbol{\Psi}^{\mathrm{T}} \boldsymbol{L}_c^{\mathrm{T}})\boldsymbol{v}_j = 0 \qquad \text{for } j = P' + 1, \ldots, M \tag{22}$$

When $\boldsymbol{\Gamma}_s$ is a full-rank matrix, we obtain

$$(\boldsymbol{\Psi}^{\mathrm{T}} \boldsymbol{L}_c^{\mathrm{T}})\boldsymbol{v}_j = 0 \qquad \text{for } j = P' + 1, \ldots, M \tag{23}$$

Equation (23) indicates that the noise-level eigenvectors of $\boldsymbol{\Gamma}_b$ are orthogonal to the lead-field vector $\boldsymbol{l}(\boldsymbol{\eta}, \boldsymbol{x})$ at the true source location. Therefore, the localizer for the frequency-domain MUSIC algorithm is given by

$$J(\boldsymbol{x}) = 1/\lambda_{min}[\boldsymbol{L}^{\mathrm{T}}(\boldsymbol{x})\boldsymbol{V}_N \boldsymbol{V}_N^{\mathrm{T}} \boldsymbol{L}(\boldsymbol{x}), \boldsymbol{L}^{\mathrm{T}}(\boldsymbol{x})\boldsymbol{L}(\boldsymbol{x})] \tag{24}$$

where the matrix $\boldsymbol{V}_N$ is defined as $\boldsymbol{V}_N = [\boldsymbol{v}_{P'+1}, \ldots, \boldsymbol{v}_M]$.

When calculating $\boldsymbol{G}_b(f)$ in practice, we cannot directly use $\boldsymbol{G}_b(f) = \langle \boldsymbol{g}_b(f)\boldsymbol{g}_b^*(f) \rangle$, because this equation requires a statistical ensemble, which is not effectively calculated in practical situations where the number of measurements is more or less limited. Therefore, instead of directly calculating the statistical ensemble, the multitaper method [12, 13] can be applied to calculate $\boldsymbol{G}_b(f)$. That is, the cross-spectrum matrix for the measurement is calculated using

$$\boldsymbol{G}_b(f) = \sum_k \bar{\boldsymbol{g}}_b(f, k)\bar{\boldsymbol{g}}_b^*(f, k) \tag{25}$$

Here, $\bar{\boldsymbol{g}}_b(f, k)$ is given by

$$\bar{\boldsymbol{g}}_b(f, k) = \int w_k(t)\boldsymbol{b}(t)e^{-2\pi itf}\, dt \tag{26}$$

where $w_k(t)$ is a windowing function and is referred to as the *kth Slepian data taper* [12, 13].

The frequency-domain MUSIC algorithm is advantageous if the source activity has specific frequency characteristics. It is known that some spontaneous activities exhibit an oscillatory nature [14]. In section 10.5.2, we apply this algorithm to source localization for the human alpha rhythm and show its validity.

10.4 Interference Rejection

10.4.1 Spatial Prewhitening MUSIC Algorithm

When applying the MUSIC algorithm to real-life MEG data, the localization accuracy is often seriously affected by interference arising from background brain activities. These external noise fields cause spatially correlated noise in neuromagnetic measurements, and the incorporation of a noise spatial correlation is needed to reduce the influence of such noise fields [15, 16, 17].

In the MUSIC algorithm, this incorporation can be done in the following manner [18]. When nonwhite noise exists, and when we denote the noise covariance matrix as $\boldsymbol{R}_n$, Equation (10) is changed to

$$\boldsymbol{R}_b = (\boldsymbol{L}_c \boldsymbol{\Psi})\boldsymbol{R}_s(\boldsymbol{\Psi}^{\mathrm{T}}\boldsymbol{L}_c^{\mathrm{T}}) + \boldsymbol{R}_n \tag{27}$$

Let us denote $\tilde{\boldsymbol{e}}_j$ as an eigenvector obtained by solving the generalized eigenvalue problem,

$$\boldsymbol{R}_b\tilde{\boldsymbol{e}}_j = \tilde{\lambda}_j\boldsymbol{R}_n\tilde{\boldsymbol{e}}_j. \tag{28}$$

Using $\tilde{\boldsymbol{e}}_j$, it is easy to show that

$$(\boldsymbol{L}\boldsymbol{\Psi})\boldsymbol{R}_s(\boldsymbol{\Psi}^{\mathrm{T}}\boldsymbol{L}^{\mathrm{T}})\tilde{\boldsymbol{e}}_j = 0 \qquad \text{for } j = P+1, \ldots, M \tag{29}$$

hence

$$(\boldsymbol{\Psi}^{\mathrm{T}}\boldsymbol{L}^{\mathrm{T}})\tilde{\boldsymbol{e}}_j = 0 \qquad \text{for } j = P+1, \ldots, M \tag{30}$$

Equation (30) indicates that the source locations are found by checking the orthogonality between the modified noise subspace projector $\tilde{\boldsymbol{E}}_N\tilde{\boldsymbol{E}}_N^{\mathrm{T}}$ and the lead-field vector $\boldsymbol{l}(\boldsymbol{\eta}, \boldsymbol{x})$. Here, $\tilde{\boldsymbol{E}}_N$ is defined as $\tilde{\boldsymbol{E}}_N = [\tilde{\boldsymbol{e}}_{P+1}, \ldots, \tilde{\boldsymbol{e}}_M]$. The localizer for nonwhite noise is thus given by

$$J(\boldsymbol{x}) = 1/\lambda_{min}[\boldsymbol{L}^{\mathrm{T}}(\boldsymbol{x})\tilde{\boldsymbol{E}}_N\tilde{\boldsymbol{E}}_N^{\mathrm{T}}\boldsymbol{L}(\boldsymbol{x}), \boldsymbol{L}^{\mathrm{T}}(\boldsymbol{x})\boldsymbol{R}_n^{-1}\boldsymbol{L}(\boldsymbol{x})] \tag{31}$$

However, to use this localizer, an accurate estimate of the noise covariance matrix is needed. For this purpose, we should find a portion of the data that contains only noise fields but does not contain any signal information. For evoked neuromagnetic experiments, such a portion can be found in a data portion taken before a stimulus is applied. When the prestimulus data portion is sufficiently long and the interstimulus interval is sufficiently large, an accurate estimate of the covariance matrix can be obtained.

10.4.2 Covariance-Difference Analysis

When the noise covariance matrix (the covariance matrix for interferences) is not available, the above-mentioned prewhitening technique cannot be used. This situation occurs when the interferences are not spontaneous but are elicited by a sensory stimulus, and such situations are rather common especially in cognitive experiments. Therefore, in most cognitive studies, neuropsychologists carefully design their experiments to extract only the target activities of interest. A common example for such experimental designs contains two kinds of stimuli: a task stimulus and a control stimulus. The task stimulus generally elicits the target cortical activities as well as other activities associated with them. The control stimulus is designed to elicit only these associated activities. Then, some kind of subtraction between these two conditions is calculated to extract the target activity.

Here, we describe a technique well suited to extracting the target activity when two measurements are conducted under different stimulus conditions [19, 20]. We assume that the measurement covariance matrix obtained from the first measurement is $\boldsymbol{R}_b^{(1)}$ and that the covariance matrix obtained from the second measurement is $\boldsymbol{R}_b^{(2)}$, while the difference between these matrices is $\Delta\boldsymbol{R}_b$. That is,

$$\Delta\boldsymbol{R}_b = \boldsymbol{R}_b^{(1)} - \boldsymbol{R}_b^{(2)} \tag{32}$$

In the covariance-difference analysis, the source locations are obtained by applying a MUSIC-like algorithm to this $\Delta\boldsymbol{R}_b$. As a result, this method can provide the difference in source configurations between these two measurements. Let us denote the eigenvectors corresponding to the zero-level eigenvalues of $\Delta\boldsymbol{R}_b$ as $\bar{e}_j$, where $j = \bar{P}+1, \ldots, M$ and $\bar{P}$ is the number of nonzero eigenvalues. The orthogonality measure here is

$$J(\boldsymbol{x}) = 1/\lambda_{min}[\boldsymbol{L}^{\mathrm{T}}(\boldsymbol{x})\boldsymbol{E}_Z\boldsymbol{E}_Z^{\mathrm{T}}\boldsymbol{L}(\boldsymbol{x}), \boldsymbol{L}^{\mathrm{T}}(\boldsymbol{x})\boldsymbol{L}(\boldsymbol{x})] \tag{33}$$

where $\boldsymbol{E}_Z = [\bar{\boldsymbol{e}}_{\bar{P}+1}, \ldots, \bar{\boldsymbol{e}}_M]$.

The procedure to implement the covariance-difference analysis can be summarized as follows:

Step 1: The difference matrix is calculated between two covariance matrices obtained under two kinds of stimulus conditions.
Step 2: Eigen-decomposition of this difference matrix is performed, and the subspace spanned by zero-level eigenvectors is defined by separating zero-level eigenvalues from nonzero eigenvalues.
Step 3: The source is localized by searching the localizer defined by equation (33) in the source space.

The advantage of the covariance-difference analysis over the conventional waveform-subtraction method is explained as follows. Let us assume that the first measurement contains an interference $\boldsymbol{d}(t)$ in addition to a signal. The second measurement only contains an interference $\boldsymbol{d}'(t)$, which may be different from $\boldsymbol{d}(t)$. The waveform-subtraction method requires that the relationship $\boldsymbol{d}(t) \approx \boldsymbol{d}'(t)$ should hold for all time points. In covariance-difference analysis, the relationship $\langle \boldsymbol{d}\boldsymbol{d}^{\mathrm{T}} \rangle \approx \langle \boldsymbol{d}'(\boldsymbol{d}')^{\mathrm{T}} \rangle$ must hold. That is, it only requires that the time averages of the squared intensities of the interference fields are equal. As a result, this method can still be effective when the onsets of the interferences are different for the two measurements or even when the waveforms are different. The usefulness of the covariance-difference analysis is experimentally demonstrated in section 10.5.7, where we apply the method to removing the interference from button-press finger movements in an auditory-evoked field measurement.

10.4.3 Interference Rejection Using Temporal Correlation

The preceding sections described two methods for removing the influence of brain activities that are not the interest of the measurements. The prewhitening technique requires information on the covariance matrix of such activities, and the covariance-difference analysis requires two measurements to be performed with different stimulus conditions. However, these prerequisites are sometimes not satisfied. In the following, a third method is presented that does not require either information on the noise covariance matrix or multiple measurements. The method utilizes the temporal correlation of the signal and noise waveforms [21]. It is effective when the temporal correlation length of interferences is shorter than that of the signal activities.

Let us define the covariance matrix of the measured magnetic field with a time lag τ as $\boldsymbol{R}_b(\tau)$, that of the source waveform as $\boldsymbol{R}_s(\tau)$, and that of the background activities as $\boldsymbol{R}_n(\tau)$. Then, using a derivation similar to that for equation (27), we have the relationship

$$\boldsymbol{R}_b(\tau) = (\boldsymbol{L}_c\boldsymbol{\Psi})\boldsymbol{R}_s(\tau)(\boldsymbol{\Psi}^{\mathrm{T}}\boldsymbol{L}_c^{\mathrm{T}}) + \boldsymbol{R}_n(\tau) \tag{34}$$

Let us define the the correlation length for the signal τ_{th}^s such that $\boldsymbol{R}_s(\tau) \approx 0$ for $\tau \geq \tau_{th}^s$. The correlation length for the noise τ_{th}^n is defined such that $\boldsymbol{R}_n(\tau) \approx 0$ for $\tau \geq \tau_{th}^n$. Thus, if we choose τ that is greater than τ_{th}^n but smaller than τ_{th}^s, we get

$$\boldsymbol{R}_b(\tau) = (\boldsymbol{L}_c\boldsymbol{\Psi})\boldsymbol{R}_s(\tau)(\boldsymbol{\Psi}^{\mathrm{T}}\boldsymbol{L}_c^{\mathrm{T}}) \tag{35}$$

We can therefore use such $\boldsymbol{R}_b(\tau)$ to localize sources free from the influences of the background interferences. It is, however, generally difficult to choose an appropriate τ because we do not usually know the noise correlation length τ_{th}^n. Consequently, if we use a single $\boldsymbol{R}_b(\tau)$, the quality of the final localization results strongly depends on the choice of τ. This difficulty can be overcome by using multiple covariance matrices $\boldsymbol{R}_b(\tau_j)$ with $j = 1, \ldots, J$. That is, the noise subspace that is common to multiple $\boldsymbol{R}_b(\tau_j)$ is estimated by using their simultaneous diagonalization [22]. Then, the source localization is performed by checking the orthogonality between this noise subspace and the lead-field vector $\boldsymbol{l}(\boldsymbol{\eta}, \boldsymbol{x})$.

10.5 Experiments

10.5.1 Applying the MUSIC Algorithm to Typical Evoked Neuromagnetic Responses

As the first example, we apply the MUSIC algorithm to source localization from typical auditory and somatosensory evoked responses, and we see how the algorithm effectively localizes sources from these sets of MEG data. The data were measured by using the 37-channel Magnes^{TM} magnetometer installed at the Biomagnetic Imaging Laboratory, University of California, San Francisco. The auditory-evoked response was measured using a 1000-Hz pure-tone auditory stimulus. The stimulus was applied to the subject's right ear. The sensor array was placed on the subject's left hemisphere and positioned to best record the M100 auditory response (see chapter 2, this volume). The somatosensory-evoked response was measured using a 30-ms-duration tactile pulse delivered to the distal segment of the subject's right index finger. These responses are shown in figures 10.3a and 10.3b.

The results of applying the MUSIC algorithm to the auditory response with the localizer given in equation (14) are shown in figure 10.4a (plate 11). The MUSIC localization function was calculated with an interval of 0.5 cm within a volume in the left hemisphere. The maximum-intensity projections of the localizer values onto the transverse, coronal, and sagittal planes are shown. In figure 10.4a, the algorithm clearly detects a single localized source near the primary auditory cortex in the left hemisphere. The results of applying the MUSIC algorithm to the somatosensory response are shown in figure 10.4b. The results show that two clear localized sources exist in the left hemisphere. These sources probably correspond to the primary somatosensory cortex (SI) and the secondary somatosensory cortex (SII).

10.5.2 Applying the Frequency-Domain MUSIC Algorithm to Alpha-Rhythm Source Localization

The frequency-domain MUSIC algorithm was applied to the source localization of the human alpha rhythm. The alpha rhythm was measured using the 148-channel whole-head magnetometer array (Magnes 2500^{TM}) installed at the Communications Research Laboratory, Akashi, Japan. A total of three measurements were successively performed. A part of the data obtained in the first measurement is shown in figure 10.5a, and the power spectrum averaged over all channels is shown in figure 10.5b. In this averaged power spectrum, a sharp peak exists near 10 Hz.

We then applied the frequency-domain MUSIC algorithm, in which the target frequency region was set at the range between 8.5 and 10.5 Hz; the region is shown by the two vertical broken lines in figure 10.5b. The results are shown in figure 10.6a (plate 12). A fairly localized single peak exists near the midline in the occipital region. This peak location as well as two other estimated locations obtained from the other two measurements were overlaid onto the subject's sagittal MRI. The results in figure 10.6b (plate 13) show that the sources obtained using the proposed algorithm are located near the parieto-occipital sulcus. These locations are in good agreement with the results obtained in previous investigations of the alpha source [14, 23].

10.5.3 Applying the Multisource MUSIC Algorithm to Detect Coherent Cortical Activities

The activations of the primary auditory cortices in the left and right hemispheres are known to be highly synchronized. Thus, using an auditory-evoked response measured

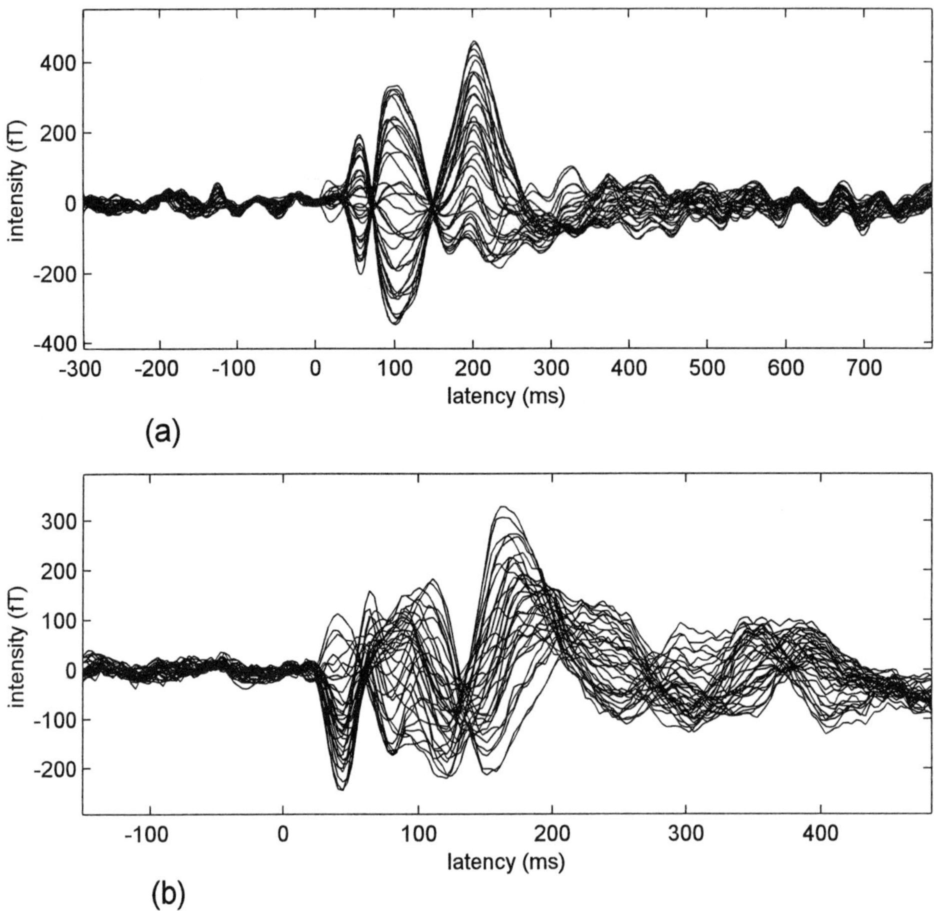

Figure 10.3
The 37-channel recordings of (*a*) auditory- and (*b*) somatosensory-evoked responses. The auditory response was measured with the 1-kHz sampling frequency and 256 epochs were averaged. The stimulus of 1000-Hz pure tone with a duration of 200 msec was applied to the subject's right ear, and the sensor array was placed on the left hemisphere. The somatosensory-evoked response was measured by using a 30-msec-duration tactile pulse (17 psi) delivered to the distal segment of the subject's right index finger. The sensor array was positioned on the subject's left hemisphere. These waveforms were digitally low-pass filtered with a cutoff frequency of 40 Hz. (The subject for (*a*) was different from that for (*b*).)

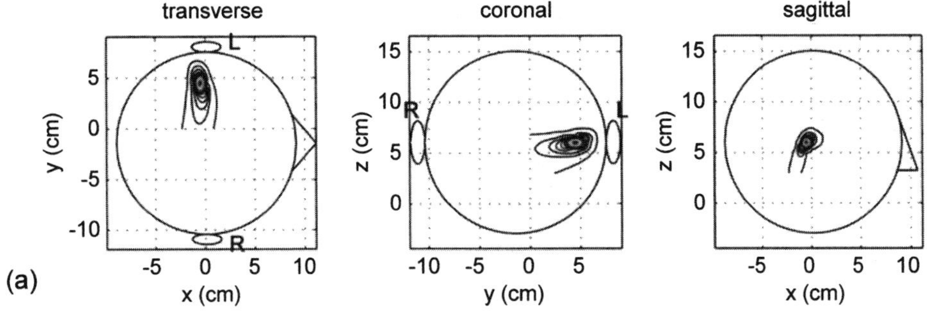

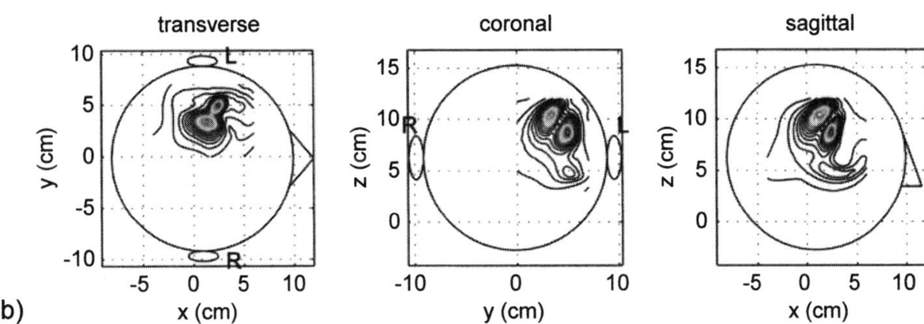

Figure 10.4
(*a*) Results of applying the time-domain MUSIC algorithm to the auditory response shown in figure 10.3a. (*b*) Results of applying the time-domain MUSIC algorithm to the somatosensory response shown in figure 10.3b. The localizer in equation (14) was calculated in a three-dimensional volume in the left hemisphere with a 0.5-cm interval. The maxium-intensity projections onto the transverse, coronal, and sagittal planes are shown. Each contour shows the relative value of the localizer, and locations where the localizer reaches a peak are considered to be the source locations. The circles depicting a human head represent approximate location of the subject's scalp surface. The letters *L* and *R* indicate the left and the right hemispheres, respectively.

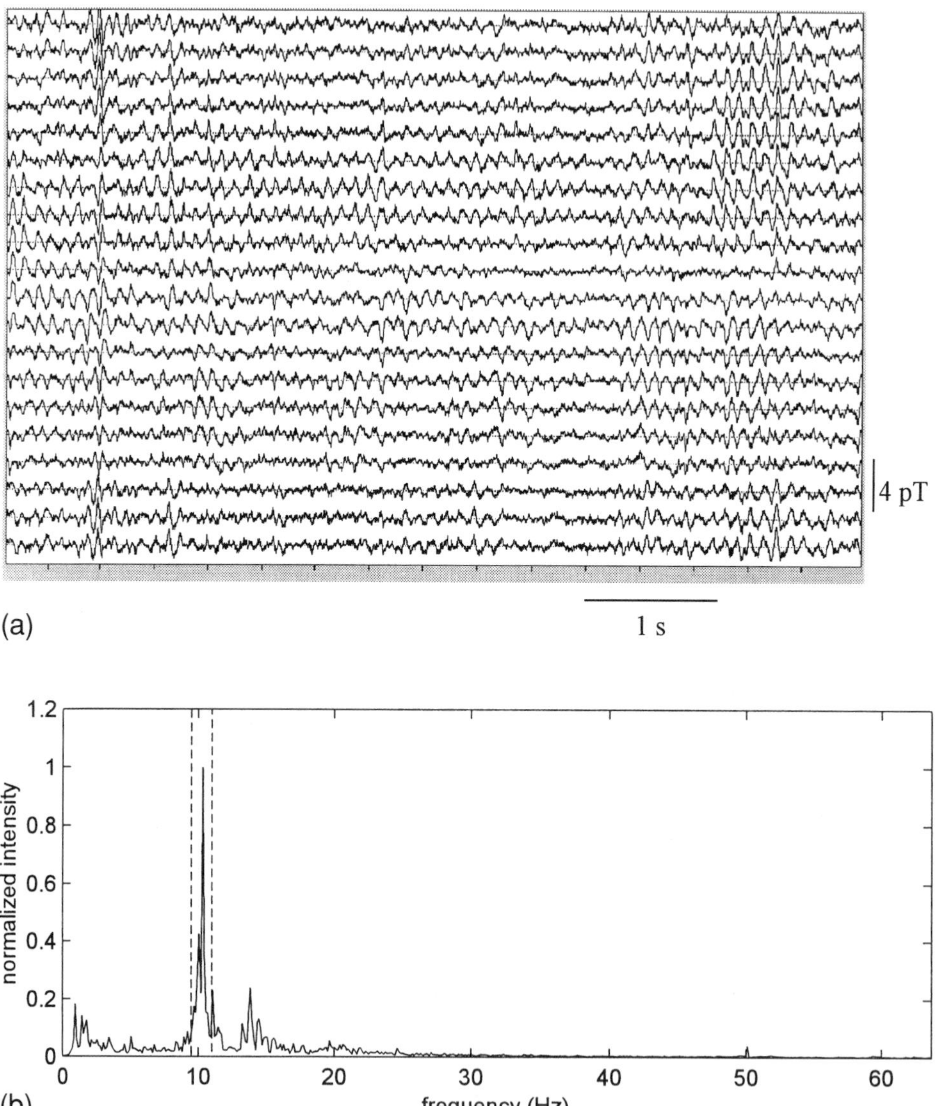

Figure 10.5
(*a*) Whole-head recordings of spontaneous neuromagnetic field. Selected 25-channel recordings are shown. The subject closed his eyes during the measurements. The data was collected during an 8-sec period with a 0.5-kHz sampling frequency, and an online bandpass filter with a bandwidth from 1 to 200 Hz was applied. The data represent one of the three identical measurements conducted successively. (*b*) The power spectrum averaged over all channels. Two vertical broken lines show the target region used to obtain the results shown in figure 10.6a.

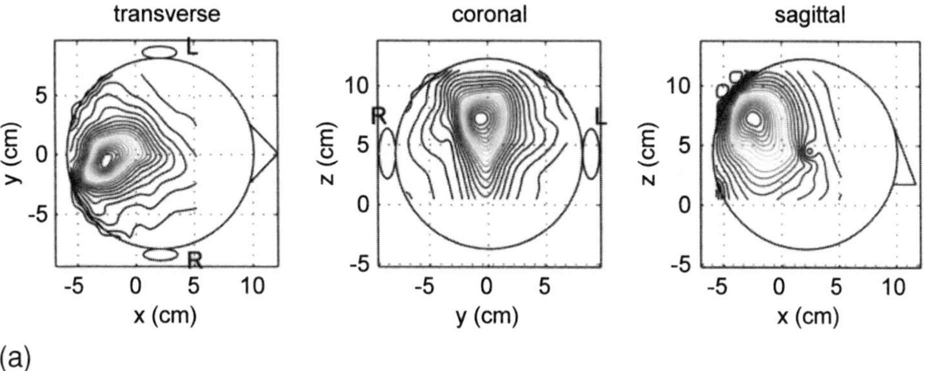

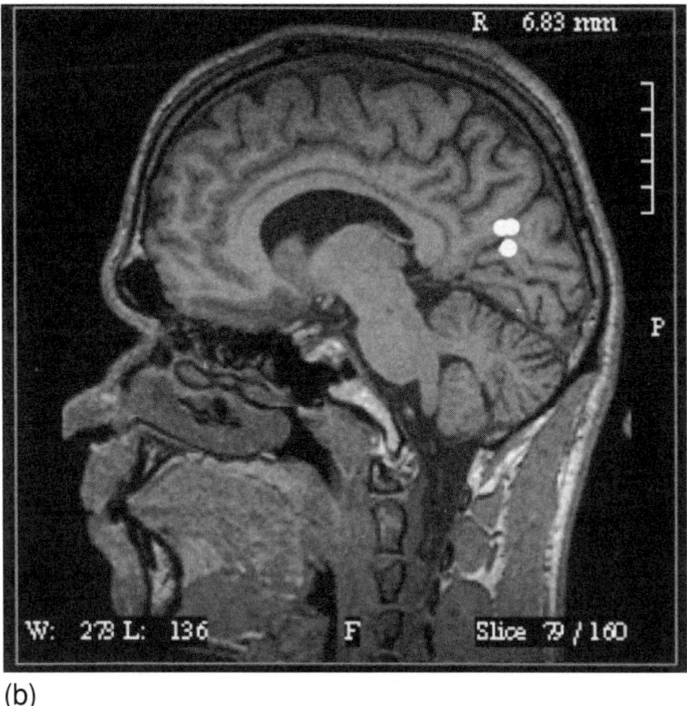

Figure 10.6
(*a*) Results of applying the frequency-domain MUSIC algorithm (equation (24)) to the spontaneous MEG data in figure 10.5a. The target region was set as shown in figure 10.5b. (*b*) Results of overlaying the peak location obtained in figure 10.6a onto the subject's MRI. The source locations estimated by using the other two identical measurements are also shown.

with a whole-head neuromagnetometer, we show that the conventional MUSIC algorithm fails to localize highly correlated sources and that this problem can be avoided by using the multidimensional MUSIC algorithm. The auditory-evoked response was measured using the 122-channel neuromagnetometer (Neuromag-122^{TM}) installed at the Basic Research Laboratory of the Nippon Telegraph and Telephone Corporation (NTT), Atsugi, Japan. The stimulus was a 1-kHz pure tone applied to the subject's right ear. The sensor-layout display of the measured auditory response is shown in figure 10.7.

We first applied the conventional MUSIC algorithm (equation (14)) to this data. The transverse and coronal projections of the resultant MUSIC localizer map are shown in figure 10.8a (plate 14). This MUSIC map is very blurred, and an accurate localization of the auditory source is hardly possible. This is probably because the responses of the auditory cortices in both hemispheres were highly synchronized and the existence of these coherent sources invalidated the basic assumption of the MUSIC algorithm.

We next calculated the two-source MUSIC localizer in equation (17). The results are shown in figures 10.8b–d (plate 14). These results were iteratively obtained by fixing one source at the location where the localizer had a maximum value in the preceding iteration. The cross mark in (a) indicates the position at which one source was fixed in order to obtain the results in (b). The left and the right auditory sources are clearly detected in the results shown in (c) and (d). Once both auditory sources are localized, we can estimate the waveforms of their source moments by fixing two sources at these locations. The estimated results of the source-moment waveforms are shown in figure 10.9. These waveforms clearly confirm that the two auditory sources were highly synchronized. The correlation coefficient between these waveforms is approximately equal to 0.95. These results demonstrate the effectiveness of the multisource MUSIC algorithm for detecting highly correlated sources.

10.5.4 Applying the Prewhitening MUSIC Algorithm to Eliminate the Influence of Background Brain Activity

The MEG data used here were taken from a series of the speech-sound auditory experiments conducted with the 37-channel Magnes^{TM} neuromagnetometer. The subject was the same male volunteer who provided the results shown in figures 10.3a and 10.4a. When measuring the particular data used here, the subject discriminated the voiced syllable /dae/ from the voiceless syllable /tae/ by pressing a response button with one of his left-hand fingers. Stimuli were presented to the subject's right ear, and the magnetometer was placed over the subject's left hemisphere. The measured auditory responses are shown in figure 10.10. The prestimulus parts of these responses indicate that some background cortical activity exists due probably to

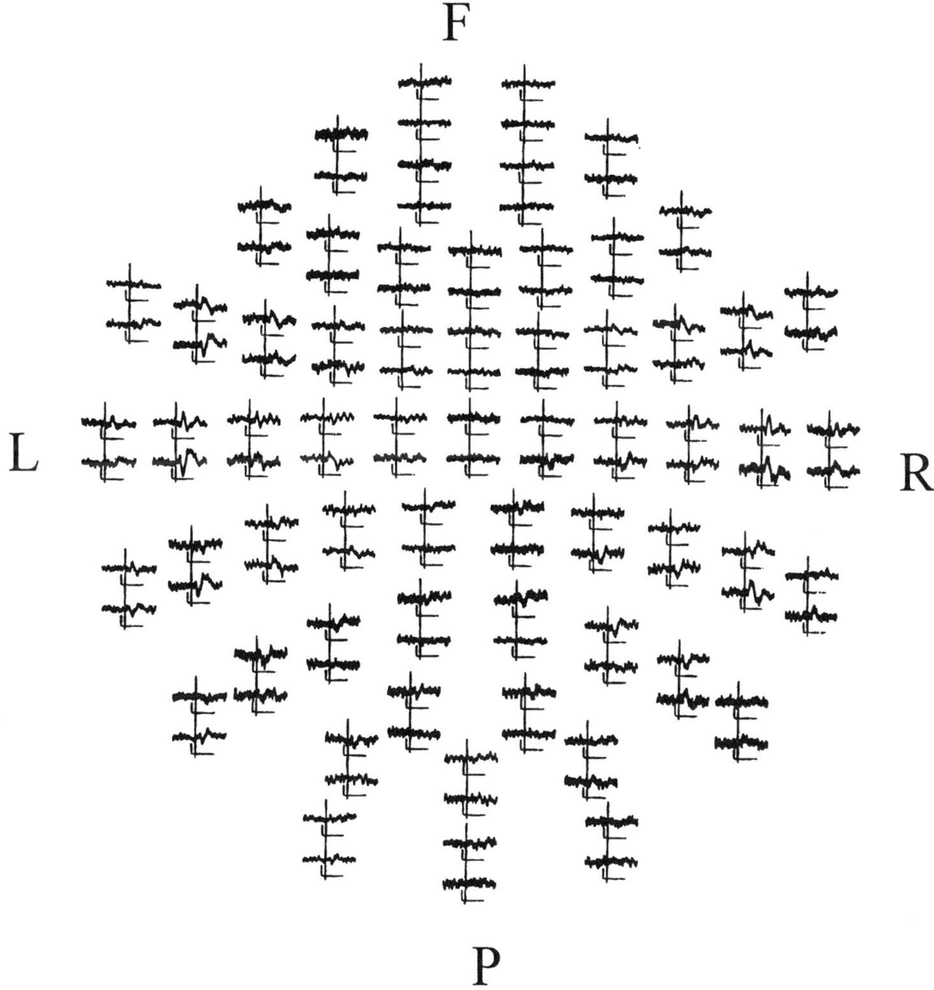

Figure 10.7
Sensor layout display of auditory-evoked response. The auditory response was measured using the 122-channel whole-head neuromagnetometer (Neuromag-122^{TM}). The stimulus was a 1-kHz pure tone applied to the subject's right ear with the average interstimulus interval of 1.5 sec. One hundred epochs were averaged. The four letters *F*, *P*, *L*, and *R* indicate frontal, parietal, left, and right hemispheres, respectively.

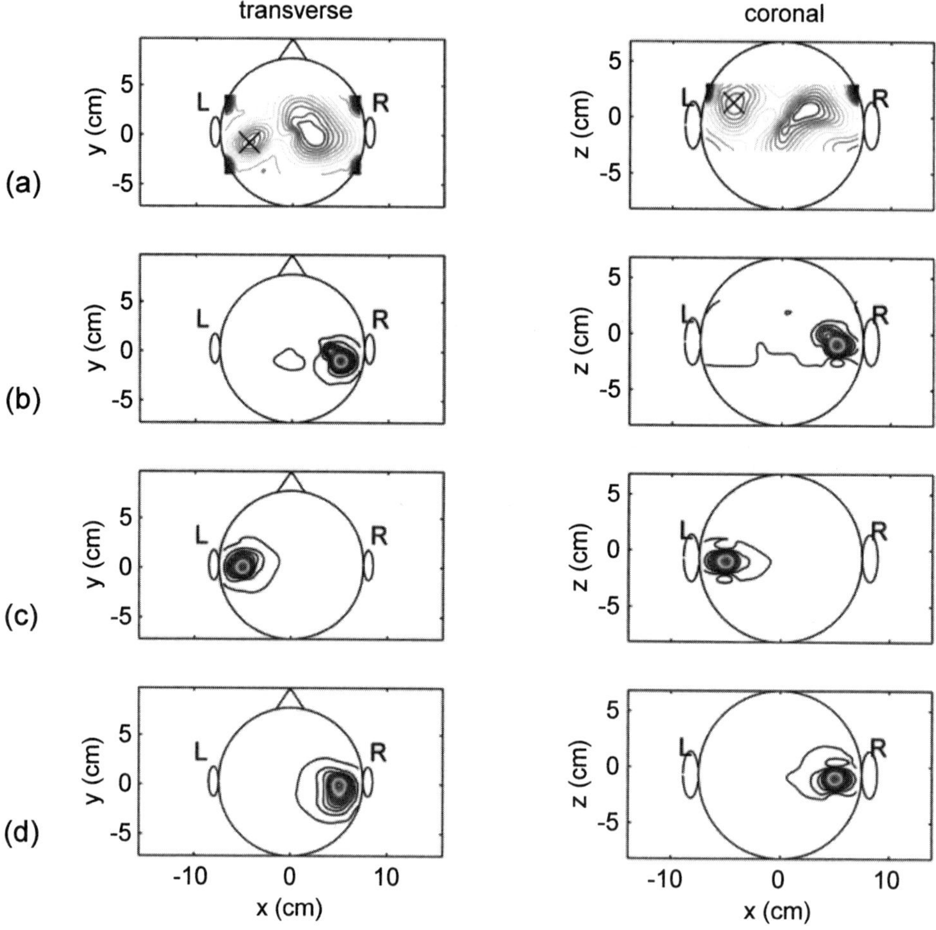

Figure 10.8
(*a*) Results of applying the single-source MUSIC algorithm (equation (14)) to the data shown in figure 10.7. (*b*)–(*d*) Results of applying the two-source MUSIC algorithm (equation (17)). The cross mark in (*a*) indicates the position at which one source was fixed to obtain the results in (*b*). Results in (*c*) and (*d*) were obtained by fixing one source at which the localizer reached its maximum in the results in (*b*) and (*c*), respectively.

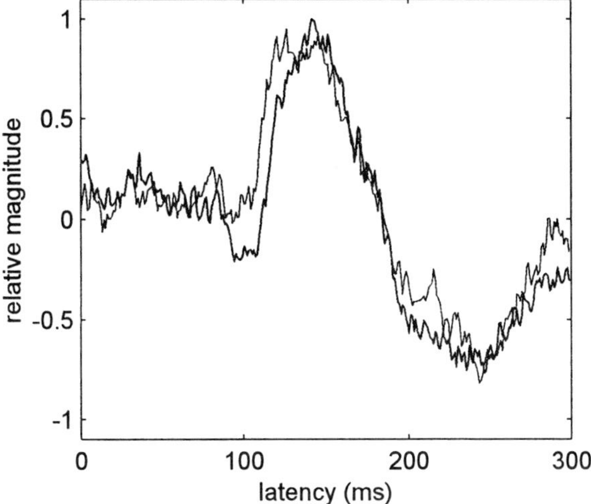

Figure 10.9
Estimated results of the moment waveforms for sources at the left and right auditory cortices. The thin line represents the left auditory cortex activation, and the thick line represents the right auditory cortex activation.

motor cortex activations elicited by pressing the button, even though the subject used his ipsilateral finger.

The results of applying the conventional localizer given in equation (14) are shown in figure 10.11 (plate 15). These results show complex source configurations caused probably by the background motor activity. The prewhitened MUSIC localizer was next applied. The results are shown in figure 10.12. The localizer clearly detects a single localized source in the primary auditory cortex area for both /dae/ and /tae/. It can be seen that both peak locations in figure 10.12 (plate 16) are very close to that in figure 10.4a, thus demonstrating the effectiveness of the prewhitening MUSIC algorithm.

10.5.5 Removal of Background Interference Influence by Using Temporal Correlation

The validity of the method described in section 10.4.3 was tested by using the data elicited by the speech-sound /dae/. The temporal correlation lengths τ_{th}^{s} and τ_{th}^{n} for this data were first estimated. The autocorrelation function from the pre- and post-stimulus parts of each channel recording was calculated and averaged over channels. The results are shown in figure 10.13a (plate 17). We assume that the prestimulus part of the recordings only contains the interferences and that the poststimulus part is dominated by the signal. The autocorrelations obtained from the pre- and post-

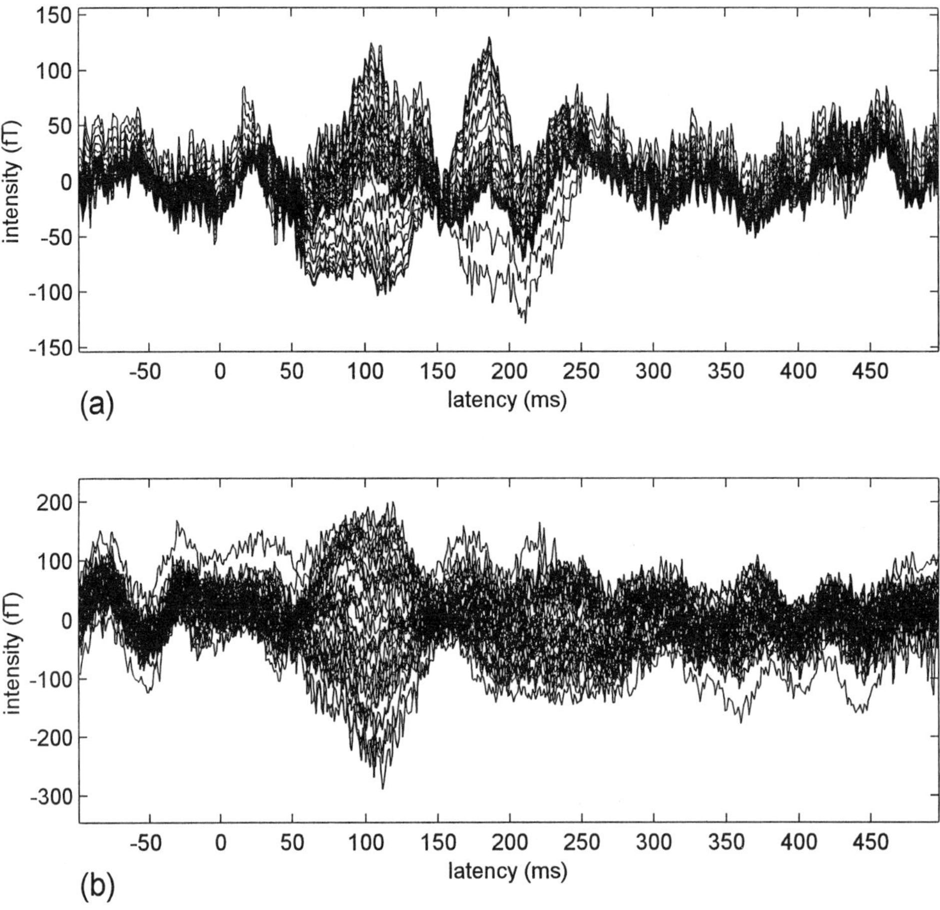

Figure 10.10
Thirty-seven-channel recordings of auditory responses elicited by speech sounds (*a*) /dae/ and (*b*) /tae/ (reproduced from [18]). The subject was the same male volunteer who provided the results in figures 10.3a and 10.4a. The data-sampling frequency was 1 kHz, a bandpass online filter with a bandwidth between 1 and 400 Hz was applied, and 100 epochs were averaged. The auditory stimulus was applied to the subject's right ear and his left hemisphere was measured. The subject pressed a button with one of his left-hand fingers.

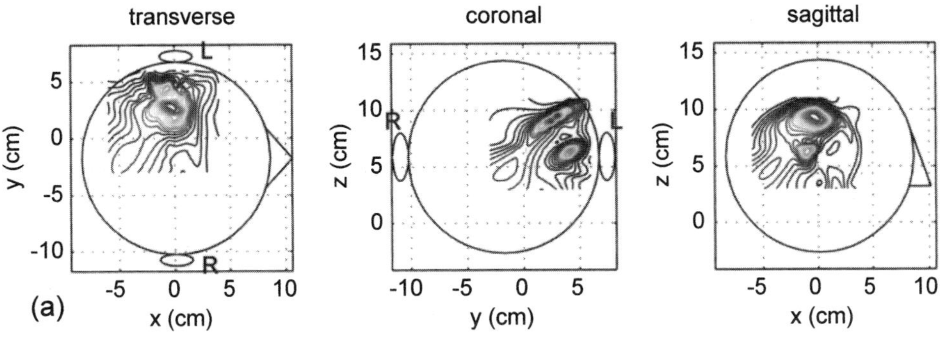

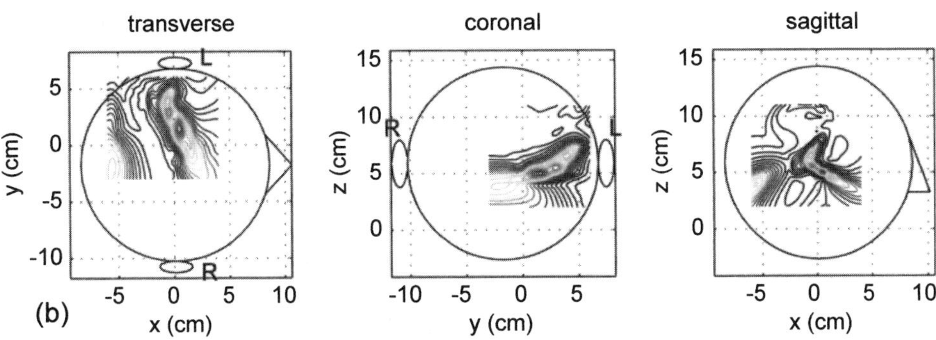

Figure 10.11
Results of applying the conventional localizer in equation (14). Results are shown for the evoked responses to (*a*) /dae/ and (*b*) /tae/ (reproduced from [18]).

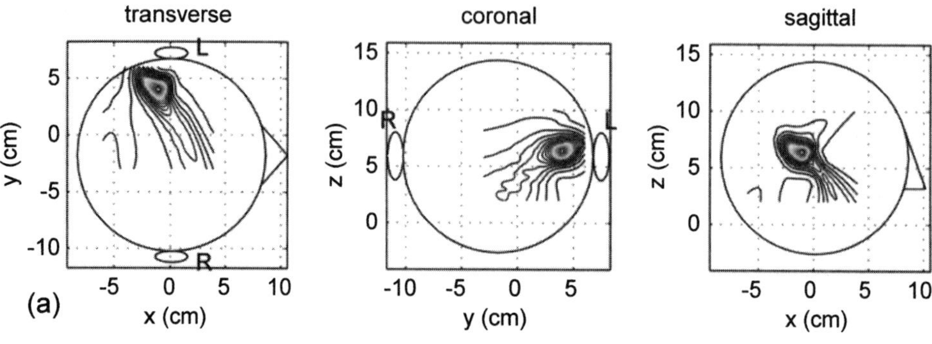

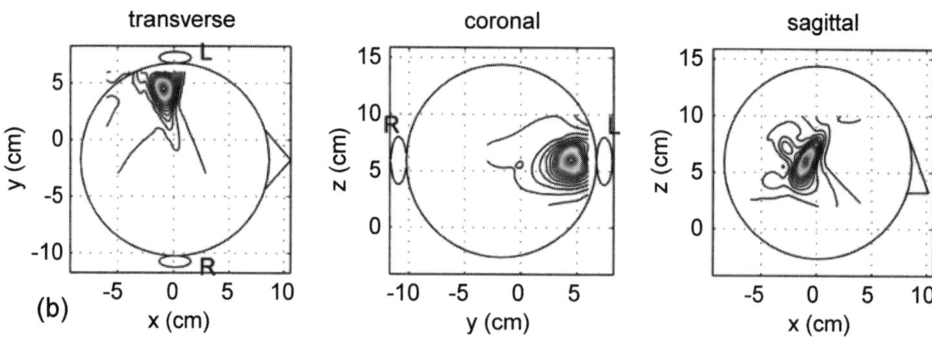

Figure 10.12
Results of applying the prewhitened localizer in equation (31). Results are for the evoked responses to (*a*) /dae/ and (*b*) /tae/ (reproduced from [18]).

stimulus parts are thus considered to represent the autocorrelations of the interferences and the signal, respectively. The results in figure 10.13a confirm that the correlation length of the interferences, τ_{th}^{n}, is shorter than that of the signal, τ_{th}^{s}. Thus, the prerequisite for the method is shown to be satisfied in these data.

We then applied the method described in section 10.4.3 to the source localization from the speech-sound data. The results are shown in figure 10.13b. To obtain these results, five covariance matrices $\boldsymbol{R}_b(\tau)$ with $\tau = 6$, 12, 18, 24, and 30 ms were used. Because the noise correlation length is generally unknown when choosing values of τ, a "safe" choice must be made—that is, a choice of τ that gives sufficiently large $\boldsymbol{R}_s(\tau)$ even though $\boldsymbol{R}_n(\tau)$ is not close enough to zero. In the above application, the maximum value of $\tau = 30$ msec was chosen such that it is equal to the half-width at half maximum of the signal-autocorrelation function's main lobe. Nonetheless, the results in figure 10.13b are almost as good as those in figure 10.12a, and they show that the method was able to eliminate the influence of the background motor activity.

10.5.6 Applying the Prewhitening MUSIC Algorithm to Localizing Sources with Time Jitter

It is common in studies of evoked neuromagnetic fields to measure many epochs by applying a stimulus repeatedly and to analyze the data averaged over these epochs. Averaging the multiple-epoch data obviously assumes that all the epochs are time-locked to the stimulus. Thus, when a non-time-locked source exists, the source estimation may also be erroneous. To avoid this problem, the measurement-covariance matrix needs to be directly calculated from nonaveraged multiple-epoch data. One difficulty with the use of nonaveraged data is that the data inevitably contain a large amount of background activity that is usually averaged out. This difficulty can be circumvented by using the prewhitening technique.

We tested the effectiveness of applying the prewhitening MUSIC algorithm to the nonaveraged raw-epoch data in detecting a source whose activation onset varies from epoch to epoch [24]. To generate the data used for this experiment, we used the same auditory data as for the averaged data shown in figure 10.3a, and we artificially created a jitter for each epoch. That is, each epoch measurement was artificially time shifted. Here the time shift was given by a uniform random number generated in a computer and distributed between 0 and 60 msec.

The covariance matrix was first calculated by using the data averaged over artificially jittered raw epochs. The results of the non-prewhitening MUSIC algorithm with this covariance matrix are shown in figure 10.14a (plate 18). These results contain severe blur, and no accurate source estimation can be made. We then calculated the covariance matrix directly from this raw-epoch data set. The noise covariance matrix was also estimated by using the prestimulus part of the raw-epoch data.

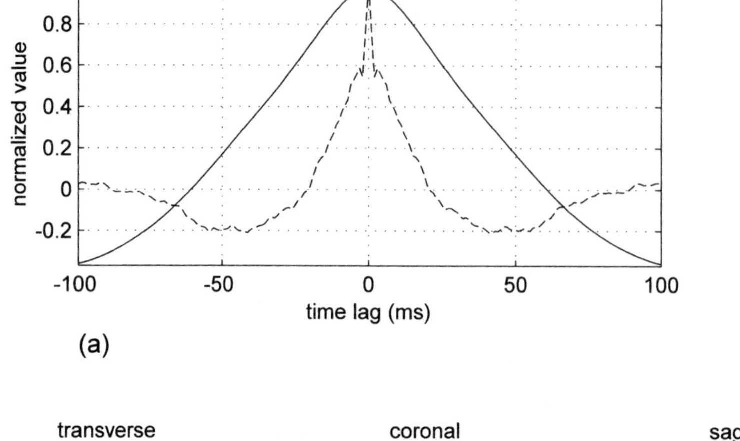

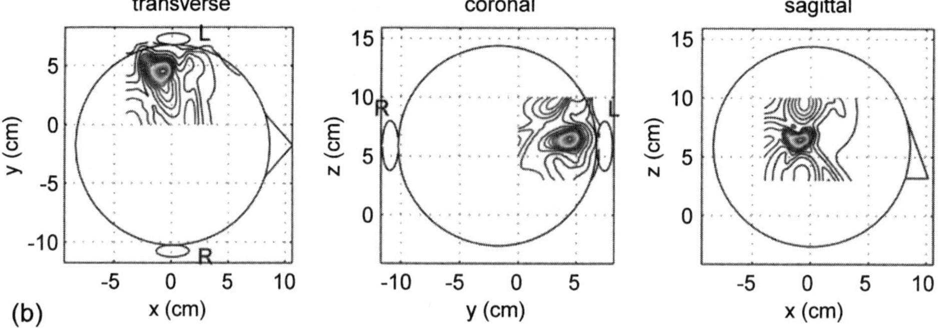

Figure 10.13
(*a*) Temporal autocorrelation function of the auditory-evoked response elicited by the speech sound /dae/. The autocorrelation function was averaged over channels. The solid line indicates the autocorrelation obtained from the poststimulus part, and the broken line indicates the autocorrelation obtained from the prestimulus part. (*b*) Results of applying the method described in section 10.4.3. Five covariance matrices $\boldsymbol{R}_b(\tau)$ with $\tau = 6$, 12, 18, 24, and 30 msec were used to estimate the noise subspace.

First, the non-prewhitening MUSIC algorithm was applied. The results are shown in figure 10.14b. Here a source that was probably caused by the spontaneous background activity was detected, instead of the M100 source in the auditory cortex area. Next, we applied the prewhitening MUSIC algorithm (equation (31)) and the results are shown in figure 10.14c. The comparison between figures 10.4a and 10.14c clearly shows that the M100 source was detected in the left temporal area, demonstrating the validity of using the raw-epoch data for detecting a source with a time jitter. The comparison between figures 10.14b and 10.14c demonstrates the necessity and the effectiveness of the prewhitening technique.

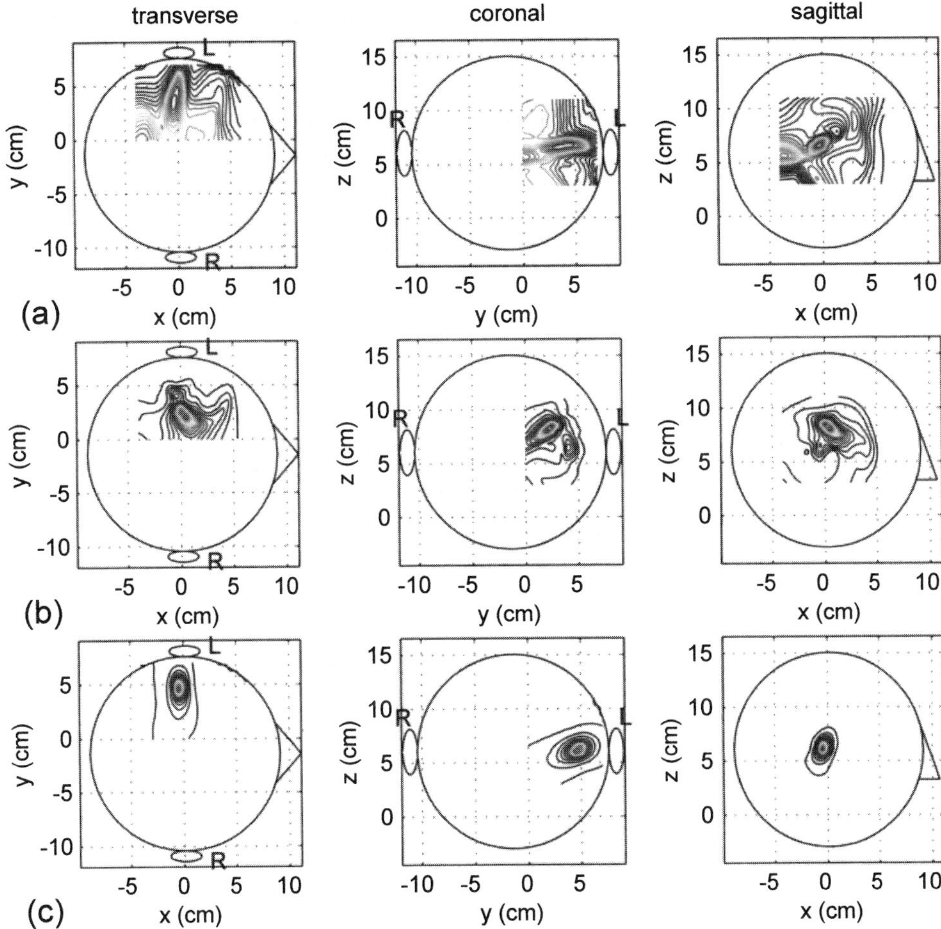

Figure 10.14
(*a*) Results of applying the conventional MUSIC algorithm to the averaged data containing the artificial time jitter. (*b*) Results of applying the conventional MUSIC algorithm to raw-epoch data. (*c*) Results of applying the prewhitening MUSIC algorithm to raw-epoch data (reproduced from [24]).

10.5.7 Applying Covariance Difference Analysis to Extract Target Activity from a Large Amount of Interference

We demonstrate the effectiveness of the covariance difference analysis for extracting the target activity from data containing a large amount of interference. Two kinds of measurements were performed. In the first measurement, a 1-kHz pure-tone auditory stimulus was applied to the subject's right ear and the subject pressed a response button when he heard the tone. The data acquisition was triggered with the onset of the auditory stimulus. In the second measurement, the subject pressed the response button every 2 sec in a self-paced manner. The data acquisition was triggered by his button presses. In both of the measurements, the subject pressed the response button with his right index finger, and subject's left hemisphere was measured. The waveforms obtained in these two measurements are shown in figure 10.15. In figure 10.15a, a very large interference, which was caused by the contralateral finger movements, overlaps onto the auditory response, so a peak in the N100m cannot be observed. In figure 10.15b, large-amplitude motor activation is observed; the activation begins at an instant before button pressing.

For comparison, the waveform-subtraction method was first applied to extract target cortical activities from these two sets of data. A data portion between 0 and 200 msec was selected from the auditory-button-press data, and it is denoted as $\boldsymbol{b}^{(1)}(t)$. The onsets for the motor activation were generally different between the auditory-button-press and self-paced button-press measurements. Thus, a portion between the latency of t_s and $t_s + 200$ msec was selected from the self-paced button-press data. It is denoted as $\boldsymbol{b}^{(2)}(t + t_s)$. We then calculated

$$\Delta\boldsymbol{b}(t) = \boldsymbol{b}^{(1)}(t) - \boldsymbol{b}^{(2)}(t + t_s) \qquad (0 \leq t \leq 200 \text{ ms}) \tag{36}$$

and the covariance matrix was calculated by using $\boldsymbol{R}_{\Delta b} = \langle \Delta\boldsymbol{b}(t)\Delta\boldsymbol{b}^{\mathrm{T}}(t)\rangle_t$, where the time average $\langle\cdot\rangle_t$ was calculated between $t = 0$ and 200 msec. Because the appropriate time difference was unknown, six cases (i.e., $t_s = -10, -30, -50, -70, -90$, and -110 msec) were tested in this experiment. The conventional MUSIC algorithm was applied with $\boldsymbol{R}_{\Delta b}$ and the results are shown in figure 10.16 (plates 19, 20). When $t_s = -50$ msec or $t_s = -70$ msec, the interferences from the motor activation were eliminated and the auditory source could be detected. When $t_s = -10, -30, -90$, or -110 msec, however, the auditory source could not be separated from motor activation.

We applied covariance difference analysis with the same six values of t_s. Denoting the covariance matrices for auditory-button-press data as $\boldsymbol{R}_b^{(1)}$ and self-paced button-press data as $\boldsymbol{R}_b^{(2)}$, the difference matrix was obtained by using $\Delta\boldsymbol{R}_b = \boldsymbol{R}_b^{(1)} - \boldsymbol{R}_b^{(2)}$. The localizer in equation (33) was then calculated, and the results are shown in figure 10.17 (plates 21, 22). The auditory source can more or less be detected for all six values of t_s. A comparison of the results in figures 10.16 and 10.17 demonstrates that

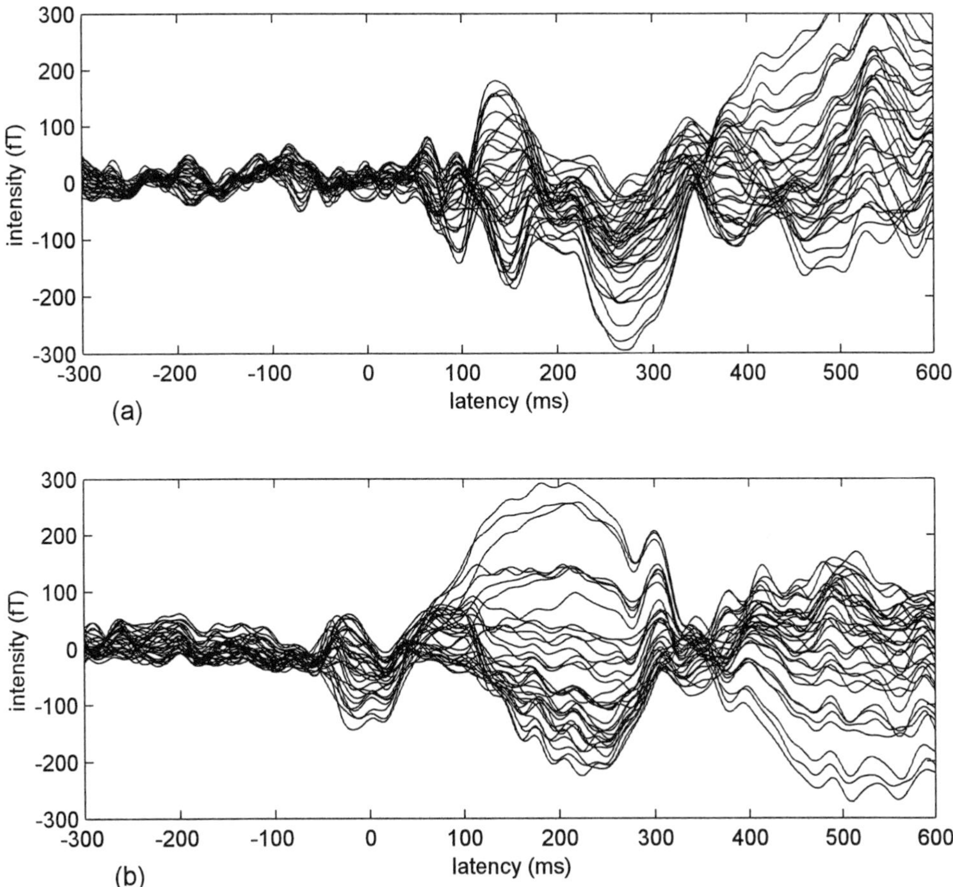

Figure 10.15
Thirty-seven channel recordings of evoked responses used in the covariance-difference experiments. (*a*) The auditory-button-press data. The 1-kHz pure-tone auditory stimulus was applied to the subject's right ear and the subject pressed a response button when he heard the tone. The data acquisition was triggered with the onset of the auditory stimulus, and the mean inter-stimulus interval was 2 sec. (*b*) The self-paced button-press data. The subject pressed a response button every 2 sec in a self-paced manner. The data acquisition was triggered by the button presses. In both measurements, the right index finger was used for button pressing, the subject's left hemisphere was measured, and a total of 256 epochs were averaged (reproduced from [20]).

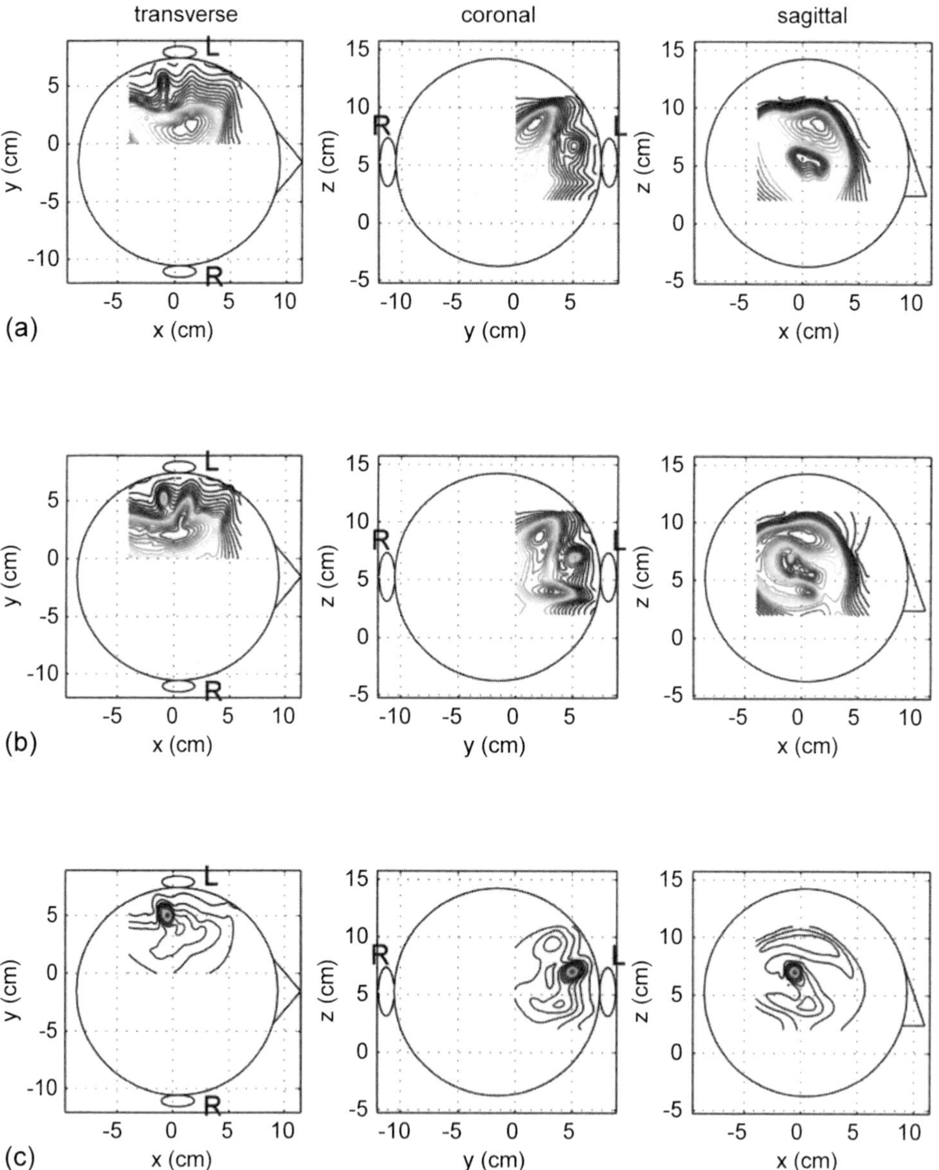

Figure 10.16
The results of applying the waveform-based subtraction method. The data portion between 0 and 200 msec was selected from the auditory-button-press data and the portion between t_s and $t_s + 200$ msec was selected from the self-paced button-press data. Results for (*a*) $t_s = -10$, (*b*) $t_s = -30$, (*c*) $t_s = -50$, (*d*) $t_s = -70$, (*e*) $t_s = -90$, and (*f*) $t_s = -110$ msec (reproduced from [20]).

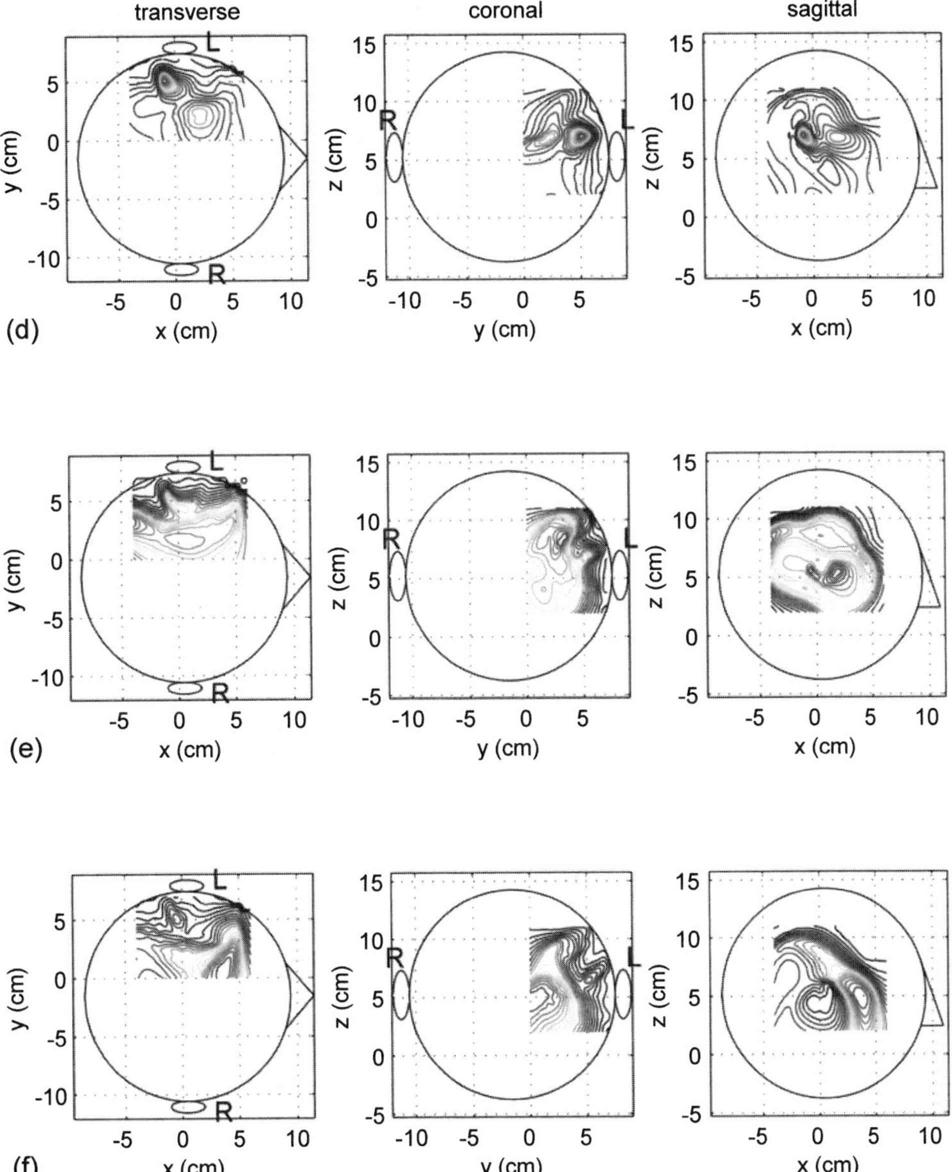

Figure 10.16 (continued)

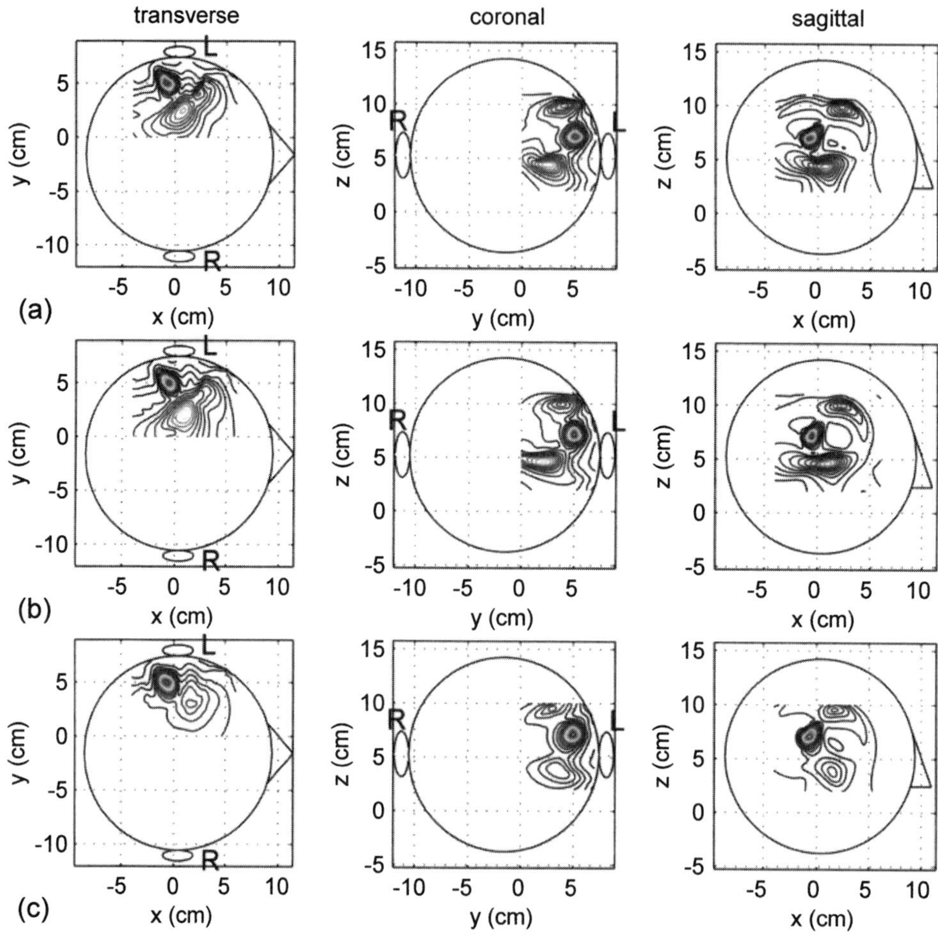

Figure 10.17
The results of applying the covariance-difference analysis. The data portion between 0 and 200 msec was selected from the auditory-button-press data and the portion between t_s and $t_s + 200$ msec was selected from the self-paced button-press data. Results for (*a*) $t_s = -10$, (*b*) $t_s = -30$, (*c*) $t_s = -50$, (*d*) $t_s = -70$, (*e*) $t_s = -90$, and (*f*) $t_s = -110$ msec (reproduced from [20]).

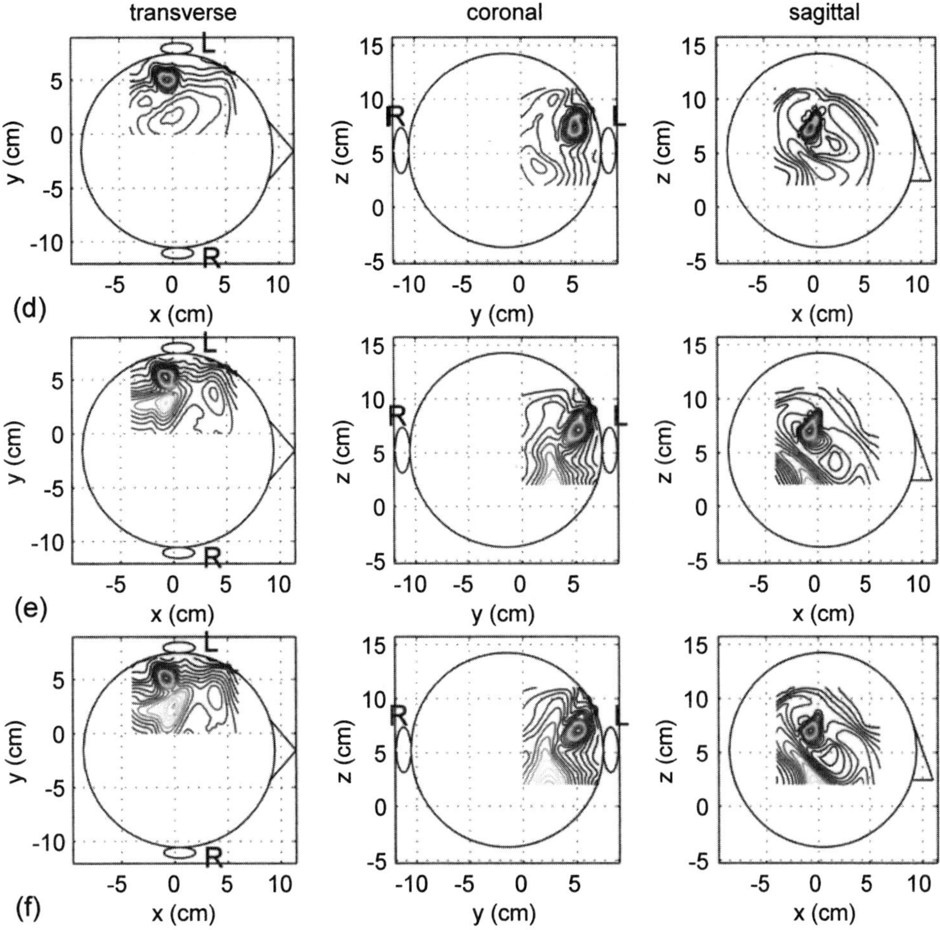

Figure 10.17 (continued)

the covariance difference analysis is less sensitive to the onset difference of the interference field than the waveform-subtraction method, showing the validity of the discussion in section 10.4.2.

Note

The authors wish to thank Susanne Honma and Tim Roberts for their help during the biomagnetic measurements, and Srikantan Nagarajan for his discussion regarding the spectral estimation. The authors are grateful to Satoru Miyauchi, Norio Fujimaki, and Ryosuke Takino for their help in the experiments using the Magnes 2500^{TM} neuromagnetometer, and to Toshiaki Imada for his help in using the Neuromag-122^{TM} neuromagnetometer. The authors are grateful to Arogyaswami J. Paulraj for his insightful comments on the eigen-structure methods. The authors also thank Deborah Won for writing the PsyScope script as well as Elron Yellin and Stephan Masterman for their help in preparing the biomagnetic data.

References

[1] M. Hämäläinen, R. Hari, R. J. Ilmoniemi, J. Knuutila, and O. V. Lounasmaa, "Magnetoencephalography—theory, instrumentation, and applications to noninvasive studies of the working human brain," *Review of Modern Physics*, vol. 65, pp. 413–497, 1993.

[2] J. Sarvas, "Basic mathematical and electromagnetic concepts of the biomagnetic inverse problem," *Physics in Medicine and Biology*, vol. 32, pp. 11–22, 1987.

[3] D. H. Johnson and D. E. Dudgeon, *Array Signal Processing: Concepts and Techniques*, Prentice Hall, Englewood Cliffs, N.J., 1993.

[4] H. Krim and M. Viberg, "Two decades of array signal processing research," *IEEE Signal Processing Magazine*, vol. 13, no. 4, pp. 67–94, 1996.

[5] R. O. Schmidt, "Multiple emitter location and signal parameter estimation," *IEEE Transactions on Antennas and Propagation*, vol. 34, pp. 276–280, 1986.

[6] R. O. Schmidt, *A signal subspace approach to multiple emitter location and spectral estimation*, Ph.D. dissertation, Stanford University, Stanford Calif., 1981.

[7] J. C. Mosher, P. S. Lewis, and R. M. Leahy, "Multiple dipole modeling and localization from spatio-temporal MEG data," *IEEE Transactions on Biomedical Engineering*, vol. 39, pp. 541–557, 1992.

[8] G. H. Golub and V. Pereyra, "The differentiation of pseudo-inverses and nonlinear least squares problems whose variables separate," *SIAM Journal of Numerical Analysis*, vol. 10, pp. 413–432, 1973.

[9] L. L. Scharf, *Statistical Signal Processing: Detection, estimation, and time series analysis*, Addison-Wesley, New York, 1991.

[10] E. R. Ferrara, Jr., and T. M. Parks, "Direction finding with an array of antennas having diverse polarizations," *IEEE Transactions on Antennas and Propagation*, vol. 31, pp. 231–236, 1983.

[11] K. Sekihara, S. Miyauchi, R. Takino, N. Fujimaki, and Y. Miyashita, "Frequency-selective MEG MUSIC algorithm: A new method for analyzing rhythmic spontaneous brain activity," *NeuroImage*, vol. 5, no. 4, p. S436, 1996.

[12] D. J. Thompson, "Spectrum estimation and harmonic analysis," *Proceedings of the IEEE*, vol. 70, pp. 1055–1096, 1982.

[13] D. B. Percival and A. T. Walden, *Spectral analysis for physical applications—multitaper and conventional univariate analysis*, Cambridge University Press, Cambridge, England, 1993.

[14] R. Hari and R. Salmelin, "Human cortical oscillations: A neuromagnetic view through the skull," *Trends in Neurosciences*, vol. 20, pp. 44–49, 1997.

[15] J. Knuutila and M. S. Hämäläinen, "Characterization of brain noise using a high sensitivity 7-channel magnmetometer," in *Proceedings of the Sixth International Conference on Biomagnetism*, pp. 186–189, 1987.

[16] K. Sekihara, K. Abramham-Fuchs, H. Stefan, and E. Hellstrandt, "Suppression of background brain activity influence in localizing epileptic spike sources from biomagnetic measurements," *Brain Topography*, vol. 8, pp. 323–328, 1996.

[17] K. Sekihara, F. Takeuchi, S. Kuriki, and H. Koizumi, "Reduction of brain noise influence in evoked neuromagnetic source localization using noise spatial correlation," *Physics in Medicine and Biology*, vol. 39, pp. 937–946, 1994.

[18] K. Sekihara, D. Poeppel, A. Marantz, H. Koizumi, and Y. Miyashita, "Noise covariance incorporated MEG-MUSIC algorithm: A method for multiple-dipole estimation tolerant of the influence of background brain activity," *IEEE Transactions on Biomedical Engineering*, vol. 44, pp. 839–847, 1997.

[19] K. Sekihara, D. Poeppel, A. Marantz, C. Phillips, H. Koizumi, and Y. Miyashita, "MEG covariance difference analysis: A method to extract target source activities by using task and control measurements," *IEEE Transactions on Biomedical Engineering*, vol. 45, pp. 87–97, 1998.

[20] K. Sekihara, D. Poeppel, A. Marantz, H. Koizumi, and Y. Miyashita, "Comparison of covariance-based and waveform-based subtraction methods in removing the interference from button-pressing finger movements," *Brain Topography*, vol. 11, pp. 95–102, 1998.

[21] A. Belouchrani, M. G. Amin, and K. Abed-Meraim, "Direction finding in correlated noise fields based on joint block-diagonalization of spatio-temporal correlation matrices," *IEEE Signal Processing Letters*, vol. 4, pp. 266–268, 1997.

[22] J.-F. Cardoso and A. Souloumiac, "Jacobi angles for simultaneous diagonalization," *SIAM Journal of Matrix Analysis and Applications*, vol. 17, pp. 161–164, 1996.

[23] S. Salenius, M. Kajora, W. L. Thompson, S. Kosslyn, and R. Hari, "Reactivity of magnetic parieto-occipital alpha rhythm during visual imagery," *Electroencephalography and Clinical Neurophysiology*, vol. 95, pp. 453–462, 1995.

[24] K. Sekihara, D. Poeppel, A. Marantz, H. Koizumi, and Y. Miyashita, "MEG spatiotemporal analysis using a covariance matrix calculated from non-averaged multiple-epoch data," *IEEE Transactions on Biomedical Engineering*, vol. 46, pp. 515–521, 1999.

Chapter 11

Competitive Mechanisms Subserve Selective Visual Attention

John H. Reynolds and Robert Desimone

11.1 Behavioral and Neuronal Limitations on Visual Processing

A typical scene is far too complicated for the visual system to process it in all its detail in a single moment. Subjectively, we are momentarily overwhelmed when looking for a misplaced object on a cluttered desk. Accordingly, psychophysical experiments have found that when one searches for a target among distractors, the addition of heterogeneous distractors typically increases the time needed to find the target, as does increasing the heterogeneity of existing distractors. Thus, the visual system is limited in its capacity to process information. However, it is equipped to overcome this constraint because it can direct this limited-capacity channel to locations or objects of interest. Subjectively, attending to a given object reduces our awareness of other objects among the clutter. As a result, our ability to identify a given object may be unaffected by the presence and number of distractors in a display (see Duncan 1980; Bundesen 1990).

We might expect to see reflections of this limited but controllable information-processing channel in the response properties of neurons involved in identifying and distinguishing between objects. The ventral stream of visual processing in the macaque is thought to serve these functions. Neurons in the areas that make up the ventral processing stream respond selectively depending on the form of visual stimuli. As activation propagates from the primary visual cortex through the ventral stream, through the thin and interstripe regions of area V2, into area V4, and onward into TEO and TE, one of the most obvious changes is that neuronal receptive fields grow steadily larger. In area V1, receptive fields are typically less than one degree of visual arc in diameter. In area TE, they typically span the entire central visual field (see Desimone and Ungerleider 1989; Boussaoud, Desimone, and Ungerleider 1991). The number of objects in a scene that fall within a single receptive field tends to increase with receptive field size. This suggests one possible explanation for why we find it difficult to simultaneously process all the information available in a complex scene.

When multiple stimuli appear within the receptive field of a ventral-stream neuron, the neuron is unable to respond to each of the objects at the same time.

If our inability to simultaneously process all the detail in a scene is related to information-processing limitations at the level of individual neurons, we should expect to find that the attentional mechanisms that enable us to overcome complexity should modulate the responses of the same neurons. Earlier experiments in the ventral stream have examined the way attention modulates responses when multiple stimuli appear within the receptive fields of ventral-stream neurons. Moran and Desimone (1985) and Luck and colleagues (1997) have found that when two stimuli are presented within the receptive field, the neuronal responses to the pair depends on which of the two stimuli is attended to. One of the stimuli was of an orientation or color that elicits a large response (the *preferred stimulus*) and the other was of an orientation or color that elicits a small response (the *poor stimulus*). The response to the pair was larger when attention was directed to the preferred stimulus, relative to when attention was directed to the poor stimulus. In contrast, when a single stimulus appeared alone inside the receptive field, attention had no effect on the neuronal response to that stimulus.

These results are consistent with the idea that the attended stimulus exerts enhanced control over the neuronal response. According to a model proposed by Desimone and Duncan (1995), the data can be explained as a result of interactions between two neuronal mechanisms: (1) automatic intracortical competition coupled with (2) a top-down attentional feedback that biases this competition. According to this *biased-competition model*, multiple stimuli appearing together activate populations of neurons that compete with one another, possibly through mutual inhibition. When attention is directed to one of the stimuli, this causes an attentional feedback signal to be directed to the neuronal population activated by the attended stimulus. This feedback biases the competition in favor of the attended stimulus, enabling it to propagate its signal forward to the next cortical area.

11.2 Do Stimuli Compete to Control Neuronal Responses?

We have recently conducted two experiments to test this model. One experiment was designed to examine how the responses elicited by a single stimulus within the receptive field (termed the *reference stimulus*) are influenced by the addition of a second receptive field stimulus (termed the *probe*), in the absence of attentional modulation. Depending on the mechanisms that govern responses to stimulus pairs, adding the probe might be expected to result in an increase, a reduction, or a more complex change in the pair response, as compared to the response elicited by the reference stimulus. An increase in response could occur as a result of additional recruitment of V1 afferents by the second stimulus. A reduction in response could occur as a result of diminished bottom-up or top-down excitatory drive. Response suppression by extrareceptive field stimuli has been observed in area V1 (Knierim and Van Essen 1992; Levitt and Lund 1997). Response suppression has also been observed in higher-order areas that provide feedback to areas V2 and V4 (Miller, Gochin, and Gross 1993; Rolls and Tovee 1995). Alternatively, the individual stimulus responses might bear *no* systematic relationship to the response elicited by the pair. For example, the pair response might depend on factors other than the firing rates elicited by the individual stimuli, such as the geometric relationships between the stimuli (Kapadia et al. 1995; Sillito et al. 1995), or their color contrast (Kiper, Fenstemaker, and Gegenfurtner 1997). Alternatively, V2 and V4 cells might simply treat the pair as a third, independent stimulus, with its own, arbitrary response.

In contrast to these alternatives, the biased-competition hypothesis predicts that the pair response should fall between the responses to the reference and probe stimuli. According to the hypothesis, different stimuli activate competing populations of neurons. To the extent that a probe stimulus has any influence on the neuronal response, it should move the pair response toward the response it would give if the probe had been presented alone. Adding a low firing-rate probe should drive down the response to a high firing-rate reference stimulus. Adding a high firing-rate probe should drive up the response to a low firing-rate reference stimulus. If probe and reference stimuli individually elicit identical responses, then the same response should be generated when they appear together as a pair.

To test these alternatives, we have recorded the responses of neurons in area V4 to pairs of stimuli appearing inside the receptive field (Reynolds, Chelazzi, and Desimone 1999). The monkey was rewarded for passively fixating a fixation spot at the center of the computer screen. Oriented rectangular stimuli could appear at one of two possible locations within the receptive field. The stimulus that would appear at position 1 was designated the reference stimulus, and its orientation and color were fixed throughout the recording session. On each trial, the stimulus that would appear at position 2, designated a probe stimulus, was selected at random from a set of sixteen possible stimuli, consisting of bars of four equiluminant colors at four different orientations. On any given trial, stimuli appeared in one of three possible configurations: (1) the reference stimulus appeared at position 1, (2) a probe stimulus appeared at position 2, or (3) the reference stimulus appeared at position 1 together with a probe stimulus at position 2.

We found that in area V4, the responses to the reference stimulus are suppressed by the addition of a poor probe, increased by the addition of a preferred probe, and unaffected by the addition of a probe that, when presented alone, elicited a response equivalent to the reference stimulus response. This is illustrated in figure 11.1 (plate 23), which shows the responses of a typical cell to the reference stimulus, the three different probes, and the resulting three stimulus pairs. For a probe that elicited a

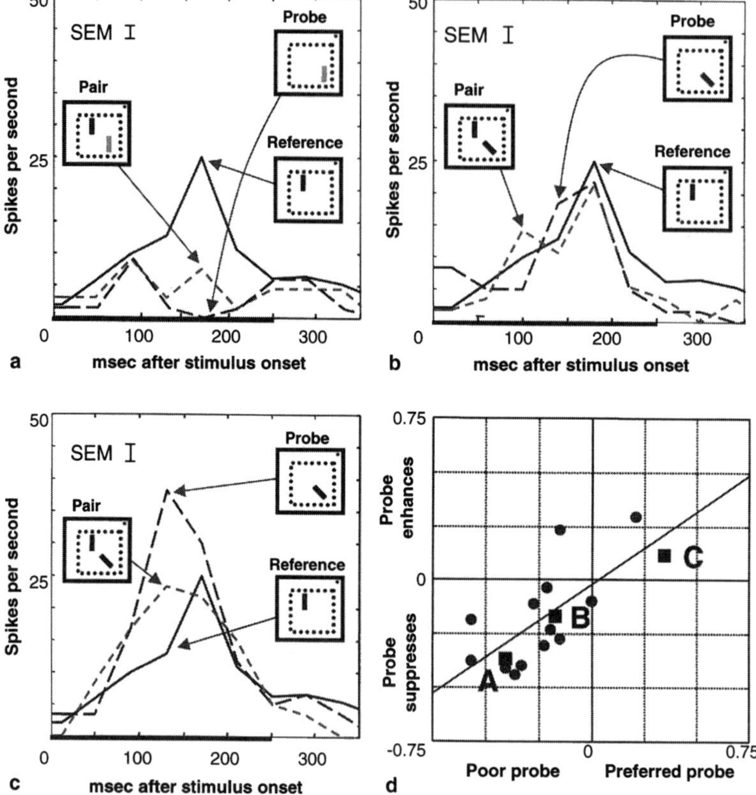

Figure 11.1
In the absence of attention, stimuli compete to control neuronal responses. The response of a single V4 neuron to the reference, a probe, and the corresponding pair is shown for three probes in each of panels a, b, and c. The horizontal axis shows time (in msec) from stimulus onset, and the thick horizontal bar indicates stimulus duration. The vertical bar in the upper left-hand corner shows the standard error of the mean (SEM) of the response of this neuron, averaged over the three stimulus conditions for each panel. The blue line that is constant across all three panels shows the response to the reference stimulus, which was a vertical green bar. (*a*) The green line indicates the response to a vertical yellow probe that drove the cell at a low average rate. The response to the pair, indicated by a red line, was strongly suppressed by the probe stimulus. (*b*) A 45° blue bar probe, which elicited a response similar to the response to the reference stimulus, caused little or no change in the cell's response. (*c*) A 45° green bar probe, which elicited a response larger than the response to the reference stimulus, increased the cell's response. (*d*) Indices of selectivity (horizontal axis) and sensory interaction (vertical axis) for all sixteen probe stimuli. The indices corresponding to each of the probes illustrated in panels a, b, and c are indicated by squares and are labeled in panel d. A negative selectivity index (indicating that the response to the probe was less than the response to the reference stimulus) was typically paired with a negative sensory interaction index (indicating that the addition of the poor probe suppressed the response of the cell). Nonselective reference-probe pairs showed little or no sensory interactions. Preferred probes increased the response to the reference stimulus.

lower mean response than the reference (figure 11.1a), the addition of the probe was suppressive. For a probe that elicited an average response roughly equal to the response elicited by the reference stimulus (figure 11.1b), the pair response was similar to responses to the probe and reference stimuli presented alone. For a probe stimulus that elicited a stronger response than the reference stimulus (figure 11.1c), the addition of the probe caused an increase in the cell's mean response.

This relationship held across all sixteen probe stimuli, as illustrated in figure 11.1d, which shows the relationship between selectivity for reference and probe (horizontal axis) versus the change in response that resulted from adding the probe (vertical axis) across all sixteen stimuli. Points labeled a–c correspond to the examples shown in panels a–c of the figure. As was typical of other neurons recorded in area V4, the effect of adding the probe was proportional to the neuron's selectivity for reference stimulus and probe. Adding a poor probe, such as a, typically suppressed the response elicited by the reference stimulus. Probes, such as b, which elicited similar responses to the reference stimulus, had little or no effect on neuronal response when they were added to the receptive field along with the reference stimulus. Adding a preferred probe, such as c, typically increased the neuronal response.

These data are incompatible with some possible models of sensory processing in areas V2 and V4. We can rule out models in which the response to a pair of stimuli is greater than the response to the preferred stimulus appearing alone or less than the response to the poor stimulus alone. We can also reject models in which the pair is treated as a third, independent stimulus, with its own, arbitrary response. However, the finding that the addition of a second stimulus drives the neuronal response toward the response elicited when that stimulus appears alone is consistent with the biased-competition model.

11.3 Are Competitive Interactions Biased by Attention?

In a related experiment, we tested the second hypothesis of the biased-competition model, namely, that attentional feedback biases this competition in favor of the attended stimulus. According to this hypothesis, when attention is directed to one of two stimuli, this should cause the population of neurons activated by the attended stimulus to suppress the responses of neurons belonging to the population activated by the ignored stimulus. As a result, neurons that respond to the attended stimulus should be active, and the neurons that do not respond to the attended stimulus should be suppressed. That is, the attended stimulus should have enhanced control over neuronal responses. At the level of the individual neuronal response, then, the biased-competition model predicts that the effect of attention will be to drive the pair response toward the response elicited by the attended stimulus when it appears alone. We tested this prediction by repeating the experiment described above, and examined the effect of directing attention to the reference stimulus.

The biased-competition model's prediction was supported, as illustrated in figure 11.2, which shows the responses of two V2 neurons. The neuron appearing in the upper panel gave a strong response when the reference stimulus appeared alone, while the monkey attended away from the receptive field (upper line). Adding the poor probe, which elicited a small response (bottom line) when presented alone, suppressed the neuron's firing rate (pair response: dashed line, middle). However, when the same pair of stimuli was presented while the monkey attended to the reference stimulus (thick gray line), this drove the neuronal response upward, almost to the magnitude of response elicited when the reference stimulus appeared alone.

Just as attention filtered out the suppression caused by the addition of a poor probe stimulus, it also filtered out the increase in response resulting from adding a preferred stimulus. The lower panel of figure 11.2 shows the responses of a neuron that responded at a low rate when the reference stimulus was presented alone (bottom, dashed line). When a preferred-orientation probe stimulus (upper, solid line) was added, this drove the neuronal response up (middle, dashed line). However, when attention was directed to the reference stimulus, this eliminated most of the increase caused by the probe, returning the firing rate to a level just above the response to the reference stimulus alone (thickened gray line, bottom).

The same pattern was observed in area V4, as illustrated in figure 11.3, which shows responses of two V4 neurons. The upper panel shows a neuron whose strong response to the reference stimulus was suppressed by the addition of a poor probe stimulus. As in V2, directing attention to the reference stimulus eliminated this suppression. Panel b shows a V4 neuron whose weak response to the reference stimulus was greatly increased by the addition of the preferred probe. As was found in V2, this increase was largely eliminated when attention was directed to the reference stimulus.

These results show that attention can either increase or decrease neuronal responses, depending on the change in response caused by the addition of the ignored stimulus. Thus, we can rule out models in which attention merely causes an increase in the gain associated with the attended stimulus. The biased-competition model offers a parsimonious explanation for results of both experiments.

11.4 An Implementation of the Biased-Competition Model

Biased competition could be implemented by the cortex in a number of ways. The model circuit appearing in figure 11.4 is a simple feedforward competitive neural network that implements the biased-competition model. It was developed to provide an existence proof that the biased-competition model can satisfy the constraints imposed by the experiments just described.

The model is defined by the four equations appearing at the bottom of figure 11.4. The model includes two classes of neurons. The circle at the top of figure 11.4 repre-

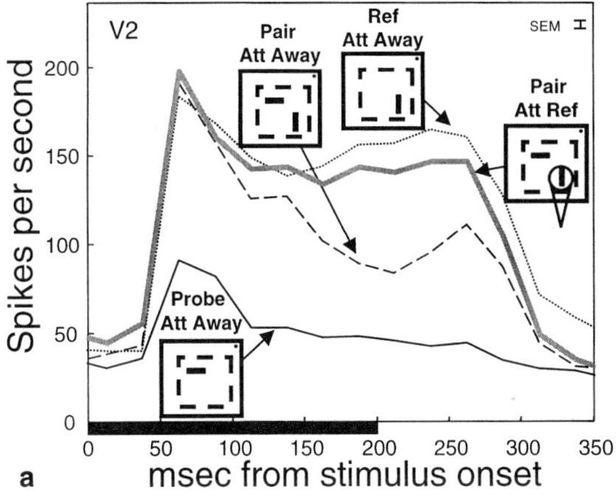

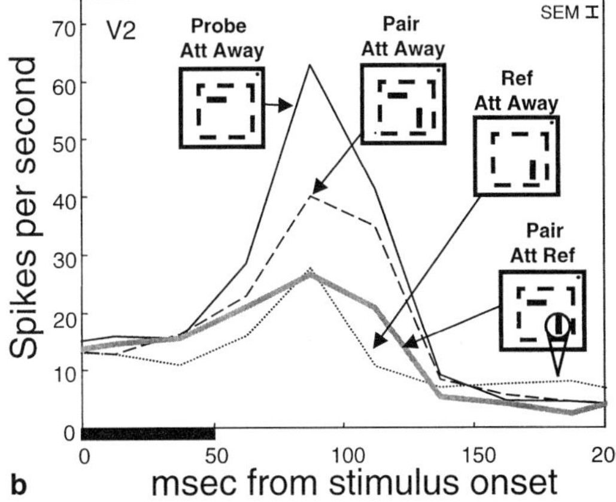

Figure 11.2
Attention filtering out the effect of a suppressive probe (*a*) and an enhancing probe (*b*) in area V2. The horizontal axis shows time (in msec) from stimulus onset, and the thick horizontal bar indicates stimulus duration. The vertical axis shows instantaneous firing rate. The vertical bar in the upper-right corner of each panel shows the standard error of the mean response for this neuron, averaged across experimental conditions. Panel a: Small iconic figures illustrate sensory conditions. The dotted line shows the response to the preferred reference stimulus. The solid line shows the response elicited by the poor probe. The response to the pair (dashed line) was suppressed by the addition of the probe. The pair response was driven back toward the reference-stimulus response by attention to the reference stimulus (thick gray line). Panel b: Facilitation filtered out of the response of a second V2 neuron. The dotted line shows the weak response to the reference stimulus. The solid line shows the strong response elicited by the preferred probe. The response to the pair (dashed line) was increased by the addition of the preferred probe. The pair response was driven back toward the reference-stimulus response by attention to the reference stimulus (thick gray line).

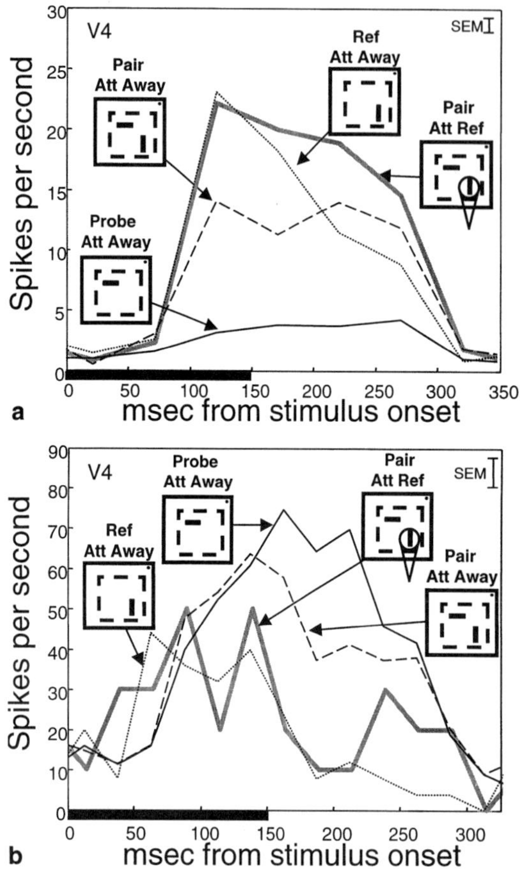

Figure 11.3

Attention filtering out the effect of a suppressive probe (*a*) and an enhancing probe (*b*) in area V4. The format is identical to figure 11.2. Panel a shows suppression by a poor probe, which was filtered out when attention was directed to the reference stimulus. Panel b shows enhancement by a preferred probe, which was filtered out when attention was directed to the reference stimulus.

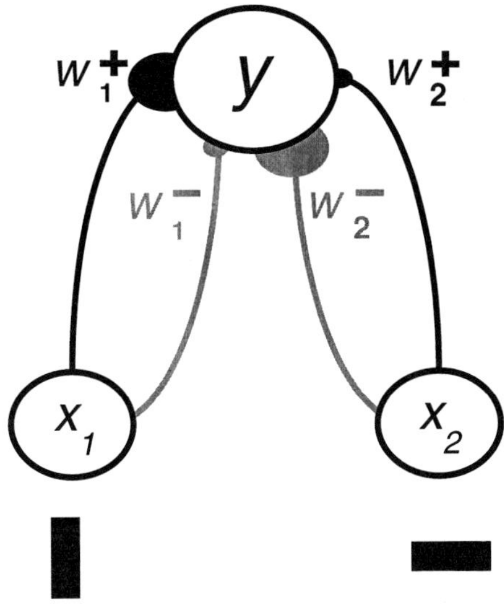

$$E = x_1 w_1^+ + x_2 w_2^+ \qquad (1)$$

$$I = x_1 w_1^- + x_2 w_2^- \qquad (2)$$

$$\frac{dy}{dt} = (B-y)\,E - y\,I - A\,y \qquad (3)$$

$$\underset{\lim t \rightarrow \text{infinity}}{y} = \frac{B\,E}{E + I + A} \qquad (4)$$

Figure 11.4
Model circuit diagram. The circle on top represents the neuron being recorded. The variable y is the firing rate of this neuron. The two circles below represent populations of "input" neurons that respond to the reference and probe stimuli, respectively, and that project to the measured cell. The average response of the ith input population is designated x_i. Black lines indicate the excitatory projections from each input population to the measured cell, and gray lines indicate the inhibitory projections, which are assumed to depend on inhibitory interneurons (not shown). The variable w_i^+ is the magnitude, or weight, of the excitatory projection from the ith input population, while w_i^- is the weight of the inhibitory projection from the ith input population.

sents the (output) neuron, which corresponds to the neuron being recorded. The two bottom circles represent populations of upstream neurons (inputs) that respond to the reference and probe stimuli, respectively. Lines connecting the inputs to the output represent feedforward excitatory and inhibitory synaptic connections.

Equations 1 and 2 describe the total excitatory and inhibitory inputs to the output neuron. The total excitatory input to the cell, E, is simply the sum of the activities of the two input populations, multiplied by their respective excitatory weights. The total inhibitory input to the cell, I, is the sum of the activities of the two input populations, multiplied by their respective inhibitory weights.

Equation 3 describes the instantaneous change in the firing rate of the output neuron, y. The first term, $(B - y)E$, governs excitatory input. B is the maximum response of the cell. Therefore, $(B - y)$ is always positive. If the excitatory input is greater than zero, then $(B - y)E$ is positive, resulting in an increase in response that grows smaller as the cell's response, y, approaches its maximum rate. The second term, $-yI$, governs inhibitory input. If inhibitory input is greater than zero, then $-yI$ is negative, resulting in a decrease in response toward zero. The third term, $-Ay$, is a passive decay term.

Equation 4 describes the equilibrium response of the output neuron. The passive decay parameter, A, and the cell's maximum response, B, are constants. Therefore, the equilibrium response depends on the relative contributions of the excitatory input, E, and the inhibitory input, I. Large values of E will drive the equilibrium firing rate toward the cell's maximum firing rate, B. Large values of I will cause the cell to remain silent.

Attention is assumed to increase the strength of the signal coming from the population of cells activated by the attended stimulus. The exact mechanism by which this increase could occur is unknown. It is implemented here by increasing the efficacy of inputs to the measured cell from the population activated by the attended stimulus. Increasing the strength of the signal from the input population causes it to have a greater influence on the total mix of excitation and inhibition. Consequently, the response of the cell is driven toward the response that would be elicited if the attended stimulus were presented alone.

Simulations of this model have shown that it is able to reproduce the relationships between individual stimulus responses and paired stimulus responses observed in the recording data (Reynolds, Chelazzi, and Desimone 1999). As a result of the inhibitory input driven by the poor stimulus, the model response to a preferred reference stimulus is suppressed by the addition of a poor stimulus. As in the recording data, when attention in the model is directed to the poor stimulus, the resulting magnification of inputs from the poor stimulus causes the response to the pair of stimuli to move toward the response generated by the poor stimulus alone. Likewise, directing attention to the preferred stimulus causes the model pair response to move toward the preferred stimulus response.

11.5 Predictions of the Biased-Competition Model

Because it is simple and relies on only three parameters, the model circuit can make clear predictions about neuronal responses under conditions that were not tested in the present experiments. First, it predicts conditions under which attention should cause an increase in the response to a single stimulus in the receptive field. According to the model, attention increases the bottom-up drive reaching the measured neuron, which forces the neuron's response upward, toward its maximum firing rate for that particular stimulus. If the bottom-up inputs driven by a particular stimulus are already strong enough that the cell's response has saturated, attention is predicted to have no influence on the response. However, if the response is not saturated, attention is predicted to increase it. Thus, a prediction of the model is that attention should increase neuronal responses to a single stimulus, if that stimulus elicits responses within the dynamic range of the cell. This would include stimuli that activate populations of afferents that project weakly to the measured cell, or stimuli of low-middle brightness or color contrast.

In addition, the model makes a novel prediction about how neuronal responses should depend on the relative salience of two stimuli in the receptive field, when attention is directed away from the receptive field. Specifically, if the salience of one receptive-field stimulus is increased relative to the salience of another receptive-field stimulus, this should cause the pair response to move toward the response elicited by the first stimulus alone. For example, suppose the response to a preferred stimulus is suppressed by the addition of a less preferred stimulus. Then, according to the model, increasing the luminance contrast of the less preferred stimulus should increase the strength of inputs from that stimulus, resulting in greater suppression of the response to the pair. This is predicted to occur even when the less preferred stimulus elicits a significant excitatory response on its own. Finally, the model predicts that the increased influence of the more salient stimulus can be offset if attention is directed to the lower-salience stimulus.

11.6 Explaining the Baseline Shift

The model can also account for a number of previously reported results, such as the observation (Luck et al. 1997) that the spontaneous firing rate of V2 and V4 neurons increases when attention is directed to a location within the receptive field. According to the model, attention increases the efficacy of synapses projecting from afferent neurons whose receptive fields are at the attended location. As a result of this increase, spontaneous activity among these afferents is predicted to be better able to activate the measured neuron, resulting in higher spontaneous activity in the measured neuron. If the synapses of inputs projecting from the afferent neurons are weak or sparse, this shift in baseline firing rate is predicted to be small. It is predicted to be larger for afferents with stronger projections to the measured cell. Consistent with this prediction, Luck and associates found that the increase in spontaneous activity is larger when attention is directed to the center of the receptive field (stronger afferent projections), versus a position near the edge of the receptive field (weaker afferent projections).

11.7 Attention to a Single Receptive-Field Stimulus

The model is also consistent with previously reported spatial attention effects in the ventral stream using single stimuli within the receptive field (Moran and Desimone 1985; Haenny, Maunsell, and Schiller 1988; Spitzer, Desimone, and Moran 1988; Maunsell et al. 1991). These studies have reported no change or small increases in responsiveness with attention directed to the receptive-field stimulus. These findings are compatible with the model's prediction that increases in response will be observed for a single stimulus, provided the stimulus has not already saturated the neuronal response. With the same parameters used to simulate the results of the present experiments, the model predicts a mean increase of 17.5% in neuronal response to a single stimulus with attention, which falls within the range of effects reported in these studies.

According to the model, these increases in response should depend on the magnitude of the attentional signal. Stronger top-down attentional feedback is assumed to result in larger increases in input strength for the attended stimulus. Therefore, the magnitude of the response increase caused by attention to a single stimulus in a difficult task is predicted to be equal to or greater than any increase observed in an easy task, using identical stimuli. Consistent with this, Spitzer, Desimone, and Moran (1988) reported moderate (18%) increases in neuronal responsiveness in V4 when attention was directed to a single stimulus in a difficult discrimination task, but not in a less demanding task.

11.8 Biased Competition from Sensory Input to Motor Output?

Other experiments suggest that similar mechanisms may be at work in a variety of cortical areas, supporting other functions in addition to spatial attention, including visual search and selection of a target for a saccadic eye movement. Earlier studies have shown that the responses of neurons in the inferior temporal cortex to a preferred stimulus are suppressed when a second, nonpreferred stimulus is added inside the receptive field (Miller, Gochin, and Gross 1993; Rolls and Tovee 1995), supporting the idea of competitive interactions in this area. Chelazzi and colleagues (1993) have found evidence that these competitive mechanisms can be modulated by a nonspatial biasing signal related to short-term memory for a stimulus. In their experiment, a monkey saw and stored in memory a visual stimulus. After the visual stimulus disappeared, a delay period ensued, during which the baseline activity of the cell was higher if the stimulus held in memory was the neuron's preferred stimulus. After the delay period, an array of randomly positioned stimuli appeared inside the receptive field, and the monkey was required to initiate a saccade to the stimulus (target) that matched the stimulus held in memory. Initially, the neuronal response to the array was independent of the identity of the target stimulus. However, about 100 msec before the onset of the saccade, the neuronal response suddenly increased or decreased, depending on whether the target was a preferred or poor stimulus for the neuron. These results suggest that during visual search for a known object at an unknown location, feedback from mechanisms for short-term memory can bias competitive interactions in much the same way as spatial attention.

A number of experiments also suggest the operation of biased competitive mechanisms in the dorsal stream of processing, which is involved in processing information about stimulus motion. Ferrera and Lisberger (1995) have reported that the onset time of a smooth-pursuit eye movement to a target moving in one direction can be increased by the presence of a distractor moving in the opposite direction, or reduced by the presence of a distractor moving with the target. They have proposed that this result is due to a winner-take-all competitive network that receives top-down feedback that biases the competition between the target and distractor. They have also reported that the responses of some neurons in areas MT and MST to a moving stimulus depend on whether the stimulus is a target of a smooth-pursuit eye movement (Ferrera and Lisberger 1997), and have proposed that this may reflect a top-down biasing signal.

In related experiments, Treue and Maunsell (1996) have found that attention modulates the responses of directionally selective MT and MST neurons in a manner similar to what we have observed for color- and shape-selective neurons in the ventral stream. They found that the response to a single stimulus is increased in magnitude when the stimulus is attended to. However, much larger attention effects were observed when attention was directed to one of two stimuli moving in opposite directions in the receptive field. When attention was directed to a stimulus moving in the neuron's preferred direction of motion, the response was greater than when attention was directed to a stimulus moving in the opposite direction. Consistent with the idea that these effects are modulated by a competitive mechanism, Recanzone, Wurtz, and Schwarz (1997) have found that neurons in areas MT and MST respond to pairs of stimuli in a manner highly consistent with what we have found in the ventral stream. That is, the response to a stimulus moving in a nonpreferred direction was increased by the addition of a second stimulus moving in the preferred direction. Likewise, the response to a stimulus moving in the nonnull direction for the cell was suppressed by the addition of a stimulus moving in the null direction.

It appears that related mechanisms may also be at work at the intersection of visual processing and motor control. Schall and Hanes (1993) found that neuronal responses in the frontal eye field were strongest when a pop-out target stimulus appeared inside the receptive field. Responses were suppressed when the target appeared outside the receptive field, near the receptive-field border. They have proposed that this results from mutual inhibition, and may serve the purpose of reducing the responses of neurons that code eye movements to locations near the target, thus reducing the probability of making an inaccurate saccade.

Basso and Wurtz (1997) have recorded from buildup neurons in the intermediate layers of the superior colliculus, which receive input from the frontal eye fields and are known to be involved in controlling eye movements. They found that when the monkey did not know in advance which of several potential targets would be selected for an eye movement, neuronal responses were diminished when additional possible targets were added to the search array. One could interpret this as arising from mutual inhibition between populations of neurons coding the different possible target locations. They then recorded neuronal responses when the monkey knew in advance which of the stimuli was to be the target of the eye movement. They found that the response was no longer suppressed when they increased the number of stimuli in the array. One can interpret these results as arising from a top-down biasing signal, possibly initiated in the frontal eye field, which specifies which of the stimuli would be selected for an eye movement. Taken together, these results appear to suggest that biased competition may be a basic computational strategy that has been adopted throughout the visual system, the occulomotor system, and possibly in other modalities as well.

References

Basso, M. A., and R. H. Wurtz. 1997. Modulation of neuronal activity by target uncertainty. *Nature* 389:66–69.

Boussaoud, D., R. Desimone, and L. G. Ungerleider. 1991. Visual topography of area TEO in the macaque. *Journal of Comparative Neurology* 306:554–575.

Bundesen, C. 1990. A theory of visual attention. *Psychological Review* 97(4):523–547.

Chelazzi, L., E. K. Miller, J. Duncan, and R. Desimone. 1993. A neural basis for visual search in inferior temporal cortex. *Nature* 363:345–347.

Desimone, R., and J. Duncan. 1995. Neural mechanisms of selective visual attention. *Annual Review of Neuroscience* 18:193–222.

Desimone, R., and L. G. Ungerleider. 1989. Neural mechanisms of visual processing in monkeys. In *Handbook of Neurophysiology*, vol. 2, ed. F. Boller and J. Grafman, pp. 267–299. New York: Elsevier.

Duncan, J. 1980. The locus of interference in the perception of simultaneous stimuli. *Psychological Review* 87(3):272–300.

Ferrera, V. P., and S. G. Lisberger. 1995. Attention and target selection for smooth pursuit eye movements. *Journal of Neuroscience* 15(11):7472–7484.

Ferrera, V. P., and S. G. Lisberger. 1997. Neuronal responses in visual areas MT and MST during smooth pursuit target selection. *Journal of Neurophysiology* 78(3):1433–1446.

Haenny, P. D., J. H. R. Maunsell, and P. H. Schiller. 1988. State dependent activity in monkey visual cortex, II: Retinal and extraretinal factors in V4. *Experimental Brain Research* 69:245–259.

Kapadia, M. K., M. Ito, C. D. Gilbert, and G. Westheimer. 1995. Improvement in visual sensitivity by changes in local context: Parallel studies in human observers and in V1 of alert monkeys. *Neuron* 15(4):843–856.

Kiper, D. C., S. B. Fenstemaker, and K. R. Gegenfurtner. 1997. Chromatic properties of neurons in macaque area V2. *Visual Neuroscience* 14(6):1061–1072.

Knierim, J. J., and D. C. Van Essen. 1992. Neuronal responses to static texture patterns in area V1 of the alert macaque monkey. *Journal of Neurophysiology* 67(4):961–980.

Levitt, J. B., and J. S. Lund. 1997. Contrast dependence of contextual effects in primate visual cortex. *Nature* 387:73–76.

Luck, S. J., L. Chelazzi, S. A. Hillyard, and R. Desimone. 1997. Neural mechanisms of spatial selective attention in areas V1, V2, and V4 of macaque visual cortex. *Journal of Neurophysiology* 77(1):24–42.

Maunsell, J. H. R., G. Sclar, T. A. Nealey, and D. DePriest. 1991. Extraretinal representations in area V4 of the macaque monkey. *Visual Neuroscience* 7:561–573.

Miller, E. K., P. M. Gochin, and C. G. Gross. 1993. Suppression of visual responses of neurons in inferior temporal cortex of the awake macaque by addition of a second stimulus. *Brain Research* 616(1–2):25–29.

Moran, J., and R. Desimone. 1985. Selective attention gates visual processing in the extrastriate cortex. *Science* 229:782–784.

Recanzone, G. H., R. H. Wurtz, and U. Schwarz. 1997. Responses of MT and MST neurons to one and two moving objects in the receptive field. *Journal of Neurophysiology* 78(6):2904–2915.

Reynolds, J. H., L. Chelazzi, and R. Desimone. 1999. Competitive mechanisms subserve attention in macaque areas V2 and V4. *Journal of Neuroscience* 19:1736–1753.

Rolls, E. T., and M. J. Tovee. 1995. The responses of single neurons in the temporal visual cortical areas of the macaque when more than one stimulus is present in the receptive field. *Experimental Brain Research* 103(3):409–420.

Schall, J. D., and D. P. Hanes. 1993. Neural basis of saccade target selection in frontal eye field during visual search. *Nature* 366:467–469.

Sillito, A. M., K. L. Grieve, H. E. Jones, J. Cudeiro, and J. Davis. 1995. Visual cortical mechanisms detecting focal orientation discontinuities. *Nature* 378:492–496.

Spitzer, H., R. Desimone, and J. Moran. 1988. Increased attention enhances both behavioral and neuronal performance. *Science* 240:338–340.

Treue, S., and S. Maunsell. 1996. Attentional modulation of visual motion processing in cortical areas MT and MST. *Nature* 382:539–541.

Chapter 12

Origin of Visual Imagery: Its Neurophysiological Basis

Yasushi Miyashita

"Create an image of the Pantheon in your mind. Can you count the columns that support its pediment?" (Alain 1926) (figure 12.1, plate 24). Our ability to "see with the mind's eye" has been of interest to philosophers and scientists for a long time. When the nature of the reflective consciousness was investigated by reflection, it was often asked whether "(strong) image" and "(weak) perception" are distinguishable along both psychological and epistemological dimensions (Sartre 1938). Recalling the Pantheon's columns is among the best-known litmus tests for such a distinction. Figure 12.1 should not be taken to suggest that mental images are actual pictures in the brain; obviously we cannot assume a homunculus in the brain that looks at the images. Nevertheless, we find imagery an important topic since it is one of the first higher cognitive abilities to be firmly rooted in the brain and since understanding this ability would provide insight into the neural basis of consciousness.

Today many approaches (including neuroimaging, electrophysiological, psychophysical, and neuropsychological ones) are being used to ask where and how in the brain pictorial representations of objects, scenes, and living beings are generated, stored, and maintained (Roland 1993; Kosslyn 1994; Miyashita 1995). Even the question of to what degree the processes involved in visual perception and imagery share a common neural substrate has partially been answered. The aim of this chapter is to provide a solid neurophysiological basis for those studies by using an animal model. In our visual memory tasks, monkeys were asked to encode visual objects in associative long-term memory and to retrieve internal representations of the objects from long-term storage according to an appropriate cue. The monkeys can recall the internal representation even without direct sensory stimulation (Hasegawa et al. 1998; Tomita et al. 1999).

The nature of the internal representation that lies in the deepest structure for "imagery" or image generation has been long debated (Pylyshyn 1981; Kosslyn 1994), but recent neuroscience investigations strongly suggest contributions of depictive representation in both humans and monkeys (Kosslyn 1994; Miyashita 1995, 1999). In humans, especially when verbal instruction triggers imagery generation,

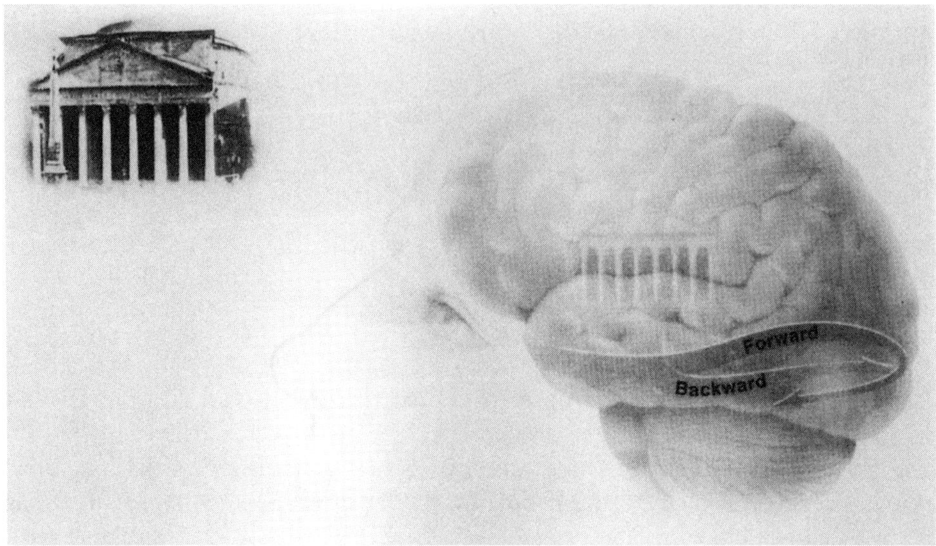

Figure 12.1
Visual perception mainly relies on the forward, bottom-up flow of information. Image retrieval or imagery experience, in contrast, highlights the backward projections as an anatomical substrate of top-down mental operations. If an imagery task requires reconstruction of the detailed local geometry of the image (as in counting the columns in a memory of the Pantheon), backward signals from higher-order representations might reach topographically organized visual areas. This illustration does not indicate that mental images are actual pictures in the brain; obviously we cannot assume a homunculus in the brain that looks at the images. Adapted from Miyashita 1995; artwork by K. Sutliff.

propositional representation may also contribute to imagery (Pylyshyn 1981), as I discuss at the end of this chapter. Therefore, in this chapter, I use the word *image* for a depictive internal representation that underlies the goal-directed behavior in the memory tasks of monkeys.

I start from a neuronal correlate of image generation in the monkey inferotemporal cortex. I demonstrate that single neurons become active when the monkey generates from its long-term memory store the image triggered by a cue stimulus (Miyashita et al. 1998; Naya, Sakai, and Miyashita 1996). Neurons in the inferotemporal cortex can respond to such a prospective object, as well as to a retrospective image in memory or a visible object (Miyashita 1988, 1993). I then ask where such a prospective activation of an object's image can originate. By using the object-object association task for monkeys, I demonstrate that inferotemporal neurons can encode associative relations between objects and can provide a kind of semantic network among objects (Miyashita 1993). We found that, in the process of encoding visual objects, the interaction between the medial temporal lobe and inferotemporal cortex plays an essential role. I analyze this interaction by a combination of electrophysiological single-unit recording, neurotoxic lesions, and molecular biological methods (Miyashita et al. 1998; Okuno and Miyashita 1996). These studies clarified how the associative long-term memory of objects is encoded and how the prospective activation of an object's image emerges. Comparisons with the human imagery system will also be made.

12.1 Neuronal Representation of Visual Long-Term Memory

Along the occipitotemporal visual pathway from the primary visual cortex (figure 12.1), the physical properties of a visual object are analyzed in the multiple subdivisions of the prestriate and posterior temporal cortices, and the inferotemporal cortex synthesizes the analyzed attributes into a unique configuration (Mishkin 1982; Van Essen, Anderson, and Felleman 1992; Miyashita 1993). The inferotemporal cortex has been proposed as the memory storehouse for object vision on the basis of behavioral experiments (Mishkin 1982; Squire 1987). But how are the memories of objects represented among neuronal networks in the inferotemporal cortex?

Most of our semantic knowledge and long-term memories of episodes are organized so that we can retrieve them by association. I propose that visual memory is organized by the same principle and encodes the forms of objects as structured bundles of associations between elementary views of objects (Miyashita, Date, and Okuno 1993). We obtained evidence for the associative mechanism by training monkeys to memorize artificial associative relations among visual patterns, and then by examining whether picture-selective activities of inferotemporal neurons encode the stimulus-stimulus associations imposed in the learning (Miyashita 1988, 1993). One such study used the pair-association (PA) learning task (Sakai and Miyashita 1991; Higuchi and Miyashita 1996) by modifying a human declarative memory task (Wechsler 1987). The results provided strong evidence that inferotemporal neurons acquire stimulus selectivity through associative learning and that the selectivity reflects a stimulus-stimulus association among geometrically different forms.

12.2 Neuronal Correlate of Mental Imagery in the Inferotemporal Cortex

In our pair-association task for monkeys, computer-generated meaningless colored pictures were sorted randomly into pairs (G1 and C1 to G12 and C12), each pair containing a green picture and a cyan/blue picture (figure 12.2, plate 25). The combination of the paired associates cannot be predicted without memorizing them beforehand, and macaque monkeys (*Macaca fuscata*) were trained to memorize these pairs. In each trial of the task, a cue stimulus was presented, and then the monkey was

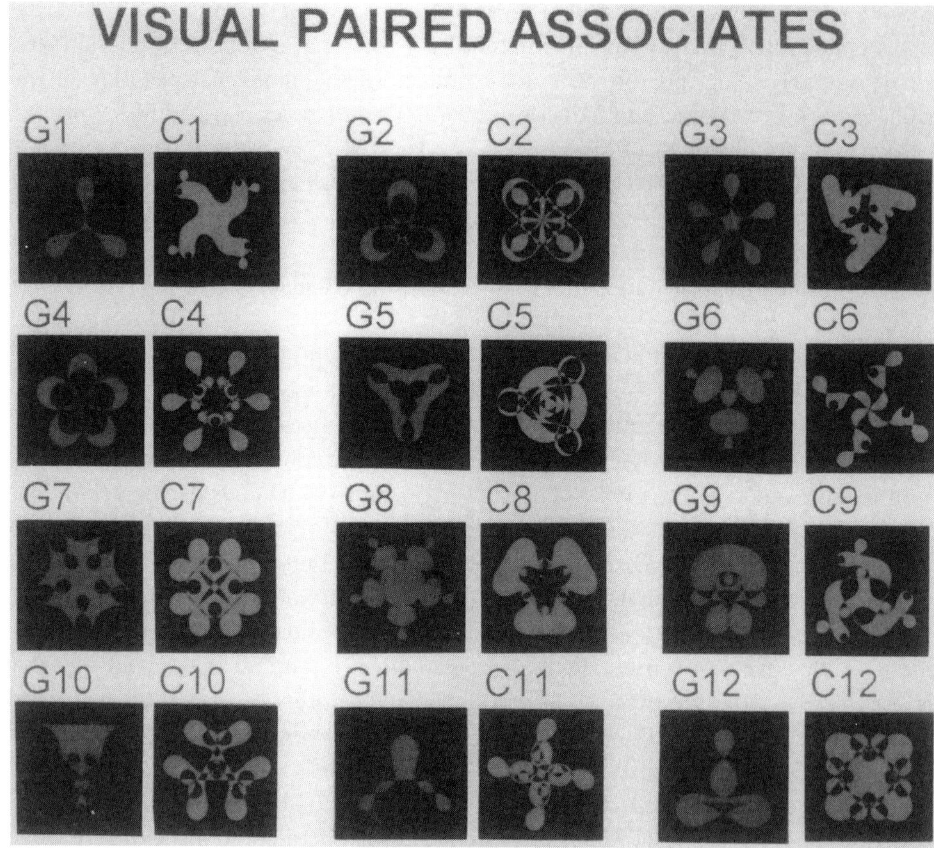

Figure 12.2
Image-retrieval task for monkeys. The pair-association with color switch (PACS) task uses twelve pairs of colored pictures. When one member of each pair is shown, trained monkeys can retrieve and choose the other member of the paired associates. The first pair consists of the picture G1 (green) and picture C1 (cyan), the second pair consists of G2 and C2, and so on.

rewarded when he or she chose the paired associate of the cue. It should be noted that this task is essentially a memory *recall* task, which demands activation of internal representation of a picture from long-term memory.

In an earlier experiment with monochromatic visual stimuli (Sakai and Miyashita 1991), we found an interesting category of neurons (*pair-recall neurons*) that exhibited a "prospective-type" delay activity before the choice appeared. The delay activity was coupled with the paired associate that is not actually seen but is to be retrieved. This finding led us to hypothesize that the pair-recall neurons were key elements of the image-generation process in the task. Then we tested this hypothesis by develop-

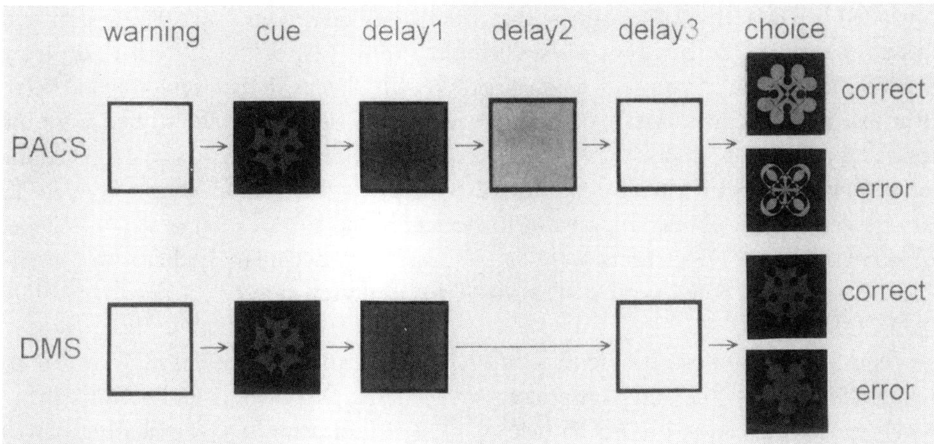

Figure 12.3
Sequence of events in the image-retrieval task. Both PACS trials and DMS trials use the same color stimuli shown in figure 12.2. In each trial of the task, a cue stimulus is presented, and then the monkey is rewarded when he or she chooses the correct stimulus. The correct stimulus is the paired associate of the cue in PACS trials and the cue itself in DMS trials. PACS trials and DMS trials were given randomly. Event sequence is the following: warning, gray square for fixation (1 sec in both trials); cue, one of twenty-four colored pictures (0.5 sec); delay period 1, fixation square that has the same color as the cue picture (2 sec in PACS trials, 5 sec in the DMS trials); delay period 2, fixation square that has the same color as the paired associate of the cue picture (3 sec in PACS trials); delay period 3, fixation gray square (1 sec in both trials); choice, a choice of two stimuli (1.2 sec in both trials).

ing a novel task, the pair-association with color switch (PACS) task, in which the necessity for image generation and its initiation time were controlled by a color switch in the middle of the delay period (Naya, Sakai, and Miyashita 1996). The PACS task consisted of PACS trials and control trials (DMS trials). The control trial, in which there is no color switch, corresponds to a trial of the conventional delayed matching-to-sample (DMS) task where the monkey chooses the same picture as a cue.

The sequence of events in a PACS trial or a DMS trial was as follows (figure 12.3, plate 26). When the monkey pressed a lever in front of the video monitor, a gray square for fixation was presented at the center of the screen for 1 sec (warning). Following the cue presentation of one of twenty-four pictures for 0.5 sec, a square was presented during the delay period. The square's color was the same as the cue's color during the first part of the delay period (delay period 1) for 2 sec in PACS trials or for 5 sec in DMS trials. In PACS trials, the square's color changed into the color of the paired associate after delay period 1, signaling the initiation of retrieval, and then the second part of the delay period (delay period 2) started. Delay period 2 was not included in DMS trials. To balance the visual stimulus conditions in the two trials, a gray square was presented for 1 sec during the third part of the delay period (delay period 3). After delay period 3, a choice of two stimuli was shown randomly in two of four possible positions (arranged in two rows of two columns). The stimuli were the paired associate of the cue (correct) and a distracter (error) in PACS trials, while the stimuli were the same picture as the cue (correct) and a distracter (error) in DMS trials. The animal obtained a reward for touching the correct picture within 1.2 sec. PACS trials and DMS trials were randomized. Extracellular discharges of single neurons were recorded with a glass-insulated tungsten microelectrode (Miyashita et al. 1989).

Figure 12.4 demonstrates activity of a single inferotemporal neuron. The neuron exhibited typical differential responses between the PACS trial and DMS trial in delay periods 2 and 3, but not in delay period 1, indicating that the neuronal firing was switched at the onset of delay period 2 in the PACS trial. In this neuron, one picture—Green7 (G7)—elicited the strongest response during the cue period in both the PACS trial and the DMS trial (we call this picture the "best picture" throughout the description of this neuron, irrespective of its delay response, although the "best picture" does not necessarily elicit the strongest delay response). The excitatory response was maintained in delay period 1 in both PACS and DMS trials. The paired associate of the best picture, Cyan7 (C7), elicited no responses during the cue period and whole delay period in the DMS trial. In contrast, when C7 was presented as a cue in the PACS trial, this neuron started to respond just after the onset of delay period 2 when the square's color changed from the cue's color (cyan) to that of the paired associate (green). Figure 12.5 (plate 27) quantifies these stimulus-specific activities of this neuron in PACS trials. Only stimulus G7 activated the cell during the cue period (figure 12.5, top). In delay period 1, this neuron continued to be active only for G7 (figure 12.5, middle). However, in delay periods 2 and 3, when the retrieval of the paired associate was required, the responses were switched from G7 to C7 (figure 12.5, bottom). In other words, in the trial when C7 was presented as a cue, the cell was not active until delay period 1, but the cell became suddenly active during delay periods 2 and 3, where the retrieval of G7 was required. Summing up, the cell became active when the image of its best picture (G7) needs to be recalled from memory. The picture-selective activation after the color switch in PACS trials is called the *pair-recall* effect.

It is important that the pair-recall effect cannot be due to the effect of the square's color, since other stimuli, either green or cyan, did not induce a similar effect at all (figure 12.5, bottom). This was also confirmed by the fact that the pair-recall effect continued from delay period 2 into delay period 3, in which the square's color was the same gray in both PACS and DMS trials, and that the pair-recall effect was only found in PACS trials but not in DMS trials (figure 12.4).

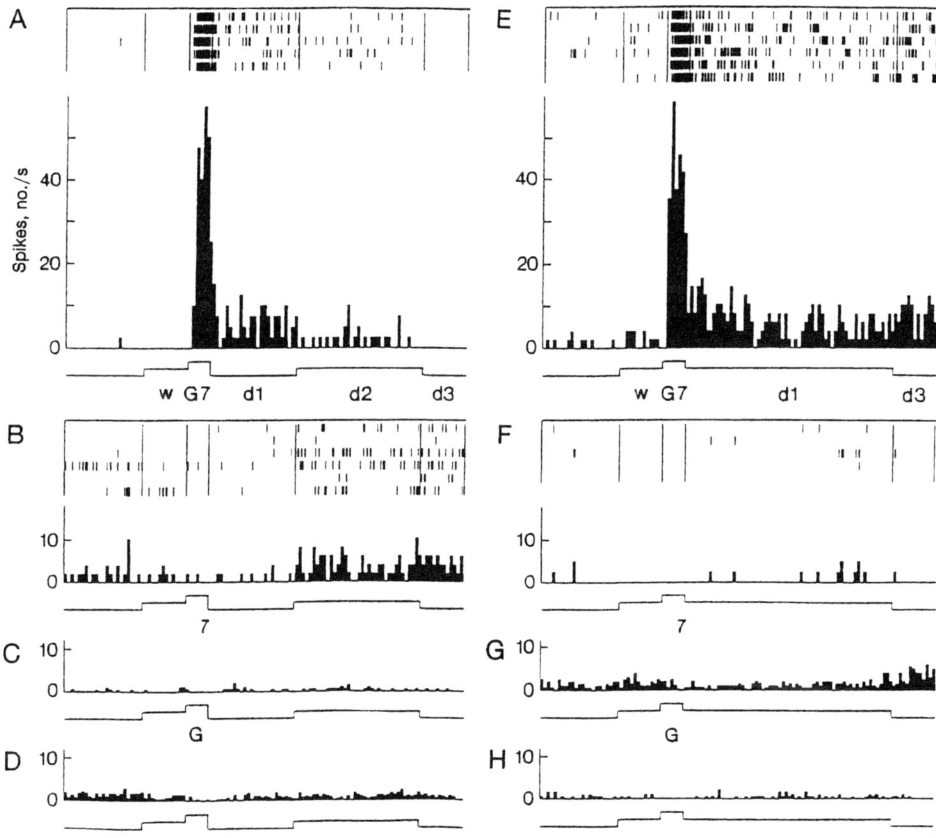

Figure 12.4
Neuronal correlate of image retrieval in the temporal cortex. Differential delay responses of a pair-recall neuron in PACS trials and DMS trials. Rastergrams of neural discharges in each trial and spike-density histograms were obtained from a single inferotemporal neuron. Bin width, 80 msec. (*a–d*) Responses in PACS trials. (*e–h*) Responses in DMS trials. (*a*, *e*) Responses in trials for picture G7 as a cue. (*b*, *f*) Responses in trials for picture C7 as a cue. (*c*, *g*) Responses in trials for pictures G1–G12 except G7 as cue pictures (*g*). (*d*, *h*) Responses in trial for pictures C1–C12 except C7 as cue pictures (c). Picture G7 elicited the strongest cue response in both tasks (*a*, *e*). Note the suppressed response during delay 2 and delay 3 in PACS trials (*a*), but not in DMS trials (*e*). We called this phenomenon the *pair-suppression effect*. In trials for picture C7 as a cue, no response was observed during the cue period in both tasks (*b*, *f*). Note the enhanced response during delay 2 and delay 3 in PACS trials (*b*), but not in DMS trials (*f*). We called this phenomenon the *pair-recall effect*. In trials for pictures g and b as cues, no responses were observed in both trials (*c*, *d*, *g*, *h*), indicating that there was no significant color effect (Naya, Sakai, and Miyashita 1996).

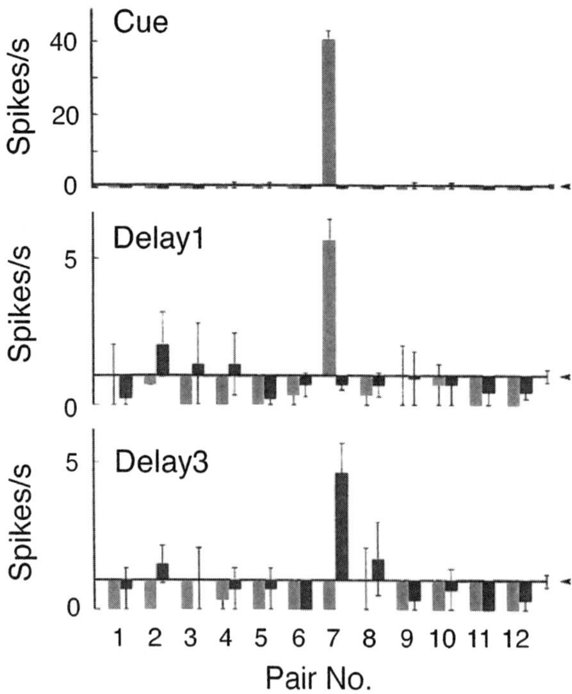

Figure 12.5
Stimulus selectivity of the inferotemporal neuron (the same as that in figure 12.4) is shown in different task periods (top, cue period; middle, delay period 1; bottom, delay period 3). The ordinate shows the mean discharge rate in each task period after the presentation of a cue stimulus; cue stimuli are labeled *Pair no.* on the abscissa (green histogram bar in no. 1: G1, cyan/blue histogram bar in no. 1: C1, and so on). This neuron selectively responded to the cue stimulus G7 during the cue period. Note that the cue stimulus C7 does not elicit any response during the cue period and delay period 1 in this neuron, but during delay periods 2 and 3 the same neuron suddenly became active.

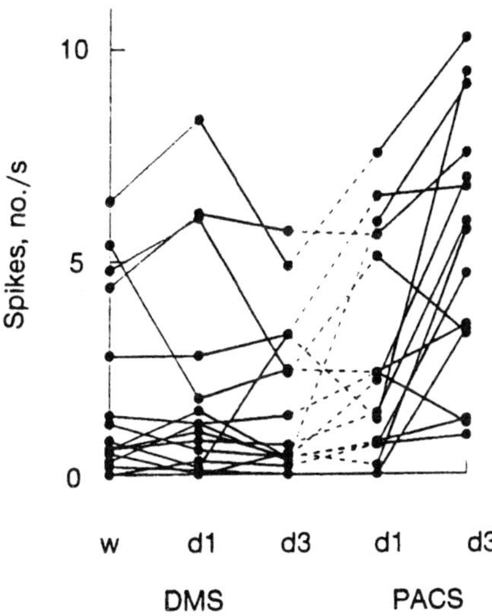

Figure 12.6
Pair-recall effect in the PACS task. Discharge rates in trials where the best picture's paired associates were used as a cue in PACS trials and DMS trials. Each circle denotes the average firing rate for one of the single inferotemporal neurons recorded ($n = 15$). In the PACS trials, activities during delay period 3 (d3) were higher than those during delay period 1 (d1) for most of the fifteen cells. In the DMS trials, activities during d3 were not significantly different from those during d1 (Naya, Sakai, and Miyashita 1996).

Figure 12.6 compares the responses of fifteen cells that showed delay responses and were held long enough to complete PACS and DMS trials with all the stimuli. The number of spikes was counted by collecting the trials whose cue picture was the best picture's associate. The effect of the trial classes (PACS vs. DMS) on the delay response was significant [$F(1, 14) = 19.8$, $P < 0.001$], and there was an interaction between the trial classes and period [$F(1, 28) = 12.2$, $P < 0.005$]. We further analyzed responses among periods in each trial class (PACS or DMS), and responses between the trial classes in each period. In both PACS and DMS, responses in delay period 1 remained equal to warning responses. These delay period 1 responses were thus independent of the trial classes. In delay period 3 of PACS, the responses were significantly stronger than those in delay period 1 ($t = 3.5$, $P < 0.005$), while the delay period 3 responses in DMS trials remained equal to the delay period 1 responses. The delay period 3 responses in PACS trials were significantly stronger than those in DMS trials ($t = 5.2$, $P < 0.001$). These results confirmed that the pair-recall effect is triggered by the color switch.

All the above results strongly support the hypothesis that these neural discharges represent the active internal representation of a specific object in mind ("image" of G7 in the case of figures 12.4 and 12.5). Then how does this neural firing arise? What kind of machinery could drive the pair-recall neuron in delay periods 2 and 3 in spite of null activity in delay period 1? It might depend on a "top-down" input from the prefrontal cortex. Indeed, we recently found that, under an experimental design with a pair-association paradigm, the prefrontal cortex could instruct the inferotemporal cortex to retrieve a correct memory of an object, even without "bottom-up" sensory input to the inferotemporal cortex (Hasegawa et al. 1998; Tomita et al. 1999). However, it was also confirmed that only the posterior association cortex—that is, the inferotemporal cortex in this context—could hold the specific information on the paired associates in long-term memory (Hasegawa et al. 1998). Thus the neural mechanism for the image generation should involve specific communication between the pair-recall neurons and the neurons that encode the paired associates in long-term memory. I will now consider the neuronal mechanisms that encode the long-term memory of objects.

12.3 Inferotemporal Neurons That Encode the Long-Term Memory of the Paired Associates

In previous studies (but with monochromatic paired associates), we found neurons that selectively encoded the associative relation between the paired associates (Sakai and Miyashita 1991). I briefly summarize the findings before examining the mechanisms of encoding process. To find out the neuronal correlates of the long-term memory of the paired associates, we trained monkeys to memorize the paired pictures (monochromatic version of figure 12.2). We recorded single-neuron activity and tested whether cells tended to preferentially respond to both of the paired associates, in spite of the fact that both stimuli had no geometrical similarity. In the anterior ventral part of area TE (TEav), we found some patchy areas in which many neurons preferentially responded to both of the paired associates (*pair-coding neuron*). We analyzed sampled cells by calculating response correlations with pair indices or correlation coefficients (Sakai and Miyashita 1991; Higuchi and Miyashita 1996). The frequency distribution of these indices revealed that the paired associates elicited significantly correlated responses in these areas. This result provides strong evidence that inferotemporal neurons acquire stimulus selectivity through associative learning and that the selectivity reflects a stimulus-stimulus association among geometrically different complex forms.

12.4 Role of the Interaction between the Medial Temporal Lobe and Inferotemporal Cortex

Now we are ready to examine the encoding mechanisms, or specifically the role of the interaction between the medial temporal lobe and inferotemporal cortex in the formation of declarative long-term memory (Milner 1968; Squire 1987). Here I examine the hypothesis that limbic neurons undergo rapid modification of synaptic connectivity and provide backward signals that guide reorganization of forward neural circuits to (and/or in) the inferotemporal cortex. This hypothesis has anatomical support in that the inferotemporal cortex receives massive backward projections from the medial temporal lobe, especially from the perirhinal cortex (Van Hoesen 1982; Webster, Ungerleider, and Bachevalier 1991; Suzuki and Amaral 1994a, 1994b). Thus the hypothesis for a role for the backward signal in the consolidation process specifically predicts that a lesion that includes the perirhinal cortex would impair the formation of the associative code for pictures in the inferotemporal neurons (figure 12.7). We now test this prediction.

We combine single-unit recording in the monkey preparation with surgical manipulation so that individual inferotemporal neurons lose the backward signals but can receive forward signals when visual stimuli are presented. We prepared a specific experimental design to carry out this project (figure 12.7). Backward neuronal connections from the limbic system to the inferotemporal cortex are to be interrupted by a lesion of the perirhinal cortices. However, a bilateral lesion would impair the monkeys' behavior in the pair-association task (Murray, Gaffan, and Mishkin 1993). Thus the perirhinal/entorhinal cortices were lesioned unilaterally. With the unilateral lesion, however, the inferotemporal cortex of the lesioned side could receive information from the contralateral inferotemporal cortex; receptive fields of inferotemporal neurons cover both hemifields before the lesion. To remove the interhemispheric signal from the healthy contralateral inferotemporal cortex, we surgically cut the anterior commissure (AC) at the beginning of the experiment. This surgery disconnected the anterior temporal cortex of each hemisphere from the other, since most commissural fibers of this area traverse the AC rather than the corpus callosum (Pandya, Karol, and Lele 1973; Demeter, Rosene, and Van Hoesen 1990). With this surgically manipulated chronic monkey preparation, we tested the ability of inferotemporal neurons to represent associations between picture pairs.

Two adult monkeys (*Macaca fuscata*) were trained in the pair-association task. The AC was transected before learning of the task (figure 12.8b). After recovery, the monkey was trained with a set of the paired associates to the criterion performance level, and then extracellular spike discharges of single neurons in the anterior inferotemporal cortex were recorded as a prelesion control, as reported in previous studies

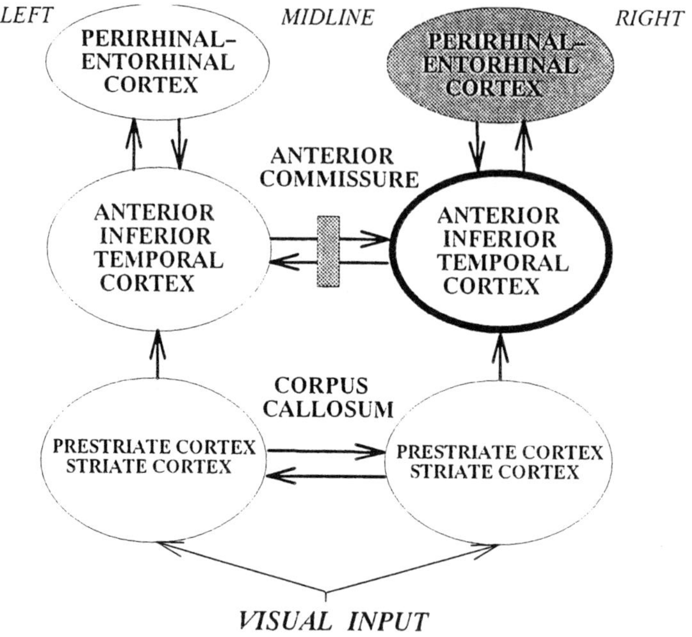

Figure 12.7
What is the role of the backward signal in memory formation? The inferotemporal cortex receives a backward signal from the limbic system as well as a forward visual signal from the prestriate cortices. This diagram shows an experimental design to answer the question (see text for details).

(Miyashita 1988; Miyashita and Chang 1988; Sakai and Miyashita 1991). Then we deprived inferotemporal neurons of backward neural information by unilateral ibotenic acid lesions of the entorhinal and perirhinal cortices. The lesion covered both the medial and lateral banks of the rhinal sulcus completely, and most of the entorhinal and perirhinal cortex (figure 12.8c–e). The lesioned cortex suffered atrophy, but fibers in the underlying white matter were left unharmed. After the ibotenic acid injection, the monkeys were trained with a new set of paired associates. Then extracellular spike discharges of single neurons were recorded from the same area as that in the prelesion control. Correlation coefficients were used to analyze pair-coding responses of these cells (Higuchi and Miyashita 1996). The response variability of the cells was evaluated before and after the lesion by a response variability index. The index was defined in each cell as the ratio of the standard deviation of firing rates among the trials for the optimum stimulus over the mean firing rate for the optimum stimulus. Larger values of this index indicate more trial-to-trial fluctuations of the responses.

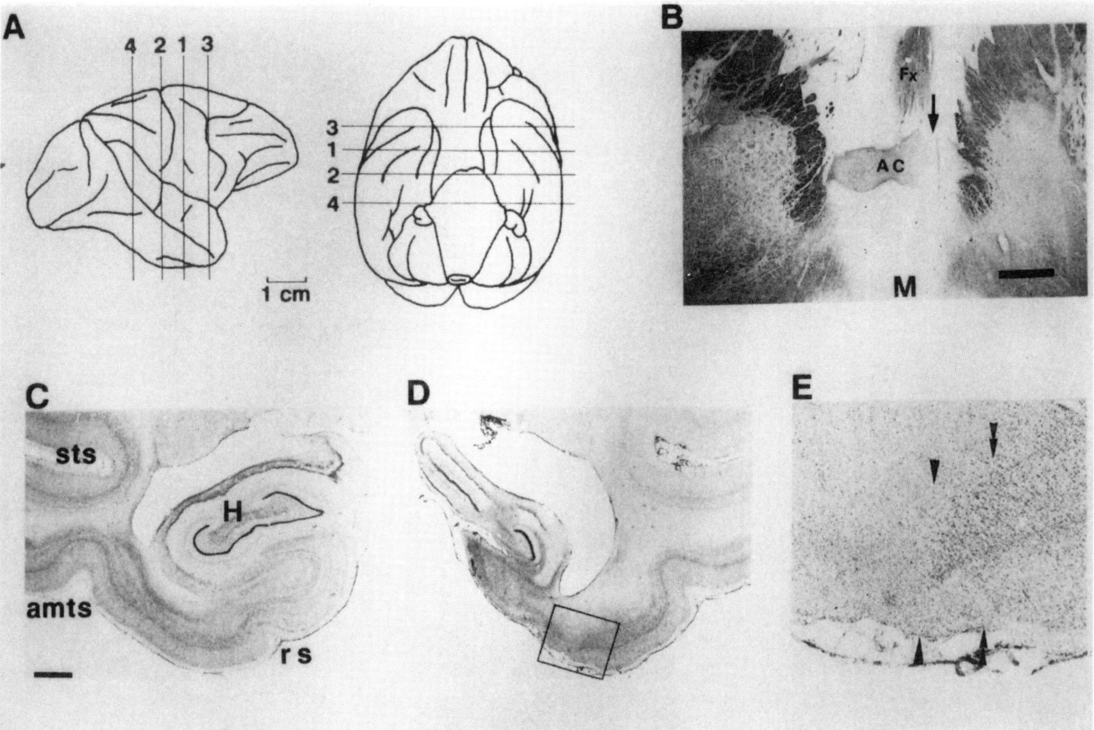

Figure 12.8
Unilateral ibotenic acid lesion of the entorhinal and perirhinal cortices. (*A*) Lateral (left) and ventral (right) view of a monkey brain, indicating the locations of sections used in the following panels (section 1 for panel *B*, 2 for *C–E*). Scale bar, 1 cm. (*B*) Fiber-stained coronal section through the anterior commissure (AC). The AC was surgically cut (arrow) just to the right of the midline (indicated by *M*). The fornix (Fx) was left intact. Scale bar, 2 mm. (*C*) Cresyl-violet-stained coronal section showing the left (intact) entorhinal and perirhinal cortices. Scale bar, 2 mm. (*D*) Same section as (*C*), but showing the right entorhinal and perirhinal cortices that were lesioned by ibotenic acid. (*E*) Higher magnification of the area outlined in (*D*). Double arrowheads indicate border between intact area (to the right) and incompletely lesioned area. Arrowheads indicate border between completely (to the left) and incompletely lesioned area. H, hippocampus. amts, anterior middle temporal sulcus. sts, superior temporal sulcus. rs, rhinal sulcus (Higuchi and Miyashita 1996).

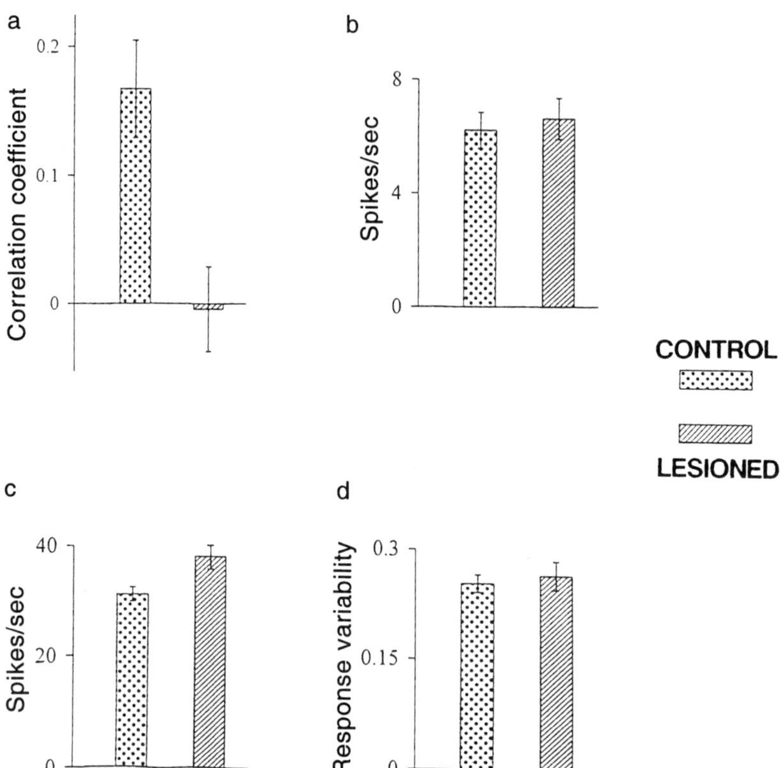

Figure 12.9
Effects of the lesion of the entorhinal and perirhinal cortices upon neuronal responsiveness in the pair-association task. (*a*) Correlation coefficient. (*b*) Spontaneous discharge rate. (*c*) Maximum discharge rate with spontaneous discharge subtracted. (*d*) Response variability. These indices were compared among two groups: (1) neurons that were recorded prior to the lesion (stippled bar, $n = 92$), (2) those recorded after the lesion (hatched with thin line, $n = 75$). Data are shown as mean $\pm$ s.e.m.

Figure 12.9 compares the responsiveness of the cells before and after the lesion. The results of two monkeys were not significantly different ($P > 0.25$) in a two-way ANOVA in any of the indices and have been pooled. Prior to the ibotenic acid lesion, we examined the responses of ninety-two cells. The distribution of the correlation coefficient showed that the paired associates elicited significantly correlated responses in the control ($P < 0.01$; Wilcoxon's signed-rank test), confirming the conclusion of our previous report (Sakai and Miyashita 1991). After the lesion, we examined the responses of seventy-five cells, and the cells responded to the pictures (38 ± 2 spikes/sec) even more strongly than in the control (31 ± 1 spikes/sec). However, the correlation coefficients were reduced ($P < 0.05$) and dropped to chance level (-0.19 ± 0.27)

after the lesion. The spontaneous discharge rates were not significantly different among the groups ($P > 0.2$). We also tested with a response variability index whether the cells exhibited any sign of pathological firing after the lesion. The index did not differ significantly between the groups ($P > 0.6$). We conclude that lesion of the entorhinal and perirhinal cortices disrupted the associative code of the inferotemporal neurons between the paired associates, without impairing the visual response to each stimulus. The results support the view that inferotemporal neurons have the ability to represent the long-term mnemonic code between picture pairs and that this ability is critically dependent on backward connections from the perirhinal cortices to the inferotemporal neurons.

12.5 Circuit Reorganization in the Primate Temporal Cortex

We now ask why the limbic-neocortical interactions are so important. As stated, I hypothesize that perirhinal neurons undergo rapid modification of synaptic connectivity and provide backward signals that guide reorganization of forward neural circuits to (and/or in) the inferotemporal cortex. Now we explore the first part of the hypothesis with a molecular biological approach. If the hypothesis is true, we should be able to detect the expressions of molecular markers for synaptic plasticity in the monkey temporal cortex (especially perirhinal cortex) during learning of the pair-association task. As the first step, we attempted to test the expression of immediate early genes (IEGs).

IEGs are a class of genes that show rapid and transient but protein synthesis-independent increases in transcription. Many IEGs encode transcription factors such as Fos, Jun, and ZIF268, and these IEGs, especially *zif268* (the gene that encodes for ZIF268), have been hypothesized to play crucial roles in the transduction of neuronal electric signals into more permanent synaptic organization (Morgan and Curran 1991; Bailey and Kandel 1993). For example, the induction of *zif268* in the dentate gyrus is closely correlated with the induction of long-term potentiation (LTP) (Abraham et al. 1993; Worley et al. 1993). We attempted to determine in which temporal cortical areas IEGs were expressed during visual long-term memory formation in the primate. We trained monkeys to learn two different cognitive memory tasks, a visual pair-association task and a visual discrimination task. The visual pair-association task required the monkeys to memorize visual stimulus-stimulus associations (Sakai and Miyashita 1991; Murray, Gaffan, and Mishkin 1993). The other task, the visual discrimination task, required them to memorize stimulus-reward associations (Iwai and Mishkin 1969). The types of learning required in these tasks are different since they are sensitive to lesions in different brain areas, and the visual pair-association task was more sensitive to lesions of the medial temporal cortex (Iwai and Mishkin 1969; Murray, Gaffan, and Mishkin 1993).

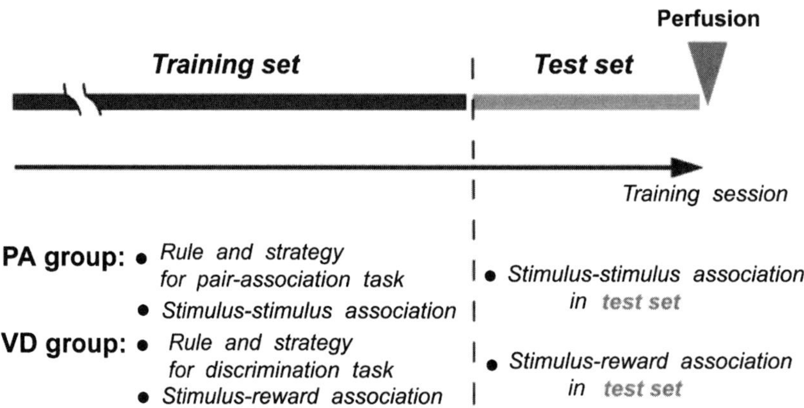

Figure 12.10
Experimental design to detect learning-induced activation of molecular markers in monkeys. To detect the expression of a gene specifically related to the paired associated learning, two different control procedures were introduced. First, the monkeys learned the rule and task strategy during the learning of the *training-set* stimuli, and then the expression of molecular markers was detected during the learning of the *test-set* stimuli. Second, the expression during paired associated learning was compared with that during visual discrimination learning. The paired associated learning and visual discrimination learning used the same visual stimuli, same motor responses, and same number of rewards.

To investigate formation of the stimulus-stimulus association memory but not the skill-based (or habitlike) memory (Mishkin 1982) incidental to the learning paradigm, we designed a specific learning procedure (figure 12.10, plate 28). We first trained the monkeys to learn a "rule" or "strategy" for the tasks, which is considered to be related to the skill-based memory, using a set of twenty-four pictures (*training set*). After the monkeys' performance reached a plateau level with the training set, a new stimulus set (*test set*) was introduced. The monkeys' performance was at a chance level in the first day with the test set. The performance improved in five to six subsequent days, but still it did not reach a plateau phase. Then the monkeys were perfused immediately after the completion of the ninety-minute learning session on the perfusion day. The brain blocks were frozen in dry-ice powder and sections (32 μm) were cut using a cryostat and stained immunohistochemically. The specificity and reactivity of the anti-ZIF268 antibody has been described (Okuno et al. 1995). The anti-ZIF268 antibody specifically recognized an 86 kDa protein in the nuclear extracts from the monkey cerebral cortex in immunoprecipitation experiments (Okuno and Miyashita 1996).

We compared expression of ZIF268 in the anterior temporal cortex of the monkeys during visual paired associate learning and visual discrimination learning. The presentation of visual stimuli, numbers of emitted motor responses, and amounts of given reward were equalized in the two tasks. In the case of visual paired associate learning, the intensely ZIF268-immunopositive neurons were accumulated in patches in the ventral surface of the inferior temporal gyrus. The patches were centered in layer IV and spread into both superficial (II/III) and deep (V and VI) layers. The patchy pattern was found in several consecutive sections and was specific to ZIF268, since other IEG products (cFos and JunD) did not show such patterns in adjacent sections (Okuno and Miyashita 1996).

The distribution of ZIF268 expression in the monkey temporal cortex was quantified by image analysis (Okuno and Miyashita 1996) and displayed on a two-dimensional unfolded map (figure 12.11, plate 29). In each monkey with visual paired associate learning, ZIF268 was expressed at high levels in a strip parallel to the rhinal sulcus in an anterior-posterior axis, particularly in several patches in this strip (PA1–PA3). ZIF268 was expressed at relatively low levels and was distributed more homogeneously in the monkeys with visual discrimination learning (VD1–VD3). The inferior temporal gyrus is composed of three cytoarchitectonically and connectionally distinct areas (area 35, area 36, and the ventral part of area TE) (Suzuki and Amaral 1994b). The expression of ZIF268 in the monkeys during visual pair-association learning was prominent in area 36. By contrast, in area 35—medially adjacent to area 36—ZIF268 expression levels were low during both types of visual learning. A two-way ANOVA on the mean expression level (two learning tasks and three brain areas) revealed a significant effect of task [$F(1,4) = 12.05$, $P = 0.025$] and of area [$F(2,8) = 17.73$, $P = 0.001$]. The expression in area 36 was significantly higher during visual paired associate learning than during visual discrimination learning [1.34 ± 0.07 and 0.96 ± 0.04 ($\pm$ s.e.m., arbitrary units), respectively; $P = 0.01$]. In area 35, the expression levels in the two monkey groups were similar and were not significantly different (pair association, 0.65 ± 0.09; discrimination, 0.58 ± 0.05; $P > 0.5$). In ventral TE, the difference did not reach statistical significance ($P = 0.22$), but there might be a tendency for higher expression of ZIF268 in the monkeys with visual paired associate learning (pair association, 1.11 ± 0.15; discrimination, 0.85 ± 0.08). These results support the hypothesis that perirhinal neurons undergo rapid modification of synaptic connectivity during learning of the visual pair-association task.

12.6 Conclusion

In this chapter, I examined neural mechanisms underlying memory retrieval and the consolidation process by single-unit recording and molecular biological methods.

A

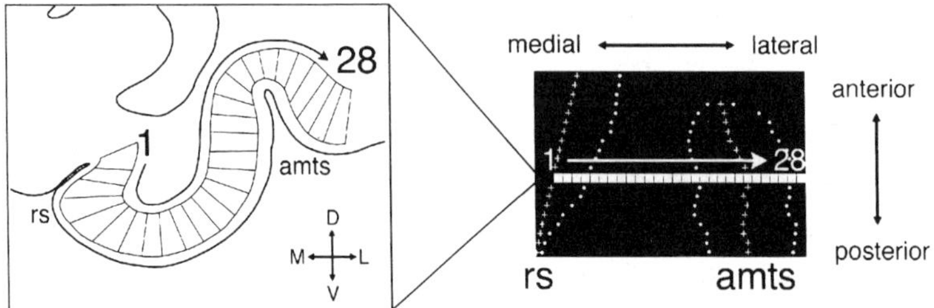

B

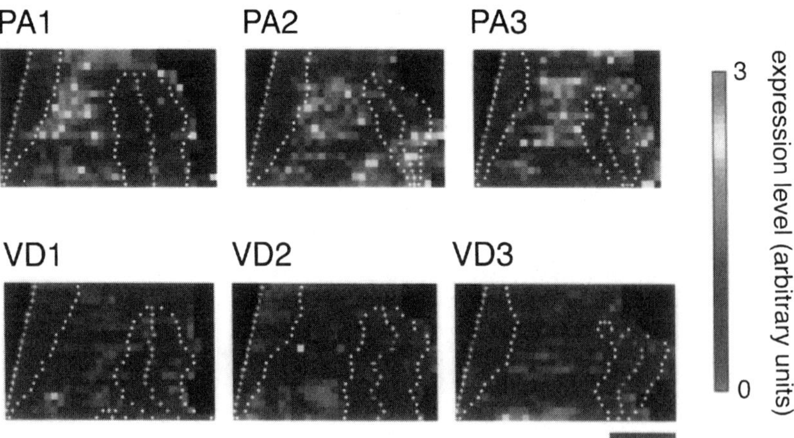

Figure 12.11
Two-dimensional unfolded maps of the monkey temporal cortex indicating ZIF268 expression levels. (*A*) Line drawing of twenty-eight radial, segmented areas in a coronal section through the right medioventral temporal cortex (left). The cortical area in each section was subdivided into a number of radial segments. To display the spatial distribution of ZIF268 expression levels, the segmented areas were reconstructed as a two-dimensional unfolded map (right). The fundus and lip of a sulcus are outlined by white crosses and dots, respectively. Serial sections were aligned along the fundus of the rhinal sulcus, rs (rhinal sulcus); amts (anterior middle temporal sulcus); D, L, V, M = dorsal, lateral, ventral, medial. (*B*) The expression levels of ZIF268 in the temporal cortex of individual monkeys. The density of reaction products of ZIF268 immunostaining in the segments is indicated on the unfolded maps (similar to the right panel in *A*) in pseudocolor representation. The maps from monkeys with visual pair-association learning (PA1–PA3) and visual discrimination learning (VD1–VD3) are shown in the upper panels and lower panels, respectively. The values are normalized so that the mean density of the reaction products of all segments from all six monkeys is 1.0 (Okuno and Miyashita 1996). The boundaries of cortical areas were indicated by gray dots. Scale bar, 10 mm (Okuno and Miyashita 1996).

For this purpose I devised a visual pair-association memory task for monkeys. The task requires the monkey to encode associative relations between visual objects and to retrieve the high-level internal representation (or the "image") of the paired associate according to a cue stimulus. I proposed that the visual memory is organized as structured bundles of associations between objects in the inferotemporal cortex (Miyashita 1993) and that the retrieved image is activated in the neural network of the inferotemporal cortex. The pair-association with color switch (PACS) task, in which the necessity for image retrieval and its initiation time were controlled by a color switch, provided particularly compelling evidence for the role of inferotemporal neurons (Naya, Sakai, and Miyashita 1996). The activated high-level representation in the inferotemporal cortex could be the origin of backward signals that appear to reach topographically organized visual areas when an imagery task requires reconstruction of the detailed local geometry of the image (as in counting the columns of the Pantheon), as demonstrated in neuroimaging and psychophysical studies (Ishai and Sagi 1995; Miyashita 1995; Kosslyn 1994; Roland 1993).

The backward signal from the medial temporal lobe to the inferotemporal cortex plays a distinct role in memory consolidation. I analyzed the interaction between the perirhinal cortex and area TEav during the formation of the visual pair-association memory in monkeys. I hypothesized that the interaction is critical since perirhinal neurons might undergo rapid modification of synaptic connectivity and could provide a backward signal to guide reorganization of forward neural circuits in (and/or to) area TEav. The results of single-unit recording combined with neurotoxic lesions, as well as the results of detection of the molecular marker expression for synaptic plasticity, supported the hypothesis. However, the study has completed only the first stage of investigation, and there are many missing links. For example, it is believed that the induced transcription factors regulate expression of late-response genes that probably contribute to morphological changes for synaptic plasticity (Bailey and Kandel 1993). So far we have no data in the monkey inferotemporal cortex supporting this line of speculation.

In the above studies, I extensively used the visual pair-association memory task for monkeys, which holds many advantages for this line of research. However, in this task (even in the PACS task), the image was generated only in a simple way, in which a subject recalled a previously seen object. We humans use imagery in more flexible ways. First, we can combine or arrange objects in novel configurations in images. Second, we can also mentally draw patterns that we have never actually seen, or we can visualize novel patterns that are not based on rearranging familiar components. To make these image computations possible, the imagery system must contain another subsystem that uses associative memory and that constructs local representations on the basis of a global image by top-down attentional shift (Farah 1990; Kosslyn 1994). The anatomical location of the subsystem might be hypothesized to be in the dorsolateral prefrontal cortex, but evidence is still scanty (Fuster 1989). It is noted that, although we believe depictive representation lies in the deepest structure for image generation (Kosslyn 1994; Miyashita 1995), propositional representation may also generate imagery by the use of this subsystem, especially in humans (Pylyshyn 1981). Characterization and neurophysiological analysis of this subsystem would provide further insight into the neural basis of imagery and its conscious activation.

References

Abraham, W. C., S. E. Mason, J. Demmer, J. M. Williams, C. L. Richardson, W. P. Tate, P. A. Lawlor, and M. Dragunow. 1993. Correlations between immediate early gene induction and the persistence of long-term potentiation. *Neuroscience* 56, 717–727.

Alain, E. A. C. 1926. *Système des Beaux-Arts*. Paris: Gallimard.

Bailey, C. H., and E. R. Kandel. 1993. Structural changes accompanying memory storage. *Annual Review of Physiology* 55, 397–426.

Demeter, S., D. L. Rosene, and G. W. Van Hoesen. 1990. Fields and origin and pathways of the interhemispheric commissures in the temporal lobe of the macaques. *Journal of Comparative Neurology* 302, 29–53.

Farah, M. J. 1990. *Visual agnosia*. Cambridge, Mass.: MIT Press.

Fuster, J. M. 1989. *The prefrontal cortex*. New York: Raven Press.

Hasegawa, I., T. Fukushima, T. Ihara, and Y. Miyashita. 1998. Callosal window between prefrontal cortices: Cognitive interaction to retrieve long-term memory. *Science* 281, 814–818.

Higuchi, S., and Y. Miyashita. 1996. Formation of mnemonic neuronal responses to visual paired associates in inferotemporal cortex is impaired by perirhinal and entorhinal lesions. *Proceedings of the National Academy of Sciences of the USA* 93, 739–743.

Ishai, A., and D. Sagi. 1995. Common mechanisms of visual imagery and perception. *Science* 268, 1772–1774.

Iwai, E., and M. Mishkin. 1969. Further evidence on the locus of the visual area in the temporal lobe of the monkey. *Experimental Neurology* 25, 585–594.

Kosslyn, S. M. 1994. *Image and brain*. Cambridge, Mass.: MIT Press.

Milner, B. 1968. Visual recognition and recall after right temporal-lobe excision in man. *Neuropsychologia* 6, 191–209.

Mishkin, M. 1982. A memory system in the monkey. *Philosophical Transactions of the Royal Society of London B* 298, 85–95.

Miyashita, Y. 1988. Neuronal correlate of visual associative long-term memory in the primate temporal cortex. *Nature* 335, 817–820.

Miyashita, Y. 1993. Inferior temporal cortex: Where visual perception meets memory. *Annual Review of Neuroscience* 16, 245–263.

Miyashita, Y. 1995. How the brain creates imagery. *Science* 268, 1719–1720.

Miyashita, Y. 1999. Visual associative long-term memory: Encoding and retrieval in inferotemporal cortex of the primate. In *The new cognitive neurosciences* (ed. M. Gazzaniga). Cambridge, Mass.: MIT Press.

Miyashita, Y., and H. S. Chang. 1988. Neuronal correlate of pictorial short-term memory in the primate temporal cortex. *Nature* 331, 68–70.

Miyashita, Y., A. Date, and H. Okuno. 1993. Configuration encoding of complex visual forms by single neurons of monkey temporal cortex. *Neuropsychologia* 31, 1119–1131.

Miyashita, Y., S. Higuchi, K. Sakai, and N. Masui. 1991. Generation of fractal patterns for probing the visual memory. *Neuroscience Research* 12, 307–311.

Miyashita, Y., M. Kameyama, I. Hasegawa, and T. Fukushima. 1998. Consolidation of visual associative long-term memory in the temporal cortex of primates. *Neurobiology of Learning and Memory* 70, 197–211.

Miyashita, Y., T. Rolls, P. M. B. Cahusac, H. Niki, and J. D. Feigenbaum. 1989. Activity of hippocampal formation neurons in the monkey related to a stimulus-response association task. *Journal of Neurophysiology* 61, 669–678.

Morgan, J. I., and T. Curran. 1991. Stimulus-transcription coupling in the nervous system: Involvement of the inducible proto-oncogenes fos and jun. *Annual Review of Neuroscience* 14, 421–451.

Murray, E., D. Gaffan, and M. Mishkin. 1993. Neural substrates of visual stimulus-stimulus association in rhesus monkeys. *Journal of Neuroscience* 13, 4549–4561.

Naya, Y., K. Sakai, and Y. Miyashita. 1996. Activity of primate inferotemporal neurons related to a sought target in a pair-association task. *Proceedings of the National Academy of Sciences of the USA* 93, 2664–2669.

Okuno, H., and Y. Miyashita. 1996. Expression of the transcription factor ZIF268 in the temporal cortex of monkeys during visual paired associate learning. *European Journal of Neuroscience* 8, 2118–2128.

Okuno, H., D. W. Saffen, and Y. Miyashita. 1995. Subdivision-specific expression of ZIF268 in the hippocampal formation of the macaque monkey. *Neuroscience* 66, 829–845.

Pandya, D. N., E. A. Karol, and P. P. Lele. 1973. The distribution of the anterior commissure in the squirrel monkey. *Brain Research* 49, 177–180.

Pylyshyn, Z. W. 1981. The imagery debate: Analogue media versus tacit knowledge. *Psychological Review* 87, 16–45.

Roland, P. E. 1993. *Brain activation*. New York: Wiley-Liss.

Sakai, K., and Y. Miyashita. 1991. Neural organization for the long-term memory of paired associates. *Nature* 354, 152–155.

Sartre, J. P. 1938. *L'imaginaire.* Paris: Gallimard.

Squire, L. R. 1987. *Memory and brain*. New York: Oxford University Press.

Squire, L. R., and S. Zola-Morgan. 1991. The medial temporal lobe memory system. *Science* 253, 1380–1386.

Suzuki, W. A., and D. G. Amaral. 1994a. Perirhinal and parahippocampal cortices of the macaque monkey: Cortical afferents. *Journal of Comparative Neuroscience* 350, 497–533.

Suzuki, W. A., and D. G. Amaral. 1994b. Topographic organization of the reciprocal connections between the monkey entorhinal cortex and the perirhinal and parahippocampal cortices. *Journal of Neuroscience* 14, 1856–1877.

Tomita, H., M. Ohbayashi, K. Nakahara, I. Hasegawa, and Y. Miyashita. 1999. Top-down signal from prefrontal cortex in executive control of memory retrieval. *Nature* 401, 699–703.

Van Essen, D. C., C. H. Anderson, and D. J. Felleman. 1992. Information processing in the primate visual system: An integrated systems perspective. *Science* 255, 419–423.

Van Hoesen, G. W. 1982. The parahippocampal gyrus: New observations regarding its cortical connections in the monkey. *Trends in Neuroscience* 5, 345–353.

Webster, M. J., L. G. Ungerleider, and J. Bachevalier. 1991. Connections of inferior temporal areas TE and TEO with medial temporal-lobe structures in infant and adult monkeys. *Journal of Neuroscience* 11, 1095–1116.

Wechsler, D. 1987. *Wechsler memory scale–revised.* San Antonio, Tex.: Harcourt Brace Jovanovich.

Worley, P. F., R. V. Bhat, J. M. Baraban, C. A. Erickson, B. L. McNaughton, and C. A. Barnes. 1993. Thresholds for synaptic activation of transcription factors in hippocampus: Correlation with long-term enhancement. *Journal of Neuroscience* 13, 4776–4786.

Contributors

Noam Chomsky Department of Linguistics and Philosophy, Massachusetts Institute of Technology, Cambridge, Mass., USA

Ann Christophe Laboratoire de Sciences Cognitives et Psycholinguistique, École des Hautes Études en Sciences Sociales, Centre National de la Recherche Scientifique, Paris, France

Robert Desimone Laboratory of Neuropsychology, National Institute of Mental Health, Bethesda, Md., USA

Richard Frackowiak Wellcome Department of Cognitive Neurology, Institute of Neurology, University College London, UK

Angela Friederici Max Planck Institut für neuropsychologische Forschung, Arbeitsbereich Neuropsychologie, Leipzig, Germany

Edward Gibson Department of Brain and Cognitive Sciences, Massachusetts Institute of Technology, Cambridge, Mass., USA

Peter Indefrey Max Planck Institute for Psycholinguistics, Nijmegen, The Netherlands

Masao Ito RIKEN Brain Science Institute, Saitama, Japan

Willem Levelt Max Planck Institute for Psycholinguistics, Nijmegen, The Netherlands

Alec Marantz Department of Linguistics and Philosophy, Massachusetts Institute of Technology, Cambridge, Mass., USA

Jacques Mehler Laboratoire de Sciences Cognitives et Psycholinguistique, École des Hautes Études en Sciences Sociales, Centre National de la Recherche Scientifique, Paris, France

Yasushi Miyashita Department of Physiology, University of Tokyo School of Medicine and Japan Science and Technology Mind Articulation Project, Tokyo, Japan

Wayne O'Neil Department of Linguistics and Philosophy and Japan Science and Technology Mind Articulation Project, Massachusetts Institute of Technology, Cambridge, Mass., USA

David Poeppel Cognitive Neuroscience of Language Laboratory, University of Maryland, College Park, Md., USA

Franck Ramus Laboratoire de Sciences Cognitives et Psycholinguistique, École des Hautes Études en Sciences Sociales, Centre National de la Recherche Scientifique, Paris, France

John Reynolds Laboratory of Neuropsychology, National Institute of Mental Health, Bethesda, Md., USA

Kensuke Sekihara Department of Electronic Systems and Engineering, Tokyo Metropolitan Institute of Technology and Japan Science and Technology Mind Articulation Project, Tokyo, Japan

Hiroshi Shibasaki Department of Neurology, Kyoto University Graduate School of Medicine, Kyoto, Japan